AFRICAN GUERRILLAS

AFRICAN GUERRILLAS

Raging Against the Machine

edited by
Morten Bøås
Kevin C. Dunn

LYNNE
RIENNER
PUBLISHERS

BOULDER
LONDON

Published in the United States of America in 2007 by
Lynne Rienner Publishers, Inc.
1800 30th Street, Boulder, Colorado 80301
www.rienner.com

and in the United Kingdom by
Lynne Rienner Publishers, Inc.
3 Henrietta Street, Covent Garden, London WC2E 8LU

Library of Congress Cataloging-in-Publication Data
African guerrillas : raging against the machine / Morten Bøås and Kevin C. Dunn.
   p. cm.
  Includes bibliographical references and index.
  ISBN 978-1-58826-495-4 (hardcover : alk. paper)
  ISBN 978-1-58826-471-8 (pbk. : alk. paper)
  1. Africa—Politics and government—1960– 2. Africa—History—
Autonomy and independence movements. 3. Insurgency—Africa.
4. Guerrillas—Africa. 5. Violence—Africa. I. Bøås, Morten, 1965–
II. Dunn, Kevin C., 1967–
  DT30.5.A35589 2007
  355.02'18096—dc22

                                            2007001105

British Cataloguing in Publication Data
A Cataloguing in Publication record for this book
is available from the British Library.

Printed and bound in the United States of America

The paper used in this publication meets the requirements
of the American National Standard for Permanence of
Paper for Printed Library Materials Z39.48-1992.

5 4

CONTENTS

Acknowledgments   vii
Map of Africa   ix

1 Introduction   1
  Morten Bøås and Kevin C. Dunn

2 African Guerrilla Politics: Raging Against the Machine?   9
  Morten Bøås and Kevin C. Dunn

3 Marginalized Youth   39
  Morten Bøås

4 Whither the Separatist Motive?   55
  Pierre Englebert

5 Liberia: The LURDs of the New Church   69
  William S. Reno

6 Côte d'Ivoire: Negotiating Identity and Citizenship   81
  Richard Banégas and Ruth Marshall-Fratani

7 The Democratic Republic of Congo:
  Militarized Politics in a "Failed State"   113
  Denis M. Tull

8 Uganda: The Lord's Resistance Army   131
  Kevin C. Dunn

9 Sudan: The Janjawiid and Government Militias   151
  Øystein H. Rolandsen

10 Senegal: The Resilient Weakness of Casamançais Separatists   171
  Vincent Foucher

11 Angola: How to Lose a Guerrilla War   199
     Assis Malaquias

12 *African Guerrillas* Revisited   221
     Christopher Clapham

List of Acronyms   235
Bibliography   239
The Contributors   255
Index   257
About the Book   275

ACKNOWLEDGMENTS

We want to first thank Stephen Ellis, Timothy Shaw, and Paul Richards for encouraging us to make this volume a reality. Special thanks to Christopher Clapham, who agreed to read the entire manuscript as it was taking shape and graciously wrote the concluding chapter. We would also like to thank Lynne Rienner and Lisa Tulchin, who supported us from the outset and who showed a great deal of patience as we completed the manuscript.

We are grateful to Erin Baines, Anna Creadick, Barrow Dunn, Anne Hatløy, Terhi Lehtinen, Pamela Mbabazi, Jane Parpart, Jon Pedersen, Richard Salter, Ian Taylor, Mark Taylor, and Mats Utas, who have all in various ways and capacities contributed to how we think about African insurgencies. Our respective institutions, Fafo–Institute for Applied International Studies and the Department of Political Science at Hobart and William Smith Colleges, also deserve some praise for tolerating our eccentric behavior and complete disregard for conventions and authority. They may be rewarded, but most likely not in this life. We also extend a big thank-you to all those we have met and talked with during the last decade or so in our travels around Africa. They have helped us far more than we will ever be able to assist them and their communities; there is unfortunately little we can do about that other than continue our engagement with Africa, in the hope that some day a new dawn will bring peace to the many troubled places we discuss in this volume.

—*Morten Bøås and Kevin C. Dunn*

Africa

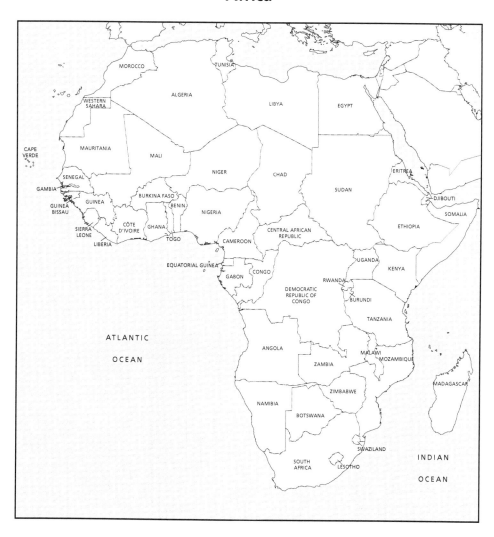

1

Introduction

MORTEN BØÅS AND KEVIN C. DUNN

Guerrilla movements occupy the center stage of violent conflict in sub-Saharan Africa. With the changing international geopolitical environment and further institutional decay of the African state, many African nations are currently facing armed insurgencies. However, it is not the scope of African guerrilla movements that makes them a significant subject for study—African civil wars are far from ubiquitous, despite popular Western imaginations to the contrary. Rather, it is the distinctive character of contemporary African guerrilla movements that seemingly challenges accepted assumptions about the motivations, manifestations, and character of armed conflict and makes them an important object for investigations and scholarly inquiry. There will be no development without security, and until sustainable solutions to the many conflicts on the African continent are identified and implemented, the quest, often externally imposed, will remain elusive.

Such solutions will appear only when the nature of these conflicts and the movements who fight them are recognized. Currently, both mainstream academia and its manifestations in policy interventions tend to be characterized by single-factor explanations that offer little possibility in this regard.[1] We are particularly worried about the dominance of what we call greed-based approaches to African conflicts, as they tell us little about the true nature of such conflicts. Treating African guerrillas as devoid of any kind of political agenda, greed-based approaches present them as bandits. Such an interpretation significantly narrows the number of possible policy interventions: you can negotiate with armed rebels with a political agenda, but bandits are to be crushed by force. We hope that the more nuanced and historically grounded studies presented in this volume will contribute to a more sober debate about the causes of conflict in Africa, the motivations of armed insurgents, and how various stakeholders can deal with these wars. Thus this volume is intended to be of use to both scholars and policymakers,

1

particularly those interested in developing a more holistic understanding of contemporary armed struggles in Africa, and perhaps elsewhere.

Armed Insurgencies

African guerrilla movements are not a new phenomenon. Numerous African states have experienced armed nationalist struggles for independence and/or postindependence civil wars. During much of the twentieth century, these conflicts were often fueled by the Cold War as the United States and the Soviet Union treated Africa as part of their zero-sum global geopolitical competition. In the years since the collapse of the Soviet Union, several Cold War–era civil wars either have collapsed or have been resolved by diplomatic initiatives. In the first category, the long-running war in Angola came to a close with the death of Uniãdo Nacional para Independência Total de Angola (UNITA) leader Jonas Savimbi in 2002. Other Cold War–fueled struggles, like that in Mozambique, reached their resolution through elaborate political negotiations. In those cases, the end of the Cold War meant that the superpower lifelines that kept the conflict alive quickly dried up, making a continuation of the struggle extremely problematic for the parties involved. Yet in other cases, long-running conflicts on the continent are entering their second or even third decade. These tend to be struggles that were peripheral to the Cold War conflict, receiving relatively little attention from either the Soviet Union or the United States. For example, northern Uganda has the unfortunate distinction of suffering almost twenty uninterrupted years of armed conflict between the forces of the Lord's Resistance Army (LRA) and the central government.

The years since the Cold War's end have also seen the creation of two relatively new fully developed regional conflict zones. The first has been caused by the intertwining of a series of localized conflicts in Western Africa, primarily around the Mano River basin (see Richards 1996; Huband 1998; Ellis 1999; Adebajo and Rashid 2004; Bøås 2001, 2005). Countries drawn into this conflict zone include Liberia, Sierra Leone, Côte d'Ivoire, and Guinea. The second conflict zone was created in Central Africa with the collapse of the Mobutist state in Zaire, now the Democratic Republic of Congo (DRC; see Mamdani 2001; Clark 2002; Dunn 2003; Bøås 2004a). As in West Africa, various localized conflicts became intertwined with the development of a regional war zone that drew in numerous countries, including Angola, Burundi, Chad, Rwanda, Namibia, Sudan, Uganda, and Zimbabwe.[2]

Armed insurgents have become an increasingly significant element of African politics given the end of the Cold War, the international geopolitical reorganization, the crises of the African neopatrimonial state, and the emergence of two fully developed conflict zones. Yet careful analysis of such movements has been an exception, be it for a lack of concise information,[3] the difficulties linked to fieldwork in conflict-ridden countries, scholarly indifference, or the deeply rooted tradition of state-centered analysis in political science. Christopher Clapham's 1998 collection *African Guerrillas* is still the only attempt to study African insurgencies in a comparative manner. Since the publication of *African Guerrillas,* the external and internal environments of African insurgencies have changed dramatically. Even Côte d'Ivoire, once the purported cornerstone of stability in West Africa, has effectively been divided into two by civil war. The long list of countries affected by insurgencies since the publication of Clapham's collection includes Liberia, where the combined pressure of the Liberians United for Democracy and Reconciliation (LURD) and the Movement for Democracy in Liberia (MODEL), together with significant external pressure, forced Charles Taylor to seek exile in Nigeria in August 2003. Since 1998, the war in the DRC has been a protracted conflict of considerable proportions, involving at least six foreign armies, two major insurgencies, half a dozen smaller movements, and a plethora of militias. In Sudan, as international efforts tried to end the war between Khartoum and the southern parts of the country, insurgencies and counterinsurgencies raised the specter of a new civil war with ramifications far beyond the Darfur region. If anything, the importance of African insurgencies both for scholarly study and for policy interventions is increasing rather than decreasing.

This volume is an attempt to revisit and discuss the insights provided by Clapham's groundbreaking *African Guerrillas,* while building upon that earlier work to substantially advance the field of inquiry. In Clapham's book four broad categories of African insurgencies are developed: liberation insurgencies (such as the anticolonial nationalist movements), separatist insurgencies (such as the Eritrean People's Liberation Front), reform insurgencies (such as Yoweri Museveni's National Resistance Army in Uganda), and warlord insurgencies (such as Charles Taylor's National Patriotic Front of Liberia [NPFL] and Foday Sankoh's Revolutionary United Front [RUF] in Sierra Leone; Clapham 1998b: 6–7). While we continue to find Clapham's typology useful, we believe the debate needs to be revisited and developed further in the light of significant changes both on the ground and in the scholarly field. For example, only the last of these four categories has been very prominent in recent debates. This is primarily because, with few exceptions, the majority of insurgencies do not easily fit into the other categories and new modes of useful understanding have yet to be developed. As we discuss in Chapter 2, much of the recent literature on insurgencies has mistakenly focused on single-factor explanations, such as greed, resources, and culture. In this volume, we argue for a more nuanced, holistic approach that is historically grounded and integrates multiple levels of analysis, from the local and national to the regional and global.

It is our belief that African insurgencies are best understood as rational responses to the composition of African states and their polities. In his edited collection *No Peace, No War,* anthropologist Paul Richards observes, "War is a long-term struggle organized for political ends, commonly but not always using violence" (2005b: 4). In many ways, this restates Clapham's earlier argument that "insurgencies derive basically from blocked political aspirations, and in some cases also from reactive desperation" (1998b: 5). Like Clapham, Richards stresses the importance of an ethnographic approach to understanding conflict. However, Richards differs from Clapham by reconceptualizing conflict as part of a continuum: "We do ethnography of war best, we will argue, not by imposing a sharp categorical distinction between 'war' and 'peace,' but by thinking in terms of a continuum" in which both cooperative and conflictive behavior shapes the dispute (2005a: 5). As Richards argues, "War only makes sense as an aspect of social process. The best analytical approach to war as process is through the ethnography of the actual practices of war and peace" (2005b: 12).

We find this an important contribution to the field, and we are disappointed by the failure of mainstream political science and international relations to take these insights seriously. In his engagement with Richards's volume, Jason Strakes questions its ability to "inform mainstream conflict studies in international relations" because "the underlying theme of the book (the skepticism of the contributors towards generalizability as an academic goal) puts it in a difficult position vis-à-vis contemporary political scientists and IR specialists" (2005: 477). We find this a damning critique not of Richards's work but of the state of "mainstream" conflict studies. It is our hope that our book—in which several contemporary political scientists and IR specialists share many of Richards's insights and examine political variables within a holistic, historically grounded approach—will provide a useful antidote to the insular, positivist-dominated field of US political science.

The Structure of the Book

This book is organized into thematic essays and country-specific case studies. The thematic essays draw together chapters examining overarching themes of the book. In Chapter 2, we explore the political agendas of African guerrillas, with specific emphasis on the internal dynamics and external contexts that are informing contemporary armed struggles. It is our contention that in order to grasp what the wars are all about, we must concern ourselves with questions regarding the composition of African states and their respective polities. The background of these wars is deeply embedded in the history of the continent, and not only in the colonial past or the transformation to independence but in the totality of African history. The chapter examines various motivations for contemporary African insurgencies, including ideology, grievances against the central government, regional and social marginalization, elite desires to capture state power, the crisis of the postcolonial state, and the extreme politicizing of autochthony debates. We also examine the external context of insurgency groups in Africa, noting the changes brought by the end of the Cold War and the global "war on terror," as well as important changes in international and regional markets. This chapter therefore promotes an understanding of African insurgency movements as both creations of and responses to the crisis of modernity and its dysfunctional institutions in Africa. Far from behaving like "classic" insurgencies such as the Ethiopian and the Eritrean ones, most of the current rebel groups seem more like manifestations of rage against the "machinery" of dysfunctional states, their equally fragmented and corrupted institutions, and the uneven impact of a globalized modernity.

In Chapter 3, Morten Bøås contextualizes the issue of marginalized youth in African insurgency movements. Africa is a continent of youth, and those who fight are mostly young men. Young African fighters are often depicted as ruthless murderers or powerless victims. Both views oversimplify by failing to account for the nature of war. War does more than merely disrupt or destroy existing social systems; it also creates new systems. Although cruel, ugly, and inhuman, war is also by nature an instrument for social restructuring. It is a site for innovation, reordering social, economic, and political life, and is best approached as a drama. War is a social drama over the distribution of ideas, identities, resources, and social positions, and it often forces the disadvantaged to design alternative survival strategies. When youth are drawn into the center stage of such conflicts, the outcome is often the emergence of militias and other types of insurgency movements. In societies torn by conflict, these entities can provide some sort of order and social organization and can represent means of social integration and upward social mobility. The only way to understand youth involvement in such processes is to take their experiences seriously, even if the narrative presented by such youthful dramas does not fit well with existing categories for understanding political behavior.

In the final thematic chapter (Chapter 4), Pierre Englebert explores the reasons behind the low number of secessionist movements in Africa. As he points out, Latin America alone has a lower propensity for separatism than Africa. Englebert offers elements for a theory of the reproduction of failed postcolonial states in Africa; he focuses on the extent to which institutions of sovereignty provide political and material resources for elites and populations at large, outweighing the potential benefits of separatist nonsovereign alternatives.

The bulk of this collection is made up of country-specific case studies. We have chosen a wide range of case studies, with the majority from the newly developed regional conflict zones of West Africa (Liberia and Côte d'Ivoire) and the Great Lakes region of Central Africa (Democratic Republic of Congo, Uganda, and Sudan). The two exceptions are Senegal and Angola. The first is included because of its arguable uniqueness—a secessionist movement with little external support and a poorly developed "war economy." In the case of Angola's UNITA, its lengthy history illustrates the multiple changes from the Cold War era of "traditional" armed insurgents to the contemporary era. Indeed, UNITA arguably represents a case of an insurgency that, despite its longevity and multiple mutations, was eventually unsuccessful in transforming itself to ensure its survival in the current context.

The first two case studies come from the regional conflict zone of West Africa. In Chapter 5, William Reno provides an examination of LURD, one of the most important factions in the second part of the Liberian civil war (i.e., 1998–2003), and draws out the differences and similarities between that group and Charles Taylor's NPFL, the group LURD eventually drove from power. One of the main differences Reno notes is that LURD faced a much more constrained regional political context than NPFL did and, as a result, LURD was more reliant on foreign politicians who had become adept at using Liberian groups to serve their own agendas. Reno argues that the politics of collapsed states operate according to a definable logic, one that is becoming more regional in its definition as individual states grow weaker and some collapse.

In Chapter 6, Richard Banégas and Ruth Marshall-Fratani seek to unravel the complex character of the ongoing armed conflict in Côte d'Ivoire. Rejecting arguments that the conflict is fueled by economic motivations or state failure, Banégas and Marshall-Fratani assert that the conflict is primarily political, with the local and international intertwined, generating a war about borders in which nation-states play a central role. Above all, the authors maintain that the conflict is a "war of modernity" focused essentially on questions of nationality and citizenship, informed by a violent nativist ideology of autochthony that is popular among the marginalized and the youth in the southern part of the country.

Turning to Central Africa, Denis Tull's chapter (Chapter 7) explores the politics of insurgency in eastern Democratic Republic of Congo, focusing mainly on the Rassemblement Congolais pour la Démocratie (RCD), the insurgency movement that, in alliance with Rwanda, triggered the second war in the DRC (1998–2003). Tull argues that given Rwanda's controlling role and changes in the international environment, the RCD lacked effective ownership of the insurgent war and was forced to privilege the quest for international recognition as a legitimate contender for Congolese state power at the expense of domestic political support—let alone legitimacy—within its host society in the Kivus. Tull considers how the failure of the

RCD to achieve local legitimacy has thwarted attempts to establish a long-term peace in eastern DRC.

Chapter 8 offers an examination of northern Uganda's LRA, evaluating several theories that seek to explain the long-running conflict from a number of angles. Rejecting the thesis that Joseph Kony and his LRA are irrational madmen, Kevin Dunn explores the local dynamics that informed the rise of the LRA and its immediate predecessors and notes the complex evolution of the war, as a localized conflict that became increasingly regionalized and institutionalized.

In Chapter 9, Øystein Rolandsen examines the recent history of government militias in Sudan, primarily the Janjawiid, the counterinsurgent militias largely blamed for the catastrophic violence in the Darfur region. Rolandsen provides a historical narrative of the conflict in Darfur, drawing out its local and regional dimensions and noting the government's use of militias as counterinsurgency tools. The chapter explores the composition and objectives of the Janjawiid, and Rolandsen argues that the use of militias by Khartoum is not new; what makes Darfur unique is the scale of the militia attacks and the level of international attention the Darfur conflict has received.

In Chapter 10, Vincent Foucher examines the motivations, character, and evolution of the Mouvement des Forces Démocratiques de Casamance (MFDC), which has been fighting since the 1980s for the independence of Casamance, the southern district of Senegal. Foucher notes that, unlike many other contemporary insurgencies, the MFDC started not as a military enterprise but as a civil society protest movement. Though it has progressively evolved, Foucher argues that the MFDC is unique among the violent sectarian movements and war-oriented movements elsewhere in the continent, given its poorly developed "war economy" and weak external support structures. Foucher argues that it is this weakness and the nature and transformations of its interactions with the local populations and with the Senegalese state that explains the resilience of the MFDC.

In the final case study (Chapter 11), Assis Malaquias examines the evolution of Angola's UNITA, an armed guerrilla group that began in 1966 but virtually imploded after the death of its leader Jonas Savimbi in 2002. Throughout most of its history, UNITA dealt with several major crises by successfully reinventing itself and adapting to the new circumstances. Malaquias maintains that the very flexibility that enabled UNITA to survive major life-threatening challenges imbued it with an exaggerated sense of confidence that, in turn, led the movement to eventually make important strategic miscalculations. Malaquias argues that UNITA's decision to fund its struggle by controlling diamond networks transformed the group from a peasant-based insurgency group into a semiconventional army, which ultimately led to its defeat.

The collection ends with a new essay by Christopher Clapham, in which he reviews the changes that have taken place since the publication of *African Guerrillas* in 1998 in light of the arguments and case studies in this book. In this concluding chapter, Clapham examines how guerrilla groups in each of the four categories of his typology evolved and mutated between 1996 and 2006.

Notes

1. A prime example is the work of former World Bank chief economist Paul Collier. See Collier 2000 and Collier and Hoeffler 1998.

2. In late December 2005, the International Court of Justice (ICJ) handed down a judgment on the case brought by the Democratic Republic of Congo (DRC) against Uganda. In the case, the DRC accused Uganda of violating its sovereignty and of massive human rights abuses, including murder, looting, and destruction. Uganda, on the other hand, claimed that its actions were only meant to protect national security along its borders. In its ruling, the ICJ said that Uganda was wrong to invade the DRC and ruled that the amount of $10 billion was appropriate compensation (see BBC 2005).

3. Important exceptions include Richards 1996, 2005a, 2005b; Abdullah 1998; Peters and Richards 1998; Utas 2003; and Kastfelt 2005.

2

African Guerrilla Politics: Raging Against the Machine?

Morten Bøås and Kevin C. Dunn

Since the mid-1980s, insurgencies and armed nonstate actors have increasingly occupied the center stage of violent conflicts in Africa. Almost every country on the continent has been faced with armed insurrection at one time or another, and many are currently dealing with armed rebellions inside their borders or from groups based in neighboring countries carrying out cross-border attacks. What explains the persistent existence of armed guerrillas in Africa? Historically, African insurgencies have enjoyed a rather poor success rate, at least if measured only against the degree to which they have been able to overthrow and replace existing regimes.[1] With the exception of the anticolonial struggles, no African insurgency was ever successful until Hissen Habré's Forces Armées du Nord (FAN) seized state power in Chad in 1979. The second successful insurgency in an independent African state did not occur until Yoweri Museveni's National Resistance Army (NRA) captured the Ugandan state in 1986. Africa's first and only successful secessionist movement did not succeed in Eritrea until after the combined forces of the Ethiopian People's Revolutionary Democratic Front (EPRDF) and the Eritrean People's Liberation Front (EPLF) toppled the central government of Ethiopia in 1991. Yet despite this poor success rate, armed insurrection has become one of the dominant features of the African political landscape.

In this chapter we examine the political motivations involved in contemporary African guerrilla movements. We begin with a brief discussion of the various theories and explanations that have gained currency in recent years. This first section explores the merits and flaws with the "greed kills," "new wars," and other theses currently in vogue. It is our general contention that these approaches tend to ignore long historical trends, diverse social forces, political motivations, and regional dimensions that have all contributed to the development of current African conflicts. In the second section, we explore the dominant characteristics of these conflicts. While each conflict is distinct, we note that some common characteristics and general features can be recognized to help make "sense" of African guerrilla wars. In this section, we explore the changing global geopolitical context, the crisis of the African state, regional and social marginalization, the politicizing of autochthony debates, and the regionalization of local conflicts, among other issues. We view contemporary African guerrilla movements as manifestations of a rage against the "machinery" of the dysfunctional neopatrimonial state and provide political opportunities as well as basic survival strategies for those navigating the continuing crises of modernity. While the individual chapters that follow provide rich material on specific cases, in this chapter we seek to observe the ways in which these conflicts are similar and to note the important ways they vary.

Explaining African Guerrillas

The staple of much international news reporting from the continent is that the only objective of these vicious youths is their own survival and the "pleasure" they seemingly find in raping and looting (Bøås 2004b). Out of Africa therefore come horror stories about red-eyed drugged monsters in the form of young men who seemingly kill without purpose or remorse. Greed and hatred seem their sole motivation. Movements such as the Revolutionary United Front (RUF) in Sierra Leone, the Lord's Resistance Army (LRA) in Uganda, the Mai Mai in Congo, and the many factions who fought in the Liberian civil war are often presented as lacking resemblance to recognizable patterns of armed resistance or political conflict. If analyzed at all, these movements typically are viewed either as unique pathologies or as solely about economic avarice.

It may be difficult to come to terms with these movements, their actions, and their motivations, but we are convinced that the reality is much more complex than single-dimension approaches would have us believe. Current mainstream debates often imply that all African wars are resource wars, fought not over political issues but in order to gain access to profits. This is what we call the "greed kills" argument (see Collier 2000; Berdal and Malone 2000; Klare 2001). Much of this literature argues that changes in the global economy have helped foster the rise of so-called "new wars" (see Kaldor 2001; Duffield 2001). Changes in the global economy, particularly the increased interconnectedness of certain markets, have certainly provided new opportunities for African guerrilla movements. One of the most pronounced trends has been the ability of armed insurgents to access and exploit regional economic markets. In many cases, primary resources such as diamonds, gold, ivory, coltan, and other precious (and relatively easily transportable) minerals are the desired goal. These goods are frequently smuggled out of the conflict zone and entered into the regional and global markets via neighboring territories. And it should not be assumed that these actors are exclusively Africans, as regional and international businesses and economic elites play a significant role in these conflicts and benefit from the opportunities they provide (see Taylor 2005).

In some African conflicts, it has been argued that for some actors the goal of armed conflict is not necessarily the defeat of the enemy in battle but the continuation of fighting and the institutionalization of violence for profit (Keen 2000: 25). Thus, the "greed kills" literature often mistakenly assumes that theft and predation are the *reasons* for the guerrilla struggle. While we recognize the complex ways in which African guerrilla movements have been exploiting opportunities provided to them by changes in the global political economy, we reject explanations of African armed struggles that focus primarily on the supposed economic agendas of these actors. Such a myopic focus may help explain how some conflicts are sustained, but it rarely tells us much about why conflicts start in the first place. It would be a mistake, for example, to assume that the recent wars in Central and West Africa started as competition over control of alluvial diamonds, coltan, or other natural resources. In fact, in both Sierra Leone and the Democratic Republic of Congo (DRC), the integration of extraction and marketing of natural resources to the conflicts occurred only once the conflicts were well under way. Nor does a "greed kills" thesis explain why these incentives have come to play such an important part in recent wars: that is, the economic agenda research assumes the profit motive on the part of the belligerents without exploring why or to what extent political-military actors become profit-seeking, market-based entities. To understand this transformation, we need to take into consideration political, cultural, and historical factors in addition to the economic dimensions of conflict. Obviously, economic agendas are an integral part of African wars, as elsewhere. But the desire to accumulate, while an important motivation, is not the only one. Even authors closely associated with the "greed" thesis have later argued that to focus excessively on material explanations and greed-inspired motivations of actors may lead to one-sided explanations of conflict (see Berdal 2003 and 2005). Making this variable the theory repeats the mistake from a few years ago, when ethnicity was presented as the decisive factor explaining war in Africa.

To understand the guerrillas of Africa, we need a more nuanced analysis of what the wars are about. Are these wars just another "resource" war, where youth are manipulated to fight on behalf of the interests of competing but equally corrupt elites? Or are these conflicts concerned with much deeper questions about the composition of African states and their respective polities? The latter assumption constitutes the vantage point both for this particular chapter and for the book as such. These conflicts are deeply embedded in the history of the continent, not only in colonial history and the transformation to independent states but in the totality of African history. In Africa, as elsewhere, recent and distant pasts relate in direct, although also sometimes rather perverse, ways. Many of the events and relationships characteristic of Africa's recent history—including politics and political violence—are closely entangled in peoples' perception of their social and ethnic identity. These perceptions of identity are social constructions, representations that change over time and are often distorted and manipulated, particularly as part of a discourse of domination emanating from those in power in successive colonial and postcolonial regimes (see Atkinson 1994).

We agree with Paul Richards that "war is a long-term struggle organized for political ends, commonly but not always using violence," and just like Richards we "object to the notion of 'new war' as some kind of 'mindless' response to stimuli such as population pressure or cultural competition" (2005b: 4). The Liberian war is instructive in this regard, as it has been portrayed as a primary example of Mary Kaldor's "new wars," drawing attention to both the economic motives and the global character of the conflict (Kaldor 2001). Our argument is that there is little "new" about the Liberian war. The conflict is deeply entrenched in history, and the only way to fully understand the Liberian war is to come to terms with this history and the ramifications it holds for current attempts to reconstruct Liberia. The Liberian war is not a "new" war but the present manifestations of social conflicts that started when the first Americo-Liberian settlers arrived in the early eighteenth century. Thus, the Liberian civil war can best be understood as a violent expression of the tendencies, organization, and attitudes toward identity, society, and class that have underpinned Liberia since its formation as a state. At the heart of the political, economic, social, and armed conflicts that have shaped and scarred Liberian society over the past two centuries is the question of how the Liberian polity should be constituted. The "new war" literature with its emphasis on economic motivations and global connections between local conflicts and international (often illegal) market-based actors helps us understand one important dimension of the Liberian conflict and the guerrilla movements that fought it. However, too much emphasis on this dimension may lead scholars and policymakers to neglect the ideational aspects of conflict. As the Liberian case illustrates, these are of immense importance to a full understanding of civil war, the actors within it, and its dynamics. This part of conflict can best be captured by a thoroughly holistic and historically grounded approach (see Bøås 2005).

Like Liberia, the violent conflict in neighboring Sierra Leone has produced multiple interpretations of the cause of the conflict and the reasons for its marked brutality (see Kaplan 1994; Richards 1996, 2005a; Abdullah 1998; Bøas 2001; Fithen and Richards 2005). Attempting to provide a socially grounded understanding of the origin and character of the RUF, Ibrahim

Abdullah focuses attention on socially marginalized youth. In particular, he regards the "revolution" of the RUF as a product of a rebellious youth culture in search of a "radical alternative" to the regime of the All People's Congress (APC; see Abdullah 1998: 204). He pays particular attention in his analysis to "lumpens"—unemployed or unemployable youths (mostly male) whom he regards as being "prone to criminal behaviour, petty theft, drugs, drunkenness and gross indiscipline" (1998: 207–208). Given the impoverishment of the social, political, and economic options facing these youths, Abdullah asserts that many would opt for a "radical alternative" to the status quo: taking up arms against the established order. This is an important contribution to the debate about the war in Sierra Leone. Nevertheless, we find Abdullah's lumpen thesis problematic for numerous reasons. First, his use of the lumpen as an analytic category is troublingly monolithic. Second, he fails to establish a causal connection between lumpen social status and their supposedly inherent violent behavior. Are we to assume that lumpens are hardwired to be brutally violent? Thus, while Abdullah does important work in underscoring the importance of youth culture and youth violence in African postcolonial politics, his analysis ends up raising more questions than it resolves. Why do some youth opt for the "bush path to destruction" and others do not? What role does gender play, given that most youths opting for a violent alternative are males? What political factors are involved in shaping these youth cultures and subcultures? What explains the turn to horrific acts of violence, beyond simplistic lumpen explanations? Is the situation really just a "wanton use of violence for the sake of violence" (1998: 235), or are more complex dynamics at work?

Thandika Mkandawire has sought to address some of those questions, claiming that because African rebel groups are made up predominantly of youths from urban areas—and thus with urban gripes—roving in the countryside amongst unreceptive peasantry, they engage in "extremely brutal and spiteful forms of violence" (2002: 181). Mkandawire argues that there are two major sources of conflict in urban spaces: ethnic rivalries and intra-elite conflicts—which fuel a sense of relative deprivation (2002: 191–192). As these conflicts move to the countryside, Mkandawire suggests, the rural terrain is inhospitable to the agendas of these angry urbanites for two reasons. First, African peasantry tend to have direct access to labor and land, which tend to be the main elements of insecurity for peasantry elsewhere (2002: 193–194). The armed rebels have little to offer the peasantry. Second, the relationship between the state and the countryside in Africa has tended to keep the peasantry relatively autonomous and thus unreceptive to the urban-focused rebels' claims of oppression and exploitation (2002: 193–198). In short, one socially marginalized group (urbanized youth) are operating in an arena populated by another, but distinctly different, socially marginalized group (the peasantry). Mkandawire's main argument is that because they are in a hostile rural setting, these roving rebels inflict violence on local populations: "they will tend to consider reluctant peasants as enemies or traitors, with death the usual penalty" (2002: 204).

While there is much that is attractive about Mkandawire's thesis, his argument about why rebels use violence against local populations in no way explains the forms and brutality of that violence, something he claims to address from the outset. Are we to resort to Abdullah's explanation that they are just ignorant and ill-tempered "lumpen" youths? More important, a number of the case studies in this volume seem to undermine Mkandawire's central claim. Members of Uganda's LRA, infamous in Western media reports for their brutality, are not dispossessed urban elites disconnected from the local population. Rather, they are semistationary (roving across the "Acholiland" of northern Uganda and southern Sudan) with direct links with their local host population—and the brutal violence is aimed at the people they are reportedly fighting for. They do regard their victims as legitimate enemies, but not for the reasons Mkandawire gives. The cases of Casamance, Côte d'Ivoire, and Angola also seem to contradict many of his assumptions and arguments, first among them being the claim that "the grievances that rebel movements claim to seek to address are often not salient in local political situations" (Mkandawire 2002: 199). Questions of labor and land are not easily negotiated in the African countryside. The case of the Banyamulenge in eastern DRC, the conflicts between agriculturalists and pastoralists in Ituri in the same part of DRC, the issue of land, labor, and migration in the Ivorian conflict, and the continued tension between the Loma and Mandingo over the right to land and belonging in Lofa County in Liberia only show all too well the insecurity of the African peasantry, the centrality of rural land conflicts in current civil wars, and how flawed one of the main assumptions behind Mkandawire's argument is. As sympathetic as we are to his desire to understand the extreme violence used in contemporary wars in Africa, his argument is unfortunately obscuring rather than unmasking the practice of violence in these cases. Nevertheless, both Abdullah and Mkandawire do well to underscore the importance of considering how socially and politically marginalized groups are drawn toward armed resistance to the state.

We agree with Paul Richards's assertion that modern African conflicts need "to be understood in relation to patterns of violence already embedded within society" (2005b: 11). Monocausal perspectives and broad-brush explanations tend to obscure more than they reveal. At the same time, while we believe that no armed movement can be properly understood without reference to its specific historical and social context, it is also wrong to assume that these movements elude any broader contextual or political analysis. The fact that guerrillas act within local social, economic, and historical contexts does not mean that their trajectories are entirely unique. Rather, we argue that almost all contemporary armed movements on the African continent share certain commonalities, which are rooted in experiences and narratives about corruption, violence (political and economic), and deep poverty.

These common experiences have over time contributed to the creation of deeply entrenched sentiments about social exclusion and marginality, especially among the young. Indeed, we argue that even members of armed movements that have bitterly opposed one another (e.g., the RUF and the Kamajors in Sierra Leone, or the factions in the Liberian war) often have more in common than what separates them. A shared experience of brutalization, abuse, and marginalization informs the worldview of those fighting for these movements. Each of these movements has also emerged within the context of a deeply dysfunctional state that was falling apart.

The question is, then, where do we turn for categories to conceptualize the trajectories of these movements? In examining the diversity of armed insurgencies in Africa at the end of the twentieth century, Christopher Clapham (1998b: 6–7) found it useful to distinguish among four broad groups of armed guerrillas. His typology offered the categories of liberation insurgencies (such as the anticolonial nationalist movements), separatist insurgencies (e.g., the EPLF and the Polisario Front), reform insurgencies (e.g., Museveni's NRA in Uganda), and warlord insurgencies (e.g., Charles Taylor's National Patriotic Front of Liberia and Foday Sankoh's RUF in Sierra Leone).

While we find Clapham's typology extremely useful, it is also our assumption that contemporary armed guerrilla movements in Africa no longer fit very well (if they ever did) with typologies based on traditional Anglo-American thinking about the political causes of conflict. Only the last of these four categories has been very prominent in recent discussions of African guerrilla movements. This is because, with a few exceptions (such as the Mouvement Patriotique de la Côte d'Ivoire), the majority of existing insurgencies do not fit easily into the other categories. While Clapham's 1998 collection is still the only attempt to study African insurgencies in a comparative manner, we believe that the external and internal environments of contemporary African insurgencies have changed significantly. The following chapters of this volume show that the characteristics, dynamics, and contexts of African insurgencies are not the same across time and space. In the next section, we discuss the characteristics, goals, and motivations of contemporary African guerrilla movements.

Characteristics of Contemporary African Guerrilla Movements

The Paucity of Ideological Motivation

Motivations vary greatly between and within different African insurgencies, but over the past few decades, there has been a noticeable shift away from ideologically informed movements. Early African armed guerrilla movements were largely characterized by their anticolonial nationalism. The specific character of these movements varied across the continent, but the common thread connecting them was their anticolonial agenda. Kenya experienced a sustained armed revolt from 1952 to 1957, while Cameroon experienced an armed rebellion from 1955 to 1960. In both of these cases, there was little outside support for the movements. Moreover, in both cases, the armed rebellions depended heavily on specific ethnic groups within the colony. In both cases, the rebellions were plagued by a lack of weapons and military skills.

In the late 1960s and 1970s, while a few liberation movements continued (most prominently in Angola, Mozambique, and Zimbabwe), several other armed insurgencies in Africa increasingly came to be characterized by their secessionist agendas. In Western Sahara and Eritrea, armed groups fought for territorial liberation against an annexing African state, Morocco and Ethiopia respectively. Nigeria was thrown into the brutal Biafran civil war when the southeast section of the country attempted to secede. Yet as Pierre Englebert notes in Chapter 4, there has been a striking absence of separatist motives among African insurgents. Historically, most armed guerrillas have been interested in capturing state power, either directly from the central government or regionally through the creation of an independent, autonomous territory. During the 1960s and 1970s, this political agenda was usually informed by a revolutionary ideological discourse often grounded in variations of Marxism-Leninism or Maoism, in combination with the influence of the Libyan gospel of Muammar Qaddafi's *Green Book*. Taking their cues from contemporary Asian anticolonial insurgencies, as well as Mao Zedong's successful revolution in China, these armed groups drew upon the emerging doctrine of guerrilla warfare. For the nationalist groups, outright victory against the better-equipped colonial armies was unlikely, but sustaining guerrilla violence against the colonial state and its infrastructure was seen as a victory in itself. Unlike their predecessors, these armed guerrillas were able to take advantage of external supporters, both from within neighboring states and from the Soviet bloc. For the most part, these armed liberation groups fought protracted guerrilla wars, in urban areas (e.g., Algeria) or, more often, in the rural countryside.

Yet it may be wise to question the extent to which armed insurgents were actually driven by ideological commitments, or whether ideology provided a convenient rhetorical cover. For example, should we characterize what happened in Kenya between 1952 and 1957 as a sustained armed revolt born out of anticolonial nationalist sentiments or as a Kikuyu revolt bent on capturing state power? The postcolonial state that finally emerged may point more to the latter than to the former. Insurgents' tenuous ideological commitments can be further illustrated by contrasting the two types of armed rebellions that emerged briefly in Congo during the 1960s. On the one hand, Pierre Mulele and his supporters led a sustained (though ethnically limited and internationally isolated) rebellion around the Kwilu district in the southwest. This group was characterized in part by its ideological adherence to a simplistic variant of Maoism. On the other hand, a more disparate collection of armed groups emerged in the northeast section of the country. Lacking ideological cohesion and often employing traditional belief systems and rituals, these groups tended to have a localized agenda, born out of the immediate "politics of place" in their area of operation and the anger and grievances of those who perceived that they had always received the "short end of the stick" in domestic political processes. As Crawford Young (2002: 20) points out, these eastern rebellions drew upon an "unrestrained social anger among the marginalized youth who filled the rebel ranks [which] led to massacres of many thousands of state personnel and others classified as *intellectuals* in the towns overrun." In this light one can only ask what is really so "new" about the more recent Congolese war. The belief systems currently informing the Mai Mai and other armed movements in the Ituri, Katanga, and North and South Kivu provinces do not constitute a sudden and swift return to premodern belief systems caused by the collapse of the Mobutist state but must be seen as a continuation, albeit reinterpreted, of traditional social practices of war. We must add that we do not understand this as an irrational retreat to paganism and magic but as a "magic of despair" under extreme circumstances (see also Gluckman 1963; Kastfeldt 2005). We will return to this issue below when we discuss the crises of the African state.

During the Cold War, it seemed that many armed groups espoused certain ideological commitments in large part to secure financial and military aid from like-minded forces. The rapidity with which many of these leaders dropped their ideological trappings at the end of the Cold War suggests the shallowness with which they had embraced their "causes" in the first place. Ghana's "Marxist-Leninist" Jerry Rawlings and Angola's "democrat" Jonas Savimbi are two good cases in point.

In the aftermath of the Cold War, ideology as understood by Western political science has rarely been a motivation for Africa's armed guerrillas. As William Reno notes in Chapter 5, on Liberians United for Reconciliation and Democracy (LURD), today's armed guerrillas no longer brand themselves with words like *revolutionary* or *resistance*. Instead, groups adopt "contemporary-sounding generic labels typical of development and human rights NGOs." Formal political ideas across a left-right continuum seem to be less relevant in Africa's armed struggles than other political motivations. The capacity of African guerrillas to adapt to changes in the global environment is illustrated by the ease with which they were able to change from the pattern of alliance during the Cold War to the global connections of business and crime in the globalized post–Cold War.

Global Geopolitical Context:
From Cold War to the "War on Terror"

The end of the Cold War affected more than just the ideologically encoded geopolitical landscape within which African guerrilla groups operated. Perhaps more important than the perceived irrelevance of leftist ideologies, the fall of the Soviet bloc meant the end of external backing for numerous African guerrillas. During the Cold War, many African armed groups benefited from direct and indirect support from either side of the Cold War. Such external support virtually vanished overnight, dramatically affecting several armed groups. For example, the evaporation of the "Soviet threat" in Africa meant that the United States no longer found it necessary to fund groups like Savimbi's União Nacional para Independência Total de Angola (UNITA) in Angola or the Resistência Nacional Mocambicana (RENAMO) in Mozambique. In both cases, these groups had to find other sources of funding or seek a negotiated accommodation with the central government. The collapse of the Soviet bloc also had some indirect and unforeseen effects on the African guerrilla movements. Most notable, the end of the Cold War meant that the international small arms market burgeoned, with cheap weaponry becoming readily available (Muggah 2002). There is little doubt groups such as RUF in Sierra Leone, the various Liberian factions, and insurgency groups in eastern Congo, who came to control mineral-rich areas, used these minerals to tap into new international markets of guns and weaponry that appeared. Beyond accessing cheap weaponry, armed groups have been able to take advantage of new advances in communication technology, most notably mobile phones and the Internet. The increasing ubiquity of cell phones and satellite phones on the African continent has increased guerrillas' ability to communicate amongst themselves, on the battlefield, and to the international community. Laurent Kabila's men used cell phones to coordinate their assault against Mobutu's shrinking forces, and this is also the means through which bands of LRA units communicate both among themselves and with local community leaders. The satellite phone is also an important medium for communication with the international community. Both Foday Sankoh and Sam Bockarie of the RUF quickly realized how powerful a tool this was when it could be used to put them directly on *BBC Africa,* for instance. For a few groups, the Internet has served as another tool by which to communicate to the "outside world." Websites are created, often by external supporters in Europe or the United States, in order to champion the cause of the rebel group, circulate their discourses and agendas more broadly, network with external supporters, and raise funds.[2] For some movements, these communicative technologies have increased their ability to articulate a narrative of their struggle, challenging the central government's authoritative voice.

While it is too early to make any definitive claims about how the US-declared "war on terror" has affected African guerrilla conflicts, we think it is important to recognize the powerful sway it now exercises over global politics. The "war on terror" has become a new frame by which policymakers and scholars engage with contemporary African guerrilla movements. One of the most pronounced ways in which Africa has figured into the "war on terror" is the United States and European Union's increased concern about failed states as breeding grounds for international terrorism. We believe this perception is built on a flawed understanding of state recession (see Dunn 2001; Bøås and Jennings 2005). Underpinning the "state failure" discourse is an assumption that all states are constituted and function in the same way: on a spectrum from good to bad. This begs the question, for whom is the state failing and how? Different actors within the state have different interests, and what is good for some (such as informal power structures that enable elite consolidation of power and profit) may not be good for ordinary citizens. In fact, the goal of the regime may be to create and sustain structures and power relations that are generally considered the consequences of state failure.

Before 11 September 2001, US and Western European security discussions paid little systemic attention to "failed" or "collapsing" states. In the immediate aftermath of the Cold War, it seemed that Western powers had little interest in addressing this phenomenon in Africa or elsewhere. But the fact that Al-Qaida planned the attacks on New York and Washington from the safe haven of Afghanistan, considered to be a "failed state," pushed the problem to the top of the security agenda in Western capitals, as evidenced by the declarations of the US National Security Strategy (White House 2002) and European Security Strategy reports (European Union 2003) that "failed states" are one of the key threats confronting the United States and the European Union, respectively. It is evident from these documents that concerns about "state failure" are essentially self-referential: failed states matter only insofar as they affect "our" security. But while few would disagree with general statements such as "The Liberian state is a failure" or "DRC is a failed state," we maintain that such pronouncements actually tell us very little about security and development within these states. Our concern is that Western policymakers employ this concept in a way that is less analytical than descriptive and categorical, lending itself to a narrow, checklist approach to policy that may result in extremely misguided planning and interventions (see Bøas and Jennings 2005).

While we are critical of Western engagement with Africa within the "war on terror" framework, we recognize that this geopolitical landscape has provided new opportunities and resources for African political elites (see Dunn 2007). In several cases, African leaders have been able to garner favors from the United States for their support of US foreign policies, particularly its invasion and occupation of Iraq. For example, Sudanese president Omar al-Bashir, once an ally of the Islamist cause, has actively cooperated with the United States since 11 September 2001. In return, the United States and the United Nations (UN) lifted the sanctions that had been in place against Sudan since 1996. In Djibouti, the United States maintains Camp Lemonier, the only true US base on the continent and home to more than 1,800 US personnel (Cowell 2003). The Central Intelligence Agency (CIA) has operated unmanned drone aircrafts from Djibouti, including the one that fired a missile at a car in Yemen in November 2002, supposedly carrying Al-Qaida operatives. In January 2003, the United States reopened the United States Agency for International Development (USAID) office in Djibouti and pledged US$8 million in education grants (Adebajo 2003: 181).

Some African leaders have publicly linked their own struggles against domestic rebel groups with the US-led "war on terror." For example, Ugandan president Yoweri Museveni frequently situates his government's war with the LRA in the larger "war on terror" context. Museveni, like others, has also sought to appropriate the rhetoric and practices of the US "war on terror" as a means of dealing with his own domestic opposition. In the fall of 2005, Uganda's main opposition leader, Kizza Besigye, was arrested and charged with treason under post-2001–inspired antiterrorist legislation. Ethiopia and Eritrea have also used the rhetoric and practices of the US "war on terror" to justify repressive measures against their domestic opposition. The government of Eritrea, which has offered the United States two sites for military bases, has accused exiled Alliance of Eritrean National Forces (AENF) dissidents of being connected to Al-Qaida. The Ethiopian government has branded opposition members in Oromo as international terrorists and has arrested hundreds of opposition leaders on the grounds of combating "terrorism." Even exiled Liberian leader Taylor has appropriated "war on terror" rhetoric. He established the Anti-Terror Unit (ATU), which rather ironically included former members of the RUF in addition to his Liberia fighters. Taylor repeatedly referred to his domestic opponents as "terrorists" and justified the detention of dissidents because they were "unlawful combatants" (Adebajo 2003: 181). In some cases, this maneuver has yielded success. Countries like Uganda, Kenya, and Tanzania have benefited from increased US military support. Some state leaders, such as Uganda's Museveni, have been successful in their appropriation of the "war on terror," while similar attempts by embattled Zimbabwean president Robert Mugabe have been notable in their failure.

In many ways, the US "war on terror" represents a return to Cold War geopolitics. African allies are again protected and strengthened regardless of their domestic governance shortcomings. The US interest in West African oil, while a significant feature of current US policy toward Africa, is not new, merely intensified. African leaders can again exploit opportunities provided by the geopolitical concerns of the (now lone) superpower. But what is perhaps most notably different in the "war on terror" is the lack of opportunities it affords to African guerrilla movements. As noted earlier, the bipolar Cold War provided both sides of African conflicts with opportunities to access resources and military materiel. African guerrilla movements could readily benefit from one bloc or the other. There is little evidence that similar opportunities exist in the current geopolitical context. In fact, the options for African guerrillas appear to be more limited. In many cases, it seems guerrilla movements are less likely to find support—material or otherwise—from an international community whose heightened sense of insecurity appears to conflate armed insurgencies overseas with terrorist threats at home. However, the more active role now played by China in Africa may point to a possible new scenario where multiple great powers once more compete for influence and resources in various spheres of interest. This may not be the case today, but clearly it is a future possibility, as it is also an issue of concern for at least some US military strategists (see Taylor 2004; Weisman 2006). If a new "great game" for Africa and African resources such as oil becomes a reality, it may yet produce new space for maneuvering for both African state leaders and African insurgency leaders.

The Crises of the Postcolonial State

One of the most important changes in the context of African guerrilla movements has been the current and ongoing crisis of the African state. The African state has entered an era of crisis—if not outright collapse in several places (e.g., Somalia, Sierra Leone, Liberia)—caused by multiple forces, such as the shrinking of the central government under structural adjustment programs and the increased marginalization of Africa in the world economy. As a result, the Westphalian sovereign state model, inherited from colonialism and modified according to the needs of African ruling elites, is increasingly in severe crisis across the continent, though the manifestations of that crisis are varied and geographically uneven.

The crisis of the state has resulted in something of a paradox. On the one hand, many African states are presented as both "failed" and "choiceless" (Mkandawire 1999; Herbst 2000). At the same time, control over the state is still much sought after and valued, as the experience from war in countries such as the DRC, Uganda, Rwanda, Liberia, Sierra Leone, and Côte d'Ivoire suggests. It may be that from the vantage point of global political economy and international relations theory this state is "choiceless," but from the perspective of its inhabitants this institution is still the main medium to negotiate order and social organization. It is precisely this "negotiation" that creates the spoils of the state and decides upon its extraction and redistribution.

How should we then approach this state? Obviously we cannot assume some sort of "sameness" between African states. Like states elsewhere, African states are both unique in their contextualizations and embeddedness and part of much larger trajectories of state formations. We believe that Jean-Francois Médard's interpretation of neopatrimonialism allows us to further explore some of these underlying assumptions (Médard 1991, 1996). In our understanding, neopatrimonialism should be considered a mixed type of rule combining to various degrees differentiation and lack of separation between public and private spheres. From a structural point of view such a state is differentiated, but from a functional perspective it is only weakly so. In short, bureaucratic and patrimonial norms coexist in neopatrimonial states. This is a general characteristic of modern life, and we will find traces of it in all states. What will often separate one state from another is the level of "patrimonialism" versus the level of "bureaucratic rationality." In their attempts to redress the colonial legacy of racially inherited privilege, the newly independent states of Africa may have created a special patrimonial path of redistribution, which divided the indigenous population along regional, religious, ethnic, and sometimes even family lines (see also Mamdani 1996). This created a state in which extraction and redistribution became privatized. This privatization of the public has three main consequences (Bøås 1997; Braathen, Bøås, and Sæther 2000):

1. Political-administrative power, instead of having the impersonal and abstract character of legal-rational domination specific to the bureaucratic state, is transformed to personalized power.
2. Politics becomes a kind of business, because political resources provide access to economic resources and vice versa.
3. Mass politics are structured around vertical client relationships.[3]

Traces of this type of socioeconomic structure can be found everywhere in the world. What is important is the level it reaches in any given society. As a system of rule, neopatrimonialism can in fact be remarkably stable and long lasting, creating states that are both "strong" and "weak" at the same time. Stated more precisely, the logic of neopatrimonialism can produce weak states with remarkably stable regimes (Bøås 2003b).

One illuminating example was the durability of the Mobutist regime in Zaire. The same example also shows us not only how a combined social and political breakdown may occur but also the cross-border ramifications the breakdown of such a neopatrimonial logic may have within a state system constituted by similar states ruled by a similar type of logic. This is illustrated equally vividly by the Sierra Leone of Siaka Stevens and Joseph Momoh, by the Liberia of the True Whig Party (TWP), and by the devastating effect of the *Ivoirité* discourse in Côte d'Ivoire. In all these cases, the argument can be made that the breakdown took place when the patrimonial logic became so dominant that it lost its integrating and legitimating aspects. This is precisely the situation referred to by Bayart as the exhaustion of the reciprocal assimilation of elites (1993). It should be a valid thesis that the logic of the state in question will influence what kind of guerrilla movement (if any) will occur when the state finds itself in a severe economic, social, and political crisis.

This brief recapitulation of the thesis of neopatrimonial politics can help illuminate the relationship between the external and the internal in such states. Drawing on Médard, Daniel Bach (1999, 2003) introduced the concept of "trans-state regionalism," which is built on the observation that in many African countries, if not the majority of them, large groups of the population, and sometimes the entire state apparatus, owe their survival to semiofficial, often illegal, flows of trade, capital, and services that go across national boundaries. The reasons behind this turn to informality are many, but there is little doubt that the increasingly diverging tariff, fiscal, and monetary policies that emerged when a number of African states began to experience severe financial difficulties in the aftermath of the "oil shock" in 1973 facilitated and sometimes required a switch to an informal economy (Bach 1999). People who had come to rely on the state and the formal economy for health, housing, education, transport, and marketing had to seek alternatives elsewhere (Mbembe 1992).

The success of African neopatrimonial states relies on the ability of political elites to carry out the expected vertical redistribution of resources through the patron-client relationship. What has happened in many African neopatrimonial states is a failure to deliver on the promises of the patronage system. Specifically, the capacity of ruling elites to maintain the vertical distribution of resources and reciprocity that the patron-client relationship relies upon has been undermined. As a result, there emerges both a crisis of legitimacy for the ruling elites and a perceived bankruptcy of the established state system. The first result is important, for it establishes a target for the resentment and frustration felt in certain sectors of domestic society—that is, the legitimacy of existing leaders is undermined and their position of power becomes increasingly challenged. While this is often the traditional trajectory in the emergence of armed insurgents against the ruling elite, what has become significant in recent years is less the perceived illegitimacy of specific ruling elites and more the perceived bankruptcy of the state model itself. This trend may have several implications.

First, the state may no longer be seen as the primary objective of the insurgency. In the past, armed struggles were aimed at seizing the reins of power—understood as control of the central government. However, with the crisis of the neopatrimonial state, control of the state may no longer be the end game. Such cases would be extreme versions of Clapham's (1998) "warlord" category. The goal may not be to change state leadership but to carve out and maintain a personal territorial fiefdom. Some movements with a strong enclave mentality (see Richards 2005a), such as LRA, RUF, or the Mai Mai, may be placed in this category.

However, the developments that have bounded these movements to specific localized territories may often be the result of the struggle rather than fruits of a deliberate strategy to carve out such a fiefdom in the first place. For example, Acholiland in northern Uganda became the LRA heartland by default because the LRA has been unable to establish itself outside this area, apart from the sporadic raids it carries out into Adjumani, Soroti, and Lira (see Bøås and Hatløy 2005). The other manner in which a personal territorial fiefdom is established is when the struggle is embedded in local conflicts and power structures. The case of Lofa County in Liberia and the "warlordism" of the deceased Francois Massaquoi of the Lofa Defence Force (LDF) and Alhaji Kromah of the United Liberation Movement of Liberia for Democracy–Kromah faction (ULIMO-K) exemplify this scenario. This part of the Liberian civil war is best interpreted as a local struggle over the right to land and belonging between the Lomas of LDF and the Mandingos of ULIMO-K. In the two respective local interpretations, Massaquoi and Kromah are not warlords but heroes who defended their people, and the establishment of their personal territorial fiefdoms during the war is understood not as an act undertaken for personal enrichment but as an attempt to protect their people under the extreme circumstance of civil war. This is also evident in the overwhelming support in the Mandingo towns along the Guinean border in Lofa County for Kromah in the Liberian presidential elections in October 2005 (see Bøås and Hatløy 2006a). Thus, in the cases where controlling the state is not the objective this is either due to default—the inability of the insurgency in question to move beyond the territory where the struggle started—or because the insurgency was motivated not by issues concerned with the state but by a local conflict, most often over rights to land and belonging. This suggests that questions concerning autochthony (discussed below) are never far away in these cases.

The second implication of the crisis of the neopatrimonial state is that the state and its institutions may not be the primary actors within the struggle. In many states, ruling elites have increasingly turned to extrastate instruments to maintain their power. In some cases, this has meant the employment of private military contractors, such as mercenaries. The recent literature on African armed conflicts has provided interesting discussions of the evolution of private military contractors in Africa. Since the emergence of Executive Outcomes in Angola in late 1992, much international attention has focused on the role and influence of these companies in stabilizing or destabilizing national and regional security in Africa (see O'Brien 2000). Another way in which ruling elites have moved beyond the state to protect their privileged positions has been in the emergence of private armed militias. In some cases militias are directly loyal to the regime in power. This is clearly the case in Côte d'Ivoire, where the Jeunes Patriotes and other militias in the southern part of the country are closely connected to the presidency of Laurent Gbagbo through an informal shadow state structure (see Chapter 6). In other situations "freelance" militias are employed by the state to do their dirty work. This is one way to interpret the Khartoum government's handling of the crisis in Darfur (see Chapter 9), and the same analysis can be applied to the employment of former "freedom fighters" by the Zimbabwean regime in its land-grabbing schemes (see MacLean 2005).

Third, the crisis of the neopatrimonial state has complicated the issue of legitimacy within African politics. Within African states, the sovereign state model is becoming increasingly irrelevant and illegitimate. Yet because of international norms, the African sovereign state (no matter how corrupt, bankrupt, or moribund) is still regarded as the sole legitimate actor within the international community. Historically, the highly qualified exceptions to this rule have been where states were considered illegitimate because of their imperialistic annexation of external regions (Morocco in the Western Sahara, Ethiopia in Eritrea), their racist foundation (Ian Smith's Rhodesia and apartheid South Africa), or where the leadership became an international pariah (Mobutu's Zaire). In these cases, armed insurgencies against the state were able to enjoy a fair degree of international legitimacy. Yet whereas the international community at large saw the Eritrean insurgency movement as a legitimate stakeholder, the same is not true for insurgencies like the RUF in Sierra Leone, the LRA in Uganda, or the Mai Mai in eastern Congo. In fact, due to the recent emphasis on warlordism in Africanist discourses, these armed groups are not just denied legitimacy as viable stakeholders but are often regarded *as the problem in itself.* This is a significant difference from the experience of previous insurgencies.

Crisis of Modernity

The crisis of the neopatrimonial state can be seen as a manifestation of a bigger phenomenon, one that can be recognized as a crisis of modernity. Before we continue, let us be clear what we do *not* mean by this term. Much of the popular Western discourse surrounding African armed conflict has focused on its exoticism to the Western eye. As a result, tired tropes of "heart of darkness," "primitivism," and "barbarism" have been reenergized (see Kaplan 1996). These explanations employ evocative imagery of Africa and of Africans incapable of existing in the "modern" world, with particular attention given to "barbaric" practices of violence and the employment of witchcraft and other forms of religious spirituality. The underlying assumption in these narratives is that Africa and Western modernity are somehow incompatible. While we outright reject such a view, we do recognize that the project of Western modernity is in crisis in Africa (as elsewhere).[4]

We see this crisis of modernity manifesting itself in several important ways. First, as discussed above, the Westphalian state system—the representation and vehicle for Western modernity as it was exported to the rest of the world—has become increasingly challenged as a concept, an institution, and a practice. Second, many African attempts to shore up the state through its neopatrimonial reinterpretation are also proving to be dysfunctional, as noted above. Third, traditional non-Western structures of power and authority are also failing to deliver. The reasons for this are varied—from their compromised appropriation by the colonial and postcolonial state to emerging generational conflicts and to the "weakening" of cultural bonds due to globalization—but the point is that these institutions and practices are failing to meet the needs within the lived experiences of most Africans. This is not to say that traditional institutions and practices are irrelevant. Rather, in this crisis of modernity, these institutions and practices, like those of Western modernity, are being reinterpreted, reinvented, and reemployed.

Often, what has emerged is a confusing amalgam of political, physical, and spiritual power that defies easy analysis, particularly from Western perspectives. Popular media attempts to explain the phenomenon tend to employ the "new barbarism" tropes mentioned earlier. A case in point is Robert Kaplan's discussion of the RUF in Sierra Leone, in which he explains the conflict in terms of the dissolution of Africa's social fabric and the inherent inability of Africans to develop into a modern society (Kaplan 1994, 1996). Both Paul Richards (1996, 2005b) and Stephen Ellis (1999) provide this dangerously misguided thesis with a sound drubbing. What is needed is an understanding of how political, physical, and spiritual power is constructed and legitimized in the popular imagination in societies under immense social stress due to a complete lack of security.

The last five years of Samuel Doe's reign are illuminating in this regard. This is a story of institutionalized corruption on a massive scale and grand theft of state resources. None of these were new in Liberia, but under Doe's rule (1980–1990) the state became an institution with one sole purpose: to be fleeced to the bone. Murder, rape, and other kinds of human rights abuses became the accepted order. In such an environment of extreme uncertainty, people will still look for answers, clues, and meanings, and as the modern structures of society fragmented, people sought refuge in magic and the many secret societies of Liberia. In previous decades these societies had clearly played an integrating effect in Liberia, but as the conflict increasingly revolved around ethnicity, they contributed to the eventual fragmentation and breakdown of Liberian society. As the civil war started, the social practice represented by the secret societies lost its embeddedness in local communities and traditional structures and was reinterpreted into the warrior cults emerging around the various armed factions (see Bøås 2005). Thus, we need to come to terms with how war and the events of war reinterpret the social fabric of different societies in order to give meaning to what is going on.

The developments in the realm of the imagination, particularly the religious imagination, should not be overlooked or simplified in analyses of war, be it in Africa or elsewhere. Ellis shows how various Liberian actors invented and employed ideas and practices from an existing range of cultural resources, and how the results were not inevitable but the product of human choices (Ellis 1999). Some of these were deliberate and intentional, but just as often they were unintended and thereby another consequence of our inability to see beyond the consequences of our immediate actions. Because there is nothing purely African about this, Richards's appeal for a functional analysis is instructive as it simply asks us to seek answers to what has been created (2005a, 2005b). "If we want to understand the behaviour of wild RUF abductees we shall have to look at the way their social worlds were pulled apart by exclusion and capture, and put together again through initiation and subsequent social control, in a violent forest world organised around a degree of practical Green Book egalitarianism" (Richards 2005a: 125). Employing the same kind of analysis to the case of the abductees who currently make up both the rank and file and increasingly the command structure of the LRA would enable actors in the international community such as the International Criminal Court (ICC) to understand why former abductees continue to fight even when an amnesty option is available.

Regional and Social Marginalization

Regions or social groups that feel they are being marginalized by the central state authority have helped foster the emergence of armed insurgencies many places in the world, and Africa is not an exception. Two important cases highlighted in this volume are the war in northern Uganda (see Chapter 8) and the Casamance conflict in Senegal (see Chapter 10). The case of northern Uganda shows us that such conflicts have a long and complicated history and that their root causes are embedded in their troubled past. The official starting point for the war in northern Uganda was resistance to the overthrow of the government of Tito Okello Lutwa by Museveni's National Resistance Army in 1986. However, the underlying cultural, political, and economic divisions are the heritage of the precolonial past, exacerbated by colonial and postcolonial projects. One of these divisions is the deep cultural (as well as political and economic) cleavage between the Bantu center and southwest of the country and the Nilotic north. The colonial administration recruited the bureaucratic elite from the center and the south, in particular from Buganda, whereas northern Uganda was mainly regarded as a reservoir of labor from which the colonial administration recruited men to the army and the police force. This ethnic division of labor reinforced already existing cleavages and differences between northern and southern Uganda and helped to harden the divide between Nilotes and Bantus that has become so significant in Uganda's political history (Bøås 2004a). This division does not represent the whole economic activity—the main economic role of Acholi and also many parts of Bantu-speaking Uganda in the colonial era was to grow cotton—but cultural differences were open to manipulation through ethnocultural politicization, so that "the Acholi, far from being born soldiers, were transformed into a military ethnocracy" during the colonial period (Doom and Vlassenroot 1999: 8).

This kind of manipulation of ethnocultural variables did not vanish with colonialism but rather increased, becoming an important tool for a string of governments from Obote I to the current National Resistance Movement (NRM) regime. As a result, resentment in the north against the central government has continued in various forms since 1986, the most durable being the LRA. Prior to the displacement of the inhabitants of Acholiland enforced by the Ugandan army, the relationship between the LRA and the local population was often more cordial; even open support was not completely unheard of. This has changed as the displacement forced LRA to attack the camps for food and other kinds of supplies. Today, the LRA is neither militarily very strong nor likely to overthrow the government. However, it should not be underestimated either. Like the insurgency in Casamance, the LRA has been able to keep its struggle alive for a remarkably long time. This is achieved "by strategically using fear to maximize perceptions of threat. Its violence is random, unpredictable, and highly visible and symbolic. Its killings, mutilations and abductions are a method implemented to institute its control over the population, and the randomness of their violence compensates for their inferiority in numbers" (Bøås and Hatløy 2005: 33). The cases of northern Uganda and Casamance also show that conflicts that take place in areas of relative isolation and that are of little interest to both the national government and the international community can last for a long, long time.

While both northern Uganda and Casamance represent cases where marginalized regions have experienced armed insurgencies, there has been some scholarship trying to explore how marginalized social groups fuel other armed conflicts. As noted earlier in the chapter, Abdullah argues that the origin and brutal character of Sierra Leone's RUF has been caused by "lumpens," the unemployed or unemployable youths, who he argues are prone to crime and violence (1998). Likewise, Thandika Mkandawire (2002) explains the brutality of African rebel movements by focusing on the violent tension between the supposed urban-generated rebels operating in a rural setting that is inimical to their struggle. As we already mentioned above, we find both of these arguments problematic for multiple reasons—from the questionable use of lumpen as an analytic category to the questionable claim that the majority of African rebels come from urban areas. Setting aside these problems, we agree with the driving motivation in both Abdullah's and Mkandawire's approaches: recognizing the significance of how socially and politically marginalized groups are drawn toward armed resistance to the state. Bøås's chapter (see Chapter 3) is an attempt to understand the African guerrilla on his or her own terms, and that chapter addresses these issues more fully than we can do here.

Recycled Elites and Warriors

To a certain extent, leadership personalities have had a significant impact on the development of African guerrilla movements. During the Cold War, the ideological disposition of these armed groups was often either augmented or superseded by the role of a charismatic leader, as illustrated by the role played by Jonas Savimbi in UNITA or Foday Sankoh in RUF. We maintain that it is impossible to understand the history of these two movements without taking into consideration their leaders' respective personalities and how their rank and file viewed them. Sankoh was the "Pa" for his fighters. Removed from their traditional structures of authority, they accepted Sankoh, or rather an imaginary Sankoh, as the majority had never met him—for a good part of the war he was either outside of the country or in jail—as their new father figure.

One important dimension that needs to be considered is the question of the professional trajectory of the leaders of various insurgencies. Often this influences the motivation of the group, particularly in its desire to capture the state. When the leaders are external to the established political elite (as is the LRA's Joseph Kony), the insurgents are often less interested in capturing the central government. But elites who have fallen from the grace of state power may be motivated to join armed struggles that are aimed at capturing the state. Elites are recycled in African societies, as elsewhere, and many armed groups are either led by or contain large numbers of people who once enjoyed the fruits of state power and now seek to recapture those benefits through force of arms. Denis Tull's discussion of the former Mobutists within the Rassemblement Congolais pour la Démocratie (RCD) in Chapter 7 provides a good example of this, and some of the leaders of the New Forces who currently control northern Côte d'Ivoire can be seen in a similar way. For example, New Forces leader Guillaumme Soro has a background as a radical student leader. In the old Houphouêtist state he would probably have been offered integration into the state machinery in exchange for his loyalty. Such practices were also an integral part of Mobutu's statesmanship in former Zaire. Bayart describes how "the success with which Field Marshal Mobutu used promotions to decimate his opposition, from 'revolutionaries' of the First Republic to the parliamentary members of the *Union pour la dèmocrati et le progrès social* (UDPS)" not only became legendary but also made the opposition look like fools (1993: 186).

Bayart also notes how Liberian president William V. S. Tubman's "unification policy" was an attempt to make opposition impossible by capturing the leadership from all popular organizations. These strategies are best viewed as attempts to enforce hegemony of a specific political regime and can be an integral part of the state practice of neopatrimonialism. In most cases of civil war in Africa, the ability of the state to pursue such a strategy was exhausted prior to the start of the war. This is a major recent development, and it explains why former elites are now to be found both in the leadership and among the rank and file of armed insurgencies.

Recycling of elites through an armed insurgency is one important aspect of civil war in Africa; another is the recycling of warriors from one place to another. Sudanese fighters originally trained by Libya for its expansionist African policies later returned to Sudan and joined various militias there (see de Waal 2004a), and the original military core of the LRA fighters in northern Uganda was the Acholi soldiers who fled to the north after the NRM captured Kampala in 1986. Concerns about similar groups in West Africa has led Human Rights Watch to focus on regional warriors in West Africa and describe them as an "insurgent diaspora" (2005). The concern is that these recycled warriors can sometimes function as seasoned mercenaries, bringing valued skills to nascent African insurgents, and further destabilize the region. But while it is correct to observe that some fighters from Liberia have fought in Sierra Leone, Guinea, and Côte d'Ivoire and that there are active fighters originating in these other three countries as well, these professional warriors constitute only a small minority of the total fighter population in these countries. The overall majority of the West African combatants, both former and current, have fought only in their country of origin. The small band of regional warriors can certainly make a conflict more brutal than it otherwise would be, given that they can operate outside of their normal context, in much the same way Mkandawire argues that urban-raised rebels can brutalize rural populations (2002).

However, as Richards et al. point out, the current situation along the border of the Mano River countries can also be compared to the mid-nineteenth-century "trade wars" in this region, when the use of "external" warrior groups was common practice—as they had "no family connections in the places they were employed to control, and therefore also little or no sympathies with local populations" (2005: 3). Brutal behavior in war is, however, not the same as the ability to set a conflict in motion. Recycled warriors may join a war if the opportunity arises, but they rarely start them in the first place. Recycled warriors are clearly a characteristic of many contemporary African guerrilla wars, but they do not provide a causal explanation for the outbreak of these conflicts.

Autochthony, Land, and Belonging

Issues of identity and belonging have not occupied an important role in traditional political science explanations of war in Africa. This should change, as questions concerning autochthony in the form of the politics of place, belonging, identity, and contested citizenship are among the most crucial and contested in African politics. *Autochthony,* literally meaning "emerging from the soil," implies localist forms of belonging, and its expressions have led to debates about the origins of candidates in election campaigns as well as violent struggles in rural areas where assertions about autochthony are used to justify land claims.

As observed by Peter Geschiere, "The recent drive towards political and economic liberalization has engendered a rapid intensification of struggles over belonging, an obsession with *autochtonie* and ever more violent forms of exclusion of so-called 'strangers,' even when they are citizens of the same country" (2004: 237). This has sometimes undermined the whole notion of national citizenship (see Geschiere and Nyamnjoh 2000). However, such controversies are not new phenomena on the African continent. Their origins are to be found in both precolonial practices and ideas about the politics of place embedded in the colonial project. With a few exceptions, most African societies are multiethnic societies. In the precolonial era, citizenship—if we can speak meaningfully of such a concept—was relatively fluid. Most often strangers of other racial and ethnic origins moved with relative ease between indigenous African polities. With land abundant and migration easy, the preferred form of political protest was exit. The colonial imposition of citizenship, which essentially tied each person to a specific territorially bounded polity, was therefore an event of revolutionary magnitude in Africa.

After independence, citizenship laws increased in importance as the new African states now had to permanently define who legitimately lived within the border of its territory and who did not. The creation of "foreigners" brought about by impending independence led to riots in many places even in the 1950s and 1960s. As Mahmood Mamdani has argued, the 1994 Rwandan genocide had its roots in such debates (2002). The Rwandan Tutsi population that had settled in Uganda after the 1959 "Hutu Revolution" were regarded as noncitizens both at home and in Uganda (despite greatly assisting the NRM's victory). Unable to resolve their noncitizen status, a group formed the Rwandan Patriotic Front (RPF) and, returning to Rwanda by force of arms, set off the civil war that eventually culminated in the 1994 genocide.

Land issues become particularly vulnerable to the politics of identity and belonging where two or more groups have "shared" the land for a period of time (Hagberg 2004). One important asset in such situations is the ability to stake your claim to land from the position of being autochthonous, that is, as a "son of the soil," whereas your counterpart is presented as a "newcomer," an "immigrant," and a "stranger." In such a situation, claiming citizenship is of primary importance, because although "citizenship does not entitle you to resources, it entitles you to enter the struggle for resources" (Mamdani 2002: 505). Due to a combination of political and economic factors, the compromise upon which cohabitation was built is increasingly unsustainable. New modes of deciding who has rights to land must therefore be established. In some cases, the conflict can be dealt with by referring to a contract, but in other cases rights to land are based on a combination of lineage-based claims and ad hoc user rights. In such situations, excluding others from the land by claiming they are not autochthonous may be a viable strategy. The examples of Côte d'Ivoire, eastern Congo, and Liberia show how disastrous such perceived and real processes of marginalization and poverty can be.

The case of Côte d'Ivoire illustrates how those able to define themselves as autochthonous demand that "migrants," who already have suffered resentment for quite some time, should be expelled. It is therefore of uttermost importance that an examination of the current crisis in Côte d'Ivoire take into account long histories of resentment, discrimination, and violence. The current crisis is an outcome of the unwillingness of the political elite to acknowledge that the system of governance for citizenship and land rights established under Félix Houphouët-Boigny increasingly is becoming dysfunctional, and that the answers to these challenges cannot be found in the attempt to change the principles of citizenship and land rights from the Boigny model of patrimonial integration to the exclusiveness of an autochthonous *Ivoirité* discourse. We believe that the way the Ivorian crisis is handled will have important consequences for similar crises of autochthony elsewhere in Africa, and the same can be said about the issue of the contested status of the Banyamulenge in eastern Congo and the "Mandingo issue" in Liberian counties such as Lofa County and Nimba County.

Autochthony and citizenship disputes are an increasingly pronounced feature of African politics, especially within polities experiencing contested elections. Debates over who belongs and who has access to resources, including the ability to vote, can become increasingly politicized, particularly by aggressive political entrepreneurs. It needs to be stressed that questions around autochthony need not necessarily lead to violence. But in some of the cases examined in this book, such questions are often a salient feature of the conflicts. In the chapters that follow, numerous authors attempt to explore the role and relevance of autochthony, providing both empirical observations and theoretical reflections on what we expect will be a continuing feature in the literature on both African politics and contemporary conflicts.

For our purposes here, we find it useful to recognize that autochthony, as a politicized discourse about who can rightfully present themselves as "sons of the soil," functions as a discourse without an end. That is, it can always be restarted, reinvented, and reemployed, with answers to questions of "which soil" and "which sons" always in flux. It is used to (temporarily) define relations, marking the constructed and shifting boundaries of "in" and "out." What is more, we see autochthony operating in three ways. First, we recognize its employment with regard to ethnicity, in the sense that it helps determine belonging to certain ethnic groups (e.g., Tutsi and Hutu, Acholi and Buganda). Second, we note its role in the construction and articulation of stereotypes (e.g., Bantu as pastoralists and Tutsi as cattle owners, Sudanese/Darfurian "Africans" as farmers and "Arabs" as semi-pastoralists). This use of autochthony often intentionally obscures nuance and ambiguity in order to create and maintain simplified cognitive frameworks, which in turn engender certain political behaviors, such as discrimination and privilege. Finally, autochthony operates on the level of geopolitics, helping to determine citizenship in the postcolonial nation-state.

In some ways, the current focus on autochthony in Côte d'Ivoire and eastern Congo (as elsewhere) can be regarded as an expedient answer to the uncertainties of the unfinished nation-building project embarked upon by the postcolonial state (specifically by Houphouët-Boigny and Mobutu, respectively). But it also functions as a response to a constitutional crisis in the rural areas over who has entitlement to speak, to represent, to vote, to access resources like land, and so forth. Thus, to varying degrees and in varying ways, autochthony informs the conflicts in Côte d'Ivoire, eastern Congo, Liberia, Sierra Leone, and elsewhere. The key to utilizing autochthony as an analytical tool, we argue, is to examine who are the speakers of autochthony, who creates the metanarratives on which the discourse is built. Here the scaling of autochthony from ethnicity as the body to the geopolitical offers a useful frame (see also Jackson 2003; Geschiere 2005).

Movement: Stationary/Roaming, Road/Bush-Path

Borrowing from Mancur Olson (2000), Thandika Mkandawire makes an important distinction between stationary and roving rebels (2002: 199–207). Stationary rebels establish physical enclaves, often setting up rudimentary structures of governance and control. Roving rebels, on the other hand, are constantly on the move. This distinction illuminates variations in the relationships between rebels and locals, as well as providing a way to understand the different methods used by movements to finance their rebellions. Stationary rebels tend to rely heavily upon the local communities in their "liberated" zones. However, in some cases they are stationary in order to secure physical control over valuable resources. Angola's UNITA is a good example of a stationary movement, or rather, a movement that became stationary. As Malaquias argues in Chapter 11, UNITA's decision to become stationary in order to control the diamond-extraction economy resulted in a change of tactics that disrupted its relationship with the local population and eventually led to its defeat on the battlefield. Roving bands, in contrast, tend to resort to predation and pillaging while they are on the move.

Mkandawire (2002: 200) points out that "no movement completely fits into either category." Indeed, the examples in this volume all tend to occupy a middle position in a stationary-roaming continuum. The clearest exception would be the New Forces in Côte d'Ivoire, which is more or less stationary due to French and UN intervention. Even regionalist movements, like the Mouvement des Forces Démocratiques de Casamance (MFDC), have elements of the roving rebels (see Chapter 10), and the LRA (see Chapter 8) is both stationary and roving. The LRA is stationary because the total displacement of Acholiland enforced by the Ugandan army gives them a physical enclave that they control by roaming the bush-paths of this space. They live, plunder, and fight within an enclaved space. However, they control it not by establishing "liberated" zones but through unpredictable movement and attacks within the frame of their enclave.

That said, we would suggest that a further useful distinction to make is noting *how* these rebel groups roam. Do they follow the main roads, as was mainly the case in Liberia? Or do they predominantly roam in the bush, like the LRA in northern Uganda or as the RUF used to do (i.e., the periods of 1993–1995 and 1998–1999)? We suggest that this distinction can have important implications for the organization, structure, and goals of various armed groups. At the risk of oversimplification, we can say that road-roaming rebel movements are usually engaged in a struggle to capture state power (either regionally or nationally), tend to fight in more conventional-style battles, and are hierarchically organized. Bush-path rebel groups, such as the LRA and RUF (during part of its existence), tend to be less interested in immediate takeover of the central government, tend to employ nonconventional tactics (such as ambushes), and are less hierarchically organized. In the case of the LRA, for instance, the movement is made up primarily of autonomous, cell-like groups that have limited and sporadic contact to the LRA's command structure. Such movements often appear incomprehensible to Western political science, and their seeming lack of a recognizable strategy or political vision is taken as proof of their primitivism. However, in line with Richards (2005a), we would argue that these movements are best understood as "enclave formations," engaged in producing an alternative "world order" based on narratives of betrayal and exile reinforced by their existence in such an enclave formation (see Bøås 2004a). Our inability to grasp what keeps these movements in existence is not their failure but ours. As the case of the LRA so vividly shows, as long as they stick to their particular modus operandi they can be very hard to defeat. In fact, an argument can be made that the death of the RUF as a viable fighting force happened only when it tried to act as a conventional force in order to protect its control over the diamond fields in Kono and Kailahun. Again, few, if any, rebel movements fit completely into either category, but we suggest that this may be a potentially useful distinction to make when analyzing contemporary African guerrilla movements.

Regionalization of Conflicts

The end of the twentieth century witnessed the emergence of two relatively new, fully developed regional conflict zones: one in West Africa around the Mano River countries and the other in the Great Lakes region of Central Africa. These regional conflict zones have been caused by the intertwining of a series of localized conflicts in Western and Central Africa, the latter largely related to the crash of the Mobutist state in Zaire/DRC. Given this, we argue that the region is an important site of analysis for understanding contemporary African guerrilla conflicts. All the chapters in this volume make explicit reference to the regional contexts. But while we recognize the rise of regional conflict zones, we reject simplified notions of interventionist regional states. This is a hallmark assigned to both Rwanda and Uganda, and also to Liberia during the rule of Taylor. We do not dispute that Rwanda and Uganda were involved in the war in the DRC, nor that Taylor's Liberia was involved in the conflicts in Sierra Leone, Guinea, and Côte d'Ivoire. What we disagree with is the tendency to see this involvement as the event that triggered these conflicts in the first place. The conflict in eastern DRC is a Congolese conflict, and to define the movements involved there simply as proxies of either Rwanda or Uganda would be a grave mistake, because it completely overlooks the historicity of the conflict. The same is true for the many attempts to blame Taylor for the war in Sierra Leone and later in Côte d'Ivoire. These conflicts are driven by their internal dynamics, but of course there are also significant cross-border ramifications.

The important issue here is the relationship between the conflicts, or how localized conflicts become intertwined and regionalized. The Great Lakes region is an example. There is war in DRC, Uganda, Sudan, the Central African Republic, and Burundi. Rwanda is currently at peace but is also an actor in these conflicts. Some, such as David Newbury (1998), argue that what we have seen in this region is a convergence of separate historical phenomena, whereas others such as William Cyrus Reed (1998) suggest that all these events are closely intertwined and should be seen as integral parts of a larger regional war. Our suggestion is that the current pattern of conflict in the Great Lakes region is best viewed as a series of local and national conflicts that do not always have much in common but become intertwined through the weakness of the state system in question (see also Dunn 2003; Bøås 2003b, 2004a). The same is true for West Africa. The Liberian war was by and large a national war, partly constituted by a series of local conflicts, most prominently between Loma and Mandingo in Lofa County and between Krahn and Mandingo on one side and Gio and Mano on the other side in Nimba County. Taylor's ability to tap into the conflict situation in Nimba helped trigger the war, but these local conflicts were the combined outcome of conflict patterns preceding the Americo-Liberians and the administrative practices of their state. The war in Côte d'Ivoire is a war about the right to land and belonging, and the Sierra Leone war started as a rebellion against a deeply dysfunctional and thoroughly cor-rupted state. Our argument is that wars in Africa are regionalized not through grand plans and criminal intention but by default, and this default is the inherent weakness of the state system.

Conclusion

We understand today's African guerrilla movements as being both the cre-ation of and a response to the crises of modernity and its dysfunctional political institutions. What this has meant is that traditional approaches to understanding African insurgents are increasingly unable to provide ade-quate guides or explanations. For example, traditional guerrilla theory as articulated by Mao and Cuban revolutionary theorists does not seem to have very much to offer when it comes to throwing light on the origins, worldviews, and narratives of insurgencies such as the RUF of Sierra Leone, the Allied Democratic Forces (ADF) and the LRA of Uganda, or the Mai Mai of eastern DRC. Far from behaving like "classic" African insurgencies such as the Ethiopian and Eritrean ones, these seem more to be manifesta-tions of rage against the patrimonial "machinery" of dysfunctional states: a largely youth rebellion organized in social movements with a cultic ele-ment. At their root, contemporary African armed rebels seem to be strug-gling to provide political opportunities as well as basic survival strategies for those navigating the continuing crises of modernity.

The "economic agendas" literature (e.g., Berdal and Malone 2000; Col-lier 2000) may be useful in explaining how armed movement are sustained, but it does not tell us much about why conflicts start in the first place. To understand this transformation, we need to take into consideration political, cultural, and historical factors as well. All current conflicts in Africa are deeply entrenched in history. The past and the present are connected in Africa as elsewhere, and the only way we can hope to understand this is to consider how current conflicts are an integral part of the total history of the area in question. Due to the privileged position of the state, both in theory and in practice, examining who controls it and for what purpose is one obvious place to start our investigations. However, we need to keep in mind that many conflicts are local in character and that not only material aspects matter, but also questions concerning belonging and identity. As the chapters in this volume show, awareness of the combination of material and ideational factors and their embeddedness in history can increase our understanding of current African wars and the guerrilla movements that fight them.

African wars are brutal, and the consequences in terms of human suffering are immense, but they are not incomprehensible. It is only our approaches that all too often make us avoid seeing the obvious: people take up arms because they are angry and scared and see no other solutions or opportunities. We do not in any way attempt to justify the killings and abuses carried out by these movements, but we still make the argument that we need to understand. Lasting solutions to the many wars on the African continent are to be found only in sober analysis of what caused these conflicts in the first place.

Notes

1. This is the standard way in Western political science to measure the "success" of armed insurgencies, but the studies in this volume suggests that this issue is far more complicated.

2. Examples include some of the rebel groups of eastern DRC, and even an LRA website existed for a little while. It is, however, doubtful whether the latter case had anything to do with the LRA. It was likely the work of Acholis in the diaspora who were trying to communicate what they believed was Kony's message.

3. According to Mahmood Mamdani, patrimonialism is "in fact a form of politics that restored an urban-rural link in the contact of the bifurcated state, albeit in a top-down fashion that facilitated the quest of bourgeois factions to strengthen and reproduce their relationship" (1996: 2).

4. For a critique, see Richards 1996 or Dunn 2003.

3

Marginalized Youth

MORTEN BØÅS

Recently the issue of youth in African insurgency movements has been a topic of much heated debate. Paul Richards's seminal contribution about youth and war in Sierra Leone (see Richards 1996) was followed in 1997 by a special issue of the journal *African Development,* which only can be described as an attempt to reduce Richards's work to pieces. The most lasting part of this critique is Ibrahim Abdullah's "lumpen" thesis (see Abdullah 1998, 2004; Abdullah and Muana 1998). Later the issue of youth was raised in Thandika Mkandawire's thesis about the "urban bias" of African insurgency movements (see Mkandawire 2002), and it has also become an integral part of what can be called a "critical anthropology of war" (see Peters and Richards 1998; Richards 2005a, 2005b; Richards et al. 2005; Abbink and Kessel 2005; Honwana and de Boeck 2005; Utas 2003, 2005; Peters 2005).[1] In addition, a number of reports from various human rights group have been concerned about this issue (see, in particular, Global Witness 2005a, 2005b; Human Rights Watch 2005).

However, despite all the recent debate, this is still a divided field of inquiry, as the young African guerrilla is often depicted either as ruthless murderer or as powerless victim. This is a pity, as almost all scholars mentioned above would probably agree that the average young guerrilla fighter is neither an angel nor a demon. He, because with a few exceptions this is a man's world, is more a "man-child" than anything else. He is fragile, damaged, and hurt. Yes, he undoubtedly commits horrific acts of human rights violation; he is a bandit, but also by all means a political actor, and sometimes he is regarded both by his peers and in his home community as a freedom fighter or a defender of certain rights, values, and identities.

One reason for the inability to avoid simple characterizations of African guerrillas may be rooted in our failure to account for the very nature of war. Our understanding of war is still cloaked both in the contemporary understanding of war emerging out of the European nation-state system and in a

liberal reading of the consequences of war. This means that we often fail
to acknowledge that war does more than merely disrupt or destroy existing
social systems; it also creates new systems. Although cruel, ugly, and inhuman, war is by its very nature an instrument for social and economic restructuring. It is a site for innovation, which reorders social, economic, and
political life, and as such it is best approached as a drama (see Bøås 2004b).
War is a social drama over the distribution of ideas, identities, resources,
and social positions, which often forces the disadvantaged to design alternative survival strategies. When youth are drawn onto the center stage of such
conflicts, the outcome is often the emergence of militias and other types of
insurgency movements. In societies torn by conflict, these entities can serve
as providers of some sort of order and social organization and can represent
means of social integration and upward social mobility. The only way to
understand youth involvement in such processes is to take their own experiences seriously, even if the narratives presented by such youthful actors
do not fit very well with existing categories of political behavior and may
also challenge our human rights ethics.

Fragile Youth

In early May 2003, the killing of the Sierra Leonean warlord Sam "Maskita"
Bockarie by Liberian troops loyal to then-president Charles Taylor was
reported.[2] Bockarie, who was forty years old when he died, was at the
height of his career. He had become a regional mercenary dealing in death
and destruction, but also a businessman and world player who anytime he
picked up his satellite phone could get access to *BBC Africa*. Bockarie was
undoubtedly a flamboyant character, having embarked on a series of coping
strategies—diamond miner, hairdresser, waiter, and disco dancer—before
he started his career as a rebel when he joined the Revolutionary United
Front (RUF) in the 1990s. First as a rank-and-file foot soldier, then later as
field commander, Bockarie emerged as the main military leader of the
movement after RUF forces and their army partners in the Armed Forces
Revolutionary Council (AFRC) were forced out of Freetown by Nigerian
forces acting under the banner of the Economic Community of West African States Monitoring Group (ECOMOG; see Keen 2005). When he died,
Bockarie was generally regarded as one of the most dangerous men in West
Africa, seen not only as a bandit but also as a regional powerbroker, trading
in murder and mayhem, whose actions were considered a threat to the stability of the whole West Africa region.

   If we look behind the labels "warlord," "regional warrior," and "mercenary"—as well as "diamond miner" and "disco dancer"—who was Sam
Bockarie? We do not know much about his life, and this chapter will not

attempt to fill those empty pages. Rather, it will attempt to use Maskita's life to say something about the background of many of the young men currently living a life by the gun in Africa. While Bockarie's rise to success makes him a remarkable case, and the details of the Sierra Leonean context have their own uniqueness, the story being told here resonates across the continent and shares numerous elements with the lived experiences of armed youths active in the numerous guerrilla struggles highlighted in this volume. This is not an attempt to redeem Maskita; he was responsible for gruesome acts and gross violations of human rights. However, we still need to understand what created Maskita and others of his kind.

Sam Bockarie was born in Koidu town in Kono district in Sierra Leone on 10 February 1964. He was the son of a diamond miner. Koidu is situated in the center of the area for alluvial diamond mining in Sierra Leone, and like many other kids growing up in Kono, Bockarie left school to become a diamond miner. Whether this was his own choice or his father's we do not know, but an inability to pay school fees has always been an important reason that teens do not go to school in this country. In later interviews with the BBC, Bockarie told reporters repeatedly about his childhood memories of having to go to bed hungry. Dropping out of school was most likely not a matter of choice but a consequence of the circumstances in which he was growing up. Most likely his father could not cover his school fees anymore and was in need of the income young Bockarie's labor could provide to the household. Parents in Sierra Leone take their children out of school not only because school fees are expensive but also because of the family income that is unavailable when children are at school instead of working. People are poor, and the combination of high school fees and loss of income is the most common reason children are taken out of school (see Kielland and Tovo 2006; Bøås and Hatløy 2006b).

The Kono district in which Bockarie lived in the first part of his life is the birthplace of diamond mining in Sierra Leone.[3] After diamonds were discovered there in the early twentieth century, the Sierra Leone economy was transformed from one depending on agricultural products (e.g., palm oil, coffee, and cocoa) to a mineral economy. These deposits are of the alluvial type, meaning that they are found out in the open air, and the work for a young boy—typically they start this work between the age of fourteen and seventeen—is to dig with a shovel, be it in mud, sand, or gravel. Mud and sand must be removed in order to get to the gravel, and after the gravel has been dug out it is transported to a place for washing and sieving. This is extremely repetitive, hard physical work. We do not know exactly how old Bockarie was when he started to work in the diamond pits, but he was around twenty when he embarked on his attempt to become a famous disco dancer. The transformation from a miner to a disco dancer is not that common, but what is typical is that most young miners do not stay in diamond-mining work for very long. The work is not only simply too demanding on the body but also boring, and only a handful of the young miners make a real profit. Diamonds may be glamorous in Amsterdam, Antwerp, or New York, but not in the alluvial pits in Kono. Many Sierra Leoneans have tried it; very few have anything else to look back on than long, hard days under the sun with muscle cramps and back and chest pains.

Sometimes these young men work for a fixed daily wage—currently around 5,000 to 6,000 leones (less than US$2.00)—or they work as members of a team under the supervision of a crew boss. In the latter case they are not paid a fixed wage but have a share in the gravel pile and the profit from any diamonds discovered in it. In this case, a supporter provides them with some food, accommodation, and limited medical services. As noted, few of these young boys make a lot of money from their work. Kono is a diamond-rich area, but still it takes time to find diamonds, and the big and really valuable stones are rare. Most diamonds are small and not of jewelry quality. Many of the boys working in the pits do not know how to evaluate the true value of the diamonds that they find. Usually they sell their diamonds to the crew boss and simply have to trust what the crew boss tells them about their value. They do not trade with the diamond dealers themselves. This is the case in Kono today, and there is no reason to believe that knowledge of diamond value was more widespread when Bockarie worked there (see Bøås and Hatløy 2006b). Bockarie was at the very bottom of the ladder of the diamond industry in Kono, and we can only imagine what it must have felt like for him and others of his kind when they later returned to Kono as RUF soldiers and commanders, establishing themselves as the new "masters" of the trade. It must have been a huge personal victory. However, his rise to power via the RUF was merely the last of his numerous attempted transformations.

Somewhere around 1985—if we are to believe the stories that are told about the life of Maskita—he left Koidu and his work as a diamond miner to embark on a career as a professional disco dancer, touring various parts of Sierra Leone, trying to make music and dance his way out of poverty and misery. Unable to get anywhere with this new career path, however, he relocated himself to Abidjan, the capital of Côte d'Ivoire, where he made a subsistence living as a hairdresser and waiter. During these days of "exile," he quite coincidentally met a group of recruits from the RUF and decided to try his luck with that lot instead. He climbed onto their truck and ended up in the densely forested border area between Liberia and Sierra Leone, undergoing military training. A new chapter was about to open up in Bockarie's life. Survival and personal gain—as well as recognition and respect—were now within the reach of the barrel of his gun. Maskita was ready to fight his way onto the center stage of political and economic life in Sierra Leone.

In this regard there is little special about Maskita. His background seems to be the same as that of many others who have ended up living a life of rebels and soldiers. They have emerged from similar marginal backgrounds, be it from diamond-rich areas such as Kono or from a rural existence of little to no possibility for progress or upward social mobility. Most of the young men who originally joined the various armed movements who fought the Liberian civil war did not come from the larger cities but from the countryside, joining a movement either as they advanced toward Monrovia or, as seems to have been the case of Lofa County, as Taylor's forces attacked the Mandingo towns in this area, escalating an already present tension between people of Mandingo and Loma origin (Bøås and Hatløy 2006a; see also Ellis 1999; Højbjerg 2005).

Although as a group these young insurgents may give an impression of menace and carelessness, when one is talking to them individually one is struck by their feeling of betrayal, of being lost and without opportunities. On their own they are not strong but fragile: a state of mind generated between the ruins of a modern state and a rural existence that seemed more and more meaningless as modern communications revealed all the things they could never enjoy.

Things Get Damaged, Things Get Broken

During the formative years of people like Maskita, not only the state was damaged and broken but the inhabitants as well, and young people were dreaming of another life. If there ever was a golden age in Sierra Leone, it must have been the very few years immediately after independence, when Sir Milton Margai ruled the country. Thereafter the country quickly went downhill. Margai's death in 1964 led to a leadership struggle along ethnic lines between his brother Albert, a Mende from the southern part of Sierra Leone, and John Karefa-Smart, a Temne from the northern part of the country. In the end, Karefa-Smart lost the leadership struggle, but as this reinforced the Sierra Leone People's Party (SLPP) as a Mende party, it also led to increased general support for the main opposition party, the All People's Congress (APC). Under Albert Margai's leadership, the SLPP lost the next general election in 1967 to the APC and its leader, former trade unionist Siaka Stevens. Under the leadership of Stevens, the APC progressively consolidated its rule. In 1973, the APC, through a combined strategy of political violence and voting irregularities, assured its candidates success and achieved control of every single seat in Parliament. De facto, the country had become a one-party state.

Under Stevens's rule, most societal institutions were completely corrupted. The APC leadership, in its bid to stay in power, deliberately weakened important sectors of civil society. Institutions, both public and private, were successfully emasculated through a combination of co-optation, bribery, intimidation, repression, and blackmail. The press was effectively controlled through violent attacks on newspapers and individual journalists but also through public regulation. The consequence of this official culture of corruption and mismanagement was the internalization in Sierra Leone society of corruption as "a way of life." It became the "order of things" (Reno 1995). The main rule for socioeconomic interaction among people at all levels of society, from the ministries and parastatals to junior bureaucrats and teachers: in order to get any work done or services conducted, you had to pay a bribe. The bribes were what people lived from, not their salaries, which were paid irregularly and were too low. Maskita must have experienced this culture of corruption, with the mismanagement and abuse of power that followed it, many times in his early years, first as a miner in Kono and later as a traveling jester and disco dancer in Sierra Leone.

His birthplace, Kono, was not only the cradle of diamond mining in Sierra Leone but also one of the primary sites for this culture of corruption. Bribery and corruption have been part of the Sierra Leone diamond "adventure" since its very beginning, when the colonial administration gave the paramount chiefs responsibility to control settlement and migration, and thereby also power to decide who belonged to the "soil" of the diamond-producing areas and who did not. Many found they could circumvent regulations by bribing local chiefs. After independence, illicit mining increased once more, and when Siaka Stevens came to power he tried to reimpose government control by sending the army to support the police in their attempt to bring an end to illicit mining. The outcome, however, was not a decrease in illicit mining but the swift establishment of a culture of corruption, as both police and army personnel accepted bribes from miners without the necessary permits. Smuggling also increased, and the few diamonds that passed through Stevens's Government Diamond Office (GDO) tended to be undervalued with regard to export tax value. The officials involved earned good money on this arrangement (see Sesay 1993). As the salaries of government officials were falling behind the inflation rate in the 1970s and 1980s, they increasingly accepted bribes to turn a blind eye to illicit diamond mining and smuggling and even took part in such operations themselves. The state structures that were supposed to control the diamond sector for the benefit of the whole country became institutions existing for the sole purpose of being fleeced to the very bone. By the late 1980s, it is estimated that up to 95 percent of the diamonds produced in Sierra Leone were being smuggled out of the country (Sesay 1993; Keen 2005).

When Joseph Momoh assumed power in January 1986, the World Bank and the International Monetary Fund (IMF) put him under pressure to control smuggling and corruption in the diamond sector to increase the nation's taxation base. Under the State of Economic Emergency Declaration of 1987, it was forbidden for private firms to deal in foreign currency, and the army was once more sent into the rural diamond-mining areas to enforce these and other new regulations. This did not improve the situation. Rather, what happened was a widening of the collaboration between mining interests and the army that also occurred during Stevens's attempt to reregulate the diamond-mining sector in the late 1960s. "Operation Clean State" of April 1990 could therefore not succeed. The army expelled about 10,000 miners from Kono. However, this not only increased the involvement of the military establishment in the diamond sector but also created a huge pool of discontented young ex-miners, who came to constitute the main recruitment pool for the RUF, the army, and the Civil Defense Force (CDF; see Abdullah 1998; Reno 1995, 1998; Fithen 1999; Richards 1996).

By then Maskita had left Kono and the mines, but he certainly must have experienced this during his time as a miner. Being exposed to bribery, corruption, mismanagement, and the abuse of power day in and day out can be a very humiliating experience and may help us understand why so many young people have willingly taken up arms in parts of sub-Saharan Africa. To understand the "African guerrillas" we need to consider their experiences with the state, the traumas caused by these experiences, and the meta-narratives constructed around these shared memories and experiences. These shared experiences and narratives create the politics of memory; and the role played by memory politics—in setting in motion not only the RUF but also movements such as the Mai Mai in the Democratic Republic of Congo (DRC), and in providing an effective call to arms in Liberia—should not be underestimated.

The state's failure to provide for its population is largely responsible for creating the nearly permanent marginalization of large segments of the public in political and economic life. This leads to intensified political conflicts over the distribution of ideas, identities, resources, and positions. In the face of state failure, people are forced to construct alternative survival strategies, usually in the informal sector. With the increased informalization of both the state and the economy, the postcolonial African state is pushed further into crisis, with the marginalized elements of society becoming further marginalized and vulnerable. These disruptions of existing patterns of authority and economic activity help shape the social settings of the armed insurgencies and the people who have fought in them. Many people suffered in recent decades from the uncertainty that these economic practices fostered. However, as states sank into seemingly permanent crisis, those hurt the most mentally were young people, emerging from an impoverished and tattered education system to seek an employment that the formal economy could not provide. The continued marginalization of young men in particular, youths such as Maskita, created the vast pool of recruitment potential that has fed the rebel movements.

The causes of conflict and motivations of those who fight are not easily delineated. But a common strand can be identified in the contexts in which these conflicts occur. Almost every movement, however distinctive, emerged as a corrupt and dysfunctional state receded, leaving behind disaffected youth with little means of achieving status or material improvement except as combatants.

The bitter truth was that there was little left to do. So few alternatives seemed viable, and this realization must have led some, obviously not all, to develop a mindset of hatred against their society, their communities, their elders, even their parents, that was unleashed in anger when a gun came within their reach. The gun became their tool, their personal revolution, and by killing they could finally prove that even they mattered. These young men are the creation of damaged and broken societies, where there is little left to do.

The Bush Devil

As the war in Sierra Leone followed its own logic of ebbs and flows, the diamond fields of Kono became one of RUF's main assets. In order to control the area and the mining, RUF burnt down nearly 85 percent of the houses in Koidu and chased away many of the residents. Just as previous governments had expelled unwanted miners from Kono, RUF tried to control the extraction of diamonds by removing what its leaders saw as a surplus work force.[4] Some people were forced to dig diamonds for RUF commanders, but as diamonds are small and the sites difficult to control, even for armed people who kill without hesitation, RUF came to rely more on installing themselves in the various roles as supporter, license holder, landowner, and machine owner than on the power of the gun solely. Maskita and his new friends in the RUF took over the roles that used to be performed by local chiefs, politicians, civil servants, soldiers, and traders. For some of those who stayed behind, the period of RUF control was one of terror and brutality, whereas for others things remained more or less the same; they just had to adapt to new faces in the roles of supporter, license holder, landowner, and machine owner.

What an amazing transformation this must have been for Maskita. What boy does not dream of returning home as a powerful man after a long adventure? For Maskita the dream was about to come true. He had left Kono in search of a dream of transformation, of making something of his life, of becoming something. Now he was returning all-powerful and omnipotent. He was no longer "only a miner's son." He was no longer just ordinary Sam Bockarie. He had become Maskita.

The "Maskita" transformation exemplifies the personal transformations of many young men who pick up the gun. Importantly, the gun represents not merely another form of survival but also the possibility of creating new meanings of self. As noted at the outset, war does more than disrupt existing social systems; it also creates new social orders. In this process, the fighters become active agents in the transformation of their social systems and their selves. They are no longer merely passive agents of a brutal system, but through the gun they gain agency in their daily lives. As they gain agency, others pay the price as victims of the violence used to establish this agency.

However, we should recognize that these new social systems are informed in large part by the old ones. Those practices of wealth accumulation, corruption, mismanagement, and physical violence that were condoned and practiced by the state become reinvented and reinterpreted in the process of social engineering opened up to these young men by the armed insurgency movements they joined and the civil wars they created. As newly forged "bush devils," members of the RUF seem to have attempted to renegotiate the old order in the enclaved areas where they now lived (see Richards 2005b), but the brave new world that they had envisioned was not as easily constructed as some of them may have thought. Old habits do not vanish that easily, and even though some aspects of camp life must be seen as a total negation of the society they had been growing up in, the "new vanguard" could be carried away by the possibility of wealth that suddenly emerged.

However, in the beginning of the Sierra Leone civil war, "get rich or die trying" does not seem to have been the main motivation for the young guerrillas. Of course, we do not know Maskita's personal hopes, but there is little to indicate that his ideas about the war were any different from those of his fellow RUF fighters in this period. The war in Sierra Leone did not start as a competition over control of alluvial diamonds. The integration and marketing of natural resources within the conflict occurred only once the conflict was well under way. While there is no doubt that international networks of clandestine dealers in diamonds and weapons assisted the RUF, it took the RUF until 1998 to get such activities organized—a fact that fatally undermines the argument that diamond mining and control was the sole objective of RUF and its fighters (Richards 2005b). The "economic agendas" literature (e.g., Berdal and Malone 2000; Collier 2000) may be useful in explaining how armed movements are sustained but does not tell us much about why conflicts start in the first place.

By the time Maskita and the RUF entered eastern Sierra Leone at Bomaru in Kailahun District (from Charles Taylor–controlled Liberian territory) in late March 1991, the Sierra Leonean state was in severe economic crisis and undermined by a near-total loss of legitimacy among the population. The RUF undoubtedly pushed this corrupted state over the edge, but the tactics used by Maskita and his RUF compatriots and the civil war that followed ripped the whole social fabric of Sierra Leone as well (Bøås 2001).

The RUF was headed by Foday Sankoh, an aging former Sierra Leone army photographer, flanked by a few other senior members such as Abu

Kanu and Rashid Mansaray; the majority of its fighting force of about 100 was made up of young men like Maskita, all determined to change the fortunes of their lives through the barrel of the gun (see Abdullah and Muana 1998). By recruiting youth—both voluntarily, by tapping into sentiments of social exclusion, and through force and coercion (for example, by making young recruits participate in atrocities against local leaders and populations)—the RUF built a viable fighting force. By summer 1991, it controlled around a fifth of southern and eastern Sierra Leone.

With the escalation of the war, the government lost nearly all of its control over the diamond trade and thereby also its ability to pay its civil servants and the soldiers fighting the RUF in the border area. In April 1992, some of these unpaid soldiers rebelled and took over power. Led by twenty-seven-year-old Captain Valentine Strasser, they formed the National Provisional Ruling Council (NPRC), initiated a major recruitment drive among youths in Freetown and other larger cities, and went on the offensive against the RUF. During 1993, the army recaptured important mining towns, including Koidu, Kailahun, and Pendembu. Most observers believed that the war would soon be over.

This was not to be. RUF was weakened, but the losses that the movement experienced led it to rethink its strategy and modus operandi. "Frankly, we were beaten and on the run, but . . . we dispersed into smaller units. We destroyed all our vehicles and heavy weapons. We now relied on light weapons, and our feet and brains and knowledge of the countryside. We moved deeper into the comforting bosom of our mother earth—the forest. The forest welcomed us and gave us succor."[5] In isolated forest bases, the RUF regrouped and retrained its fighters and also engaged in the first trade in diamonds—often with government soldiers. These first deals were small and haphazardly done, mainly constituting an exchange of diamonds for arms and ammunition with government soldiers who had been too long unpaid.

This camp experience is yet another time of "exile" that we must recognize when we discuss the life of Maskita and his peers. As these people understood their own actions, they were fighting for a new Sierra Leone, putting their lives at risk for a revolution that would save Sierra Leone from the years of corruption and mismanagement that had followed after independence. Now they had to seek refuge in the forest, as their project was generally not well received in rural communities. This may very well have increased the frustration and hatred that these young men already had toward rural life and traditional structures of authority. In the worldview facilitated by the exile experience in isolated bush camps, Sierra Leone may have been seen as a society beyond any salvation than the one that could emerge from a "baptism of fire." RUF launched a major new offensive just before Christmas 1994. One year later the movement got as close to Freetown as Waterloo, just a few miles outside the capital.

During this part of the war, a major RUF bush camp was established in the Makondu Hills, off the highway between Masiaka Junction and Mile 91, the area known as the "death zone" during the war. This camp, called Bush Camp 44, was a twenty-minute walk from a village called Makandu. The camp was established in 1994, and in that first year an uneasy truce was established between the village population and the RUF fighters in the camp. However, in 1995 the village was suddenly attacked. The RUF burnt it down entirely and even stuffed the village well—the only source of clean water in the area—with the bodies of villagers killed in the attack (Bøås and Hatløy 2005).

From a military point of view, this action simply does not make sense. Even if the target was the village population, why not just drive them away and occupy the place? There was nothing to be gained from burning down the town and destroying the well. The reason for this and many other violent acts orchestrated by Maskita and his fellow RUF fighters must be sought at another level. Most likely the war was just as much about symbolic acts as about ordinary warfare. RUF was an armed insurgency, but just like other insurgency movements analyzed in this book, it must be seen as much as drama as actual warfare. Maskita's war was not simply a war of arms but also an attempt to reconstruct the societal structures of Sierra Leone through violent but basically discursive means. The "bush devils" emerging from the isolated forest camps seemingly all over Sierra Leone wanted to create a new Sierra Leone for themselves through a baptism of fire.

The Kids Are on High Street

In an attempt to reverse the tide of the war, Strasser announced a return to multiparty democracy, making unconditional offers to the RUF to discuss a ceasefire and RUF participation in the forthcoming elections. At the same time, however, he also employed the services of Executive Outcomes, a South African private military company with strong links to various international mining and oil interests and other African regimes (notably in Angola). Supported by Executive Outcomes, the army managed to stop the RUF offensive (see Howe 1998).

In 1996, the situation seemed to be improving. The NPRC stepped down and elections were held, with Achmed Tejan Kabbah and the SLPP victorious. However, the nascent, fragile process of peace and reconciliation did not last long. The peace process soon encountered a dead end, and the international community—which should have helped the warring parties to reach out to each other—by and large abandoned the scene. Additionally, the Sierra Leonean army felt threatened by the support the new government gave to the CDF, which was increasingly transforming from a southeastern-based local defense force into a government-controlled (SLPP) militia.[6] This was the immediate precipitant of the coup in May 1997 and the establishment of the AFRC, which included both army soldiers and RUF members.

The kids were now certainly on high street as former marginalized sons of diamond miners and farmers established themselves as the new "masters" of Freetown. Everything they ever wanted was suddenly within their reach. Finally they could embrace a life many of them felt rightfully belonged to them. Maskita certainly enjoyed his new status as a "big man" in Freetown. Now he was both the disco-dancing champion of Freetown nightlife and the one giving the orders during the day. This could not last very long, however, as the AFRC was completely isolated politically.

The AFRC stayed in power for less than a year. In March 1998, Freetown was "liberated" by Nigerian soldiers acting under the banner of ECO-MOG (see Keen 2005). But still the war persisted. The RUF and Maskita in particular had spent their time in Freetown well, cultivating connections with the international underworld of illicit arms trading, and they now used their continued control of diamond-rich areas such as Kono to restock their supplies of arms. As in 1993, the movement withdrew into the hinterland to reorganize and rearm—but this time on the basis of a resource base they had learned to master. It is only after the RUF was chased away from Freetown in March 1998 that control of diamonds became the movement's modus operandi (Bøås and Hatløy 2006b). One of its key sites was Koidu, Maskita's old hometown, and the surrounding diamond areas. Diamonds extracted from these and other areas under RUF control were sold for cash and exchanged for arms and ammunition. A considerable amount of this trade was organized through Liberia, but international merchants of arms and diamonds also dealt directly with RUF commanders in Koidu and other such places. In the midst of all of this, Maskita was busy transforming himself from a national insurgent into a regional warlord.

Just prior to Christmas 1998, the movement reemerged again and, in a daring and violent offensive, planned and led by Maskita, broke through ECOMOG's defenses around Freetown. The RUF managed to take control of substantial parts of the city for over a week in January 1999. Now the kids were once more on high street, and the result was an orgy of violence, looting, and human suffering documented, for example, in the movie *Cry Freetown*. However, this attack led to subsequent negotiations that prepared the ground for a peace agreement and the deployment of the United Nations Mission in Sierra Leone (UNAMSIL).

The UN peacekeepers stumbled initially: after a series of errors, 500 peacekeepers were temporarily captured by RUF insurgents under Maskita's command (Bøås 2000), and more UN troops—assisted by a British intervention force and more ECOMOG soldiers—were eventually needed to control the situation. However, as the UN force increased to approximately 15,000 peacekeepers, RUF came under considerable pressure, and the movement eventually fragmented. Maskita's days in Sierra Leone were now numbered, and after falling out with RUF leader Foday Sankoh, he left Sierra Leone for Liberia, where he was employed by President Charles Taylor in various military operations. Masikta also participated in the Ivorian civil war, in the western region; whether and how much this was under Taylor's orders is still unclear.

Maskita was now a regional warlord, a much-feared businessman of death and destruction, preying on the decaying state structures of West Africa. To the very end, he was a kid on the high street of insurgent activity in West Africa. He took things to extremes, yet there is a clear line of continuity between the behavior of previous Sierra Leonean "big men" and Maskita's actions. Every institution or aspect of society was there for the taking, to be milked dry. What had started out as a social revolt (we do not know if Bockarie ever shared RUF's initial ideology) ended up as a perverted version of the state the movement initially rebelled against. This is not unique to Bockarie and the RUF but seems to be a common pattern among current armed insurgencies all over Africa.

We can relate this to greed, or we can seek explanations elsewhere. I believe that such practices as we saw in the latter part of the RUF war in Sierra Leone represent direct connections between the old social systems of the dysfunctional state and the new social orders practiced by the armed insurgents. If acceptable modes of social (to say nothing of political and economic) behavior are cast so openly and violently into question in the wake of dysfunctional states, is it so striking that some of the young, marginalized, and vulnerable elements of society eventually gravitate to extremes? In very real ways, these young men are only putting into practice what they have learned from their elders. We have trained them well. And for those like Maskita, their story can be seen as a success: the successful reinvention of the self, of doing something, of becoming someone.

Bockarie once stated in a satellite phone interview, "I never wanted myself to be overlooked by fellow men. Now I think I am at a stage where I am satisfied. I have heard my name all over. I have become famous" (BBC News 2003b). Indeed, Bockarie was a wanted man, sought by the UN-backed war crimes tribunal (i.e., the Special Court for Sierra Leone) as it prosecuted atrocities committed during the war in Sierra Leone. Though he had been hired by Taylor in Liberia, Taylor's forces would end Maskita's life in May 2003. But by the time he was gunned down, the forty-year-old had become a "self-made man" several times over. He had made history. He became something as he reinvented himself as a disco dancer, a hairdresser, a seeker of fortune in Abidjan, a guerrilla, a field commander, the RUF commander, and finally the ultimate regional warrior. He had become a "man in full." For many angry and marginalized young men, he no doubt had become a role model as well. The full tragedy of the situation is exposed only when we take into consideration that by Sierra Leonean standards Bockarie lived a successful life. Yes, he was gunned down at only forty, but that's one year older than the average life expectancy at birth in Sierra Leone, and whereas the ordinary Sierra Leonean dies as a poor man whom nobody knows about or pays much attention to, Bockarie died as a rich and famous man (see UNDP 2005).

Conclusion

Maskita is dead and at the time of writing Sierra Leone is quite peaceful, but what we need to keep in mind is that there is not only one Bockarie but many. As the Cockney Rejects argued so brilliantly in the 1980s, "the East-side is everywhere," and unfortunately, a Maskita-in-the-making is everywhere in the countries dealt with in this volume. In any slum area, be it the Magazine or the Sawa Grounds in Victoria Park in Freetown, Sierra Leone, or Monrovia, Voinjama, Koidu, the IDP camps in northern Uganda, or any other forlorn and forgotten place, there they are sitting in a palm wine shack, hanging out on the street outside a bar or a restaurant, or at a bus stop. At such places you find them: idle young men, seeing little if any opportunity to make the transformation from their present state of despair and exclusion into something else and better. All it takes is one individual with an idea about something else and the means to transform his ideas into action—call it resistance, call it revolt, call it violence, robbery—and they are game, eager to settle the score of humiliation and marginalization.

What can we offer them to redefine these frames of hopelessness and exclusion? No matter what we choose and how we position ourselves, we should base our approach on respect for their perception of their lived realities and take their views seriously. These youth should be seen as a resource, not as a problem.

Notes

1. For an extended account and critique of the "lumpen" and "urban bias" theses, see Chapter 2. What is here termed a "critical anthropology of war" relates to the new interest in anthropology for conflict research, for questioning the causes for conflict and the background for people's motives and actions. It pays attention to the historical dimensions of the conflict in question and is based on in-depth field-work. An excellent example of this kind of work is Paul Richards's edited volume *No Peace, No War,* which presents the work of scholars connected to Uppsala University's Living Beyond Conflict seminar.

2. Bockarie was indicted by the Special Court for Sierra Leone (SCSL) on seventeen charges of war crimes, including acts of terrorism, collective punishment, unlawful killings, sexual violence, physical violence, crimes against humanity, use of child soldiers, abductions and forced labor, looting and burning, and attacks on United Nations Mission in Sierra Leone (UNAMSIL) personnel. The indictment was withdrawn after his death was confirmed on 2 June 2003.

3. This section draws on Bøås and Hatløy 2006b.

4. David Keen describes Kono as a persistent focus of rebel activity and relates how the RUF expelled thousands of people from this district (Keen 2005: 51). People claim that Maskita planned to blow up the bridge across the River Bagbe at Njaiama-Sewafe, in order to improve RUF's ability to control the movement of people in and out of this territory. This plan is reminiscent of previous attempts at regulation and control, such as the checkpoint system of the De Beers subsidiary in the 1950s.

5. Statement by Foday Sankoh in *Footpaths to Democracy: Towards a New Sierra Leone,* RUF's main political manifesto, probably written in 1994–1995 in the Gola Forest headquarters of the RUF.

6. Other local community-based militias for self-defense existed, such as the Tamaboras in Koindadugu District. The Tamaboras also fought outside their own district, mainly in Kono, but never became an integral part of the CDF structure. The increased ethnification of CDF as a Mende project may be the main reason for this.

4

Whither the Separatist Motive?

Pierre Englebert

In his landmark contributions to the study of African politics and guerrillas, Christopher Clapham (1996, 1998a) identifies separatism as one of four purposes of African insurgencies, together with colonial liberation, reform of the state, and warlordism. In addition to the examples of Eritrea and southern Sudan discussed in *African Guerrillas* (Clapham 1998a), readers will be familiar with the secessionist context of several other recent or ongoing African civil conflicts, including the Casamance war in Senegal, the Oromo and Ogaden rebellions in Ethiopia, the Azawad movements in Niger and Mali, the struggle over Cabinda in Angola, and the unilateral withdrawal of Somaliland from the rest of Somalia since 1991. Yet rather than providing revelations about the nature of political insurgency in Africa, the salience of these conflicts actually hides the surprising fact that separatist warfare is relatively rare across the continent. Indeed, if one adds the Biafra, Kasai, and Katanga secessions of the 1960s, the above enumeration represents nearly all the instances of secession attempts in Africa since independence. In contrast, more than thirty African countries have undergone one or more nonseparatist conflicts since 1960. All together, if one were to add all the years of conflict of every country from 1960 to 2002, 27 percent of those in Africa would have separatist content, as against 44 percent in the Middle East and North Africa, 47 percent in Asia, and no less than 84 percent in Europe.[1] Only Latin America would have a lesser propensity for separatism than Africa, but the lack of domestic territorial conflict in Latin America is not unexpected. Its states are older than those of Africa, its populations more homogeneous, its political divisions based on class more than regional identities, and its economies less reliant on primary commodities.

In the case of African insurgencies, the relative scarcity of separatist motive is puzzling. After all, African states are youthful and very heterogeneous, dispose of large and decentralized reserves of natural resources, which could sustain separatist groups (Collier and Hoeffler 2002), and have

55

a poor record of providing for their citizens. African states are also more culturally alien to their populations than most states in other regions of the world. Moreover, politics on the continent often amounts to zero-sum games, as states are captured by one ethnic group or coalition, which frequently exerts its domination over others, largely excluding them from state benefits if not persecuting them (Deng 2002). That these dominated groups do not resort to separatism with greater frequency is perplexing, especially given the continent's propensity for other types of violent conflict. How are we to explain the relative contemporary absence of significant separatist demands from long dominated or excluded regions such as the Democratic Republic of Congo's Kivu, Kasai, and Katanga provinces; Congo-Brazzaville's south; Côte d'Ivoire's north; Nigeria's Igboland, Yorubaland, and northern states (alternately); South Africa's Zululand; Angola's Lunda Norte and Lunda Sul; Zambia's Barotseland; Zimbabwe's Matabeleland; Cameroon's Anglophone western region; and so forth?[2]

Several answers have been suggested, but each has its shortcomings. In their seminal essay "Why Africa's Weak States Persist," Robert Jackson and Carl Rosberg (1982) focused on international dynamics, suggesting that the granting of "juridical statehood" by the international community to former colonial entities allowed their reproduction despite their empirical shortcomings, because it froze African states in their inherited colonial jurisdictions and impeded self-determination movements. Their argument was about the resistance of the African juridical state, thanks to its international legitimacy, to domestic challenges. What they did not explain or even identify, however, was the relative lack of such challenges to the state. Although they pointed to a relationship between juridical statehood and continued poverty, they did not explain why Africans do not reject the poverty, chaos, and institutional weakness perpetuated by juridical statehood. How do international norms of recognition of sovereignty translate into the actions of Africans, especially those excluded from power?

Another argument highlights the depth and territorial specificity of nationalist feelings generated in Africa over the last several decades and through the colonial episode. According to Crawford Young, African nationalism originates in the shared experience of "common colonial subjugation" (2002). For this reason, he contends, there has been no real confrontation between territorial nationalism and political ethnicity. Furthermore, the effective ties of territorial nationalism appear impervious to negative popular perceptions of the state and have so far shielded states torn by civil strife or prolonged economic crises from disintegrating completely. While much is appealing about Young's argument, the origins of territorial nationalism remain unclear, especially given the territorial and institutional fluidity of colonial states, many of which were not finalized in their current shape until well after World War II. Further, Young does not account for the exclusive character of some of Africa's nationalisms, such as *Ivoirité,* which purports to exclude large segment of citizens from the benefits of belonging to the state (see Chapter 6). Finally, it does not explain the few actual instances of separatist conflict in Africa.

A third type of answer has suggested that artificial and heterogeneous African states have been integrated and kept together thanks in large part to the distribution of state resources to group elites. This model of "fusion" (Sklar 1963; Boone 2003) or "reciprocal assimilation" (Bayart 1993) of elites has indeed promoted the reproduction of Africa's weak states. Yet in the post-1990 era of financial failure and institutional collapse of many African states, it is getting increasingly hard to impute the resilience of states to neopatrimonial redistribution. Clearly, redistributive politics cannot explain why the Congolese rebels of the Rassemblement Congolais pour la Démocratie (RCD), radically excluded from the benefits of power at the center until 2003, nevertheless promoted the institutional reproduction and territorial integrity of the DRC while simultaneously occupying three or more of its provinces (see Chapter 7). Similarly, the increasingly restricted basis of power in Côte d'Ivoire following Félix Houphouët-Boigny's death in 1993 led to the exclusion, dispossession, and nearly literal alienation of large segments of the northern populations. Yet the "New Forces" rebellion has not so far challenged Côte d'Ivoire's territorial integrity, despite its exclusive control of the northern half of the country and the probable benevolence of neighboring Burkina Faso. It may well be that, despite repeated peace agreements, the intransigence of the Ivorian actors will eventually solidify the country's current partition, but it should be stressed that separatism has never been part of the New Forces' agenda (see Chapter 6). These examples highlight the need to account for the reproduction of the African state after the bankruptcy of nationwide neopatrimonial arrangements.

A fourth type of explanation has stressed the extent to which early-independence African rulers erected particularly rigid rules of territorial integrity in order to mutually protect their fledgling polities (Neuberger 1991; Bartkus 1999). These rules, embodied in international legal documents such as the 1960 United Nations' General Assembly Resolution 1514.15 on the granting of independence to colonial countries and peoples, the 1963 charter of the Organization of African Unity (OAU), and the latter's Resolution 16.i on border disputes among African states, adopted in Cairo in 1964, have indeed provided African rulers with a formidable juridical arsenal in favor of territorial inertia and may have occasionally played a deterrent role among would-be separatists. Yet in practice, separatist movements in other regions of the world have not met with easier circumstances in terms of recognition, which remains broadly limited across the world to entities that can demonstrate separate colonial or previous sovereign existence (Crawford

1997; Dahlitz 2003). Hence, the argument that the low odds of recognition reduce the likelihood of separatist insurgencies in Africa is not supported by the evidence of intense and prolonged insurgencies without recognition by separatist groups elsewhere. Furthermore, the idea that OAU rules inhibit separatism fails to account for the few actual instances of African secession attempts. What, indeed, would make Casamance or southern Sudan impervious to this disincentive? Finally, the incapacity of weak African states to enforce their rule of territorial integrity (as shown by the widespread violations of borders in the DRC and Sierra Leone conflicts) suggests that it may not be per se an impediment to separatist action.

This chapter offers a theory for why relatively few peripheral regions of Africa develop separatist agendas and why so few of the regions and movements that do engage in violent conflict with the state have separatist motives. In essence, it provides elements for a theory of the reproduction of failed postcolonial states in Africa, while also accounting for the few instances of separatism. As the next section will show, its main focus is the extent to which institutions of sovereign statehood represent a political and material resource for communal elites and populations at large, the benefits of which often outweigh the potential returns of separatist nonsovereign alternatives.

The Domestic Benefits of Sovereign Institutions

In Africa as elsewhere, separatist mobilization can be expected if the potential rewards of a separatist state, in the absence of international recognition, outweigh the potential rewards associated with control or partial control of institutions of the sovereign national state. While African would-be separatists face odds of recognition similar to those in other parts of the world, what essentially distinguishes them are the relatively greater local material returns to sovereignty that they anticipate. Given its dramatic dearth of private alternative paths of accumulation or welfare enhancement, the continent offers a significant material premium to internationally recognized sovereignty, tilting the odds for regional groups in favor of staying within the state, even if they do not immediately benefit from power at the center.

While in no way contradictory to other theories that highlight the patronage benefits of sovereignty for political elites, such as the resources from foreign aid (Clapham 1996) or the benefits from foreign direct investments (Reno 2001), my argument focuses on the domestic translation of (mostly symbolic) sovereignty into a political and material resource for both national and local elites as well as commoners. Indeed, while it is true that positions in sovereign institutions provide politicians and bureaucrats with access to international financial resources, they also allow them to easily dominate, predate, and exploit their fellow citizens in a manner that would not be possible without the backing of state sovereignty. The following paragraphs articulate and illustrate this argument.

My departure point is the now well documented weakness of the African state and the advantages that such weakness can represent for African elites and regular citizens.[3] The capacities to privately appropriate the resources of the weak state or to use it as an instrument of predation, because of its widespread lack of accountability, are crucial elements of the logic of its survival and reproduction (Joseph 1984; Bayart 1993). At many levels of society, people with parcels of state authority, however limited, can market them and extract resources from their fellow citizens, while others, not directly associated with the state, can also benefit from these practices through the networks that link them to their political patrons.[4]

How does the sovereign weak state offer such returns in Africa? First of all, sovereignty facilitates the reproduction of the weak state, making feasible strategies of predation and private appropriation of state resources and institutions. The juridical guarantee of the state's existence that is the by-product of international sovereignty reduces pressures for capacity building. International sovereignty allows the state to enforce itself upon its citizens without having to resort to continuous violence and without the capacity to truly penetrate society. To refer to Joel Migdal's classic terminology, sovereignty shields political elites from the penalties associated with the "weak state–strong society" dichotomy (Migdal 1988). It prevents failed institutions from disappearing and allows them to outlive their functional existence. The weaker the state and the greater the reliance on it in elites' strategies of accumulation, the more important is this dimension of sovereignty.

Second, state agents derive domestic power from the evidence of their international legitimacy, which facilitates their instrumentalization of the state and predatory activities. Sovereignty, with its international sanction, gives state institutions and personnel substance, structure, and power and makes them hard to escape for grassroots Africans. This is in part why visits of African heads of state abroad and their meetings with other heads of state tend to receive disproportionate coverage in African media. For sure, external recognition is not the only source of control over local populations. In the absence of such recognition, rebel groups are occasionally able to develop strong local control based on local legitimacy or social structure. Yoweri Museveni's National Resistance Army (NRA) in Uganda in the 1980s or the Eritrean People's Liberation Front (EPLF) in Ethiopia until the early 1990s are cases in point. Yet in the absence of such strong domestic legitimacy, the evidence of international legitimacy provided by the recognition of the sovereign status of a government can be used as an instrument of political control. One of its main benefits is to allow governments to present predation as policy, which somewhat shields it from challenges. The capacity to act as sovereign ruler has allowed individuals in the DRC government, for example, to engage in what the United Nations has called "asset stripping." According to the UN, an "elite network" of DRC and Zimbabwean state and military interests "transferred ownership of at least US$5 billion of assets from the state mining sector to private companies under its control in the past three years with no compensation or benefit for the State Treasury of the Democratic Republic of Congo" (United Nations 2003a). In this case, sovereignty is a legal artifice that protects the exploitation of Congo's resources by state elites and their allies. African governments' capacity to act as sovereign rulers confers the seal of legality to robbery and persecution and contributes to the elites' strategies of accumulation. The instruments of predation are policy instruments that are reserved to states, regardless of their own empirical weakness.

While the relevance of this mechanism is particularly striking at the national level of government, it is also at work at regional levels, where it largely accounts for the satisfaction of local elites with the central state even when they are not directly associated to its networks of resource redistribution. Local elites want access to sovereign state institutions (such as provincial governments, regional bureaucratic agencies, parastatals, or recognized chiefdoms) in order to better establish their hegemony over local populations. Association with the sovereign state provides for cheap avenues of control, predation, and exploitation, with few demands for actual use of force. For example, in the Western Province of Zambia, which is culturally and geographically distinct from the rest of the country and has a separate precolonial and colonial past, the Barotse Royal Establishment does not seek separatism (despite its province's poverty-driven grievances), because it benefits locally from the recognition by Zambia of its powers over land and natural resources. The Barotse king is permitted to use regional assets, such as timber, in apparently private business deals and to enforce his hegemony over his subjects.[5] A similar dynamic of access to the local appendages of sovereignty is also partly responsible for the tendency of some states to seemingly endlessly federalize or decentralize, as is the case with Nigeria and Uganda.

International sovereignty is not only a domestic currency. It also shields weak governments from outside interference, as they can raise the principle of nonintervention in their domestic affairs against outside attempts to check their excesses. Only in the most outrageous cases of genocide and crimes against humanity is this principle bent in international law, and even then hardly so (as witnessed by the lack of serious intervention on behalf of Rwanda's Tutsis in 1994). For daily economic exploitation at the hands of a sovereign state, there is no international legal recourse for domestic populations. When governments do end up accused of abuses, they can still hide behind their sovereignty to dodge the bullet, with the likely sympathy of many other governments. As the DRC government spokesman, Kikaya Bin Karubi, told the BBC in 2003 in reference to accusations against members of the government in the UN report, "The Congolese government is the legitimate government of this country. . . . Whatever we do is legitimate" (BBC News 2003a). Of course, this line of reasoning is not always successful. Yet it is a line of defense that other actors do not have. Although it can be overturned, there is a favorable presumption toward sovereign governments. There are also few recourses in international law against the validity of contracts signed by governments with foreign companies for the exploitation of natural resources.

To some extent, analytical statements about the empirical weakness of the African state have been exaggerated. The authority of state agencies to issue (however arbitrary) regulations and make extractive demands and their power to enforce them are very rarely challenged, even at the local level. There is weakness of state performance, but not of state "command," to borrow from Achille Mbembe's lexicon (2001). This residual capacity of the weak state, magnified in fact by the very weakness of mechanisms of accountability, promotes its continued appeal for many local elites and would-be elites, as well as for lower-ranking agents of the state and those whose livelihoods depend on them.

Sovereignty is the ingredient that makes such authority and power possible without systematic recourse to the use of force. Evidence of the external legitimacy of the state—Jackson and Rosberg's "juridical statehood"—is a domestic as much as an international resource, for it contributes to the effective authority and power of its institutions at the domestic level. Sovereignty is the gold standard that guarantees the convertibility of state institutions into credible instruments of domination, extraction, and predation at the local level and makes such institutions so appealing to rulers and opponents alike, uniting them in their embrace of the state while pitting them against each other in their competition for it.

As a result, political insurgencies are widespread in Africa yet rarely represent the expression of exit strategies. Instead, African political violence usually provides marginalized and excluded groups with the means to fight for (re)insertion into the system. It does not represent attempts to challenge, reform, revolutionize, or break away from the state. The association of political violence with a universal nationalist discourse is thus only superficially paradoxical. While competing for state access for the benefit of the particularistic interests of their own group, political elites use a nationalist discourse as a platform to build a minimum winning coalition and to define others as nonpatriotic and keep them on the outside. Competition in the display of nationalism can thus be perceived as competition for power. The nationalist discourse becomes the foundation for the reproduction of the state's otherwise failed and predatory institutions, denying legitimacy to alternative scenarios and confining challenges to military factionalism for control of the state itself or to the nonthreatening realm of "civil society." By reinforcing the reproduction of the state, it guarantees the predatory potential of its institutions.

Leaders of culturally distinct, oppressed, or otherwise polarized groups or regions may well initially prefer to go their own way but find it hard to sustainably pursue separatist strategies in Africa's sovereignty-constrained environment. With international recognition elusive, they face a greater problem of time inconsistency than do would-be separatists in more developed or industrialized regions, so they derive greater benefits from joining "national unity" governments than from continuing their original struggle. To borrow from a popular typology, "grievance" has a greater propensity to turn to "greed" in Africa than elsewhere (Berdal and Malone 2000). Such outcomes are further facilitated by the recent tendency of Western governments to foster power-sharing agreements as a solution to civil conflicts in Africa (e.g., Sudan, Côte d'Ivoire, DRC, Burundi). In these agreements, the integrity of the state usually trumps other considerations.

Making Sense of Separatist Insurgencies

If the above argument is valid, how are we to make sense of the few existing cases of separatist guerrillas in Africa? There are two possible explanations. First, some of Africa's secessionist movements make a historical claim to a separate colonial existence from the state to which they are now deemed to belong. To some extent, these movements may attempt to use the norms of international recognition of sovereignty in their favor. Indeed, while the international system is in general opposed to the recognition of new states through secession, it considers decolonization an acceptable form of self-determination. Both the United Nations and the Organization of African Unity enshrined this principle in the resolutions mentioned earlier, with the explicit stipulation that colonies have a right to sovereign independence only within their colonial boundaries, which are considered intangible. This principle of postcolonial sovereignty may have had for consequence the perception that an ambiguous colonial status raises the odds of regional recognition, thereby offering an opportunity for local elites to make a claim for separate sovereignty. Eritrea provides the textbook example of this type of secession. In their war against the Ethiopian government, the Eritrean Liberation Front (ELF) and the EPLF clearly articulated their separated status under Italian colonial rule. The historical validity of this argument eventually guaranteed their success and their recognition by the international community.

Although Eritrea stands alone as a successful case of secession in Africa, several other movements have used similar claims of past existence as a distinct colony to legitimate separatist claims. To some extent, Western Sahara's war against Morocco derives from the same principle, as it was a colony of Spain, which accounts for the support of a majority of OAU states for the Sahrawi government, although its accession to full-fledged international sovereignty remains so far elusive. The Front for the Liberation of the Enclave of Cabinda (FLEC) has also used the history of Portuguese colonization as justification for its secessionist drive from Angola. The FLEC notes that the Portuguese administered Cabinda separately from the rest of Angola until it was formally incorporated in 1956. In Somalia, the northern secessionist territory that emerged in 1991 as the Somaliland Republic also traces its claim to sovereignty to the fact that it was once a British colony whereas the south was administered by Italy.

Although their cases are weaker, southern Sudan, Senegal's Casamance region, and Congo's Katanga province have at times made similar historical claims. It is indeed part of the Sudan's People Liberation Army's (SPLA) argument for independence that the three southern provinces of Sudan were administered by the British separately from the rest of the country and that the options of annexation by another East African colony or of outright independence were considered by the British (Deng 2002). Rebels from the Mouvement des Forces Démocratiques de Casamance (MFDC) have also argued that historical differences in colonial administration justified their claim for separate independence from Senegal (see Chapter 10). A 1994 French arbitration found no definitive evidence, however, of Casamance's separate status during the colonial era (Republic of Senegal 1994). Since then, the civilian leadership of the MFDC has repeatedly professed its intention to bring an end to the conflict, which endures mainly because the movement's armed wing hopes to leverage better terms of integration in the state for its members and may find material benefits in continuing low-intensity warfare throughout the region (Gasser 2002). Although it was by and large an affair of traditional Lunda chiefs and Belgian settlers, the secession of Katanga from Congo in 1960–1963 also partly relied on the argument that the province had been integrated late to the rest of Congo and had been for the most part administered by Belgium separately from the rest of the colony (Lemarchand 1962; Gérard-Libois 1963).

In all these cases, regional political elites embarked upon separatist strategies based on the claim that their region should qualify for postcolonial sovereign status. The fact that none of them has so far obtained any international recognition, however, suggests that the past existence of a region as a separate colonial entity does not really raise its odds of recognition. As a consequence, the reasons for adopting such strategy must be sought elsewhere. In keeping with my earlier argument, I suggest that these claims may be aimed at regional domestic audiences more than at the rest of the world. The fact that a region had colonial status at some point means there are remnants of institutions—such as borders, administrative agencies, or public buildings—that serve as a skeletal institutional framework for local elites to work with, making popular mobilization easier by providing symbolic appeal and credibility to a claim for statehood. Writing about ethnic nationalism in the Russian Federation, Dmitry Gorenburg argues that existing institutional resources facilitated mobilization around "real" demands for autonomy, by which he implies that such demands were made more credible to the local populations as they could witness the real albeit incomplete institutional expression of the state (Gorenburg 2001). Henry Hale's evidence that already autonomous Soviet regions were more likely to demand sovereignty supports Gorenburg's argument and my interpretation of postcolonial claims by African separatist movements, as these regions benefited from a more developed institutional apparatus (Hale 2000: 49).

One can take this point even further in the case of Africa, based on my earlier theoretical argument regarding the relative absence of separatism in Africa. Indeed, not only are remnants of colonial institutions useful for mobilization, but in fact they represent quasi-sovereign resources for regional elites. If local populations recognize some historical validity to these formerly colonial state institutions or remember their effective presence, they can be used by regional elites as instruments of power over these populations, competing in this respect with the recognized sovereign state and altering the cost-benefit calculations of separatism versus nationalism. This will be particularly true if these regional elites are otherwise prevented access to official state institutions, as was for example the case among the Lunda of Katanga and still is among the Diola of Casamance.[6]

My second explanation deals with the timing rather than the substance of secessionist claims. There appear to be two secessionist moments in Africa: in the 1960s, immediately following the main decolonization period; and in the 1990s, after the end of the Cold War and the breakup of the Soviet Union and Yugoslavia. I suggest that time variations in the benefits of sovereign statehood in Africa and in the norms of recognition of states account for these two peaks of separatism.

In the early 1960s, the principle of postcolonial sovereignty was not yet fully entrenched, and the benefits of weak sovereignty were not yet fully apparent. The future of the African nation-state was still uncertain. It made sense, therefore, for regional elites to hedge their national bets with alternative local strategies. Congolese secessions fit such a model. The fragility of the new Congolese state in 1960, the army mutinies, and the stalemate between Prime Minister Patrice Lumumba and President Joseph Kasavubu in Leopoldville made it rational for Moise Tshombe to declare the secession of Katanga, especially as he hoped to benefit from Western support given the large proportion of expatriates in his province. The "Great Mining State of South Kasai" followed suit in 1961. But the UN intervention in Congo and the lack of foreign recognition of the breakaway states affirmed the principle of territorial integrity of Africa's postcolonies and doomed these experiments. It is not surprising, in view of my argument, that Tshombe later became prime minister of Congo and that Albert Kalonji, the leader of Kasai's secession, ended up minister of agriculture in the national government. These were elites who adjusted their strategies of access to power as a function of the opportunities and constraints they identified at different levels of political action.

As international support confirmed the sovereignty of Congo, the secessionist momentum of the early 1960s subsided. Following the Congolese stabilization, the international community's display of its willingness to intervene on behalf of territorial integrity, and the proclamation of the principle of territorial integrity by the OAU in 1963, challenges to state authority no longer took on separatist dimensions. The only exception was Biafra, which fought a war of secession against the Nigerian federal government as late as the period 1967–1970. It should be noted, however, that for the Igbo leaders of the secession it was clearly a second-best option. Their first choice had been to take over power in Nigeria as a whole. It was only after the Igbo officers' coup of January 1966 had been reverted by the counter-coup of northerner General Yakubu Gowon in July (followed by numerous massacres of Igbos throughout the north) that the military governor of the Eastern Region, Lt.-Col. Odumegwu Ojukwu, proclaimed its independence as the Republic of Biafra.

The period from the end of the Biafra secession to 1990 was characterized by the virtual absence of separatism from Africa (with Sudan and Ethiopia the lone exceptions). African regional elites could no longer entertain hopes for favorable rules of self-determination on the continent, and the benefits of collaborating in the weak postcolonial state project became more appealing. The global changes in the 1990s as a result of the end of the Cold War, the partition of the Soviet Union, and the West's ideological push for the spread of electoral democracy combined to affect, and in many cases undermine, the existing international legitimacy of African states. The perception of changing international norms regarding territorial integrity led to a resurgence of autonomy-seeking activities by regional political leaders around the world, Africa included. The secession of Somaliland, which occurred in 1991 after Somalia had all but collapsed as a functional state (not unlike Yugoslavia), provides a case in point. Senegal's Casamance conflict, although it had begun in 1982, also took on renewed military vigor in 1990. In Mali, the Azawad People's Movement and the Islamic Arab Front of Azawad concentrated their fighting for Tuareg separatism during the 1990–1994 period.[7] In Niger too, Tuareg secessionism emerged as a violent political project in the early 1990s (but subsided by 1997). By the mid- to late 1990s, Western donors, faced with increased conflicts in the developing world, returned to policies supporting state integrity rather than democratization and contributed to closing this second window of separatist opportunity.

Conclusion

With the effective rules for recognition of new states by and large similar around the world, this chapter has argued that Africa's secessionist deficit derives from the greater relative returns to sovereignty which prevail on the continent. Given the presence in their region of factors contributing to separatism, local elites everywhere compare the rewards of seceding without recognition to those associated with control or partial control of institutions of the sovereign recognized state. Because there are few opportunities in Africa for controlling and exploiting resources and people outside the realm of the sovereign state, the continent offers a significant material premium to internationally recognized sovereignty, tilting the odds for political elites in favor of staying within the state.

This argument is not merely a gratuitous discussion of an empirical paradox, for Africa's weak-sovereignty equilibrium may well contribute to its underdevelopment. This is so at least for three reasons. First, the irony of nationalism and antisecessionism in Africa is that they create a context that is favorable to the dismemberment of these countries' wealth. African countries are maintained so they can be taken apart. The UN reports on the illegal exploitation of DRC's assets confirmed that African politicians use weak but sovereign institutions as instruments to appropriate wealth. The conditions under which many African states are reproduced guarantee their institutional weakness. This weakness facilitates in turn the exploitation of state power by political elites for their personal strategies of accumulation. In essence, the failure of the public domain engenders the private successes of political entrepreneurs. Sovereignty liberates states from the consequences of robbing their societies.

Second, the sovereign reproduction of African states undermines the emergence of forces that could contribute toward greater institutional accountability and better governance. The stigmatization of alternative solutions to the nation-state deprives Africans of credible exit options. It matters little in the end whether Africans would avail themselves of such options if they were given to them; making territorial partition politically feasible by altering the norms of recognition would at least modify the parameters of African elites' political calculus. Should the international community substitute a norm of institutional effectiveness for the currently prevailing norm of postcolonial territorial continuity, as suggested by Jeffrey Herbst (2000), African elites could find benefits in the promotion of regional rather than national levels of societal aggregation. Theoretically, elites would then choose the level of political action that maximized the development of state capacity to the extent that this level would also maximize the revenues from aid and other benefits from sovereignty. Although political elites can be expected to continue to seek the appropriation of the rents from state control for their private advantage, they would now do so in a context that would neutralize the benefits of sovereignty associated with weak statehood and make such pursuits compatible with public welfare. This context could be subnational, promote the adoption of a new developmental social contract at the national level, or even encourage regional integration. It is not likely, however, that such a normative shift would open a Pandora's box of territorial realignments, as is often feared, if only because of the high costs associated with this option for political elites, not least the uncertainty with respect to the dynamics unleashed by such realignments.

Third, postcolonial nationalism dialectically produces ethnic polarization, which results in social conflicts and retards development. Power strategies that transform the state into a resource, and their accompanying nationalist discourses, repress the political expression of local cultural identities, which find outlets in "tribal" clientelism, differentiation, and ethnic polarization. This is why Africans express nationalist views while simultaneously complaining of their compatriots' tribalism. Hence, the perpetuation of the African state in its current alienating form reinforces micro-identity formation as a cultural escape from the anomie of the public domain. African nationalism engenders ethnicity. The ethnic differentiation process is thus used not so much to challenge the nation-building exercise of state elites as to justify access to the benefits of the system. This leads to local ethnic competition and conflict and to economic and social policies biased toward the groups whose elites have access to the state. In both instances, state capacity and economic development come out on the losing side.

These arguments combine to suggest that the sovereign reproduction of weak African states comes at a high price for Africans. The continued deterioration of Africa's economic conditions, despite a litany of policy reforms, may provide the opportunity for a reconsideration of the merits of territorial integrity. As a first step, and while there is no contesting the short-term benefits of pacifying countries, donors may want to revisit their systematic emphasis on state reconstruction, which further contributes to the reproduction of dysfunctional states.

Notes

By permission of Oxford University Press, this chapter is adapted and reproduces large sections from Pierre Englebert and Rebecca Hummel, "Let's Stick Together:

Understanding Africa's Secessionist Deficit," *African Affairs* 104, no. 416 (2005): 399–427.

1. Based on data from Gleditsch et al. 2002.

2. Of course, there have been groups with separatist agendas in some of these regions, such as the Caprivi Liberation Army in Namibia, the South Cameroon's National Council (SCNC) in Anglophone Cameroon, or the Movement for the Actualization of the Sovereign State of Biafra (MASSOB) in Nigeria, but these have fallen short of a minimum threshold of mobilization and political violence to be credible.

3. On the benefits of state weakness to elites, see Reno 2003; on the ability of Africans at large to live with weak state institutions, see Chabal and Daloz 1998.

4. For a detailed case study of the predatory logic of a weak state, see Englebert 2003.

5. It was only when the Zambian government decided to nationalize land in 1995 that the Barotse Royal Establishment began to grumble about separatism. In the end, the government's continued implicit recognition of their rights over land placated local elites.

6. Moise Tshombe was kept out of the ruling Congolese coalition in 1960. Regarding the failure of Senegalese co-optation with Casamance's Diola, see Boone 2003: 94–96.

7. The last Malian Tuareg revolt before that dated back to 1964, during the first separatist moment.

5

Liberia:
The LURDs of the New Church

WILLIAM S. RENO

Fighters who eventually joined Liberians United for Reconciliation and Democracy (LURD) played a major role in reviving Liberia's conflict in 1999. These insurgents fit Christopher Clapham's definition of warlords, who have "poorly defined aims, and could largely be associated with the personal ambitions of their leaders" (Clapham 1998a: 212). Like other warlords, LURD's leaders sought external patronage on an opportunistic basis. In this it resembled the National Patriotic Front of Liberia (NPFL) regime that it fought. Those insurgents had invaded Liberia in December 1989 with help from neighboring countries. Other groups soon emerged, and by conservative estimates widespread fighting led to the deaths of about 80,000 people in a country of some 3 million (Ellis 1999: 316). Charles Taylor, head of the NPFL, managed to get himself elected president of the country in July 1997 as his armed supporters sang their campaign song, "He killed my Pa, He killed my Ma, I'll vote for him." LURD's leaders appeared to want the same thing, to become the next rulers of Liberia, a goal that contributed to the fracturing of the organization much as personal ambitions plagued the NPFL.

At first glance, LURD seemed to come from the same church as the NPFL. However this chapter highlights how LURD differs from the NPFL and other warlord insurgencies that fought in Liberia between 1989 and the start of the deployment of the 15,000-strong United Nations Mission in Liberia (UNMIL). These differences reflect the emergence of a "new church" warlord category.

In Liberia, I distinguish between the old church's "Class of '89" and the new church's "Class of '99," which restarted the war and of which LURD was a part. Heads of the "Class of '89" exploited their powerful positions in prewar political networks to commandeer resources that they already managed. They used these to recruit fighters from throughout the West Africa region and to conduct their own "international relations" in an area where formal state structures were collapsing and chaotic borderlands offered sanctuary to fighters. Some politicians in neighboring states took interest in that conflict and offered aid to the NPFL and to its rivals, but the interests of these Liberian warlords guided the pace and location of fighting.

Much of the "Class of '99" arose from among junior commanders who fought for these earlier leaders. The newcomers also involved neighboring states in their cause. A crucial difference, however, was that foreign politicians had by now become more adept at using Liberian groups like LURD to serve their own agendas. Though LURD continued to reflect the local politics out of which it emerged, these changes in external ties played a big role in reshaping the organization and behavior of armed groups like LURD. Even though many states in regions like West Africa are weaker than they were in the late 1980s and conflict has spread to include low-level struggles to control urban areas and the heartlands of regime opponents, politicians compensate for this. They find new ways to incorporate insurgencies like LURD into their political strategies and to conduct a kind of "international relations" in an increasingly stateless region. Paradoxically, as LURD's history shows, Taylor himself found ways to exploit LURD's presence for internal and external political gain while it posed a real threat to his power. Even officials in the United States and Great Britain saw how LURD could be used in indirect ways to pursue goals in a region where the diplomacy of peace agreements and the usual tools of state-to-state relations were becoming less relevant. In short, LURD's leaders faced a regional political context that constrained them more than it had their predecessors. The lesson here is that the politics of collapsed states and their regions evolve and operate according to a definable logic, even if it is violent and unstable in the long run, and this logic is becoming more regional in its definition as individual states grow weaker and some collapse.

The argument here is that the changing political strategies of major political actors in stateless areas are reflected in the evolving character of their warfare, which strengthens a new kind of "international relations." In this regard, the pages below divide LURD's operation into a period of the "Fake LURD," in which Taylor used real and fabricated instances of LURD violence to bolster his own political position, and "Real LURD," when the insurgency posed a true threat to his regime as Guinea and other foreign governments used it as a proxy to pressure him. This shows how armed insurgency in collapsed states is not just a battle between "the government" and "the rebels." At one level, it is a struggle for power, as the "Real LURD" shows. At another level, considering Taylor's response to LURD, what I call "Fake LURD," provides insights about the wider interstate political context in which new-church warlord insurgents fight. More than for the old church, regional personal-alliance politics shape what has become more than just a fight to be the next president of Liberia. Let us examine this context.

The Context

Taylor's regime, which LURD fought from 1999 until its inclusion in a post-conflict coalition government in 2003, was distinguished by its extreme personalization of authority. For example, United Nations investigators estimated that commercial operations under Taylor's personal control in 2001 generated an income of about $250 million. This was about twenty-five times the Liberian state's sources of domestic revenue (UN Security Council 2002a: 23–24; IMF 2002: pars. 35–36). He used this income to assist Sierra Leone's Revolutionary United Front (RUF) well into 2002 (UN Security Council 2002b: 15) and to support numerous militias that fought on his behalf and for members of his political network. Taylor's involvement in ostensibly private business concerns such as telecommunications also gave him the capacity to equip his associates with mobile telephone handsets to keep in contact with them. More significant was the company's routing of calls through Monaco (and the use of Monaco's 377 country code for calls to Monrovia) as a means to buffer overseas business transactions after his regime faced UN economic sanctions (interview with Liberian telecom businessman, 12 January 2002).

Wars in neighboring states dominated LURD's wider context. War formally ended in Liberia's western neighbor Sierra Leone in January 2002, only to break out in Liberia's eastern neighbor Côte d'Ivoire in September of that year (see Chapter 6). Guinea, LURD's rear base, had suffered years of political uncertainty amidst factional jockeying to succeed its terminally ill but durable president.

Liberia under Taylor was a prime example of a system of personal rule constructed behind a facade of statehood. This system of authority is founded on the ruler's ability to control his subordinates' access to markets. Control over a state and the prerogatives of sovereignty that global recognition accords gives the ruler opportunities to manipulate laws and regulations to favor his associates. This and the capacity to issue passports and conceal transactions of business partners give such rulers the ability to control even clandestine markets. In its more extreme forms in places like Taylor's Liberia, rulers end up controlling people and building political networks through domination of markets, not the expensive and potentially dangerous institutions of a functioning bureaucratic state.

As old-church warfare in Liberia demonstrated, the collapse of such networks leaves key people in possession of resources and connections that they can use to mobilize for war. Thus the "Class of '89" insurgent leaders, prior to an ill-fated 1995 UN-brokered Abuja peace agreement, came from high positions in the political network of President Samuel K. Doe (1980–1990). For example, George Boley, minister of state for presidential affairs in the 1980s, established the Liberian Peace Council (LPC) as an armed force in 1993. Prince Johnson, head of a breakaway faction of the NPFL that killed former president Doe in 1990, had earlier served as a lieutenant in the Armed Forces of Liberia. Alhaji G. V. Kromah emerged as head of a faction of the United Liberation Movement of Liberia for Democracy (ULIMO) in 1994 after serving in the office of the vice president and as minister of information in prewar governments. These personalities included Taylor, head of the National Patriotic Front of Liberia after he had run Doe's overseas procurement agency. As the pages below show, the intertwining of old political networks, their connections to clandestine economic opportunities, and their cross-border informal political alliances weighed heavily in the rise of LURD, though in different ways from those the "Class of '89" experienced. In particular, they lacked direct control over these resources and had to adjust their behavior to serve the interests of their backers.

Like old-church warlords, however, they shared an absence of strong ideological principles, a fact that highlights the nature of new proxy relations. In the realm of ideas, gone are the days when an insurgency could call upon a superpower to provide arms, finances, and diplomatic support. That backing and recognition from old agencies such as the Organization of African Unity's Liberation Committee required that rebels articulate a vision of the future for which they fought. This change may encourage armed oppositions to define themselves in contrast to their enemies rather than in reference to an abstract idea. Words like *resistance* and *revolutionary* have become scarce in names of contemporary insurgencies in Africa. LURD adopted contemporary-sounding generic labels typical of development and human rights NGOs, as did other Liberian insurgencies such as the LPC, ULIMO, the Movement for Democracy in Liberia (MODEL), and the shadowy New Horizons.

Despite optimistic labels, one does not easily rally fighters around the promise of free markets and elections. Alternatives such as Muammar Qaddafi's *Little Green Book* offer few details about how to create the ideal society. Besides, the Libyan colonel's recent accommodation with the United States and Britain strips him of his radical chic. North Korea's Juche Idea suffers in translation. Islamism is not a good fit for Liberia's situation. This is not to say that Liberians fail to think about politics or that it lacks ideologically motivated people with leadership potential. It is just that the recession of ideological alternatives and of material support for them clears the field for warlords who are closely tied to the politics of the regimes that they fight. In short, this is another reason that warlord insurgencies reflect the nature of their enemies.

Thus LURD commanders found themselves in 1999 in an environment dominated by regional informal political networks of powerful individuals. People like Taylor had developed clandestine cross-border commercial and political ties to field fighters from neighboring countries. Taylor's opponents had to battle him on the same terrain, since striking at the government of Liberia would not have a significant effect on the resources at his disposal. Power lay in controlling these informal relationships and transactions, something that the personalist regimes of the 1970s and 1980s in Liberia had equipped the old-church warlord leaders to do. Those of the new church, the "Class of '99," did not have the advantage of first-comers. To oppose Taylor they had to adapt to an environment in which both their foes and their potential allies dominated most of the instruments of political control. This context meant that even Taylor was able to use LURD's appearance to his advantage, even while it threatened him.

Fake LURD

LURD indeed existed, formally founded in a meeting in Freetown, Sierra Leone, in February 2000. The coalition that became LURD grew out of the conviction among many politicians and former fighters that Charles Taylor had manipulated the internationally mediated 1995 Abuja Agreement, which ended the first phase of Liberia's civil war. Taylor used his control of the country's largest faction to avoid full disarmament and to intimidate other factions. He also used this control to intimidate voters into electing him in the July 1997 elections, convincing many that he would return the country to war if he lost (Harris 1999). He made his point in his public statements. In a Baptist church in Monrovia, for example, Taylor proclaimed "how bad I am" and promised, "I will be ferocious."

Once firmly entrenched, Taylor systematically targeted his wartime rivals and the civilians who campaigned against him in the elections. Such incidents continued a pattern that began with the elimination of most of Taylor's associates from the "Class of '89" and resumed with mysterious attacks on critics, opponents, and their family members after he assumed the presidency in 1997. (A lengthy list is found in *New Democrat* 2000.)

Thus it is not surprising that LURD really took shape in a meeting in Freetown several months after the 18 September 1998 "Camp Johnson Road" incident, in which at least several hundred members of the United Liberation Movement of Liberia for Democracy–Johnson faction (ULIMO-J), Taylor's main opponents during the 1989–1995 phase of Liberia's war, were murdered. The flight of survivors of this incident and other ULIMO fighters' presence in refugee camps gave this new leadership access to experienced field commanders and fighters. Like several other groups that formed at this time, its leaders declared that their primary objective was to rid Liberia of Taylor.

LURD appeared to be a real factor in Liberian politics in 2000 amidst reports of serious fighting in Lofa County. Wire services reported clashes starting on 8 July 2000, soon leading to the capture of Voinjama, the county headquarters. The departure of about 13,000 refugees lent credence to reports of a humanitarian crisis in the region.

The attack also came several days after news of the death of Ennoch Dogolea, Taylor's vice president, allegedly after his visit to the presidential farm, had become public knowledge. Dogolea was among forty ethnic Gio fighters who broke with Taylor in 1990 to form the Prince Johnson faction. Dogolea wrote a letter to Taylor's Libyan backers, accusing him of ties to the US Central Intelligence Agency (CIA). Libyan officials allegedly later told Taylor who authored the letter. Despite this activity—or perhaps so that Taylor could better watch him—Dogolea was included on Taylor's slate of candidates in the 1997 election. Within several weeks of Dogolea's death, Nowai Flomo, an influential Monrovia market woman, was killed. Human rights lawyer Kofi Samuel Woods was forced into exile. Amos Sawyer, a former interim president, was physically attacked, as was a civilian opposition figure, Conmany Wesseh.

At the same time, Taylor's government would not grant clearance to international journalists to visit the area of fighting. The BBC's Jonathan Paye-Layleh had to report from Monrovia; on 12 July the BBC broadcast a telephone call from Emmanuel Moore, who claimed to be calling from Liberia, where he was leading the attack on Voinjama on behalf of LURD. At the same time that Taylor's government was claiming that LURD had occupied significant portions of Liberia, Guinea's government complained of a series of cross-border raids into its territory. Liberian officials replied that these were defeated LURD units that were looting as they retreated into Guinea. But I observed that the destructive and systematic arson attacks seemed to have been focused on destroying, not looting, these sites. Guinean officials and local residents blamed those attacks on Liberian army units and militias that were supporting a new insurgent group, the Rassemblement des Forces Democratiques de Guinée (RFDG).

This discrepancy, especially the lack of evidence of an extensive LURD occupation of Liberian territory, raises the question of how LURD fit into the Liberian president's political strategy. It is plausible that Taylor enhanced LURD's reputation to develop a cover for shipping men and arms to Lofa County to support the RUF in neighboring Sierra Leone, not just to fight LURD. Taylor had to be careful about how he did this, since foreign diplomats had accused him of aiding RUF and prolonging the Sierra Leone war.

The US Department of State publicly condemned Taylor's commercial and military relationship with the RUF on 28 December 1998. Pressure grew in March 1999 as Susan Rice, US undersecretary of state for Africa, testified before the US Congress about "clear evidence of Liberian involvement with the RUF" (US Congress, House of Representatives 1999). On 5

July 2000, several days before LURD allegedly started its rapid drive into Liberia, the UN Security Council passed Resolution 1306, charging a panel to investigate Taylor's commercial and military relationship with the RUF. In December, this panel produced a report that confirmed suspicions about Taylor's close ties to the RUF and led to the imposition of a wide range of sanctions on Taylor's regime (UN 2000).

Meanwhile, on 15 June, the British government succeeded in convincing European Union (EU) foreign ministers to block a $53 million aid package to Liberia, in retaliation for Taylor's material support for Sierra Leone's RUF rebels. This measure followed soon after the May deployment of British troops in Sierra Leone to rescue UN peacekeepers whom RUF fighters had kidnapped.

Other evidence pointed to the benefits of a strategy of diversion. In October 2000, RUF fighters were found to be using new weapons to attack the Kambia region in eastern Sierra Leone and occupy the Guinean border town of Pamelap (interview, UK Military, 16 May 2001). It also appeared that Taylor was positioning himself to exploit a split in the RUF that occurred as the British military force's intervention in Sierra Leone began to result in serious reversals for RUF fortunes. Those who remained committed to fighting and who rejected a UN- and US-brokered 1999 peace agreement had the option of joining with RUF commanders whom Taylor supported. Most prominent among these was Sam "Maskita" Bockarie, who had been RUF battlefield commander until he broke with the RUF leader (see Chapter 3).

Taylor emerged as a far more sophisticated strategist than most media or negotiators were willing to credit. He was extremely bright and was a careful collector of data on people and events that he thought important to his situation. The impression of an embattled president and a strong LURD gave him additional means to collect data. The RUF attacks in the second half of 2000 also gave Taylor a chance to assess whether the United Nations and the new British force were serious about fighting back. He knew as well as British trainers did that the Sierra Leone army had "a serious leadership problem" and was not likely to be effective in combat (interview, UK Military, 12 May 2001). He also could test for a reaction from the UN Security Council, which on 17 October 2000 had voiced support for enforcing ceasefires but not for an armed assault on rebels or their backers. This statement continued what appeared in West Africa to be a UN tendency to waver in its pressure on Taylor. One "Class of '89" leader of an anti-Taylor faction surmised: "When Taylor is losing, he tells guys to go on a rampage. The international community has no stomach for this. They always come back to the bargaining table" (interview, 30 October 2001).

A resurgent RUF offered bigger prizes to Taylor. The overall model for his thinking appeared to have been his own election in 1997 to the Liberian presidency. Like Liberia in the mid-1990s, a multinational intervention force was overseeing the end of fighting and arrangements for an election. Thus a well-armed RUF that could intimidate foreign peacekeepers would be a good bet to win Sierra Leone's election. If an RUF government in Sierra Leone had been elected under the mandate of a peace agreement, it would have lessened Taylor's diplomatic isolation and left him and his partners in possession of a lucrative commercial network that was critical to their political strategies. International efforts to sanction Taylor's government would have been much more difficult if they could not obtain support from an elected government in Sierra Leone that their own peace agreements had installed.

Real LURD

Meanwhile, Taylor really did face a military threat, if not precisely as he wished the world to believe. Taylor's aid to his RUF partners drew the attention of the Nigerian commander of a West African peacekeeping force in Sierra Leone. In August 1998, General Maxwell Khobe announced that he believed that Taylor was helping the RUF. At the same time a group of Liberian dissidents, many drawn from the ranks of the old ULIMO and from fighters who had fled Liberia after the April Camp Johnson Road incident, staged an incursion into Liberian territory. Calling themselves the Justice Coalition for Liberia (JCL), they announced that they were forming an alliance to get rid of Taylor. Its head, a former NPFL commander, explained that Taylor had his family members murdered after he wanted to quit the NPFL.

The resurgence of the RUF later in 1998 removed Sierra Leone territory as a possible base for invading Liberia. Fortunately for Taylor, Western officials, especially those from the United States, pressured Sierra Leone's President Ahmed Tejan Kabbah to crack down on belligerent Liberian dissident organizations after the July 1999 signing of the (soon to fail) Lomé peace agreement between the Sierra Leone government and RUF.

Consequently, the next JCL incursion in October 1999 came from Guinea. Like General Khobe, Guinea's President Lansana Conté had good reason to want Taylor gone. Taylor had once given sanctuary to General Gbago Zoumanigui, who had been a minister in Conté's government until he attempted to organize a coup against the president in 1996. After fleeing to Côte d'Ivoire, Zoumanigui returned to Liberia, where he sought Taylor's protection. Other Liberian dissident groups appeared in Guinea (*Standard Times* 2000). Another group, the Organization of Displaced Liberians, launched a raid from Guinea on 1 April 1999, while the Union of Democratic Forces of Liberia under the leadership of a former Taylor associate issued communiqués.

Thus LURD already existed as a coalition of anti-Taylor forces when the organization's founding was announced in Freetown in February 2000.

But the center of gravity of the organization was in Guinea. Conté's personal backing of the organization was reflected in the emergence of Sekou Conneh at its head. A used-car dealer from Bong County in Liberia, Conneh was attractive to his Guinean patron mainly because of his wife, Ayesha. A onetime market trader, she had become President Conté's spiritual adviser on the basis of her premonitions of the 1996 coup attempt and a warning that allowed him to prepare for the event. Her family commercial networks, shared with intimates of the Conté regime, also eased the flow of weapons to LURD.

Though the organization claimed responsibility for earlier attacks, more significant "Real LURD" fighting came in October 2000, as Taylor was experimenting with his strategy for aiding the RUF and probing the extent of international commitment to sanctions against him. Even more than sanctions, Taylor found that his foes were willing to allow Liberian dissident forces to join Guinea's military to attack RUF positions inside Guinea and to launch attacks into northern Sierra Leone. This, along with significant British and UN military offensives inside Sierra Leone, led to the end of an armed RUF challenge to Sierra Leone's government by mid-2001. This, along with the UN report about Taylor's RUF ties (UN 2000), appeared to be sufficient to convince Taylor to start professing support for a Sierra Leone peace process.

LURD launched more concerted offensives in 2001, as Taylor was losing his Sierra Leone allies. Observers reported that LURD forces, about 3,000 fighters, were more disciplined than those of a year earlier (Brabazon 2003: 7). One observer noted that "civilians inside Lofa report that LURD have largely ceased serious human rights violations since June 2001" and that LURD was setting up administrative structures in captured territory (ICG 2002: 9). Such manifestations of discipline would not be expected to be enforced by the group's own leaders. The same report stressed that among the group's leaders, "almost all of the members [harbored] presidential ambitions" (ICG 2002: 10). Given the factionalized nature of the group's founding and its disorganized initial attacks, it is possible that the close connection with Guinea's armed forces was behind the newfound discipline among forces in the field—a considerable contrast to the behavior of most warlord insurgencies and to LURD's later record.

LURD's behavior in the field and its position as a proxy for Conté highlighted distinctive features of Guinea's politics. On the one hand, often counted as a collapsing state, Guinea has government institutions that lack real capacity to deliver services. On the other hand, Conté's skills as a personalist leader have been considerable. Analysts rarely recognize the degree of political control that his network exercises in Guinea, separate from the formal institutions of the state.

A test of this discipline occurred in mid-2001, when Conté's political operatives and military officers began distributing weapons to citizens along the Liberian border. Taylor reportedly approved of this policy, as he anticipated a "normal" response in which these people who did not share Conte's ethnic kinship would side with Zoumanigui and Taylor's proxy Guinea rebel group. After all, Conté should have been an easy target for rebels since he had rigged an election in December 1998 and remained unpopular in many quarters. More surprising was the distribution of weapons to members of Taylor's own ethnic group, a community that had a history of antagonistic relations with groups from which LURD was recruiting. Nevertheless, local army commanders and government officials were able to discipline and direct these civilian militias to keep Liberian incursions at bay. Only as the threat from Taylor receded did these militia members use weapons to set up informal roadblocks to extort money from travelers.

Taylor did not anticipate the extent to which these informal political ties crossed into ethnic groups that Taylor had hoped would undermine his rival and create a friendly rear base for his RUF allies (interview with Liberian official, London, 16 October 2001). The durability of these ties and the extent to which they are built upon indigenous social structures that predate the brief sixty-year period of colonial rule in most of Guinea's hinterland give them a greater stability than ostensibly similar personalist networks in Sierra Leone and Liberia enjoy.

Taylor had to rely upon his RUF allies to turn back this offensive in September 2001, a pattern repeated later in the year. By February 2002, LURD was driving deeper into Liberia along the Sierra Leone border. The efficiency of the offensive raised questions among regional observers over whether British or US officials were providing covert aid or advice. "There is circumstantial evidence," reported one observer, "that U.S. officials, particularly from the Department of Defense, played an important role in coordinating military and other activity designed to rid Liberia of Charles Taylor" (ICG 2003c: 3).

Taylor's forces turned the tide once more from June to October 2002. Meanwhile, Taylor's efforts to help the RUF into power had failed. The May 2002 elections in Sierra Leone resulted in a 2.2 percent vote for the RUF's candidate for president. According to UN investigators, he turned to foreign arms dealers in violation of UN sanctions (UN Security Council 2002b). With these weapons and fighters from the region, Taylor's forces retook territory from LURD.

By February 2003, however, LURD forces controlled major highway junctions outside Monrovia, cutting off Taylor's forces from their rear bases. Despite these quick advances, however, LURD forces were not able to advance much farther as international negotiators tried to convince Taylor to seek exile. Taylor still appeared willing to try to manipulate perceptions of LURD attacks for his personal political gain. In March 2003, for example, he cited "LURD attacks" as a justification to relocate displaced families from Rick's Institute to a position in the path of LURD's expected advance (UN Security Council 2003: par. 33). Government reports on 13 May 2003 of battles with LURD in Arthington, Taylor's birthplace just twenty kilometers from Monrovia (but with little evidence of subsequent damage), accompanied a wave of arrests within Taylor's security forces.

This behavior supported the assessment that Taylor still regarded his own security forces as at least as much of a threat as LURD. The March claims also coincided with the start of the US and British invasion of Iraq. Taylor again showed himself to be a keen observer of international events, one who scrutinized them for personal opportunities.

The Trouble with Being a Proxy

Taylor finally left Liberia on 11 August 2003 for exile in Nigeria, but not because LURD had overthrown him. Instead, he accepted a bargain with an international contact group that included US, British, and French officials that if he left Monrovia he would not be prosecuted before a war crimes tribunal in Sierra Leone. While secret at the time, in March the UN-sanctioned war crimes tribunal had issued an indictment of Taylor, accusing him of crimes against humanity for his aid to the RUF (Special Court for Sierra Leone 2003).

Thus LURD commanders got positions in a new government and the protection of a new UN peacekeeping force without completing their conquest of the country. LURD's leaders were not allowed to claim the prize of forcing Taylor out and installing themselves in power. Leaders of non-African states that backed the UN deployment in Sierra Leone understood that the core weakness of Taylor's alliance with RUF was its reliance on interests, not ideology. On the level of interests, Taylor was easy to defeat. With a little guidance, LURD forces in the field could be armed and deployed effectively, provided politically reliable elements of Conté's army could pick the right people. But LURD was not effective enough as an organization to give its fighters their own capacity to march into the capital.

LURD's backers knew full well that to allow its leaders to assume control over Liberia would subject the country to continued predatory personalist rule. Instead, US and British diplomats had to recruit new leaders at a conference in Accra. Though the post-Taylor government contained members of LURD's leadership and other representatives of armed groups, Liberia's interim president, Gyude Bryant, was not directly connected with the recent conflict. These strategies showed how a little bit of organization and material backing for an armed group by outsiders goes a long way in a regional context of very weak institutions and political instability.

Subsequent behavior confirmed that members of the "Class of '99" were as prone to factional splits as their "Class of '89" colleagues, however. By January 2004, UN observers reported fighting among LURD factions. More widespread battles broke out in March and April as competition between factions heated up access to customs and ports positions allocated to LURD (UN Security Council 2004: 3). This split found a visible expression in the estrangement of Ayisha Conneh from her husband, who had become marginalized after Taylor's departure. In the final analysis, LURD was settling into the same pattern of exploiting resources of the state for members' benefits. This happened in a very different context, however, as the UN prepared to deploy 15,000 peacekeepers. LURD had served its usefulness to the government of a neighboring state and to a coalition of non-African states that needed to address the problem of state collapse at low cost and low risk. The new church of the "Class of '99" warlords in DRC, Somalia, Sudan, Uganda, and elsewhere would likewise become tools of more powerful neighbors. These pursuits were not coordinated in the same way as in Liberia. Nonetheless, the age of high warlord politics when rebel leaders charted their own course had come to an end.

6

Côte d'Ivoire: Negotiating Identity and Citizenship

RICHARD BAÉGAS AND RUTH MARSHALL-FRATANI

> This war, it's a war of identification. The Minister of State—rest in peace—Emile Boga Doudou, wanted us to be able to identify all the Ivorians. And that caused a general outcry, 'cause there's lots that are foreigners, Malians and Burkinabè, who came here. They've been here for such a long time, they managed to have the same documents as us, even the same birth certificates as us. Those people, they're the same ones who are opposed to identification. Because it's a problem for them. Because in the new formula of identification, when you go to get your card, you have to tell them the name of your village, so they can go and find out if you're really from that region. Because if I take the case of our Dioula brothers, when they arrive, as soon as they find a city like Yamoussouko and they settle there, have children there, do everything there, they don't return to their country of origin. And then they say they are Ivorians. We saw that it isn't right, that we have to be able to tell who is Ivorian, who isn't Ivorian. That's why they're making war on us.[1]

Long considered a haven of peace and prosperity, Côte d'Ivoire was victim on 19 September 2002 of an attempted coup d'état, which plunged the country into a war whose consequences have threatened the stability of the whole West African region (Banégas 2003; Banégas and Marshall-Fratani 2003). A cease-fire line policed by multinational forces under UN mandate now marks the geographical division of the country, and the body politic is increasingly divided into two opposed camps: on the one hand, a protean rebellion occupying the north of the country, seconded by the major opposition parties, grouped together since 2003 under a loose coalition, the G7, and on the other, the Gbagbo regime, seconded by the "patriotic galaxy," a nebulous group of youth organizations and militias, largely controlled by power holders at the presidency and in Laurent Gbagbo's party, the Front Populaire Ivoirien (FPI).[2] While theoretically all working together in the reconciliation government put in place after peace talks in Linas-Marcoussis (France) and Accra, these two camps confront one another in a zero-sum

81

game of winner takes all. The loose and fragile G7 coalition wants to project the image of a "republican response" to the political crisis brought to a head by the rebellion, an ambition seriously compromised by its alliance with armed rebels and its intransigence vis-à-vis Gbagbo. The Gbagbo regime, in an increasingly minority position, has from the outset refused any form of political compromise likely to weaken its grip on power; instead it has engaged in a process of ultranationalist radicalization via a vast apparatus of propaganda and parallel forms of control, surveillance, and violence, most notably via informal militias and paramilitary forces.

How can we account for Côte d'Ivoire's dramatic downfall? From a country famous for its stability and tolerance, Côte d'Ivoire has come to be characterized by xenophobia and hatred, engaged in a regional system of conflicts previously touching only those countries of the Mano River Union. Why has violence become the principal resource of political struggle? How should we interpret the emergence of rebel movements in the light of the Gbagbo regime's political trajectory? Should we see these movements as the result of a "spillover" effect or contagion from neighboring conflicts in Liberia and Sierra Leone as some claim (Galy 2003)? In this view, the conflict in the west is interpreted by some as evidence of state "weakness," where, incapable of controlling its borders, the state finds itself faced with "ethnic leagues" and transnational rebellions recruiting mercenaries from throughout the subregion. Following the now classic, but nevertheless debatable double thesis of "war economies" and "failed states" (Collier 2000; Zartman 1995; Reno 1998), other observers argue that the Ivorian conflict is fueled above all by the search for profit and the greed of actors: "much of the rhetoric of division and ethno-nationalist hatred on both sides of the conflict is highly theatrical and a cover for illicit economic gain" (ICG 2004a: 2–3).

We do not share these interpretations of the rebellion and conflict in Côte d'Ivoire. Rather than the result of "spillover" or transnational ethnic solidarity, we argue, this "war without borders" is also, and perhaps above all, a war about borders in which nation-states play a central role. Behind these so-called uncontrolled phenomena of transborder circulation hide state strategies, policies of direct or indirect interference directed from the highest spheres of neighboring capitals. Against the received wisdom of the transnational thesis, the Ivorian conflict shows that cross-border dynamics are not necessary in opposition to state logics, since the latter often exploit the former to their advantage. This is typically the case in the subregion, where, as in the Great Lakes crisis (see Chapter 7), we can observe the mutual instrumentalization by neighboring states of transnational rebellions, increasing the potential for local violence and contributing to the conflict's encystment. As we will see below, this is the mode whereby veritable systems of regional wars take form, mixing local and international interests to the point where they can no longer be distinguished. Against the view of a purely internal conflict, a position taken by many in the early stages of the crisis, we now know that the internal and external dynamics are inextricably linked. Our position is that if these local and international dimensions are so closely intertwined, it is not only because the war involves confrontation among neighboring states but also, and above all, because this crisis engages questions that, by their very nature, find themselves at the interface of the internal and the external.

In opposition to approaches that see the rebellions and nationalist mobilization as the expression of a struggle over resources, we argue that the conflict is eminently political. It's a "war of modernity" focused essentially on the questions of nationality and citizenship, and it seeks to answer a few deceptively simple questions:

- Who is Ivorian, and who a foreigner?
- What are the fundamental principles of our nation?
- Who should belong to it?

More prosaically, it is a conflict over rights (political, economic, land, educational, cultural, etc.), which the possession of identity papers confers, in which are opposed two distinct conceptions of citizenship, one open and the other based on the political ideology of autochthony, which carries within it the seeds of exclusion. In other words, it is a war of identification, whose history is long and complex (Marshall-Fratani 2006). While in many respects the current conflict is the indirect result of struggles for succession following the death of Félix Houphouët-Boigny, beyond these recent events it is above all the latest phase of a structural crisis rooted in the colonial period. The current war entails the violent reenactment of a debate, unresolved since independence, over the foundations of sovereignty and citizenship. We argue that this debate, which finds its current expression in ambivalent claims for a "second independence" and the nativist ideology of autochthony, is all the more violent because it entails the "revenge" of certain autochthonous populations, hitherto marginalized, and above all the youth, who have come to constitute a central actor in the political arena.

It will be impossible to account for all the dimensions of the current conflict here. This chapter will attempt first to briefly account for how, on the basis of long-standing divisions, violence has imposed itself in a relatively short period as a central element structuring the political field. We argue for both the historicity of this process and its contingency. We will then discuss how Ivorian society is engaged in a double process of "militianization" and paramilitarization, taking the form of, on the one hand, the emergence, consolidation, and decomposition of rebel movements and, on the other, the paramilitarization of an increasingly radical and ultranationalist

regime. We underline the interpenetration of the internal and external dynamics in this process, fueled by both highly local conflicts and the regionalization of violence. Finally, we hope to show that the "popularization of
violence" produces significant sociopolitical transformations, in particular
between generations, but also mutations in imaginaries of power, itineraries
of accumulation, and lifestyles.[3]

Genealogies of Violence

From Ivoirité to Ultranationalism

As we noted above, the war that broke out in September 2002 is not merely
circumstantial. It expresses the exacerbation of deep lines of fracture, the
degeneration of conflicts brought to the fore by the theme of *Ivoirité* and
the failure of a mode of political regulation that had enabled the peaceful
coexistence between autochthons and strangers.[4] Houphouët had consolidated and extended the colonial policy of intensive agricultural development, encouraging migration from throughout Côte d'Ivoire and neighboring countries to exploit the fertile but underpopulated southern region. He
instituted a political system of extraversion founded on the exploitation of
rents (coffee and cocoa but also the strategic rent of the nation's position
at the heart of what is known as the Françafrique) and based on a triple
alliance with the former colonial power, the planters, and immigrant workers. This "colonial compromise" depended above all on an institutionalized
form of clientelism, oiled by revenues from cocoa, via the famous Caistab
(Caisse de Stabilisation des Produits Agricoles, Fund for the Stabilization
of Agricultural Produce; Mbembe 1992). From the early 1980s on, the
foundations of this clientelist system crumbled under the effects of economic crisis, the rise of new generations (both civil and military), and the
political ambitions of Houphouët's heirs.

    Since the mid-1990s, the country has been victim of an unprecedented
financial and economic crisis, which the policies of liberalization dictated
by the World Bank (in particular the cocoa and coffee sector) have only
worsened. At stake in the liberalization of export sectors was not merely the
success of structural adjustment but also a mode of regulating political tension that had enabled the acceptance of a highly unequal social division of
labor. The dissolution of the Caistab and the opening up of the sector to
international competition led to the gradual breakdown of the mechanisms
of political regulation. The traditional social base supporting the regime—
the Baoulé planters and the urban middle classes, principal beneficiaries of
clientelist redistribution—were profoundly affected by these changes. Henri

Bédié's government paid the price, as has Gbagbo, both failing to renew the "postcolonial compromise" made by Houphouët. On the contrary, Gbagbo greatly exacerbated latent conflict among different communities without managing to build new sociopolitical alliances.

The progressive erosion of this model of political regulation was accompanied by the rejection of the second principle founding the Ivorian "miracle": the acceptance of massive numbers of immigrants into the fertile planting regions, populations that from the colonial period on were the veritable artisans of Côte d'Ivoire's growth and that today constitute a third of the country's population. In fact, this process of rejection, whose first public expression can be found as early as the 1930s, was already well under way in the 1970s, leading to the policy of "Ivorianization" of the civil service. These longstanding latent tensions were profoundly aggravated under President Bédié, who opened the Pandora's box of *Ivoirité,* partly for electoral reasons (Losch 2000; Dozon 2000). Conceived and instrumentalized by the organic intellectuals of the ruling Parti Démocratique de Côte d'Ivoire (PDCI) to prevent the leading opposition leader, Alassane Ouattara, from running for office, the theme of *Ivoirité* rapidly came to be used as a powerful instrument of exclusion, at the service of every maneuver of stigmatization and discrimination throughout the entire society (Touré 1996). Laurent Gbagbo, who in 1990 was one of the first to stigmatize Houphouët's use of foreigners as "electoral cattle," as he delicately put it (Dozon 2000), likewise mobilized this register (even if he never used the term itself) as the basis of political mobilization.[5] Since the elections of 2000, the FPI and its propaganda press have become the principal purveyors of a discourse that promotes a radically "nativist" vision of citizenship. Following the outbreak of the crisis in 2002, this discourse of autochthony has taken a resolutely xenophobic and ultranationalist form, designating "foreigners" and northerners as the "enemies" of Côte d'Ivoire.

We can partially explain the diffusion of this ideology of hatred among a population renowned for its tolerance by evoking the role of hate media, political propagandists, and groups of "young patriots" instrumentalized by the regime. However, in order to fully understand the rapid appropriation of this discourse by a significant proportion of Ivorians, we must remember that behind the idealized image of a Côte d'Ivoire, "country of welcome," the real nature of social relations has always been much more fraught. Rather than a "melting pot," we find a form of cohabitation and division of labor among communities where each group occupies a specific "economic niche," as Ousmane Dembelé explains, in a system severely strained by the economic crisis (Dembelé 2002; Le Pape and Vidal 2002). Second, this ethnonationalist mobilization is nourished by the crisis in urban employment and serious tensions around land tenure and land shortage (Chauveau 1997,

2000, 2002). Houphouët's liberal land policy ("the land belongs to those that cultivate it") encouraged massive migratory movements, to the extent that in many villages and towns in the far and central southwest, autochthons make up less than half of the population, and in some places less than 30 percent. These immigrants and internal migrants (respectively, Burkinabés, Malians, and Guinéans and Ivorian Baoulé, Senoufo, and Malinke) dramatically reduced remaining arable land, giving rise to disputes among newcomers and autochthons. During the 1990s the land crisis came to a head, notably as many youth returned to the rural areas to find that their fathers had sold or ceded remaining land to migrants. Numerous conflicts broke out, initially between autochthons and Baoulé, then from 1998 on between autochthons and northern immigrants and migrants (notably Burkinabés, of whom there are some 2.5 million in Côte d'Ivoire). In the western regions, the multiplication of militia groups imbued with the political ideology of autochthony has gravely exacerbated these conflicts, and tens of thousands of strangers have been chased off their land since 2003. Finally, the problem of growing xenophobia should be regarded from the point of view of long-term state formation and agrarian colonization. *Ivoirité* and its ethnonationalist successors have deep historical roots: since the creation in the 1930s of the Association of Defense of Autochthons' Interests of Côte d'Ivoire (ADIACI), the relations between autochthons and strangers has been a central theme of the Ivorian political debate, giving rise on numerous occasions to xenophobic violence against immigrants and strangers. However, never in the past had this question been so politicized and radically divisive.

With the outbreak of the war, not only have relations among communities become radically politicized, but the sources of tension have changed: originally principally economic and land related, they have become political and cultural. Today, the reasons for hatred and violence are not only socioeconomic but dress themselves in political, military, and even religious clothing. The perception of foreigners has become "ethnicized," and criteria of identification based on local belonging, autochthony, "culture," lifestyles, and religion have replaced the social and economic criteria that previously served to determine difference. This slippage is heavy with consequences, since the foreigner is now not simply the immigrant but has become the "Dioula," the northerner or the Muslim, or indeed any stranger, even one's own neighbor or family member. These tensions among communities have also changed scale, creating new confrontations, both geopolitical—the north against the south—and sociopolitical, northerners versus southerners. Despite decades of shared history and despite their own internal divisions, these broad groups now think of themselves as radically separate and opposed.

In fact, what is at stake in the conflict is not only the borders between groups but also the question of what constitutes the nation and who may be considered a legitimate member. It is telling that one of the poles around which the current conflict has crystallized is the process of establishing the new identity card. Far from clarifying the debate about citizenship, the program of identification established by the Gbagbo regime in early 2002 has only deepened the divisions among communities. There has been a long-standing polemic in the country over the naturalization of immigrants and their purported "usurpation of identity," exacerbated by the introduction of national identity cards and resident's cards for immigrants under the Ouattara government. The question of national identification grew increasingly contentious during the Bédié and Gueï regimes; through the promulgation of exclusive texts concerning electoral eligibility, the exclusion of former prime minister Ouattara on the grounds that he was Burkinabé, and alarmist press reports concerning the level of immigration and falsification of documents, these regimes attempted to resolve the question of "real-fake" identity cards (and by extension, "real" and "fake" Ivorians). Under Gbagbo's FPI government, the situation worsened dramatically when the regime attempted to impose a new identification process based on the ideology of autochthony. The problem with this operation lay less with the legal texts governing access to citizenship than with the administrative procedures engaged in their application. Under the aegis of Minister of the Interior Emile Boga Doudou (later killed during the attacks in Abidjan on 19 September 2002), the Office National d'Identification (ONI, created by the Gbagbo government) imposed the obligation on all individuals seeking their identity card to prove their nationality by citing witnesses in their "village of origin," claims that were to be validated by commissions composed of local dignitaries and political party leaders.[6] The process of identification makes the "ancestral home" the principal site for the production of identity and the basis of citizenship. As Sery Wayoro, assistant director of the ONI, puts it: "The village of an Ivorian, it's firstly from the ancient Côte d'Ivoire. . . . Authentically [sic], people were sedentary, they stayed on their homelands, where their parents, their elders and ancestors were born. That's what we consider as a village, the place where a person finds members of his family at their origin, before the urban phenomenon" (*Patriote* 2003).

We can measure the inanity of such a program for a highly urbanized population, where the relations with a "village of origin" are weak, to say the least, and where individuals and groups have proved highly mobile, both socially and geographically. We can also observe the perverse effects of such measures, which relegate to the margins of the national community all those unable to prove the local origins of their national belonging, in particular those whose northern surname does not rhyme with those in southern villages. Reinforced by official discourse and rooted in daily practices, this process has contributed to the diffusion of a "nativist" conception of citizenship, founded on localized belonging, and constitutes the structuring principle of the FPI's project of "refounding" the nation. Cited by numerous rebel soldiers and their recruits as the principal reason for taking up arms, these procedures were formally abandoned following the peace accords in Marcoussis and Accra. But they continue to weigh in political imaginaries and administrative practices. In this context, semantic slippages are highly significant: since the outbreak of the war, the accent has been placed on "patriotism," both by the government and by the rebellion. This patriotism is measured by the defense of an imagined community that refers formally to the space of the national territory but has its historical foundations in the belonging to a localized space, leading to the progressive affirmation of a localized citizenship and the banishment of local strangers to the margins of the nation.

Political Violence and the Culture of Impunity

While the radicalization of conflicts over identity and citizenship is the production of historically unresolved tensions, the historicity of these issues does not fully explain the outbreak of violence. In order to understand the extent and forms of violence, we need to take into account the negative effects of the coup d'état of 1999 and the military transition. We argue that it is also during the brief period of the *annus horribilus* (Le Pape and Vidal 2002) and the contingency of political struggles that marked the transition that we can situate, in part at least, the origins of the "militianization" and paramilitarization of the Ivorian political field.

Violence was, of course, present in political life under Houphouët. Indeed, it was even a principle of government, as the numerous "false plots" and repression of dissension testify. Under Bédié, coercion and repression were likewise commonplace. Nevertheless, political violence was never massive nor the centerpiece of the regime, as was the case of totalitarian regimes such as Guinea under Sékou Touré or Idi Amin's Uganda. Rather, the regime's stability was guaranteed principally by institutionalized clientelism and an official tolerance of a certain degree of corruption. (As Houphouët put it, "One doesn't look into the peanut-griller's mouth.") The army occupied a significant place in the state apparatus, in particular within the administration (e.g., customs, *prefets,* public enterprises). However, on a symbolic level Houphouët was careful to separate the military apparatus from the process of political legitimation. Houphouët, the planter-president, attempted to cultivate an aura far removed from force and violence. Always wary of his army, he depended almost exclusively on French military assistance to assure the country's security and relegated to the FANCI (Forces Armées Nationales de Côte d'Ivoire), led by loyal officers, the job of keeping public order.

The putsch of December 1999, when young noncommissioned officers (NCOs) handed power over to General Robert Gueï, the "Father Christmas in fatigues," marked the end of this tradition and inaugurated a new cycle of violence, characterized by the multiplication of attempted coups and the increasing politicization and division of an army that had become a central political actor. Without undertaking a detailed analysis of this process, we can nevertheless underline some of its principal effects. First, the military transition brought armed violence into the heart of political arbitrage: from this point on, soldiers in revolt and young NCOs became the kingmakers and central referees of political competition. While these young soldiers may not be masters of the political game, the old class of politicians can no longer govern without them.

The second major effect of this period was rapid acceleration of a process of "militianization" of the army and society.[7] From the early stages of the junta, we can observe the rapid disintegration of the security apparatus and its division into multiple factions, which obeyed less an official hierarchy than informal networks and personal clans. In fact, this process was already under way under Bédié, who feared the army and sowed the seeds of division not only by imposing strict budgetary austerity but also by discriminating against officers thought to be close to his political rivals and promoting an increasing number of Baoulé, his own ethnic group.[8] Divided and increasingly undisciplined, the regular soldiers and NCOs obeyed their hierarchy less and less and considered them fundamentally corrupt. Following the coup of 1999 carried out by these *jeunes gens,* they constituted informal and more or less autonomous military factions (such as the PC-Crise) and parallel forces, which rapidly turned into urban militias, more or less affiliated with a political leader but in reality obeying their own small military chiefs. The two most infamous were Lieutenant Boka Yapi and Staff Sergeant Ibrahim Coulibaly (the famous IB who was to head the rebellion of 2002). These group's exotic names—the Camorra, Cosa Nostra, Red Brigades—indicate the criminal turn taken by the military regime, and the population was at the mercy of these militias operating with complete impunity. Gueï attempted to rein in the excesses of these groups, disbanding the PC-Crise in the summer of 2000 and operating brutal purges among those young leaders whose loyalty he doubted. Nevertheless, he was incapable of controlling them and was in fact hostage to these young soldiers, who had handed him the presidency and considered themselves above the law.

Finally, these events led to a third effect—the rapid diffusion of violence throughout the public space and the dramatic growth of a feeling of impunity on the part of those who used it to accumulate power and wealth.

Far from stopping this process, Laurent Gbagbo's election as president paradoxically reinforced the idea that armed or street violence constituted an acceptable means for gaining and keeping power. This was brought home during the presidential elections of October 2000, when, following the exclusion of the candidates from the main political parties (the PDCI and the Rassemblement des Républicains, RDR) and Gueï's attempt to pull off an electoral holdup, Gbagbo and the FPI threw their "troops" into the street, plunging Abidjan and other towns into three days of extreme violence. Hundreds of thousands of demonstrators thronged the streets, among them several thousand RDR militants, demanding new elections, only to be violently repressed by the gendarmerie, loyal to Gbagbo.

In Youpougon, a poor neighborhood in Abidjan and an FPI stronghold, a mass grave of fifty-seven bodies was discovered—all of whom were northerners and many of whom had been close to the RDR. The Youpougon massacre shook the Ivorian nation and profoundly exacerbated the reign of impunity on the part of security forces, who were acquitted during a sham trial. Indeed, many of the recruits to the Mouvement Patriotique de la Côte d'Ivoire (MPCI) justified their participation in the rebellion by evoking this massacre.

The legislative elections of December 2000 only aggravated tensions further, as the Supreme Court invalidated Alassane Ouattara's candidacy on the grounds that he was not Ivorian. RDR militants demonstrated in Abidjan, leading once again to extremely violent confrontations with youth from the FPI and the pro-FPI student organization FESCI (Fédération Estudiantin et Scolarie de Côte d'Ivoire). These demonstrations were savagely repressed by the gendarmes, with the assistance, as in October, of pro-FPI student leaders and militants.

The organization of a Forum for National Reconciliation in late 2001 did not help overcome these conflicts, rather the opposite. The event turned into an opportunity for political grandstanding and mudslinging of the most odious sort. From early 2001 until the attacks of 2002, the regime lived in an intense paranoia about potential coups d'états, especially following the mysterious attacks of January 2001, and state repression, impunity, and political radicalization became the norm.

This brief overview demonstrates the extent to which the use of violence has become a central part of political struggle in Côte d'Ivoire since the fall of the Bédié regime. While it is essential to examine the long history of state formation and the postcolonial political economy in order to understand this development and the nature of the divisions that now polarize Ivorian society, we must not underestimate the effects of recent events, in the sense of a "history of events" (*histoire événementiel*). It is in the short instants of violent confrontation that violence imposes itself as a way of "doing politics," and through them the street and the gun have become principal resources for the conquest of power. It is also in this particular context that the main political actors came to consider political competition as a struggle to the death between Us and the Others.

Rebellions and the Regionalization of the Ivorian Conflict

As we stated in our introduction, the internal and external dynamics of the conflict are inextricably linked. The long history of internal sociopolitical relations detailed above naturally involves, directly and indirectly, neighboring states and their populations. The relations between the internal and external dynamics in the Ivorian conflict are extremely complex and are rooted in the long history of migration and immigration, as well as Houphouët's regional interventionism. While at the heart of the war is a deep and long-standing political conflict over the content of citizenship and the foundations of the nation-state, this conflict is by its very nature transnational. The politics of identification and land introduced by the Bédié and Gbagbo regimes directly affect the futures of the some 30 percent of the Ivorian population considered as foreigners and thus inevitably involve those nation-states from which these immigrant populations originate. Furthermore, the long history of Houphouët's interference in other conflicts in the region, notably the first Liberian war, and the presence on Ivorian soil of some 60,000 Liberian refugees have had their impact on internal relations, sowing the seeds of cross-border solidarities with Liberian protagonists. Finally, with the regionalization of the war and the involvement of Liberian fighters on both sides, the growth of violence, impunity, and the paramilitarization of society, which itself made armed rebellion a possible political practice, have accelerated wildly and served to radicalize positions on both sides.

Contrary to what many international observers and journalists maintained in the first year of the conflict, the involvement of countries from the subregion goes well beyond the activities of poorly controlled armed groups, some of whom "spilled over" from the Mano River conflicts, looking for bounty and adventure. Rather, states and their leaders, highly placed political officials, army officers, politicofinancial networks, and entrepreneurs find themselves involved in a complex game of alliances and networks that, beyond purely economic or financial considerations, tends to follow the logic of "the enemy of my enemy is my ally," against a somber and often sordid background of treachery and revenge. However, with the appearance of the three rebel movements in Côte d'Ivoire, we can observe the encystment of the Mano River system and the continued implication of nation-states and their interests behind the various insurgent groups. The principal rebel movement, the MPCI, has been directly supported by Burkina Faso and indirectly by Mali. The Mouvement Populaire du Grand Ouest (MPIGO) and the Mouvement pour la Justice et la Paix (MJP) in the west of the country were created to a large extent with the direct involvement of the MPCI and Charles Taylor, with the assistance of the notorious ex-commander of the RUF in Sierra Leone, Sam Bockarie, whose fighters led attacks in Côte d'Ivoire together with their Ivorian rebel allies. In short, far from a situation in which groups of transnational desperados and their unscrupulous financiers motivated by pillage and gain (the famous "greed" theory) continue to expand the borders of regional conflict, the direct intervention of states, governments, and national armies can be observed to extend this conflict, all in the pursuit of precise internal political agendas (Marshall-Fratani 2004).

The MPCI: From Attempted Coup to Armed Rebellion

Despite its subsequent development of a political platform, developed over long months of negotiation, the MPCI was a military operation designed from the outset to remove Gbagbo. Its preparation in Ouagadougou was long and meticulous, and by many accounts almost successful. The planners and leaders of the coup were Ivorian soldiers, many of whom were leaders or members of the infamous parallel military groups (Cosa Nostra, Camorra, Red Brigades) that were formed under General Gueï's junta but chased from the army by Guéï and Gbagbo, and that had sought refuge in Burkina Faso in successive waves from September 2000 on. The support they needed was provided in part by President Blaise Compaoré, whose relations with Gbagbo had been execrable from the outset and in particular in the wake of his policy of identification. This support enabled them not only to launch attacks but also to recruit, arm, and organize during the stalemate imposed by the creation of a cease-fire line and negotiations. On 15 October 2002, Staff Sergeant Tuo Fozié revealed the existence of a political leadership, and Guillaume Soro, former leader of the student organization FESCI, onetime FPI sympathizer and recent RDR collaborator, declared himself the group's general secretary.[9] Few Ivorians took him seriously at the time; it was thought that he, at age thirty-one, could only be a screen behind which RDR barons were hiding. However, time has shown that Soro, like many other young political and military figures, is a force to be reckoned with. On 6 November Soro and an ex-FPI heavyweight, Louis Dacoury-Tabley, presented political claims that went beyond simply taking power.[10]

The direct involvement of opposition leaders in the planning of the coup has not been established, despite the regime's repeated claims affirming their complicity. Indeed, the immediate targets of government reprisal, L'Union Pour la Démocratie et la Paix en Côte d'Ivoire (UDPCI) leader Guéï and RDR leader Ouattara, were taken by surprise on the morning of 19 September 2002. Guéï was killed by members of Gbagbo's Presidential Guard and Ouattara narrowly escaped with his life, thanks to the direct intervention of the French ambassador. However, along with grievances related to its members' status within the army, the political platform outlined by the MPCI during the first peace talks held in Lomé in October and November 2002 echoed positions held by the RDR, in particular concerning the conditions in which the elections of 2000 had taken place, the conditions of presidential eligibility, and the government's policy of national identification.[11] These positions were reinforced during the peace talks held in Linas-Marcoussis in France in January 2003, and the peace agreement signed by the three rebel movements and principal political parties provided not only for the installation of an interim government but also for the satisfaction of many of the central political claims of the rebellion.

The mastermind and original leader of the MPCI was Sergeant-Chief Ibrahim Coulibaly, popularly known as IB. Having been a bodyguard for opposition leader Ouattara during his period as prime minister, IB had also been one of the leaders of the coup that ousted Bédié on 24 December 1999 and a central figure during the military junta of 1999–2000. A member of Gueï's Presidential Guard, he was finally suspected of plotting against the general in the summer of 2000 and was sent to Canada as a military attaché. Following a supposed assassination attempt against Gueï in September 2000, Ibrahim Coulibaly left his post in Canada and went into exile in Ouagadougou, where he was to be joined by other members of Gueï's guard, the Cosa Nostra, the Camorra, and other *jeunes gens* targeted by the Gbagbo government. The great majority were in exile in Ouagadougou throughout 2001–2002. IB was the military mastermind despite (or perhaps because of) the fact that he stayed mainly in Ouagadougou, at least until his arrest in France in August 2003.[12] However, his lack of presence on the ground and the importance accorded to other rebel leaders during the peace talks in Linas-Marcoussis created a split between pro-IB and pro-Soro forces, which has led to a series of bloody account settlings and ongoing conflict.

These exiled soldiers had been lodged by the Burkinabé government in Ouagadougou's Somgandé neighborhood. According to various accounts, coup preparations began in early 2001, most probably after the arrests that followed the mysterious attacks in Abidjan of 7–8 January and the subsequent trials in absentia of army deserters. Tracts reportedly circulated in Ouagadougou that announced the preparation of an armed movement (Banégas and Otayek 2003). Clearly well looked after by their hosts throughout the earlier part of 2002, the deserters frequented the hot bars and nightclubs of Ouagadougou, drove expensive cars, trained openly, and made no secret of their plans to overturn the Gbagbo government (Smith 2002). Despite the accusations of the Ivorian government, preparations for the 19 September coup attempt did not involve the training of significant numbers of soldiers but rather the discreet formation and training of the rebellion's military leaders in logistics, communication, and clandestine operations—all areas in which the Burkinabé army excels (Banégas and Otayek 2003).

Once they had taken and held the central city of Bouaké and towns and cities in the north, the MPCI organized recruitment. Only some 800 soldiers on 19 September 2002, by Christmas of the same year the MPCI's ranks had been swelled not only by thousands of young recruits from the northern territory under their control but also by some 800 traditional hunters, the *dozo* from northern Côte d'Ivoire, Mali, and Burkina Faso. Youths from the region of Bobo Dioulasso also joined ranks with the MPCI, and numerous mercenaries from the Mano River conflicts grabbed this new opportunity. At the same time, following witch hunts in the armed forces and security services by the Gbagbo regime against those thought to be sympathetic to the rebellion, many members of the defense and security forces crossed the cease-fire line and joined the ranks of their erstwhile companions-in-arms.[13] Two and a half years later, the combined rebel forces counted some 35,000 fighters.

Organized in companies with the same sorts of exotic names as under the military junta, the MPCI leaders and their young recruits tore around Bouaké and other towns in stolen pickups mounted with RPG-7 launchers. Until November 2002, the MPCI appeared not to count with any senior officers.[14] Rather, their leaders were and have remained the young NCOs so instrumental during the junta. These young soldiers, tracked by the regime, many having escaped torture and death, have indeed little to lose. All the MPCI's leading NCOs are northern soldiers who passed through the school system during the violent years of FESCI-led protest and the struggle against Bédié's authoritarianism. A number of them participated in the UN Mission in the Central African Republican (MINURCA) in the late 1990s, an experience that altered their view of the Ivorian army, opening their eyes to the corruption, difficulties for upward mobility, and poor material conditions. Victims of antinorthern discrimination under the Gbagbo regime, many other young NCOs, seeing their careers compromised, grew increasingly politicized. It took little to convince many of them to cross the lines and join the struggle.

While Colonels Michel Gueu and Ismaël Soumaïla Bakayoko have been placed in positions of responsibility because of their rank, the real power lies in the hands of the young NCOs who planned the coup. These MPCI strongmen include Staff Sergeant Tuo Fozié, the commander of operations in Bouaké, present at the peace talks in Marcoussis, and from 2003 minister of youth and civic service in the reconciliation government; Chérif Ousmane, a member of the Force d'Intervention Rapide Para-commando created by Gueï under the Ouattara government, part of Gueï's presidential guard and head of the notorious Guépard Company[15] in Bouaké, and real military "boss" of the rebellion since IB's arrest; Issiaka Ouattara (alias Wattao), assistant chief of military staff, of the Forces Nouvelles since early 2005, and chief leader of the Anaconda Company in Bouaké; and Massamba Koné, commander of Korhogo and minister of development and planning in the reconciliation government.

One would have expected the same sort of wild indiscipline from these young soldiers as had been witnessed under the junta. However, for the first few months at least, while they still had ready cash, the MPCI forces appeared to be running a charm operation in relation to the population. Indiscipline, pillage, and extortion were exceptional and often punished with summary executions. While they showed little clemency toward loyalist security forces, as the summary execution of some forty gendarmes and thirty of their adult children in Bouaké between 6 and 8 October 2002 testifies (Amnesty International 2003), those returning to their homes in Bouaké in late November were amazed to find their belongings intact.

However, this situation did not last past Christmas 2002. As time has gone on, indiscipline, warlordism, racketeering, and pillage have become more frequent and widespread; in particular since the rift between those forces loyal to Soro and Ousmane and those close to IB. From April 2003 to early 2005, a series of more or less bloody reorganizations, "cleanups," and purges have taken place, purportedly to improve discipline but also to keep control over increasing dissent and undisciplined individuals. Summary executions of dissident fighters have become fairly frequent, and many of IB's most faithful commanders have either been killed or left the country. Populations, transporters, and other economic operators are held for ransom at the numerous roadblocks throughout the region, and a parallel informal economy has grown up, where cocoa, cotton, and other agricultural products leave the country under MPCI control through its porous northern borders. Major bank holdups in Bouaké and Man have also provided the rebellion with cash, although the change of notes through the Banque Centrale des Etats de l'Afrique de l'Ouest has enabled the recuperation of a significant amount of this bounty.

The northern regions have been more or less administrated through the rebellion since September 2002—schools, hospitals, press, and state security are being run with varying degrees of success by members of the rebellion, NGOs, civilians, and volunteers. Since the peace talks in Linas-Marcoussis in January 2003, the MPCI has tried to give itself a resolutely political image. Participating in the reconciliation government, its ministers, mostly ex-soldiers, and its charismatic and populist leader Soro have multiplied tours of their regions, grandstanding before populations and attempting to limit exactions in a bid to keep popular support. A certain amount of violence and intimidation is involved; nevertheless, in the absence of any systematic study, various anecdotal accounts from well-informed sources suggest that in early 2005, while the populations were exceedingly tired of the occupation, they still appeared supportive of the rebellion's political agenda, in particular in the face of the "patriotic" radicalism and ultranationalism coming from Abidjan and the government's bomb attacks carried out against northern targets in November 2004. It must be remembered that these regions never saw any real fighting, as towns and cities in the north were abandoned practically without a struggle in September 2002 and the cease-fire line has more or less contained fighting between the two protagonists.

The same cannot be said for the west of the country, where from December 2002 to April 2003, extremely violent combat raged between loyalist and rebel forces, combat in which Liberian and Sierra Leonean fighters played a central role. During this period, the civilian populations on both sides were victims of savage and brutal acts of killing, torture, rape, and pillage. Thousands were killed, maimed, and raped, and tens of thousands crossed and recrossed the borders with Liberia and Guinea, hiding for months in the bush in desperate attempts to find safety. The extremity of this violence, introduced largely by the Liberian protagonists, fundamentally changed the face of the war and had far-reaching consequences for the radicalization of youth, the rise of militias, and interethnic violence among civilians.

MPIGO, MJP, MODEL, and FLGO:
Rebellions and Counterinsurgency in the Wild West

With the involvement of Liberian protagonists in the western conflict, and despite the UN peacekeeping operations in Côte d'Ivoire (UNOCI) and Liberia (UNMIL), we observe the extension of the "system of conflicts" crystallized around the Liberian war of 1989 and involving the Mano River countries. Rather than using the logic of the "spillover" concept, which says little or nothing about the particular reasons for which a given conflict advances or recedes, we want to examine the particularities of the space in which internal and external dynamics meet, creating a sort of regional system. Armed conflict, even a conflict already regionalized, such as in the Mano River case, does not have an a priori vocation for extending its territory. The conditions of its extension and systematization obey a historical logic, which is to say a logic of struggle, contingency, and incertitude.

Second, this process is largely tributary to the internal politics and dynamics of the individual nation-states involved. In order to understand the regional implications of the Ivorian conflict, we must bear in mind that, as Roland Marchal puts it, "a system of conflict is characterised by the intimate links between inter or trans-national and civil conflict" (Marchal 2002: 9). Armed conflicts, produced by distinct national circumstances and depending upon distinct actors, modalities, and interests, find themselves mutually articulated, blurring the spatial, social, and political borders that initially distinguished them, and in the process, they transform their conditions of reproduction, the protagonists, stakes, and objectives. Yet while such wars appear to be conflicts without borders, they are in fact, and perhaps above all, conflicts *about* borders, underlying the political and economic importance of frontier spaces and the "floating populations" that transit through them (Marchal 2002). All observers have confirmed that the involvement of Liberian and Sierra Leonean fighters fundamentally changed the nature of the Ivorian war. The extreme violence of the fighting has provoked an interethnic conflict and radicalized the xenophobic nationalism of autochthonous populations, providing grist for the mill of politicians in Abidjan, only too happy to instrumentalize the ongoing violence, and, finally, has provoked major social upheaval, giving the youth unprecedented power in their local communities.

The MPIGO and the MJP burst onto the scene on 28 November 2002, arriving over the border from Liberia and attacking, respectively, the cities of Danané and Man. The MJP appeared immediately as a satellite of the MPCI and included numerous Liberian, Sierra Leonean, and Burkinabé mercenaries. Its organization appears to have been the work of IB, together with senior Burkinabé officers, ex-RUF commander Sam Bockarie, and the infamous Ibrahim Bah, diamond dealer and Taylor collaborator. While the cease-fire line ran from east to west, this region of the west was not controlled by French forces. With peace talks at Lomé stalled, the MPCI needed to open a new front that would give access to the port of San Pedro and the wealthy cocoa-coffee belt. The MPIGO appears to have been set up largely by Taylor in concert with certain Ivorian soldiers, notably Felix Doh (whose real name is N'dri N'guessan). Until April 2003, MPIGO zones and controls were distinct from those of the MJP-MPCI. Apparently, Taylor feared the incursions of the MPCI via the MJP into his "territory" and counted on having a force faithful to him in the hopes of gaining access to the port of San Pedro, as well as a base for retreat in the event things turned against his forces in eastern Liberia. Taylor was also aware that Gbagbo was recruiting Liberians who had fought against him and that he had developed close ties to the Krahn branch of the LURD (ICG 2003b). According to converging accounts, the 28 November attacks on Danané and Man were likely planned and coordinated through the mediation of IB, Bockarie, Doh, and top Taylor generals. The attacks were led on the ground by Taylor's men: Kuku Dennis, Sam Bockarie, Roland Duo, Adolphus Dolo, and "Jack the Rebel" (ICG 2003a: 14).

Beyond their interests in gaining access to resources and central axes in Côte d'Ivoire, the MPCI and Taylor needed to provide a common front that would contain the menace arising from Gbagbo's support of LURD forces, who more than six months before 19 September claimed to have some 500 fighters based in the west and supported by the Ivorian president (see Chapter 5). From November 2002 on, Gbagbo began actively recruiting anti-Taylor forces. Confronted from the outset by the FANCI's incapacity and unwillingness to crush the rebellion, Gbagbo set out to constitute a force willing to fight his war. Alongside the recruitment of numerous mercenaries from South Africa, Angola, and Eastern Europe, Ggbago recruited Liberians with the help of agents from the Krahn branch of LURD or ex-ULIMO-J, many of whom had been living in Côte d'Ivoire since the first Liberian war (ICG 2003a, 2003b; Marshall and Ero 2003). The anti-Taylor movement LURD, supported by Lasana Conté of Guinea, underwent a scission in early 2003, giving birth, through the generous assistance of Gbagbo, to a new movement, the Movement for Democracy in Liberia (MODEL). MODEL, based in Côte d'Ivoire and armed and equipped by Gbagbo, joined forces with the FANCI and with local "patriotic" youth organized into militias, notably the Front de Libération du Grand Ouest (FLGO).

Recruitment was undertaken in refugee and transit camps in Ghana, Abidjan, and Nicla, near Guiglo in the west, principally by two LURD agents, Edward Slanger and Eric Dagbeson, and by a network of Ivorians close to Gbagbo and the FPI, in particular a group of Guéré (or Wê) politicians and businessmen.[16] These agents also recruited several thousand young Guéré "patriots" in the poorer neighborhoods of Abidjan and in the towns and villages in the west. These new recruits, many of whom were promised large sums of money and training by the FANCI, were formed into ethnic militias, the best known being the FLGO. The majority of these young recruits were sent into combat without training and used as cannon fodder, either in Côte d'Ivoire or in Liberia, most often under the command of Liberian fighters. Both the Liberian troops and the Guéré recruits received arms and equipment from the Gbagbo regime, through a network of Guéré army officers headed by Colonel Mathias Doué, then chief of army staff, and Colonel Denis Bombet, commander of ground forces.

These heterogeneous forces, in which regular soldiers more or less willing to fight for Gbagbo rubbed shoulders with hardened Liberian fighters and eager but totally inexperienced youth—FANCI, MODEL, FLGO—began combat on 6 December 2002 in an attempt to take the town of Bloléquin, held by the MPIGO. On 16 January they managed to take Toulépleu. In the months that followed, battles led by Liberian protagonists set fire to the west, with Liberians on both sides committing atrocious acts of indiscriminate killing, torture, and rape. Whole villages were deserted, and the Liberians pillaged everything that could be taken. The Liberian forces loyal to Gbagbo, under the command of MODEL leader General Amos Chayee, used the west as their base, and FANCI and FLGO forces assisted them in attacks on Liberian soil, helping take Zwedru and Buchanan. This collaboration ended when the Liberian cease-fire came into effect in the summer of 2003.

During the six months of combat, the autochthonous Guéré paid a horrific price at the hands of the MPIGO and the MJP, especially in the early stages of combat. The confrontation between Ivorian Yacoubas, fighting in the MPIGO and the MJP with their Liberian Gio "cousins," and the Guérés, loyal to Gbagbo and forming a common front with their Krahn "cousins" from MODEL, provoked a grave interethnic conflict among populations that had always lived together peacefully. Even more deadly has been the conflict between Guéré and northerners, Burkinabé and Malians. Motivated by a politics of xenophobia, the desire to revenge the hundreds of Guérés tortured and brutally murdered by the rebellion, and the hope of appropriating the strangers' land and harvests, a systematic policy of targeting and murdering northerners has provoked a spiral of revenge and counter-revenge that continues to claim victims.

The rebellions' collaboration with the Liberians ended in April 2003, when MPCI commanders were sent from Bouaké to get rid of their extremely undisciplined and cumbersome allies. These were chased back over the border or summarily executed, and both Doh and Bockarie were among those killed. Nevertheless, certain commanders, in particular those close to IB, retained Liberian soldiers as personal bodyguards, and unverified accounts claim that a certain number of Liberians are still present among rebel forces. During the disarmament, demobilization, and reintegration (DDR) program run by UNMIL in Liberia from November 2004 on, peacekeeping officers not only noted the disappearance of most of MODEL's heavy arms and a significant number of light weapons, clearly repatriated over the border in Côte d'Ivoire, but also claimed that many Liberians who had fought with Ivorian militia forces were hoping to benefit from the DDR program that was being planned in Côte d'Ivoire, considered more lucrative. Numerous fighters, both pro-Taylor and MODEL, continue to maintain links with the rebellion and the government's forces, and many Liberians still hang about in the border regions, hoping for either action or largesse. Gbagbo has intervened in the composition of the Liberian interim government in favor of MODEL candidates and continues to count Conté of Guinea as one of his few remaining West African supporters.

It is clear that the involvement of Liberian forces in the Ivorian conflict has involved more than a circumstantial alliance among mercenary fighters. The international community calls MODEL fighters present in Côte d'Ivoire the "Lima force," considering that they are merely mercenary extras on Gbagbo's side, but it is obvious that without Gbagbo's support and their Ivorian base, MODEL would never have seen the light of day. Taylor's forces fighting for the rebellion have been treated as uncontrolled armed gangs of killers. These terms tend to mask the involvement of states and their leaders and the true international character of these conflicts. The various interests, forces, and networks at play are the proof of a growing systemization of war in the subregion. At the same time, the participation of these forces in the Ivorian conflict has greatly contributed to the radicalization and paramilitarization of the civilian population, rendering violence and impunity terrifyingly commonplace.

The Paramilitarization of an Ultranationalist Regime

The participation of these various forces in the Ivorian conflict has thus radicalized both protagonists and civilian populations, as well as furthering the systematization of regional conflict. Beyond these developments, the creation of armed groups such as the FLGO, as well as the massive recruitment of youth into the rebellion, has contributed to a broader process of what we call the "militianization" of Ivorian society, the privatization of violence, and the militarization of the youth loyal to the FPI and the rebellion. From the early stages of the conflict, in particular in the west, President Gbagbo and his advisers realized that the FANCI, weakened and divided, was both unable and unwilling to fight their war. To compensate for this structural weakness in the state security forces, they followed a double strategy of privatization and "paramilitarization"—recruiting foreign mercenaries (e.g., Angolans, South Africans, Israelis, French, Eastern Europeans) used principally, but not exclusively, in positions of trainers, technical assistants, pilots, and espionage, and also creating diverse paramilitary movements for combat as well as the political defense of the regime.

Among these various movements, we can identify three types along a continuum of a more general process of informalization, radicalization, and criminalization of the FPI regime. This typology is, however, purely analytical, since seen from the ground, the lines separating these movements are extremely porous, and all these movements belong to a large and nebulous patriotic network of parallel forces and organizations, structured and financed by the inner circles of the presidency and the FPI. While they are not homogenous nor always coordinated and are often victims of internal tensions and schism, these diverse parallel forces form a continuum in the process of the privatization of violence and the paramilitarization of power, where poorly armed and trained village self-defense groups rub shoulders with the highly politicized urban groups of "young patriots," structured into myriad associations, as well as mercenaries of diverse nationalities, paramilitary groups, and "tribal" militias, well trained and armed, officially or unofficially integrated into the state security apparatus.

The "Militianization" of the Rural Areas (West and Central West)

As discussed above, it is above all in the west that this strategy of counterinsurgency has been used, with the creation of veritable paramilitary organizations, similar, *mutatis mutandis,* in their structure and function to those developed by Latin American governments in their fight against narcoguerrillas (Lair and Sánchez 2004). In concert with the FANCI, a parallel army was developed through Gbagbo's support for the creation of MODEL, in the context of the transnationalization of the war, and these forces were instrumental for the training and veritable "baptism by fire" of the young Ivorian militiamen.

Yet this type of organization has been developed in other regions as well. Beyond the theater of war in the far west, regions in the central and southwestern cocoa belt have not been spared the growth of militias and patriotic self-defense groups, in particular in the Bété regions, home to President Gbagbo. Here, the war and the regime's ultranationalist propaganda have further radicalized the autochthons and whetted the youth's appetite for strangers' land and harvests. For example, in November and December 2003, violent attacks against strangers broke out in Bété country, following which numerous Burkinabé and Baoulé fled their plantations in the middle of the cocoa harvest. Despite the declaration of the end of the war in June 2003, another paramilitary movement similar to the FLGO has seen the light in the region: the Forces de Securité du Centre Ouest (FSCO), led by "commanders" Bertrand Gnatoa and Hippolyte Légré Biaka. Composed of young Bétés, in their majority from the region of Gagnoa, this group has considerably aggravated the violence between autochthons and strangers. From the end of February 2004, northerners have been systemically targeted in the Gagnoa region, and journalists' inquiries reveal that hundreds have been killed (F. Konaté 2004a). The same type of violence was witnessed during the period of harvest in 2004, and the bomb raids by the army against the north and the subsequent anti-French violence in Abidjan in November 2004 likewise triggered further attacks in the region. These attacks have given rise, as in the far west, to a spiral of revenge and counterrevenge that continues to claim more victims.

While this violence is profoundly rooted in local history and conflicts over land and resources, it is also directly linked to a determined paramilitary strategy initiated in Abidjan as well as to the processes of regionalization discussed above. Detailed reports claim that the FSCO underwent training in Liberia between December 2003 and February 2004, under MODEL commander General Paye Duoway. Before leaving for Liberia, this militia group apparently received training by sixteen members of the First Battalion of the Commando of Parachutists (BCP). The reports claim that this operation was set up by one of Gbagbo's ex-ministers of defense, Bertin Kadet, well known for his radical and warmongering positions (*Patriote* 2004).[17]

In the context of the FPI's global strategy of resistance, involving the creation of parallel forces and paramilitary groups, the regime has also encouraged the formation of a multitude of militias and "self-defense" groups in the rural areas, in particular in the west and central west. In Toulépleu, for example, where the war was particularly atrocious, local youths took up arms to defend their villages against rebel attacks. In a context of growing insecurity, groups of self-defense have developed in every southern town and village. Their creation was publicly solicited from the outset of the conflict as a form of "patriotic resistance," and their form follows that of village militias, comparable to urban vigilantes. These informal patrols were rapidly organized with the help of local officials into hierarchic organizations of "rural young patriots," in reference to their comrades in Abidjan. In many localities we can now find highly structured village associations of "young patriots," complete with president, treasurer, and posts linked to different activities such as security, fundraising, and mobilization. These groups receive visits from the national "patriotic leaders" on tour in the south, and contacts exist among local leaders and the "patriotic stars" in Abidjan. At times, different village groups will coordinate their actions on a regional level. This process of politicoadministrative organization is accompanied by the registration and identification of volunteers, as Jean-Pierre Chauveau and Koffi Samuel Bobo observe; "All possess an identity card proving that they are patriots serving their country, with their names, age and village of origin. These cards are used as laissez-passer on instructions given by the Préfet [local state administrator]" (Chauveau and Bobo 2003: 20).

The relations between these village militias and local authorities (be they locally elected officials, MPs, or members of the local administration) are extremely close, and these authorities play a vital role in the mobilization and coordination in the dynamic of "militianization" of rural space. In Oumé, for example, each volunteer has received presents and money from the local authorities. In Guiglo, Denis Mao Glofeï, the third assistant to the mayor, is himself the commander of the FLGO. According to the International Crisis Group,

> Mr. Mao is the President of the Association of Wê chiefs, and has been called an FLGO warlord. He is also a member of the Central Committee of the FPI. Although his title does not suggest that he might be influential, sources in both the west and Abidjan agree that he gives orders to all other elected or appointed government officials of the Government in the region around Guiglo. According to the same sources, Mao is the relay in a parallel chain of command that goes from the Présidence through him to the various militia forces (both Ivorian "patriots" and Liberian Lima/MODEL fighters) on the Guiglo-Touléplen and Guiglo-Bangolo axes. One source close to the Présidence confirmed that he had daily phone contact with either former Minister of Defence Kadet Bertin or Minister of Civil Service and Employment, Hubert Oulaï, who is from Troya, a village near Guiglo. Mao has become an almost mythical figure in the far west region, and his militias patrol Guiglo town and neighbouring areas. (International Crisis Group 2004a: 18)

He is not the only one: Octave Yahi, second vice president of the Guiglo General Council, and Pastor Diomandé Gammi also head militias, which continue to multiply (Konaté 2004b). These examples demonstrate the double process of paramilitarization and informalization of the FPI regime, which increasingly depends upon parallel structures and organizations and secret hierarchies where political, economic, military, paramilitary, and criminal networks are all inextricably linked.

What is the sociological makeup of these local militias, and what are their modes of action? In the absence of recent fieldwork, precise and detailed information is hard to come by.[18] Nevertheless, it appears from available sources that their activities and number vary considerably according to local situations. In the early stages of the conflict, it appears that these militias or self-defense groups, comprising in their majority young men under the age of thirty, were made up of three types of recruits. First, young autochthons have been the most numerous in volunteering to defend their village and "fatherland" and above all chase "strangers" off their lands and appropriate their goods (be they northerners, Baoulés, or Burkinabé or Malian immigrants). In this group, note Chauveau and Bobo (2003: 28–29), we often find individuals who have experienced professional or educational difficulties and have already been in conflict with migrants over land questions. After an initial phase of general mobilization of local self-defense groups, when these youth were often armed with the hunting weapons of their elders, it appears that those having regular professional activities went back to work, leaving the control of these groups to young school dropouts, who saw in them an opportunity for social mobility. Among these young "barragists" turned militiamen, we also find a number of urban youth who had returned to their villages following professional or scholastic failures, often in quest of land. Some of these youth were politicized via youth organizations on campus, or unionized during their time in the city, and now sought to put the "organizational competence" thus acquired to work for the local "patriotic struggle." While these recruits are relatively rare, they constitute important cogs in the FPI's patriotic "machine." Finally, certain internally displaced persons (IDPs), victims of violence and seeking revenge, have also come to join these village groups. While it is extremely hard to determine the political affiliations of these various youth, their "patriotic" discourse and proximity (both material and symbolic) to the FPI, given the growing polarization between the FPI regime and the "rebel bloc" (as they call the G7 coalition), means that the majority are supporters, if not militants, of the FPI.

These rural patriotic organizations undertake a variety of tasks, which vary according to the situation yet which obey the double and potentially contradictory logic of protection and extortion. As noted above, these structures were initiated in a "spontaneous" movement early in the crisis, incited by national politicians and pro-FPI press to defend villages against attack and prevent "rebel infiltration." Village elders conferred on these youth the responsibility of defending their homelands by creating informal roadblocks and filtering and controlling access to the village. Progressively, in many cases, this function of policing and controlling identities was "recognized" by public authorities and security forces. The gendarmes (part of the FANCI but responsible for internal security) gave a mitigated welcome to these newcomers. While typically sharing a "patriotic" discourse with them and anxious not to appear opposed to any national defense initiative, many gendarmes took a dim view of their ascendancy, the support they received from local authorities (whereas the gendarmes themselves often failed to receive their official "war bonuses"), and their often insolent autonomy, indiscipline, and growing monopoly over racketeering and extortion.

Indeed, roadblocks sprang up by the thousands throughout the south; in some places and during certain periods of high tension, one could find them every two kilometers! This situation created terrible problems of circulation and, during the harvest season, caused grave economic prejudice for growers, buyers, and transporters. The reason for this exponential growth, apart from any security concerns and the fact that they had been formally legitimated by national and local authorities, was clearly that the roadblocks were highly lucrative. While those set up in 2002 were above all designed to prevent rebel infiltration, very rapidly the activity of "barragists" consisted in extorting travelers and vehicles, according to increasingly structured principles, using intimidation, humiliation, and occasionally outright violence. Chauveau and Bobo calculated that in the Oumé region in 2003, each roadblock brought in a minimum of 20,000 FCFA (US$40) per day. On the road to Man, travelers with their identity papers could get away with paying a forfeit of 1,000 FCFA ($2), whereas those without papers have to hand over the astronomical sum of 10,000 FCFA ($20; Konaté 2004b).

But that is not all: as well as their role as "tax collectors," the village militias have been delegated power over land, which increasingly takes the form of violent expropriation. With the encouragement of local authorities and certain regional dignitaries with important positions in Abidjan, groups of "young village patriots" have created a climate of terror in which strangers (northerners and Burkinabè but also Baoulé) are chased off their lands, which are subsequently recuperated "legally" by local big men. In this process of expropriation, the youth use violence but pose as defenders of a "tradition" that they accuse their elders of having abandoned and thus reaffirm their autochthonous rights to land.

Last but not least, in certain cases local militias have served as fighters properly speaking in the war in the west, as discussed above. On the ground, the distinctions among types of groups are fairly tenuous. For example, associations of "young patriots" from the region of Guiglo and Gagnoa are in close contact with the FLGO and the FSCO, veritable paramilitary organizations. During the month of October 2004, in preparation for the counteroffensive undertaken by Gbagbo on 4 and 5 November, many of these militias underwent military training, notably in Daloa, Bloléquin, and Duékoué, where numerous training camps were set up for several thousand youths, some of whom had been bused in from Abidjan and all of whom were dressed in fatigues and given Kalashnikovs. Finally, working under the mistaken hypothesis that presidential elections would be held as planned in October 2005, the FPI and the presidency gave these militias a more political mission, consisting of preventing opposition party members from campaigning in, or even visiting, their electoral fiefs in the southwest. Thus PDCI health minister Mabri Toikeusse was prevented on two occasions in late 2004 and early 2005 from entering the towns of Guiglo, Bloléquin, and

Toulépleu, where he was to deliver ambulances and medicines (*Nouveau Réveil* 2005). As one observer remarks:

> Failing an attack from the ex-rebels, the militiamen's mission has been modified to adapt itself to the current combat. In the forest zones of the south-west, the instructions given to the militias are clear. They consist, on the one hand, in protecting the zones held by the party in power [FPI] against any incursions from the opposition. In regions like Gagnoa, Guibéroua, Divo, . . . the elective posts (MPs, Mayors, and Presidents of General Councils) must remain the exclusive property of the FPI. At the same time, the regime's militiamen are to "chase" all opposition parties from the zones where they hold elected posts. . . . "In the upcoming elections, there will be no Mayor, no MP, nor President of the General Council from the PDCI or the RDR in our region. These parties are rebel parties, and we're going to prevent the votes of their militants," explained a militiaman from Diégonéfla. (Konaté 2005)

Abidjan's Young Patriots

This phenomenon of "militianization" and militarization of the youth is central in the rural areas. But it is also and above all rampant in Abidjan, where, under the direction of highly visible and popular leaders, stars of the pro-Gbagbo media, the "young patriots" have taken the streets by storm. This movement, in all its organizational, sociological, and ideological complexity, is doubtless the most emblematic expression of the Gbagbo regime's evolution during the war—a regime that, incapable of relying on a powerful army and solid international alliances, has used a process of paramilitarization and militianization of society to impose its political order through terror, and an ultranationalist radicalization in order to legitimate its resistance to any form of external interference.

The Alliance des Jeunes Patriotes pour le Sursaut National, led by the self-styled "general" Charles Blé Goudé, was born just after the attacks of 19 September 2002 as a movement supporting the government in its resistance to the assailants from the north. Benefiting from extremely generous presidential largesse, this movement managed to mobilize hundreds of thousands at rallies held in Abidjan in the first few months of the conflict. While the first rallies were attended by citizens from every political party, region, and age group, the increasingly ultranationalist and pro-FPI discourse very rapidly discouraged the participation of more moderate populations and militants from other parties. Stigmatizing in the most virulent terms a whole range of "enemies" (e.g., the rebels and neighboring countries, in particular Burkina Faso and its citizens, as well as the rebels' supposed external supporters, principally France but also the United Nations), the young patriots have rapidly become central political actors in the crisis. They also very rapidly developed into militia forces working for the regime, charged with surveying the opposition and denouncing "suspicious" or "enemy" behavior, controlling popular neighborhoods, and creating a climate of terror throughout the city, even assisting at times the famous death squads responsible for numerous disappearances and summary executions.

At its origins, however, the Alliance was conceived as an alternative political movement, grouping together in a heterogeneous coalition a half a dozen or so associations or unions that had already participated as representatives of "civil society" under the junta in the Commission Consultative Constitutionnelle et Électorale (Consultative Constitutional and Electoral Commission, CCCE), where they had militated in favor of the restriction of political rights to autochthons only (Y. Konaté 2003). Alongside Charles Blé Goudé, ex-leader of the FESCI, the powerful students' union close to the FPI, we find Geneviève Bro-Grébé, ex-minister of sports in the first government of the Second Republic and president of the Réseau Ivoirien des Organisations Féminines; Laurent Tapé Koulou, director of the ultranationalist daily *Le National,* originally financed by Bédié but since rallied to Gbagbo; Konaté Navigué, leader of the youth wing of the FPI; Eugène Djué, also ex-leader of the FESCI, president of the Union pour la Libération Totale de la Côte d'Ivoire; Hilaire Gomé, president of the Federation of NGOs of Côte d'Ivoire, close to the FPI; Thierry Legré, president of the Cercle Alassane Dramane Ouattara before rejoining the patriotic union; Serge Kassy, famous reggae singer and mentor of the FESCI; and a multitude of more or less informal organizations, like the famous Sorbonne, led by Richard Dakoury (Konaté 2003).

From the outset of the crisis, the young patriots of Abidjan have constituted the shock troops of the FPI regime. Instrumentalized by the regime, which richly remunerates their leaders, the young patriots play a central role in the highly ambivalent relations with France, as shown by the extremely violent and destructive demonstrations following the Marcoussis peace accords in January 2003 and again in November 2004. Recruited, armed, and in daily training in Abidjan's streets, they constitute a formidable apparatus of social and political control. "Parliaments," "agoras," and "senates" have multiplied throughout most Abidjan neighborhoods, on the model of the "Sorbonne" (originally an Ivorian version of Hyde Park Corner, where soapboxing on politics and other subjects was open to all comers). These informal associations have been organized on a national level and are engaged in a process of "gridding" the entire city, enabling the least compound and its occupants to be identified and watched and even going so far as to have painted marks on some compounds. These associations were instrumental in the identification of opposition militants during their demonstration, which ended in the killing of some 300 opposition marchers, many of them in their homes, between 24 and 27 March 2004.

This movement is growing but is also increasingly divided. As time has gone on, the "patriotic galaxy" has become increasingly schismatic, giving birth to a multitude of groups led by petty chiefs fighting for the monopoly of the patriotic label and especially the presidential largesse that accompanies it: the Alliance and the Congress of Pan-African Youth, both led by Blé Goudé; the infamous GPP (Groupement Patriotique pour la Paix) led by Moussa Touré, alias "Zéguen"; Eugène Djué's Front National de Libération Totale de la Côte d'Ivoire, which claims to have 70,000 recruits; the Convention des Patriotes pour la Paix of Charles Groghué; the Front de Libération National; and others too numerous to name. As in the case of the rebellion, its internal divisions serve not only to weaken the movement but also, and more dangerously, to radicalize it. The repeated anti-French demonstrations can be interpreted in the light of this internal competition to keep the "patriotic flame" alive and the advantages that go with it (e.g., armed escort, luxury cars, access to the presidency, wealth, and beautiful women).

The regime has proclaimed its willingness to control this very dangerous phenomenon; in 2003, following renewed violence, the decision was taken to disband the GPP (for falsification of official documents). However, far from ceasing to exist, the organization simply changed its name for a short period and was soon back on Abidjan's streets. At the same time, when the minister of interior announced the disbandment, Gbagbo immediately reiterated his support for the "young patriots," whom he claimed were unarmed and were simply "young people who enjoyed doing exercise." In any case, the militia's leader announced clearly that he was not bothered by any decision coming from the Reconciliation government and its prime minister, Seydou Diarra, for these had no legitimacy in his eyes. ("It's not within the power of the government to disband us," boasted Zeguen.) The very day after the announcement was made, the GPP militiamen marched through Youpougon, openly defying police. More recently, in January 2005, the GPP were involved in extremely violent confrontations with local traders and transporters, who had become enraged by the constant racketeering, violence, and extortion inflicted on them by the militiamen, who had taken up illegal residence in a girls' boarding school. Several days later, a shootout between the GPP and students from the Police Academy left three dead, an incident that led Minister for Human Rights Victorine Wodié, who had been generally conciliatory to the Gbagbo regime, to demand their immediate removal from the school and disbandment.

This dynamic of militianization and paramilitarization of urban space is one of the central issues of the crisis, and it bodes extremely ill not only for the evolution of the peace process but also for the stability of the regime. Among the young patriots, as with the rebels, the high life led by leaders has led to growing frustration and indiscipline among the base, who are tired of seeing their leaders getting rich at their expense.[19] If the movement of patriots was tightly controlled by the presidency in its early stages, it seems unlikely that this is still the case, given the extent of their growth and the diverse logics and fluctuating networks that animate them. Today, these urban militias have become a veritable state within the state, a sort of youth counterpower at the heart of the regime which weighs heavily on decisions taken in the presidential palace. Some feel that Gbagbo has become, like Gueï before him, hostage to his "young people," who no longer hesitate to criticize decisions or even proffer indirect threats if the president fails to follow his hawks' hard line.

In the same vein, the regime is confronted with the increasingly pressing claims of certain western paramilitary fighters from the FLGO and the FSCO, particularly those who saw direct action in early 2003 and felt abandoned following the end of hostilities, without recognition or remuneration. Numerous FLGO fighters undertook a sit-in and hunger strike in 2004 at the cathedral in Abidjan to draw attention to their situation. Demonstrations by the FSCO led to the arrest and imprisonment of their leader, Bertrand Gnatoa. One anonymous fighter claimed in the press:

> Up until now, we haven't received a thing, while the mercenaries have everything. We're sickened by the fact that they've given millions to certain people like the Blé Goudés and the rest for organizing demonstrations, and we, who offered our breast to the bullets to save our country, we haven't been given anything. Not even a simple thank you. . . . If they want to see us hand over our arms, then they'll have to meet certain conditions, in particular, solve our financial problems. We believe the state has the means to compensate us. Today, they call us militiamen, but we're the ones that defended the Côte d'Ivoire, not the FANCI. . . . I fought for my country for nothing. Despite the danger I faced for my country, I'm invisible, without any respect, not even a word of encouragement from the regime I helped to save. This situation can lead us to revolt. . . . Today, given my financial situation, I'm ready to offer my services to anybody. (*Patriote* 2004: 3)

The rapid rise of these patriotic militias bears witness to two major political transformations. First, through the political influence they have acquired, they demonstrate that sovereignty and legitimacy are no longer to be found principally within official institutions but also and above all in the popular neighborhoods and on the streets where their law, made of violence and racketeering, rules. The fact that "General" Blé Goudé has proclaimed himself "President of the Street" is in this sense telling. Behind the boast lies a significant evolution of modes of government, of mobilization and control of the public space. Second, the "patriotic" mobilization in Abidjan and throughout the rural areas, as well as the mobilization of the youth by the rebellion, reflects a major sociological phenomenon: youths becoming men through war and affirming their power in the face of their elders. These youths have seized a unique opportunity to impose themselves as power holders in local politics. Despite the fact that these conflicts are largely provoked and controlled by local politicians in concert with power holders in Abidjan, youth groups have shown that they are a force to be reckoned with, capable of making or breaking local chiefs and officehold-ers and even openly defying state security forces.

This reconfiguration of intergenerational relations and rise of a new political generation is not only due to the war. This process of affirmation and search for autonomy is not new but has been greatly accelerated by the crisis, which has transformed the youth into an independent political cate-gory. While it is true that the great majority of the patriotic youth are mobi-lized and instrumentalized by the presidency in its strategy of populist and nationalist mobilization, the central role they hold shows that they have gained a considerable influence on the running of public affairs. On the rebellion's side, we can also observe the rise of new politicomilitary fig-ures, some of whom are now ministers in the reconciliation government at under thirty-five and tend to eclipse the old generation of politicians from the Houphouët era. In other words, what is at stake in the Ivorian war is also the rise of a new political generation, which, even if it has not entirely broken with old practices, carries with it a new political style and ethos.

Even if it is too early to measure the consequences of these develop-ments, understanding this major sociological transformation is central to explaining the current violence. In the image of these new political leaders formed by the FESCI, the patriotic youth in Abidjan, the roadblockers in the countryside, and the young western militia fighters from the FLGO, as well as the rebel recruits, all tragically imitating their Liberian comrades, the Ivorian youth are experiencing a new form of political subjectification through war, one that, with its warrior lifestyles and ethos of liberty through violence, does not augur well for a peaceful renegotiation of the contours of the nation.

Notes

1. Ferdinand, young patriot from the "Parlement" in Marcory, interview with Richard Banégas, September 2003.

2. The G7 is composed of seven of the ten signatories of the Marcoussis peace accords of January 2003. Apart from the three rebel movements—the MPCI, MPIGO, and MJP, now grouped together under the term "Forces Nouvelles"—the G7 counts the two largest political parties, the Parti Démocratique de Côte d'Ivoire (PDCI), ruling party from independence to 1999, and the Rassemblement des Répub-licains (RDR), led by Alassane Dramane Ouattara, prime minister from 1990 to 1993, as well as the Union pour la Démocracie et la Paix de Côte d'Ivoire, created by ex-president General Gueï, and the small Mouvement des Forces de l'Avenir (MFA).

3. We borrow this notion from Rémi Bazenguissa-Ganga, who uses the term to designate the double process of a generalization of violence and its popular reappro-priation (Bazenguissa-Ganga and Yengo 1999).

4. We will use the term *stranger* for the French term *allogène,* which has no English equivalent. *Allogène* does not necessarily imply a relation to nationality: *allogènes* may be either nationals or nonnationals.

5. All African foreigners had the right to vote in Ivorian elections until 1995.

6. For the leaders of the ONI, "whoever claims to be Ivorian must have a village. Whoever has done everything to forget the name of his village or who is incapable of showing he belongs to a village is a person without bearings and is so dangerous that we must ask him where he comes from" (M. Sery Wayoro, assistant director of the ONI, in *Notre Voie,* 27–28 July 2002).

7. We borrow the distinction between "militianization" of the army and the "militianization of society" outlined by Roland Marchal and Christine Messiant (1997).

8. Himself Baoulé, Houphouët nevertheless was careful not to "baouléanise" the army and recruited numerous officers from the west and especially the north.

9. Guillaume Soro was the running mate of Henriette Diabaté, general secretary of the RDR, in the legislative elections of December 2000. According to Diabaté's campaign organizers, Soro had originally refused to run on an RDR ticket, preferring to campaign as an independent.

10. Louis Dacoury-Tabley has a serious personal ax to grind with Gbagbo. When they were childhood friends, Gbagbo was accepted into the powerful Dacoury-Tabley family, which assisted him in his studies. As cofounder of the FPI, Dacoury-Tabley, a former police officer, was in charge of security issues for the party and also liaised with Compaoré, repatriating the funds that he donated for over ten years to the FPI. The two friends fell out in 1999 over the party's policies. Dacoury-Tabley started a newspaper, *Le Front,* which strongly criticized the Gbagbo government, revealing financial and political scandals. Dacoury-Tabley's brother Benoît was arrested by armed men on 8 November 2002 and found shot dead two days later.

11. Some 600 members of the initial attacking force belonged to special corps set up by Gueï during the transition: the Zinzins (crazy ones) and the Bahefoué (sorcerers). These troops faced demobilization with little or no compensation. Others were soldiers who had been forced into exile or court-martialed under the Gbagbo regime.

12. While IB on occasions left Ouagadougou for the border and a few times was seen in Korhogo, he remained based in Burkina Faso. Some reports have him at Danané in April 2003.

13. Gbagbo had good reasons for seriously questioning the loyalty of the national armed forces, FANCI. During the 19 September attacks on Abidjan, neither of its two military bases was attacked. Instead the rebels concentrated on the camps and schools of the gendarmerie and police. Contacted by French military officers immediately following the outbreak of shooting, the army took several hours to respond. According to one French official, they were "waiting to see which way things would go and intervened only when it appeared that the insurgents had lost the upper hand."

14. Colonel Michel Gueu and Colonel Ismaël Soumaïla Bakayoko made their first appearance during the peace talks in Lomé in November 2002. Colonel Bakayoko is chief of army staff for the Forces Nouvelles.

15. One of the four leading MPCI military units in Bouaké.

16 At the head of this network was Pouho Richard, an FPI financier from Toulépleu with interests in the logging industry in Monrovia and Toe Town in Liberia (Eloï Oulaï, director of Radio Côte d'Ivoire, and Pol Dokui, assistant director of programming at Radio Côte d'Ivoire).

17. These accusations were confirmed in interviews with Western military intelligence officers.

18. Given the climate of insecurity in this zone, there are few inquiries into these phenomena. The only scholarly fieldwork available is that of Koffi Samuel

Bobo cited below, seconded by relatively thin NGO reports, anecdotal information from interviews, and relatively rare press articles.

19. "When elements from the Cojep [another Blé Goudé movement] came to mobilize us to go out and march, they told us if we fought for Gbagbo, he would finance our projects," admitted Séry Antoine, who presents himself as a patriot from Youpougon military camp. He regrets, with other comrades enrolled in the pro-Gbagbo militia GPP (comrades who claim that Zéguen, the rebel chief of this militia, had promised them that they would be integrated into the army), that none of these promises had been kept. "What do we see after more than a year of resistance?" asks Séry, who answers himself: "Thierry Legré is married. Serges Kassy is married. Richard Dakoury is married. They all drive around in big cars with armed bodyguards, even Ahoua Stallone. They've all used us. These patriots complain that they've been treated like children. Like sheep, they followed people who were struggling for their stomachs more than their country" (Konan 2003).

7

The Democratic Republic of Congo: Militarized Politics in a "Failed State"

DENIS M. TULL

This chapter will examine the genesis and trajectory of the Rassemblement Congolais pour la Démocratie (RCD), the insurgency movement that, in alliance with Rwanda, triggered the second war in the Democratic Republic of Congo (DRC) (1998–2003). Given the unprecedented political and military involvement of outside forces in that conflict, this chapter will disentangle the interests and strategies that have been pursued by the RCD insurgency and its Rwandan backers throughout the various stages of the conflict.

Following a short overview of the political crisis in the former Zaire and the course of the war, the chapter will sketch the incipient period of the insurrection to probe the relative weight and interests of its founding parties, that is, the Congolese rebels and their Rwandan allies. Pondering this question is vitally important to the extent that the origins of an insurgency and the nexus of internal and external factors determine the legitimacy and, by extension, the trajectory of its armed conquest of power (Clapham 1998a).

Given the preponderance of Rwandan interests, the RCD lacked effective ownership of the insurgent war. The extent to which its largely externally induced nature bore on the RCD's political strategies will be analyzed in regard to the insurgents' international diplomacy and their record of domestic governance in the occupied territories of eastern DRC. It will be argued that both Rwanda's heavy hand and changes in the international post–Cold War environment induced the RCD to privilege the quest for international recognition as a legitimate contender for state power at the expense of domestic political support—let alone legitimacy—within its host society in the Kivus. Its shortcut to state power in Kinshasa through violent and diplomatic means proved extremely successful as international actors advocated its inclusion into a power-sharing agreement with the incumbent regime of President Laurent Kabila. Even so, external involvement did not bring about peace in the DRC. The reasons for this failure of external conflict resolution will be examined in the final section of the chapter, notably the neglect of colluding local and regional actors in the Kivus and Rwanda respectively who, for political and economic reasons, have a vested interest in the maintenance of the status quo.

Crisis and Warfare in the Former Zaire

At least two decades before the outbreak of the wars in the 1990s, the Zairian state had entered a severe crisis.[1] Never a strong bureaucratic state in the first place, it began a downward spiral with the disastrous "Zairian-ization" of foreign-held commercial enterprises in 1973–1974 (Young and Turner 1985). Initially, however, the economic crisis barely affected the power of the regime. President Mobutu Sese Seko quietly abandoned his ambition to erect an integral state (C. Young 1994) and set up an informal system of rule that, in addition to foreign military and economic aid, relied primarily on informal levers of power such as patronage, intermediary institutions, and control over clandestine markets. By the late 1980s, the informalization and privatization of the state in conjunction with the deepening economic crisis showed unmistakable signs of political reverberations. Increasing pressure from inside and outside the country forced Mobutu in 1990 to reluctantly announce the end of single-party rule (Callaghy 2001: 102–137).

As a result of the political liberalization, Mobutu and the opposition were soon engulfed in a fierce power struggle in Kinshasa. The deadlock utterly paralyzed the country's political system, and entire regions, such as Kasai, informally seceded (Herbst 2000: 147). In the Kivus and Katanga, the political crisis ushered in violent conflict as Mobutu's henchmen unleashed vicious xenophobic campaigns against "foreigners" in an attempt to garner support for electoral purposes. In addition, the already disintegrating Zairian army was allowed to run riot to intimidate the population and to create a degree of political disorder, intent on demonstrating to the West that Mobutu remained an indispensable factor to keep the anarchy-bound country together (Lemarchand 2001: 23–25). On the eve of the Rwandan genocide in 1994, Zaire was thus deprived of even remotely functional state institutions, including the army. At the same time, the patronage networks forming the political backbone of Mobutu's power underwent serious distress, which rendered the country more and more ungovernable. Still, internal turmoil barely threatened the survival of the regime, as Mobutu succeeded in outflanking the rising tide of domestic political opposition. His eventual downfall in 1997 owed more to regional dynamics than to domestic political challenges.

Like most of its African contemporaries, the Zairian state was never conceived to defend itself against threats coming from the exterior. In the flipside of the state's judicial sovereignty, the Mobutu regime had always focused on controlling domestic contenders. The Shaba invasions in 1977– 1978, which were suppressed only with the help of Western military support, were early indicators of the regime's feeble military capacities. In the post-1989 period, Mobutu and his cronies were entrapped in this structural feature of postcolonial statehood and were unable to adapt to the changed international environment, notably the erosion of the hitherto sacred principle of noninterference in the domestic affairs of a sovereign state.

As a result, the Zairian state was ill-prepared to confront the new challenges arising from regional processes such as the repercussions of the Rwandan genocide and the refugee crisis of 1994 (Reed 1998). The Alliances des Forces Démocratiques pour la Libération du Congo (AFDL) insurgency, led by Laurent Kabila and his regional backers (Angola, Rwanda, Uganda), whose security concerns had been threatened by Mobutu's tacit or open support for rebel groups, met with little organized resistance when they ousted Mobutu after a sweeping military campaign in May 1997 (Reyntjens 1999). Kabila, now the freshly inaugurated president of the DRC, inherited this legacy and was barely able to put up with his own violent contenders.

On 27 July 1998 Kabila put a term on the military presence of the Rwandan troops that had helped his AFDL insurgency to topple Mobutu in 1997. Barely one week later, the North Kivu–based battalion of the DRC army staged a mutiny against Kabila, which quickly turned into a fully fledged insurrection spearheaded by a hitherto unknown group called the Rassemblement Congolais pour la Démocratie. Supporting the insurgents, Kabila's former allies Rwanda and Uganda invaded the eastern DRC provinces of North Kivu and South Kivu alongside the RCD. In a parallel military operation, on 4 August 1998, Rwanda airlifted 400 troops to Western Bas Congo Province to take control of the capital Kinshasa, a move that was obstructed by the intervention of Angolan troops. Zimbabwe and Namibia joined Angola to save the beleaguered Kabila, and the hopes of the rebel coalition for a swift military takeover were dashed. As a consequence, the insurgents were forced to concentrate on their military campaign in eastern DRC. Meeting scant resistance, they rapidly occupied vast stretches of territory and advanced toward the Kasai provinces. Meanwhile, the northern parts of the country fell under the control of a newly created insurgency group, the Mouvement pour la Libération du Congo (MLC), backed by Uganda.

In July 1999, subregional mediators backed by Western governments brokered the Lusaka cease-fire agreement, which was subsequently observed by the United Nations Organization Mission in the Democratic Repubic of the Congo (MONUC).[2] The accord froze the war along the 2,400-kilometer-long conventional frontline. The country remained divided into three vast zones of influence controlled by Kabila, the MLC, and the RCD.

It was only in late 2002 that all the foreign armies withdrew from the DRC. This paved the way for the holding of the Intercongolese Dialogue in Pretoria in December 2002. President Joseph Kabila (Laurent Kabila's son, who ascended to power following his father's 2001 assassination), the RCD, the MLC, three smaller insurgent groups, and representatives of political opposition parties and civil society agreed on a power-sharing formula for a two-year-long political transition. Flanked by four vice presidents, Joseph Kabila remained head of state and presided over the government of national unity that took oath in July 2003.

However, hopes for a smooth transition from war to peace were soon dashed by the utter paralysis of the government and the profound distrust and competing interests among its composite factions. A flare-up of violence in the Kivu provinces in 2004 brought the fragile government to the verge of collapse (Wolters 2004). Coupled with massive logistical problems, pervasive insecurity led to a postponement of the elections, originally scheduled for mid-2005, to July 2006, with a run-off held in October 2006.

Permanent low-intensity warfare and pervasive insecurity took an appalling humanitarian toll. It is estimated that 80 percent of the population living in the provinces of Orientale, North Kivu, and South Kivu left their home at least once during the war. By 2003, internal displacement reached a peak of 3.4 million people, the vast majority of whom were living in eastern DRC (Norwegian Refugee Council and Global IDP Project 2003: 51). It has been alleged that some 4 million people have died as a direct or indirect result of the war (*Economist* 2005).

Regional Power Play

Although the insurgency of 1998 was more than just a remake of the AFDL war, a number of similarities among the context, origins, and actors of the uprisings are noteworthy. Much as in 1996, the war was driven by strong regional interests, as the DRC insurgents received decisive military support by Rwanda and Uganda. Their decision to overthrow Kabila—whom they had installed as Congo's president barely fourteen months before—did not come as a surprise. Already shortly after the AFDL had entered Kinshasa in May 1997, popular resentment against Rwanda's heavy military presence had risen steadily both in the DRC capital and in the Kivu provinces in the east of the country. Having alienated Kinshasa's political circles and lacking a domestic political powerbase, Kabila was caught between a rock and a hard place. He could either maintain his close links with his external godfathers, thus nurturing the domestic perception of being a stooge of foreigners, or disengage from Kigali and Kampala at a yet unforeseeable price. In July 1998, he cut the Gordian knot by opting for domestic legitimacy and demanding the withdrawal of the Rwandan and Ugandan forces from the country.

Following Kabila's move to free himself of the overpowering influence of his erstwhile allies, Rwanda and Uganda once more conceived the power holders in Kinshasa as a threat to their security. These concerns were particularly strong in Kigali, whose assaults on the refugee camps in the Kivus, where the former Hutu regime had regrouped since 1994, had not resulted in the ultimate elimination of the former Forces Armées Rwandaises (FAR) and Interahamwe militias responsible for the Rwanda genocide. Given that not even the Rwandan army in conjunction with the AFDL had succeeded in defeating the Hutu *génocidaires,* as evidenced by an upsurge of rebel activities in northeastern Rwanda since late 1997, how could Kabila, in whom Kigali had lost confidence anyway, be trusted to deal with the problem on his own?[3] The Rwandan leaders had come to the conclusion that Kabila was unwilling or, more likely, unable to address its security concerns (Reyntjens 1999: 177). The ultimate turning point came on 14 July 1998, when Kabila dismissed the Rwandan officer James Kabare as chief of staff of the DRC army. This, however, was but an accelerating factor leading up to a new war. As a top RCD official was later to admit, the war had been under preparation for several months (BBC Monitoring 1998h). And as early as spring 1998, Rwanda had allegedly convinced Uganda to once more invade the DRC (Prunier 1999: 53). At the same time, the Rwandan government had been busy regrouping a number of DRC personalities who were willing to serve as a national smokescreen for the invasion (De Villers et al. 2001: 43; Nzongola-Ntalaja 2002: 228).

Broadly speaking, the leadership of the insurgency was composed of four groups (Misser 1998). A first group consisted of former AFDL lieutenants, most of whom were members of South Kivu's Rwandophone minority group (the so-called Banyamulenge), including Moise Nyarugabo, Bizima Kahara, and Azarias Ruberwa. Former followers of the late Mobutu made up a second group, notably Alexis Thambwe, José Endundo, and Lunda Bululu.[4] A third component comprised some well-known academics and professionals who were to provide the insurgency with some measure of political credibility to shield it against the predictable accusations of being a foreign proxy, such as Ernest Wamba dia Wamba, Jacques Depelchin, and Zahidi Ngoma. A fourth group consisted of various individuals disappointed or marginalized by Kabila, including Emile Ilunga and Joseph Mudumbi.

Thus the RCD assembled some odd bedfellows, and it seems almost inconceivable that this motley crew of would-be insurgents had come together without the impetus of a third party's hidden hand (i.e., Rwanda and Uganda). For example, that prominent members of the former Mobutu regime joined some of their erstwhile enemies from the AFDL appears indeed remarkable. The assemblage is likewise remarkable in light of the well-known disgust that the leading intellectuals (Wamba, Ngoma) of the rebellion harbored for the "Mobutists."[5] Exchanging their purported principles for pragmatism, however, the intellectuals jumped at the opportunity offered by foreign powers to play, at last, a political role in their country.[6] If the political opportunity to seize state power was the common denominator that brought these groups together, it would have been in itself insufficient to counterbalance the diverging interests within the insurgency, in particular between Wamba and Ngoma on the one hand and the three remaining factions on the other.

And indeed, serious cracks within the alliance were brought to light by a falling out between the rebels' Rwandan and Ugandan backers. Having failed to anticipate Angolan intervention on behalf of Kabila, the allies became divided over their divergent views regarding strategies.[7] While personal rivalries between Presidents Museveni and Paul Kagame certainly played a role, competing economic interests in northeastern Congo's diamond-rich Orientale Province also came to the fore.[8] In November 1998, Uganda left the alliance and sponsored the creation of a rival rebel movement to the RCD, Jean-Pierre Bemba's MLC.

As a result of Kampala's walkout, RCD president Wamba dia Wamba, who had arguably been installed at the behest of Museveni, lost his influential patron. Lacking any constituency within the movement, Wamba was ousted from the RCD leadership in March 1999 (BBC News Online 1999; *Humanité* 1999).[9] Aside from his feud with the "Mobutists," Wamba's departure was primarily prompted by insurmountable divergences with Rwanda. His ostensible advocacy for a more political approach to the rebellion was by and large incompatible with Kigali's penchant for a military solution. By the same token, the deeply suspicious Rwandan government never permitted the former Mobutists to benefit from later leadership overhauls of the movement. In fact, the former AFDL leaders hailing from the Kivus proved to be the only rebel faction Kigali regarded as trustworthy. As a result, they came to play a preponderant role within the rebellion, though they did not take over the leadership until 2003, when Azarias Ruberwa became president of the RCD. Not incidentally, the Rwandophone leaders remain today the only sizable group that was part of the initial nucleus of the RCD. Suffering a series of defections under Ruberwa's predecessors Emile Ilunga and Adolphe Onusumba, the movement lost an estimated 80 percent of its founding members (International Crisis Group 2003b: 15).[10]

If dependence on Rwanda and political bickering characterized the RCD for most of its existence, its internal problems were compounded by the elite origins of its leaders, who shared few commonalities beyond the goal of regime change in Kinshasa. With the notable exceptions of Wamba and a few others, the vast majority of the rebel leaders had formerly served in senior government positions under Presidents Mobutu or Kabila. Now excluded from power, the Rwandan impetus provided these former state elites with an opportunity to recycle themselves politically. Contrary to their foot soldiers, the RCD rebel leaders were not social outcasts but members of the political establishment. As such, they did not fight to address societal grievances but in order to reintegrate into a system from which they had been excluded. Former ministers or prime ministers under Mobutu, Bululu, Endundo, and Thambwe as well as the former followers of Kabila, Kahara, Nyarugabo, and Ruberwa, among others, fall into this category. Due to their past positions, they possess the connections and resources to organize a rebellion as a means to enforce their inclusion into a profitable political system that, as a result, they do not want to change (Reno 2002: 841f). This lends support to Clapham's observation that "insurgencies derive basically from blocked political aspirations" (Clapham 1998b: 5). It comes as no surprise, then, that the more reform-minded group around political newcomers like Wamba was fairly quickly sidelined by the well-entrenched political elites of the Mobutu and Kabila period, whose vision was exclusively focused on capturing state power (IRIN News 1999). The political pastoralism that not a few defecting RCD leaders later embarked upon further underscores this point. For example, Vice President Ngoma, who left the RCD in February 1999, reconverted into a civilian politician. In 2003, with President Joseph Kabila's help, he secured one of the four vice presidencies of the republic which the Pretoria accords had reserved for civilian opposition parties in the transitional government. Other noteworthy figures who changed sides included the former "Mobutists" Thambwe and Endundo, who joined Bemba's MLC rebellion and reemerged as ministers in the government of national unity in 2003.

As the rest of the chapter will show, the circumstances and interests surrounding the creation of the RCD had a significant impact on the trajectory of the insurgency.

International Relations: The Quest for Recognition

Like many of its contemporaries elsewhere, the RCD consistently put emphasis on the garnering of external rather than domestic support. For one thing, this outward-oriented approach matched the RCD's lack of any domestic agenda other than conquering state power. For another, it reflected realpolitik insofar as the rebels were accurately aware that their international recognition as contenders of power was both more vital and easier to achieve than the burdensome mustering of domestic constituencies. This rationale was considerably enhanced in the wake of the Angolan intervention and the signing of the Lusaka accords. Since negotiations seemed inevitable, mobilizing international diplomatic backing turned into a crucible of the rebels' conquest for power.

But even before Lusaka, the RCD insurgents had attached considerable importance to international relations. This was arguably the very reason that eloquent intellectuals like Wamba and former UNESCO official Ngoma were granted the formal leadership of the movement. Like many other insurgents, the RCD also hired lobbying firms to represent its interests in Washington (*Lettre du Continent* 1999). Valuable help came from President Laurent Kabila himself. Having alienated the Western audience due to his dealings with so-called rogue states like Libya and North Korea, the RCD justifiably regarded Kabila "as its best asset" and portrayed itself on the international level as a preferable political alternative to the erratic leader (*Africa Confidential* 1998a).

In the final analysis, it remains an open question whether the tacit international backing for the rebels was due to the RCD's successful international diplomacy or to Kabila's propensity to make an art of making enemies. Except for Angola, Namibia, and Zimbabwe, no other countries in the subregion responded positively to Kabila's demand to condemn the insurgency (BBC Monitoring 1998b).

The RCD, for its part, was extremely successful in the diplomatic realm and achieved de facto recognition by Western states. In early November 1998, US assistant secretary of state for African affairs Susan Rice traveled to Kigali to hold discussions with RCD officials (BBC Monitoring 1998k). Given past diplomatic practices, the talks in the capital with the RCD's Rwandan godfathers were a spectacular act of recognition and fell just one step short of visiting the insurgents in their headquarters in Goma. The talks were not the first contact between the insurgents and Western state officials. Several RCD delegations had visited Western capitals (Paris, Brussels, Washington) in the early days of the rebellion (BBC Monitoring 1998d, 1998f, 1998i). After a trip to Paris, Vice President Ngoma was reported to have "welcomed the way Western countries were reacting and the French position on the dispute in particular. . . . 'France is a country that has understood what we are about, I am pleased to say. The fact that it is keeping out of current events is a good sign [a reference to Paris's strained relations with the RCD's Rwandan backers]. Of course, we are labeled rebels, which makes it difficult for the international community to adopt a stance, but it is encouraging for us to see that, in Africa as elsewhere, we are not alone in this battle'" (BBC Monitoring 1998g). Ngoma's comment is remarkable, for it reflects both a sensitivity to the convention of juridical statehood and, more important, an understanding of its changed operational nature in the international realm.

As subsequent developments were to indicate, the RCD's vice president was not the only one to grasp this issue. For it cannot be ignored that the numerous international attempts to broker a peace agreement—a stunning 23 by one count—provided a powerful incentive to other ambitious would-be leaders to follow the RCD on its pathway to state power: a shortcut that appeared promising exactly because both subregional and international actors strongly advocated a political deal between Kabila and the insurgents (*Africa Confidential* 1999a). Intriguingly enough, one of the main obstacles that outside peace brokers encountered while establishing the terms of the Lusaka agreement of 1999 was exactly the row over which parties to the conflict qualified as belligerents—that is, who was militarily strong enough to deserve a place at the bargaining table that was to distribute political spoils among the warring factions (International Crisis Group 1999: 5–7). Unsurprisingly, as soon as the Lusaka accords foreseeing the holding of a "national dialogue" (read: power sharing) had been signed, the issue asserted itself with a vengeance, and defections from the RDC and the proliferation of smaller insurgencies started in earnest. This process included the creation of the RCD-ML (RCD–Mouvement de Liberation), which progressively fragmented even further into factions led by Wamba, Jean-Baptiste Tibasima, Mbusa Nyamwisi, and Thomas Lubanga.[11] Given the underlying logic of power-sharing agreements, according to which all armed insurgents are to be included in negotiations, the new factions understandably expected to be handled by the mediators as the RCD was. Indeed, this was the very reason they had been created.

In retrospect, the violent insurgencies instigated by the RCD and Bemba's MLC proved extremely successful. The 1999 Lusaka cease-fire agreement and the subsequent implementation process, however cumbersome, gave the rebels and their foreign backers almost everything they had asked for. Four years later, a transitional government in Kinshasa was installed in which the RCD and the MLC each took one of the four vice presidencies and numerous other posts.

Insurgency Governance in the Kivus

Throughout the war, the RCD insurgency entertained difficult relations with its host society in eastern DRC, and as Vice President Ngoma admitted barely one month after the start of the rebellion: "We are conscious of a certain unpopularity of our movement among the population" (Tull 2005: chap. 4; BBC Monitoring 1998a). For a start, the insurgents' explanation for yet another uprising fell on deaf ears. Though Laurent Kabila's popularity plummeted after only a few months in office, a population tired by almost a decade of violent conflict was unwilling to suffer the costs of another war. What is more, the rebels were reluctant but somewhat forced to "administer" the vast territories in eastern DRC they had occupied. As RCD vice president Ngoma conceded, "We hadn't realized that we would have to set up what is more or less a government so fast, but it's an obligation now" (BBC Monitoring 1998d).

This obligation never translated into a coherent political approach (Tull 2003). The insurgents took charge of the feeble state apparatus it found in place and converted the provincial branches of the central government into its "ministries." By claiming to administer the occupied territories in accordance with DRC law, the RCD portrayed itself as the provisional inheritor of the state in the eastern part of the country. If only on the symbolic level, this decidedly statist approach was arguably conceived as a tactical move to address Western anxieties about the maintenance of a resemblance of administrative-bureaucratic order. However, this could barely conceal the group's exceedingly poor performance. As the self-declared legitimate political authority in eastern DRC, the rebels claimed prerogatives of statehood without delivering public goods. Much like its rivals from the MLC and RCD-ML, it asserted, for instance, its right to collect monies and custom duties in accordance with DRC's legal code directing matters of taxation. At the same time, it changed these regulations at will for its own economic benefit and allegedly raised tax levels by 200 to 300 percent (United Nations 2003a: para. 89). It also introduced new taxes to pay for "security" and the "war effort." These were particularly resented by the local population on account of both its hostility toward the war and the RCD and the blatant lack of reinvestment to pay civil servants and soldiers or to finance public services such as security, education, and health. The RCD justified this state of affairs by explaining that 70 percent of its revenues was consumed by the war effort (*Africa Confidential* 1999b).

Even so, no single factor corroborated the RCD's unpopularity more than its close links with the Rwandan regime and the widespread Congolese resentment of living under foreign occupation. Excessive human rights abuses and systematic pillages that were attributed to the Rwandan army only aggravated the situation (BBC Monitoring 1998c). A Kisangani resident described what turned out to be the leitmotif determining popular attitudes vis-à-vis the movement: "If a Congolese soldier misbehaves, the population is hurt, but they can stomach it . . . because Congolese soldiers have been like that from Mobutu's days. But we can't stand it if it's a foreigner who came here saying he wanted to help us have freedom and democracy!" (Aliro 1998).

In the frontier provinces of North Kivu and South Kivu, where the insurgency took off and established its headquarters, outright hostility to the RCD and its Rwandan backers was particularly pronounced. These attitudes built on sentiments that had arisen during and after the AFDL insurrection in 1996–1997 when large parts of Kivu society leveled accusations against rebel-cum-president Kabila of being a Rwandan stooge. Rwanda's military presence provoked an uprising of indigenous militias, the so-called Mai Mai, to counter Rwanda's grip over eastern DRC (Willame 1999: 135). Under the RCD regime, armed and unarmed resistance grew even stronger and persisted throughout the war. The vicious repression with which the rebel alliance responded only added fuel to local resentment.[12]

The fierce resistance against the RCD was rooted in the fact that the Kivus were the theater of three intertwined and mutually reinforcing levels of conflict. The local and national dimensions of the war—foreign intervention and the violent struggle for DRC state power, respectively—exacerbated long-standing local ethnic tensions, which came to determine both the RCD's relations with its host society and the protracted nature of the conflict. Local conflicts first erupted in 1992, when discourses of autochthony took root in the Kivus which, inter alia, targeted Rwandophone "foreigners," that is, people of Rwandan origin who had migrated to eastern Congo during various periods in the course of the twentieth century and even before: the so-called Banyarwanda (Hutu and Tutsi) of North Kivu and the so-called Banyamulenge (Tutsi) of South Kivu. The ideology of autochthony covered the instrumentalization of simmering communal tensions and was, to a certain degree, a result of the announced democratization of the country in 1990. With the Banyarwanda forming a demographic majority in many parts of North Kivu, the anticipated elections sparked "indigenous" fears of political marginalization. Local politicians claiming authentic "nativeness" in the Kivus mobilized their ethnic communities (Nande, Hunde, Nyanga, Tembo, etc.) to garner electoral majorities and to politically exclude the Banyarwanda. Ensuing violent clashes between the groups left several thousand people dead.

Taking recourse to autochthony, the attempted political exclusion of the Banyarwanda built on the fact that their citizenship had been a contentious issue for a considerable time. Due to Mobutu's divide-and-rule strategies and the political jockeying of North Kivu's ethnic groups in search of political and economic patronage, several contradictory nationality laws had been passed in the last decades (Nguya-Ndila Malengana 2001). In effect, however, the root causes of the violent clashes between the Banyarwanda and the indigenous communities were essentially linked to conflicts over local resources such as political power and access to land. The arrival of more than a million Hutu refugees in the wake of the 1994 Rwandan genocide aggravated tensions even further. In South Kivu, by contrast, violent conflicts erupted only in 1996, when local administrators called on the Banyamulenge to leave the country. The attempted expulsion led to a military uprising by the Banyamulenge, who shortly thereafter joined forces with the invading AFDL rebels and the Rwandan army (Vlassenroot 2000).

As a result of Rwanda's continued military presence in eastern Congo—first in alliance with the AFDL, later with the RCD—autochthonous and xenophobic sentiments were exacerbated to an unprecedented degree. They culminated in narratives of "genocide" of indigenous people by Rwandophones and even the creation of a "Tutsi-Hima Empire" in the Great Lakes region.[13] Rwanda's cynical claims to be protecting the Banyarwanda and preventing another genocide, this time of Congolese Tutsi, only added fuel to discourses of autochthony and xenophobia directed against Kivu's Rwandophone groups. This reinforced the intersection of local conflicts with the national and regional war of 1998, insofar as large parts of Kivu's so-called indigenous groups considered the RCD to be dominated by Banyamulenge and Banyarwanda elements. Although this perception was largely inaccurate in the initial stage of the rebellion, a deeply flawed but powerful equation emerged among the indigenous groups of North Kivu and even more so in South Kivu: RCD equals Rwandophone (Tutsi) equals Rwanda. Civil society activists in the urban centers were quick to decry the "Tutsification" of the Kivu provinces and their imminent annexation by Rwanda. These discourses struck a powerful chord among vast segments of the indigenous population, and a plethora of "indigenous" Mai Mai militias formed its military equivalent. Casting themselves as a nationalist resistance movement, the Mai Mai realigned with Kabila and Rwandan Hutu rebels to fight their common "Tutsi" enemies, that is, Rwanda, the RCD, and the local Banyarwanda communities.

In summary, Kivu's local conflicts were not at the root of the second Congo war, but the rebel alliance buttressed societal divisions along ethnic lines. These divide-and-rule strategies were instrumental in dealing efficiently with societal resistance and instigated the progressive interconnectedness of both local and regional conflicts. They left a legacy of ethnic antagonisms in the Kivus that will endure for many years to come (Tull 2005: 234–257). Unfortunately, international interveners and mediators (e.g., the United Nations and its mission, MONUC) seeking to resolve the DRC war neglect this local dimension, thereby effectively undermining their attempts to build peace on the national and regional level.[14] As a result, instability in eastern DRC endured well after the enthroning of the government in 2003, thus endangering the larger peace process. This was most dramatically exposed in spring 2004 in South Kivu, when renegade commanders of the RCD briefly captured the city of Bukavu and Banyamulenge civilians were attacked by Mai Mai militias and Kabila's troops. The crisis provoked the flight of several thousand Banyamulenege to Burundi and Rwanda and plunged the whole transition process into a severe crisis (Wolters 2004).

New Strategies—Same Old Story?

The interplay of local, national, and regional conflicts entered a new phase during the second half of the war, when the strategies by Rwanda and some of its DRC allies underwent a decisive shift. Beginning in 2001, the ceasefire on the conventional frontline was respected, and negotiations were to lead to "a new political dispensation" in the DRC. This so-called Intercongolese Dialogue was based on the principle that all the participants in the negotiations "shall enjoy equal status."[15] This formula significantly strengthened the political standing of the rebels to the detriment of the government, as it laid down the basis for the sharing of political power between the government and the rebels. The likelihood of this outcome increased when Joseph Kabila took up the reins of his murdered father in January 2001. Although the talks were not completed until December 2002, the revamped peace negotiations, beginning in October 2001 in Addis Ababa, heightened international pressure for the implementation of the third central provision of the Lusaka accord, the withdrawal of foreign armies.

For Rwanda the direct implications of this new dynamic were twofold. First, the pullout of its 23,000 soldiers from Congo had become inevitable and was finally executed in October 2002. Second, the possibility loomed on the horizon that the RCD leaders would eventually leave the Kivus to partake in a government of national unity in Kinshasa, a move that would inevitably diminish the political value accorded to the rebels by Kigali. Against that backdrop, after 2001 the Rwandan regime embarked on a strategy to retain control over the Kivus without an overt military presence there and, if necessary, without direct recourse to the RCD. Eugène Serufuli, a founding member of the RCD, was at the heart of this tactical shift. At the instigation of Kigali, Serufuli was appointed as the governor of North Kivu Province in 2000. Subsequently, he received strong Rwandan backing enabling him to construct his own power structure first inside the RCD and later independent of the formal insurgency structure. In other words, Serufuli replaced the RCD as Kigali's key ally in North Kivu.

The reasons behind Serufuli's rise were related to Rwanda's weak grip on the province. The unpopularity of the RCD and the presence of Rwandan Hutu rebels of the Forces Démocratiques de Libération du Rwanda (FDLR) had created concerns that the Hutu could start to collaborate with the FDLR, particularly in the Hutu strongholds of Rutshuru and Masisi. Serufuli, himself a Hutu from Rutshuru district and a former member of a Hutu militia, was given the task of countering this threat by mobilizing the Hutu in line with Kigali's interests and to succeed where the RCD had failed—that is, to build a local power base (Tull 2003: 441–442). By constructing patronage networks, Serufuli established himself as the most important intermediary powerbroker between Kigali and his local Hutu constituency. In the process, he recruited some 10,000 mostly Hutu young men into his Local Defense Forces, which formed the coercive pillar of his rapidly increasing power. By 2002, he had grown largely autonomous of Ruberwa and other RCD leaders conducting the peace negotiations with Kabila (Tegera 2003). Unimpressed by the national power-sharing arrangement, he also hung on to his political autonomy vis-à-vis the transitional government that took oath in July 2003.

Thanks to Rwanda's covert support and his own military power, Serufuli thus established himself as a major stumbling block for President Joseph Kabila's efforts to extend his power to eastern DRC. When it was time to appoint new governors to the country's provinces in May 2004, the helpless Kabila had little choice but to formally confirm Serufuli's governorship of North Kivu. A subsequent attempt to remove Serufuli by force only confirmed Kabila's lack of leverage over the autonomous-minded strongman. Unlike South Kivu, which Kabila's troops in conjunction with Mai Mai militias occupied in spring 2004, military attempts to "liberate" North Kivu ended in pathetic failure in late 2004, amid rumors that Rwandan troops had entered North Kivu (*Africa Confidential* 2004).

Rwanda's sponsorship of Serufuli raises questions about Rwanda's real interests in the DRC, beyond its purported security predicament. First, after at least five years of direct presence of the reputedly effective Rwandan army in Congo, the Hutu rebels have not been dismantled and still number 8,000 to 10,000 fighters. Recurrent allegations have centered on the discrepancies between Kigali's zealous security rhetoric and the often indecisive approach of its army on the ground (African Rights 2000; United Nations 2003a: para. 66). In addition, Rwanda's latitude with the rebels is bigger than Kigali is ready to admit. In 2003, for example, it successfully negotiated the surrender and repatriation of senior Hutu rebel commander Paul Rwarakabije and 100 of his fighters without the knowledge of either the Kinshasa government or the MONUC (*Africa Confidential* 2003). This suggests that Rwanda's secret service maintains contacts with the rebels and that if Kigali has political will, the repatriation of substantial numbers of Hutu rebels and their leaders is by no means impossible.

Generally speaking, the Rwandan government has lacked the resolve to resolutely tackle the problem of Hutu rebels by either political or military means. Instead, Kigali took a backseat and appeared to relish bashing the hapless disarmament approach of MONUC and the international community. In so doing, it retained a convenient justification for its continued interference in the DRC. While it is unlikely that economic agendas were an original motive of Rwanda's intervention, abundant evidence suggests that predatory objectives became central to Kigali's rationale. The large scale and systematic exploitation of mineral resources (e.g., gold, diamonds, coltan), often under the direct surveillance of military officers, demonstrate that economic objectives have superseded security interests as the primary motive of the continued Rwandan presence in Congo.[16] In 1999 alone, the UN Panel of Experts estimated Rwanda's overall revenues from its military commercialism in the DRC to have been on the order of $320 million, amounting to 20 percent of the country's gross national product for that year (United Nations 2003a: para. 71). According to numerous sources, the systematic exploitation of natural resources in eastern DRC by Rwanda and its ally Serufuli continued unabated in spite of intensified international attention to the issue (United Nations 2004: para. 65–84, 91–100; *Africa Confidential* 2005).

Moreover, Rwanda stands accused of having recurrently violated the arms embargo that the United Nations Security Council imposed on eastern Congo in 2003 by providing weapons to the RCD renegade commanders who briefly captured the capital of South Kivu (Bukavu) in May 2004 (United Nations 2005; Wolters 2004). All of this suggests that Rwanda has little intention of relinquishing its at least indirect political control over Kivu, particularly its northern part. Tending to regard the province as its backyard, Kigali does not hesitate to use its security concerns as a convenient cover for its continued resource exploitation.

Given recent scholarly emphasis on economic greed as a driving force of contemporary African insurgencies, it is instructive to note that Rwanda's economic imperatives have also informed its relations with the RCD insurgency. The United Nations in particular has placed much emphasis on the fact that the sharing out of resources gained from violent resource exploitation over the course of the war was fairly lopsided, observing that Kigali "perennially deprived its junior partner, RCD-Goma, of any significant share in resources and prerogatives" (United Nations 2003a: para. 74, 78; *Africa Confidential* 1999a). According to RCD officials, between one-third and two-thirds of the total coltan production was directly transported from the Kivus to Rwanda without passing through the channels of the insurgency (International Crisis Group 2003b: 25).

While uneven distribution patterns to the detriment of the RCD are indeed plausible, it remains true that the rents siphoned off by the insurgents were substantial. Still, the evidence is insufficient to determine whether the RCD insurgents were primarily driven by economic interests or not. Moreover, successive RCD leaders throughout the war followed a consistent policy of negotiations and international diplomacy intent on accessing state power in Kinshasa.

In the end, it may be of only limited value to analyze insurgency-ruled eastern DRC by resorting to often misleading binaries such as "political versus economic" and "greed versus grievance." These may provide seemingly comforting certainties but are inadequate to capture the complexities and ambiguities that characterize the political situation in eastern DRC and other war-torn zones. What, for example, is "illegal" resource exploitation in a country where any notion of state-sponsored juridical order has been a chimera for decades? How do we comprehend that mineral exploitation may fuel insurgent warfare while at the same time it is a crucial element of the survival economy of thousands of eastern Congolese (Pole Institute 2002)? Government officials in Kinshasa and their Zimbabwean allies have transferred assets worth at least US$5 billion from the DRC's state mining sector to their private companies with no compensation for the DRC—does that differ qualitatively from the machinations of rebel alliances (United Nations 2002: para. 22)?

Conclusion

The second war was just the latest manifestation of the ongoing political crisis in the former Zaire. Now, as in the late 1970s, a national army and bureaucracy worth the name barely exist, and public services are not offered by the state. Given this, the current scholarly emphasis on state collapse is misleading. What collapsed in the early 1990s were not so much formal state structures but the patronage networks that had underpinned President Mobutu's rule. With the crumbling of the regime, the conflicts and pogroms ravaging the Kivus and Katanga in 1992–1993 signaled the dawn of an era in which already violent politics became thoroughly militarized.[17] Ruthless politicians and local strongmen embarked on violent strategies to push into the political vacuum that the ailing regime was leaving behind. While the ease of the 1996–1997 AFDL rebellion was a manifestation of that void, the political system was catalyzed out of its paralysis by the political liberalization since 1990. It unleashed centrifugal political forces at the very moment that the state was weakest. Thus the aborted democratization process was a major turning point in its own right and is to a large, albeit overlooked, degree related to the wars of the 1990s. Both wars are central components of the ongoing violent transformation of Congo's political order.

Ultimately, the novel phenomenon that has characterized the DRC from 1994 onward was the extent to which external (and violent) actors have directly influenced and shaped political outcomes in the country. By intersecting with local and national processes, regional actors fomented the militarization of politics to a hitherto unprecedented degree. Their overpowering influence was such that DRC's civilian political actors have been largely excluded from any meaningful participation in shaping the country's future. This, of course, is not to downplay the role of the Congolese protagonists who have been active agents of the crisis, on both sides of the war.

What appears remarkable, however, is the fact that neither the AFDL nor the RCD rebellion aimed at posing a challenge to the notion of Congolese statehood. Seeking state power in Kinshasa rather than secession, the strategies of both insurgencies were framed by the notion of juridical statehood (Englebert 2003). Its salience was bolstered by Western powers' categorical refusal to consider a new territorial configuration in Congo, instead brokering a political solution within the country's current borders via power sharing. Given the decline of vital Western interests in Africa in the post-1989 period, power sharing has become the preferred instrument of low-key engagement by outsiders concerned to achieve conflict resolution and state-sponsored order. To some extent, its recurrent use in the 1990s for the sake of "peace" has created an incentive structure for would-be insurgents to have recourse to violence to conquer state power or at least to receive a seat at the bargaining table. As such, the much-decried lack of political agendas that the RCD and other contemporary insurgencies reveal is intrinsically linked to changes in the post-1989 international environment, whereby ideological pretenses have been largely replaced by raw military power. Sadly, power sharing has more often than not failed to bring about sustainable peace. This has been particularly true in cases such as the DRC, where the political solutions proposed by external conflict brokers have failed to address the interests of the most powerful player, Rwanda.

Regardless of the outcome of the current peace process, the enduring importance Western powers ascribe to the notion of juridical statehood forestalls any perspective for a fresh start of the Congolese state. In spite of the rhetoric of state building, it is blatantly obvious that Western states lack the political will and the resources necessary to put this objective into practice. Failing to address the root causes of warfare, their apparent opting for quick-fix solutions in so-called failed states such as the DRC will at best result in a state resembling the political system that was at the core of the violent crisis since the early 1990s.

Notes

1. Zaire was renamed Democratic Republic of Congo by incoming president Laurent Kabila in May 1997.

2. In 2003, due to the political impasse of the peace process and continued fighting in eastern DRC, MONUC was transformed into a peacekeeping force consisting of 10,800 personnel.

3. See various IRIN reports in November and December 1997. Rwandan intelligence sources also claimed that the DRC president had begun supporting the ex-FAR and Interahamwe in September 1997. See International Crisis Group 2000: 12.

4. For biographical sketches of the RCD leaders, see BERCI 2002; IRIN News 1998.

5. See, for example, the remarks by Wamba in IRIN News 1999.

6. For Wamba's explanation for his joining the RCD, see BBC Monitoring 1998e.

7. The surprise in this turn of events was articulated in an interview with James Kabare. See *Observatoire de l'Afrique Centrale* 2003.

8. For an account of the origins of the "family feud," see International Crisis Group 2001: 6–9.

9. With Ugandan help, he moved his new faction, the RCD-ML, to Kisangani. A few months later, Rwanda and Uganda came to military blows in that city. The defeat of the Ugandan army forced Wamba to move his headquarters to Bunia.

10. For a scathing review of Onusumba's rule and rare insights into the RCD's internal workings, see Mulumba 2003.

11. However, many of these insurgent factions were located in the northeastern district of Ituri, which saw a very peculiar political trajectory during the war. For a good overview of the background see Human Rights Watch 2001.

12. As a result, the RCD stood little chance of gaining a significant number of votes in the postconflict election. In the July 2006 election, neither Kabila nor Bemba secured a majority of votes, and a run-off election was held in October 2006.

13. For an illuminating account, see Lemarchand 1999.

14. It was only in 2003 that the MONUC belatedly recognized that the provinces in eastern Congo held the "key" to a successful peace process in Congo. Even so, this translated only into the deployment of additional peacekeepers to the Kivus and little concrete action (e.g., local peace-building programs) was undertaken to address local conflicts. See United Nations 2003b: par. 29.

15. Lusaka Ceasefire Agreement, annex a, chapter 5, article 5.1 and 5.2.b.

16. The United Nations assembled a panel of experts that issued several reports on the topic (all of them are accessible at www.monuc.org). See also All Parliamentary Group on the Great Lakes Region and Genocide Prevention 2002.

17. The phrase "militarized politics" is borrowed from Stephen Ellis 2003.

8

Uganda:
The Lord's Resistance Army

KEVIN C. DUNN

For two decades, northern Uganda has been devastated by a conflict involving the central government, the local population, and the Lord's Resistance Army (LRA), an armed group, led by Joseph Kony, that has been active in the region since 1987. But the conflict in northern Uganda has attracted surprisingly little international attention. In fact, Western media coverage of the conflict has tended to be highly sensational, focusing on the brutality of the LRA and its practice of kidnapping children. More often than not, the LRA war is held up as an example of barbarism and irrationality in contemporary Africa, with little attempt to contextualize, historicize, or even explain the conflict.

It is true that the conflict in the north has affected children the most. The LRA targets children, kidnapping thousands of them and often forcing them to become soldiers, temporary porters, or sexual concubines for LRA officers.[1] According to Amnesty International estimates, nearly 80 percent of the LRA combatants are abducted children (2001: 2). Many of the kidnapped children are forced to carry out atrocities, such as killing other children who were caught trying to escape. For this reason, every night thousands of children leave their homes in the bush and suburbs, fearful of being abducted, and walk to nearby towns to sleep in shelters or on the streets. These "night commuters," as they have become known, mainly crowd into Gulu, where their numbers fluctuate between 1,000 and 40,000, depending on local security conditions.

Resolution of the conflict remains highly elusive. Ugandan president Yoweri Museveni proclaimed that 2002 would be a year of peace for all Ugandans, but the LRA's activity actually increased. At the beginning of 2003, Museveni promised to end the war by April. Instead, the LRA stepped up its attacks on the civilian population, striking targets outside its usual zone of conflict. The number of people living in the displacement camps in the north rose from 500,000 to 800,000—more than half the Acholi population.

Many of the internally displaced persons (IDPs) have been living in camps for over six years, where health and sanitation facilities are very poor and daily life is rather dire. In early 2005, the government again proclaimed that peace was close at hand. The peace initiatives, however, quickly collapsed, and the military conflict intensified, with no sign of diminishing. As this volume went to press (January 2007), peace talks were taking place in Juba, Sudan, driven by the Sudanese vice president Riek Machar. Despite being heralded by many as the best chance yet for peace, the success of the talks face numerous hurdles, as this chapter will explore.

Very little is actually known about the LRA, but numerous theories abound. This chapter weighs the merits of the main theories for the causes and continuation of the conflict. There seem to be five main theories put forth, both within and outside of Uganda. First, Kony is described as a "madman" who is engaging in an irrational campaign of violence and terror with no purpose or ultimate goal. Second, the conflict is regarded as the result of serious and legitimate complaints that the Acholi and other peoples in the north have against the central government of Uganda. Third, the conflict is understood as a by-product of the larger geopolitical rivalry between the Sudanese government and Uganda. Within this theory, Kony and his soldiers are seen as hired guns who are used by the Sudanese government to destabilize Uganda. Fourth, it is held that the army and government of Museveni actually have no interest in defeating the LRA at all. Either the government doesn't consider it a major concern, or political leaders are exploiting the conflict for their own political purposes. Finally, there is the view that a "political economy of conflict" has emerged in northern Uganda, where various actors are economically benefiting from the continuation of the war and thus have no interest in bringing about its conclusion.

This chapter examines each of these five theories at some length. The goal is to clear up some confusion surrounding the conflict and provide readers with a more nuanced understanding of what is a rather complicated conflict. Before examining the merits of these theories, I provide a brief historical summary of the rise of the LRA and the government's responses. These elements provide necessary background for any understanding of the war in northern Uganda.

From Alice Lakwena's Holy Spirits
to Joseph Kony's Lord's Resistance

In July 1985, as the beleaguered government of Milton Obote faced the advancing forces of Yoweri Museveni's National Resistance Army (NRA), a group of Acholi soldiers led by Bazilio Okello mutinied, ousted Obote, and installed Tito Okello, another Acholi, as the new president. This marked the first time that a group of Acholi controlled state power in Uganda. Following the tradition of previous postcolonial regimes in Uganda, they generally used state power for personal enrichment and as a weapon against their enemies, including the Langi and people from the West Nile (Behrend 1998b: 108).

Around this same time, a young woman named Alice Auma from Gulu in Acholi claimed to be possessed by a Christian spirit named Lakwena.[2] Under the guidance of this spirit, Alice established herself as a spirit medium and began working as a healer and diviner in the region. The following year, the Okello regime was toppled, and Museveni's NRA established itself in Kampala. Thousands of Acholi soldiers, who had been deployed in brutal fighting against the NRA in the Luwero triangle, fled home to the north, most fearing reprisals from the victorious NRA. In Acholi, a power struggle began between the returning young soldiers and the Acholi elders, who regarded the soldiers as the root of all evil. During their struggle with the NRA, these soldiers had plundered, tortured, murdered, and, in the eyes of Acholi elders, become "impure of heart." Moreover, they brought *cen,* the vengeful spirits of those they had killed, back to Acholi, and these threatened the lives of all the people in the north (Behrend 1998a: 248). Thus, the "impure" soldiers and the *cen* they had brought north were generally blamed for the misfortunes that struck Acholi. The returning soldiers also represented a direct threat to Acholi, as they began to plunder the villages and terrorize anyone whom they didn't like. The Acholi elders attempted to reassert their political and moral authority but were unsuccessful (Behrend 1998b: 108). It was within this crisis in the north that the Alice Lakwena's Holy Spirit Mobile Forces emerged.

In August 1986, the spirit Lakwena instructed Alice to stop working as a healer and to establish the Holy Spirit Mobile Forces (HSMF) to wage war against witches, impure soldiers, and the government. She recruited many of the former (Acholi) soldiers from the Uganda National Liberation Army (UNLA) and the rebel group Ugandan People's Democratic Army (UPDA). The HSMF gained increasing support from the civilian population (including various other ethnic groups, such as the Langi, Teso, and Jopadhola), especially after its initial military successes against the central government. As Heike Behrend notes, "The HSMF was alone in responding to the crisis [in northern Uganda] with a moral discourse" (Behrend 1998b: 109). From the beginning, Alice Lakwena created a purification ritual to cleanse her soldiers from witchcraft and the *cen.* By seeking to purify her followers and the Acholi in general, she sought to reconstitute a moral order.

As Behrend has pointed out, "The HSMF waged war not only against an external enemy, the NRA government, but also against internal enemies: against rival resistance movements like the UPDA and the Uganda's People Army [UPA], against witches . . . and impure soldiers. Thus, destruction was not only directed against the government troops but also against people in Acholi who were held responsible for all the evil in the world" (Behrend 1998a: 247). Fighting a more or less conventional war and led by the spirit Lakwena, Alice marched toward Kampala with between 7,000 and 10,000 men and women. Near Jinja, around fifty kilometers east of Kampala, she and her followers were defeated by government forces. Alice crossed into Kenya, where she reportedly remains today.

After Alice's defeat in October 1987, many of her surviving soldiers tried to retreat back to Acholi. Some joined the UPA in Teso, while others joined the UPDA or Joseph Kony's own Holy Spirit Movement (HSM). Others joined Alice's father, Severino Lukoya, who decided to continue her struggle by creating the Lord's Army. During the rise of the HSMF, Lakwena had possessed Alice and instructed her father not to get involved in the movement. He had abided by the command and remained in Kitgum. Only after her defeat did he succeed in gathering a following, which was estimated to number around 2,000 men and women. Unlike Alice's HSMF, the Lord's Army conducted mainly a guerrilla campaign, mostly around Kitgum District. Moreover, Severino's movement was more focused on healing and cleansing people than Alice's had been. Severino's struggle ended in 1989, when he was captured by fighters loyal to Kony. He eventually managed to escape, but he was subsequently captured by government soldiers and imprisoned until 1992, when he returned to Gulu.

It is often incorrectly suggested that Kony's LRA was the continuation of Alice's HSMF. In fact, Kony started his movement around 1987. At the time, he was a young school dropout from Gulu and claimed to be the cousin of Alice. Depending on the historical account one follows, Kony was possessed either by the spirit Lakwena or by Juma Oris, a onetime minister under Idi Amin who was living in Sudan and would resurface in 1993 to lead the West Nile Bank Front (WNBF). Creating his Holy Spirit Movement, Kony recruited soldiers from around Gulu while Alice's HSMF marched on Kampala. Reportedly, Kony offered to form an alliance with Alice, but Lakwena snubbed him. Seeking revenge for the rejection, Kony started cutting off the food supply to Alice's troops and directly attacked some of her forces. By the time of Alice's defeat, the two Holy Spirit Movement groups were in direct competition. However, in the wake of her defeat, several of her soldiers joined Kony's forces, and Kony adopted the discourses Alice had created, establishing a complex initiation and cleansing ritual (Behrend 1998b: 115).

Kony began fighting a guerrilla war, using small, quasi-independent armed groups that mostly operated in Acholi and southern Sudan. In May 1988, Kony's group received a boost when they were joined by a group of renegade UPDA rebels who refused to abide by the peace agreement between the UPDA and Museveni's government. After 1990, the LRA gained a further boost when it began receiving direct aid from the Sudanese government. For a brief time, one of the ex-UPDA leaders, Odong Latek, rose to prominence in the group (renamed the Uganda People's Democratic Christian Army, UPDCA), and the group's religious discourse was partially replaced by more explicit guerrilla tactics. After Latek was killed, Kony rechristened the group the Lord's Resistance Army and reasserted its religious rituals (Behrend 1998b: 116). The religious elements of the movement seem to continue to date. Escaped children tell of numerous rituals involving water, stones, special prayers, and medicines. As Rosa Ehrenreich observes, "Such reports suggest that the rebels remain motivated by a variant of Alice Lakwena's millenarian beliefs" (Ehrenreich 1998: 85; see also Human Rights Watch 1997, 2003).

Throughout the 1990s, Uganda suffered from the war of attrition between the LRA and the government—or, more correctly, the LRA and local populations in northern Uganda. The LRA's activities were generally limited to armed attacks on trading posts, schools, and villages in northern Uganda and to sending small groups to fight against the Sudan People's Liberation Army (SPLA) in southern Sudan on behalf of the Sudanese government. Describing the increased banality of the conflict, Carlos Rodriguez of the Acholi Religious Leaders' Peace Initiative (ARLPI) wrote, "Insecurity in Acholi was rather limited to certain areas. The scenario would go like this: A group of one or two hundred rebels would enter from Sudan and for two or three months people knew that they had to exercise caution. Usually, their movement could be monitored and one knew that certain roads had to be avoided" (Rodriguez 2003).

In what many regarded as a major breakthrough, the governments of Uganda and Sudan signed a peace agreement in 1999. The Nairobi agreement committed the two governments to cease hostilities against each other and not to harbor, sponsor, or give military or logistical support to any rebel or hostile elements from each other's territory (Mayanja 2003). Many observers assumed that with the withdrawal of Sudanese support, the LRA "rebellion" would peter out. Hoping to further that process along, in December Uganda's parliament passed an amnesty bill for rebels who surrendered. That same month, the *Economist* predicted that the conflict was drawing to a close. Morale among the LRA was low, and Kony was reportedly "a spent force" (*Economist* 1999: 40).

But reports of the LRA's demise were greatly exaggerated. The LRA continued to attack the north and continued to employ bases within southern Sudan. In an attempt to rout out the LRA once and for all, in March 2002 Sudan signed a protocol with Uganda that allowed Ugandan troops to be deployed in southern Sudan to carry out search-and-destroy operations against LRA bases (Mayanja 2003). Thousands of Ugandan People's

Defence Forces (UPDF) soldiers were deployed in Sudan in what was named Operation Iron Fist. Army commander Major-General James Kazini promised if he couldn't deliver Kony's head by December, he would quit.

The UPDF was relatively successful in dismantling the LRA's infrastructure behind the lines, but Operation Iron Fist had the unintended consequences of pushing the LRA more deeply into northern Uganda. In the words of Giulio Cederna, "Reports say the LRA has ordered its fighters to return to Sudan, spreading them over the territory in small groups of 10 or 15 and has changed its objectives: they are not only to attack the 34 refugee camps into which four-fifths of the district's inhabitants are crowded (380,000 displaced out of a population of 460,000), but also the survivors in the villages surrounding the main cities" (Cederna 2003). The rebels also began kidnapping even younger children.

More than 20,000 UPDF soldiers were deployed in the north, and several thousand more were in southern Sudan under Operation Iron Fist. Yet since the beginning of Operation Iron Fist, the number of people living in displaced people's camps across northern Uganda grew to more than 800,000 (Kaiza 2003). By summer 2003, the situation seemed to have reached an all-time low. The LRA was increasing its field of activity, kidnapping more and younger children, while the UPDF seemed increasingly ineffective in stopping it. All the major roads in the north of Uganda were inaccessible. In May 2003, Museveni dropped Kazini in a reshuffle of the army leadership. Minister of State for Defense Ruth Nankabirwa understandably banned security officers from issuing ultimatums for ending the war in the north.

Throughout 2004 and 2005, the Ugandan government announced several military victories in its struggle against the LRA, including the killing, capture, or defection of numerous high- and mid-level LRA fighters, most notably Brigadier Samuel Kollo. With each seeming blow to the LRA, pronouncements of the imminent collapse of the LRA were routinely aired. A temporary cease-fire was established in early 2005, and the beleaguered peace process was revived. The peace talks collapsed, however, after the International Criminal Court, at President Museveni's urging, announced that it was preparing arrest warrants for Kony and four of his commanders (see Allen 2006). After that the military campaign intensified, with attacks by the LRA increasing in number and severity, while the Ugandan army yet again proclaimed that the end of the conflict was close at hand. In 2005, LRA rebels had reportedly established themselves in eastern Democratic Republic of Congo (DRC), around the Garamba region. Indeed, it emerged in 2006 that Kony himself was in the DRC when the BBC was able to conduct a rare interview with him (BBC Two 2006). The interview was seemingly inspired by Sudanese vice president Machar's active role as mediator in a new round of peace talks. Fearing for his security despite Museveni's promise of amnesty, Kony was refusing to attend those formal peace talks at the time of this writing.

Trying to Understand the LRA

How does one go about understanding why the LRA exists and why the conflict continues? In the remainder of this chapter, I will attempt to grapple with the five primary theories put forth to answer those questions.[3]

Kony as Madman

Relatively little is known about Joseph Kony. Even less seems to be known about the LRA's ultimate agenda. Dialogue has repeatedly failed because the LRA has not produced a list of grievances that could form the basis of talks. In March 2004, the Sudanese magazine *Referendum* reportedly interviewed Kony, and the transcript was widely circulated throughout the region. In that interview, Kony stated, "LRA is fighting for the application of Ten Commandments of God and we are also fighting to liberate people living in occupied Northern Uganda" (*Monitor* 2004: 12). The claim that the LRA is fighting for the Acholi is often seen as ironic, since it has largely targeted the Acholi population. Beyond this supposed interview, the few pronouncements made by the LRA underscore its goal of installing the biblical Ten Commandments as the rule of law in Uganda. How the LRA can reconcile this goal with its almost daily violation of "thou shalt not kill" is unclear but not unique, as this contradiction is a quandary for many religious militants. In his 2006 BBC interview, Kony spent little time articulating his reasons for fighting, focusing instead on denying charges of brutality (BBC Two 2006).

Referring to her interviews with former LRA child-soldiers who managed to escape, Ehrenreich observed, "None of the children we met seemed to have any real understanding of the rebels' aims and motivations. They frequently told us that the rebels wanted to 'overthrow the government,' and that Kony claimed to be doing the bidding of the Holy Spirit. Beyond that, the children could not go" (Ehrenreich 1998: 94). The vagueness of the LRA's agenda and its clear hypocrisy in pursuing its stated goals have led many to conclude that Kony and his comrades are either madmen or irrational, or both. Indeed, the Ugandan press regularly depicts Kony as a dreadlocked, drug-addled witchdoctor and madman, surrounded by skulls on pikes, cauldrons with human flesh, and other tropes meant to convey savagery, barbarism, and irrationality. During my various trips to the region, explanations of the war based on Kony's insanity and irrationality are a constant refrain heard from both local Ugandans and foreign observers.

But writing off Kony and the LRA as crazed, drug-fueled madmen is too easy and ignores facts that suggest Kony is neither crazy nor irrational. For example, the military practices of the LRA suggest a clear and consistent rationality—acting in a coordinated manner through an extensive radio network with alarming efficiency and employing advanced weaponry such as automatic weapons and land mines. Ehrenreich correctly notes that the insanity thesis is deeply grounded in the Western-scripted "heart of darkness" paradigm frequently used to write off the complexities of African conflicts (1998: 83). For example, an article on the LRA in the *Los Angeles Times* concluded, "Brutal and bizarre insurgencies are hardly new in Africa, where rebels without a coherent ideology have laid waste to Sierra Leone, Liberia, Somalia and other nations in recent years" (Drogin 1996: A1). Actually those conflicts, though often illogical to the outsider (and especially to the Western media), contained an internal logic that has made them highly rational to the participants.

In a discussion of the Revolutionary United Front (RUF) rebels in Sierra Leone, who were similarly portrayed as irrational madmen with a practice of kidnapping children and mutilating their victims, the anthropologist Paul Richards argues that "once a decision to resort to violence had been taken, hand cutting, throat slitting and other acts of terror [became] rational ways of achieving intended strategic outcomes" (1996: xx). For Richards it is important to understand war as a practice, a performance, and a discourse. With regards to the performative aspect of Kony's war, one can examine how the LRA generates power through managing violence and terror as expressive resources (think of the US "Shock and Awe" strategy against Iraq). Moreover, I maintain that Kony's actions can rationally be understood as part of a discourse of violence, where the LRA is engaged in a "conversation" with other social and political groups, particularly among the people in the north. What perhaps makes this discourse bewildering to Western observers is the integration of religious discourses with political and violent discourses. But as Behrend points out, "It seems that, in contemporary Africa, political issues are increasingly expressed in religious discourses. To gain or conquer the central power, i.e. the state, religious discourses are invented" (Behrend 1998a: 245–246). Indeed, as I will elaborate below, the LRA's violence against civilians can be understood when we examine how the LRA views the conflict through the lenses of religion and ethnicity.

The Legitimate Complaints of the North

Those who reject the insanity thesis often cite the legitimate problems and complaints of the Acholi and other people in the north as reasons that the LRA conflict continues. Indeed, there is a lengthy history of antagonism between the Acholi and central authorities. On one hand, one of the common "metanarratives" in Acholi society features the historical memory of deception and antagonism at the hands of the government (Bøås 2004b: 286–290). On the other hand, in recent decades northern Uganda has been further marginalized, both politically and economically. While Museveni's

Uganda is sometimes portrayed as a development success story, it is clear that the north has not benefited from the economic growth enjoyed by many others in the rest of the country.

Under the British colonial system, the practice of ethnic division was imposed in Uganda, as a result of which the peoples of the north came to dominate the ranks of the colonial army while generally being economically and politically disadvantaged. A major colonial betrayal of the Acholi occurred in 1913, when the British colonial government promised that all Acholi men who turned in their rifles would get them back after they had been registered. But instead of returning the rifles, the colonial administration had them burned. Under the regimes of Milton Obote and Idi Amin, the colonial practice of ethnic division continued, particularly in the army, where roughly three-quarters were from northern Uganda (Museveni 1997: 38). In 1971 and 1972, Amin ordered thousands of Acholi soldiers into the barracks, where he had them murdered. During the Obote government's brutal struggle against Museveni's NRA, Obote chose to deploy mostly Acholi troops to the Luwero triangle, where many assumed they were being sacrificed (Omara-Otunnu 1987: 162–163). When the National Resistance Army came to power and established itself in the north, many of the NRA soldiers took their revenge on the Acholi soldiers and their brethren by plundering, raping, and murdering.[4] In 1986, the new National Resistance Movement (NRM) government ordered the Acholi to surrender their weapons, which had increased in number during the preceding civil wars. This time, many Acholi kept their weapons and fled to the bush to join resistance movements.

Over the course of the LRA war, government officials and soldiers have repeatedly complained of a lack of cooperation from the local civilian population in the north (*New Vision* 2003b: 2). Yet it is fairly obvious why that might be the case. Reported atrocities committed by soldiers against the local Acholi population are common and accounts of them are well circulated throughout the north. For example, a report by the ARLPI accuses the army of routinely raping civilians, especially those venturing from camps in search of food (Ross 2003: 20). The government's paramilitary organizations, such as the Kalangala Action Plan (which was active in Museveni's 2001 presidential campaign), are also notorious abusers of the northern population. In December 2005, government soldiers opened fire on civilians in the Lalogi IDP camp, killing at least seven and wounding many more (BBC News 2005).

Such abuses by the government's representatives have strengthened the north's historic distrust of, if not outright hostility toward, the central government. It is not uncommon to hear residents of the refugee camps describe their situation as being "trapped between the two warring groups and trust[ing] neither" (Ross 2003: 20). As Behrend has noted, the mere existence of these "protected camps" has alienated people from the government:

"purportedly to protect the people from the 'rebels' . . . these camps served to prevent people from supporting Kony's soldiers, and to punish them for alleged collaboration with the LRA" (Behrend 1998b: 117). Many in the north believe that the counterinsurgent tactics employed by Museveni's government are actually part of a strategy aimed at "the disappearance of the Acholi people" (Finnström 2003: 145).

The economic marginalization of the north is also a major source of the political animosity toward the central government. Since coming into power, Museveni has launched a series of neoliberal economic reforms in hopes of increasing Uganda's development. While various sectors and regions of Uganda, most notably the western sections of the country, have enjoyed increased economic growth under Museveni, the north has certainly not. The north's economic and political marginalization has further fueled many northerners' distrust of Kampala and animosity toward Museveni. Citing several supposed LRA manifestos that were circulating in northern Uganda, Sverker Finnström claims that the LRA "evidently feed on an increasing local discontent with neoliberal developments in Uganda, particularly structural adjustment and other development measures demanded by the donor community" (Finnström 2003: 159). For many in the north, the belittling of the LRA and its political agenda by the government and most media devalues and erases the legitimate complaints of many northerners.

But while one may understand the animosity of the Acholi and other northerners toward the central government, it is not immediately apparent why these same people would support Kony and the LRA. As mentioned above, the LRA has not put forth any significant political agenda, so it is unclear whether it is truly fighting "for" the people in the north. Finnström himself is quick to recognize that the manifestos critiquing Museveni's neoliberal economic policies are probably not authentic products of the LRA (2003: 169). While the northerners may consider their complaints against Museveni legitimate reasons for armed resistance against Kampala, it is unclear that the LRA actually represent those concerns. It has failed to produce any serious political alternatives or correctives. In his study of Sierra Leone's RUF, Ibrahim Abdullah suggests that a lack of a clear-cut ideology explains why the rebels tolerated terror and anarchy as part of their struggle (1998: 234). In the case of Uganda, LRA fighters predominantly attacked, raped, kidnapped, and killed exactly the people they are purportedly fighting for: their fellow Acholi and other northerners.

This seemingly bewildering contradiction can be partly explained by the fact that because the government soldiers' current ill-treatment of the Acholi continues a lengthy tradition of abuse from the central government, the LRA has been tolerated in some parts of Acholi. But an even more nuanced understanding emerges when we shift our focus beyond strict political considerations to the larger social belief systems in the north. As Morten Bøås has pointed out, the dialectic "between healing and killing is a constant theme in the history of the Acholi, and the narratives connected to this dialectic are integral to the social practice surrounding both the Holy Spirit Movement of Alice Lakwena and its successor, the LRA" (Bøås 2004b: 286). Discussing the "anthropological" causes of the conflict, Ehrenreich writes:

> While Kony's activities may seem bizarre to outsiders, they in fact form part of a coherent belief system. Kony has vowed to rid the Acholi of witches and believes that killing a witch is not a wrongful act in the same way that killing a person is wrongful. The rebels kill those they believe are working with evil spirits. The rebels view the conflict through the lenses of religion and ethnicity. From such a perspective, all those not with Kony are against him, and anyone against Kony—and, by implication, against the Holy Spirit—must be working with evil spirits. Thus, the apparently senseless violence against civilians, though tragic, is not senseless when viewed in context. (Ehrenreich 1998: 85)

I agree that this is an important element for understanding the LRA war. In fact, Heike Behrend's *Alice Lakwena and the Holy Spirits* examines the movement's socioreligious belief structure and, in my opinion, remains one of the most insightful discussions of the roots of the LRA conflict.

Yet while Alice Lakwena, Joseph Kony, and their immediate followers have employed a coherent belief system that resonates with many in the north, it is equally clear that many northern Ugandans appear bewildered and tragically numbed by the conflict's persistence, unable to understand, let alone justify, the brutal murder of fellow Acholi and the kidnapping of young children. Moreover, as the war spread into eastern Uganda during 2003, it no longer remained a "northern" war. More important, the LRA's relationship to local populations seems inconsequential to its ability to attack government and civilian targets.

Sudanese Hired Gun? The Regional Geopolitical Dimension

An alternative explanation for the conflict argues the LRA is part of a larger regional geopolitical struggle between Uganda and Sudan. For various reasons, there has been a history of animosity between the Khartoum government of Sudan and Museveni in Uganda. For several years, each side directly supported a rebel group active in the other's territory. While Uganda provided direct assistance to the SPLA, Sudan countered by aiding Kony's LRA. The Khartoum government not only provided military and financial assistance to the LRA but also allowed it to use parts of southern Sudan as its base of operations. Many reports note that the LRA would often join the Sudanese army in operations against the SPLA. This situation led many to view Kony as little more than a Sudanese mercenary, a hired gun.

The 1999 Uganda-Sudan agreement was seen as a major blow to both the SPLA and the LRA, as it severed what many considered to be their life-lines. The agreement required Kampala and Khartoum to cease hostilities against each other and not to harbor, sponsor, or give military or logistical support to any rebel groups from each other's territory. This agreement was followed in March 2002 with a surprising protocol that allowed Ugandan troops to be deployed in southern Sudan to carry out search-and-destroy operations against LRA bases. With Ugandan troops operating freely in parts of southern Sudan, evidence emerged in the summer of 2003 that the LRA was receiving fresh military supplies from elements in the Sudan People's Armed Forces (SPAF). This evidence came largely from rescued abductees and documents captured in battle (*New Vision* 2003b: 2). The ARLPI released a report substantiating these charges. As Rodriguez wrote: "Eyewitnesses have told me of a meeting in Nisitu at that time [July 2002] in which Mr. Kony was given a good amount of military supplies, and the same sources have indicated that during the battle for the recapture of Torit in November LRA forces (commanded by Tabuley) fought alongside the Sudanese army against the Sudanese People's Liberation Army" (Rodriguez 2003). Thus, by summer 2003, not only was Operation Iron Fist a failure but the LRA was actively fighting in new parts of Uganda and the Sudanese support seemed to have been reactivated.

For some, the resurgence of the LRA, especially in eastern Uganda, was directly related to Sudanese support. Reflecting on the connections between Kony and Khartoum, Museveni stated on 27 June 2003 that the lengthy LRA war was the manifestation of Sudan-Ugandan competition: "In fact it was a war between us and the Sudan. We had to support the black people there. If you throw stones at us we shall do that to you too. Last year they promised to stop supporting Kony but they have continued. If you want to understand a snail, see where it came from. The snail has its trail" (quoted in *New Vision* 2003a: 2).

Despite Museveni's attempt to blame the Sudanese government for the survival and successes of the LRA, it actually appears that the aid the LRA is receiving is coming from specific elements within the Sudanese army and does not reflect a change of policy by Khartoum. Ugandan defense minister Amama Mbabazi sought to clarify the situation by pointing out that it was elements in the Sudanese army, possibly those allied to opponents of President Omar el Bashir, who had resumed arms supplies to the LRA. Mbabazi stressed that apart from specific elements in the army, he did not believe that Sudan had resumed support for the LRA (Mayanja 2003). Speculation has centered on two influential figures in Khartoum, former speaker of Parliament Hassan el-Tourabi and Vice President Ali Osman Taha, for supporting the resumption of assistance to the LRA in hopes of reversing the larger trend of détente between the two countries (Mayanja 2003).

Sudanese assistance has definitely been significant to the survival of the LRA, but it does not address the reasons for the LRA's existence. The resumption of aid partly explains why the LRA has been successful in its recent attacks in eastern Uganda, but it is simply a gross exaggeration to view Kony as a Sudanese hired gun, as Museveni and others occasionally suggest. The geopolitical competition between Khartoum and Kampala has helped shape the LRA war, but the roots of the conflict exist outside the dynamics of this regional power struggle.

Museveni Doesn't Want Peace

Personal experience suggests that one of the most popular theories about why the LRA conflict continues is because the government really has no desire to end it. Across Uganda, it is not uncommon to hear the view that Museveni could eliminate a tiny group of rebels if he really tried to do so, particularly given his own history as one of Africa's most successful rebel leaders. Ehrenreich summarized this argument thus:

> But after all, why should the government try hard to destroy the rebels? For the most part, it is Acholi destroying Acholi; the rebels do little damage to the government, but they kill and abduct many civilians. The government hates the Acholi and wants us to destroy ourselves, so they do not intervene to end this conflict. Fighting against the rebels is also designed to kill the Acholi, since the government knows full well that most of the rebels' soldiers are captive Acholi children. (Ehrenreich 1998: 88)

This theory is not only held among northerners but is articulated throughout Uganda. In an editorial defending the Museveni government against such conspiratorial charges, the *East African* wrote: "There have been other groups such as the Uganda National Rescue Front, that have opposed Museveni's rule in northern Uganda but because their grievances were more discernible, it has been possible to meet them half-way and end hostilities. On that count alone, the accusation that the government has turned a deaf ear to peaceful initiatives does not hold water" (*East African* 2003). Yet an examination of the historical record suggests that such accusations in fact do hold water.

For example, when the first peace process between the LRA and the government fell apart, members of the president's own peace team pointed to Museveni's "lack of seriousness" as a serious obstacle for peace (Kaiza 2003). In 1994, Museveni thwarted a peace initiative being spearheaded by Betty Bigombe (former minister of state in charge of northern Uganda) by demanding that all the rebels come out of the bush in two weeks. Such a demand not only was unrealistic but seemingly indicated that Museveni was not seriously committed to a peaceful solution. This interpretation was strengthened when Museveni's government then charged Yusuf Adek, the person responsible for arranging contacts with the rebels, with treason. Okot Ogoni and Olanya Lagoni, two Acholi elders who pressed for political negotiations with the LRA, were murdered in 1996 (Behrend 1998b: 117). Understandably, civilians are now highly reluctant to come forward as possible contacts with the rebels. Further evidence to support this fear came in October 2001, when a local contact named Oyike was arrested and charged with treason (Kaiza 2003).

The government's response during 2002 to the possibility of a peace initiative suggested once again that a nonmilitary solution was not seriously considered by Museveni and his government. In June, Museveni publicly said, "Please, I do not want to hear of talks with Kony" (quoted in Ross 2003: 21). A few months later, the LRA announced a cease-fire, but the Ugandan government insisted once again that the rebels gather in specific locations before the cease-fire could be implemented, something the rebels understandably refused to do (Ross 2003: 21). In responding to the LRA's offer, the government was reluctant to put together a negotiating team but finally issued letters in October. The team was finally inaugurated toward the end of November. Following months of working with the parish priest in Pajule, the team won a 6 April appointment with the LRA. But before the meeting could take place, the Ugandan army flooded the area, wrecking any chance for direct negotiations (Kaiza 2003). The 2005 peace initiatives were likewise thwarted when Museveni brought in the International Criminal Court to prepare arrest warrants for a number of rebel leaders. With the exception of offering Kony and his commanders amnesty, the Ugandan government has had limited involvement in the peace talks taking place in southern Sudan. Museveni made a highly publicized day trip to Juba in October 2006, but was reluctant to meet with LRA representatives. A twenty-minute meeting eventually took place, during which Museveni reportedly verbally abused the LRA contingent.

Many Ugandans place the blame for these failures directly on Museveni. Gulu Municipality member of Parliament Nobert Mao, then a member of the peace team, stated: "Some of us in the team are not sure that Museveni is serious about the peace process" (quoted in Kaiza 2003). Reagan Okumu, a member of Parliament for Aswa County and a peace team member, claims that Museveni's actions "right from the start show that he never intended to support the process" (Kaiza 2003).

While I don't subscribe to the most extreme conspiracy theories regarding Museveni's desire for the LRA to act as a surrogate genocidal force against the Acholi, it is clear that Museveni and his administration have frequently failed to pursue nonmilitary solutions and have even undermined existing peace initiatives.

The Political Economies of Violence

In explaining the Museveni government's failure to resolve the LRA conflict through either military or nonmilitary means, reference is sometimes made to the political economy of violence thesis. Put simply, the theory posits that in a war economy, the goal of the conflict is not necessarily the defeat of the enemy in battle but the continuation of fighting and the institutionalization of violence for profit. Mats Berdal and David M. Malone's edited volume *Greed and Grievance: Economic Agendas in Civil Wars* (2000) is perhaps the clearest articulation of this thesis. In the case of the LRA conflict in Uganda, some evidence seems to support the view that a "political economy of violence" has been institutionalized in northern Uganda.

With regard to the Ugandan army, there are well-established and widely circulated claims that senior military officials are profiting from the war by picking up salaries of "ghost soldiers" and engaging in other corrupt practices (Ross 2003: 20). A visit to Gulu and surrounding areas indicates that many Ugandan officers are enriching themselves from the conflict through corruption, predation, or exploitation. Indeed, there is much evidence that government officers and soldiers are more interested in profiting from the war than in directly confronting the LRA. Operation Iron Fist was reportedly transformed into a lucrative moneymaking venture by many UPDF officers with connections, using the conflict for both predation and market exploitation, selling beer, cigarettes, and other luxury goods for sizable profits. In general, the war in the north led to numerous opportunities for extraction, exploitation, and corruption. As David Kaiza reports, "Some of the 23 per cent budget cut across ministries to support the war effort is said to have ended up in private pockets. Soldiers were not paid on time, and when questioned why, it was blamed on the Ministry of Finance. Water and fuel trucks were grounded because money to run them was diverted. Some of the money was put into Kampala's moneylenders' hands, generating interest before being taken to the operation at a later date" (Kaiza 2003). In Kampala, it seems that everyone has their favorite example of how the institutionalization of the war has led to profit-taking behavior by the government and the army.

But the political economy of violence thesis argues that both sides of a conflict have an interest in continuing the violence for their self-enrichment. Museveni himself has argued that Kony fights only for personal enrichment. During his address at the opening of Parliament on 28 April 1997,

Museveni claimed, "Kony is not fighting for political aims but for a style of living that he cannot afford through legal toil" (quoted in Ehrenreich 1998: 101). Unsubstantiated rumors abound regarding the lifestyle enjoyed by the elusive Kony, from lavish living arrangements in Khartoum to extravagant shopping sprees in Nairobi. Yet the beneficiaries of the conflict are reportedly not only limited to the combatants. Yakobo Komakech, the Pader District chairman, created a minor stir when he alleged that several people in government and nongovernment organizations were profiteering from the LRA war. Interviewed by Uganda's independent English-language daily *The Monitor,* he stated, "Several NGOs were now organising seminars and conferences in the name of ending the conflict, yet the aim was just to make money through allowances" (Lapoti 2003: 5). Several NGOs vehemently denied the allegations, but perhaps their vehemence suggests that Komakech's charge cut a bit too close to the bone. Finally, one of the interesting yet unspoken facts of the conflict is that the war economy has often benefited some members of the civilian population in the regions of combat. There are considerable indications that civilians in the north often collude with the rebels, with goods stolen during LRA raids subsequently showing up in town shops (Kaiza 2003).

While these various examples of the profitability of the emergent war economy certainly support the political economy of violence thesis, there are limitations to such an approach. There is the occasional tendency to conflate the existence of a war economy with the dynamics of the conflict itself. That is, the reasons for a conflict are explained through the lens of the political economy of violence thesis, suggesting that the cause of the conflict is simply greed. This is not the case. I wholeheartedly agree with Behrend's observation that beginning in the early 1990s "the war became a mode of production, and created a form of life which 'normalized' and banalized violence and brutality, and blurred the distinction between war and peace. For most of the soldiers, whether they fought on the side of the government or that of its opponents, war became a business which was more profitable than peace" (Behrend 1998b: 116). But it is important to realize that that war *became* a profitable business—and only for a select few. The causes of a conflict are often separate from the development of a war economy. In northern Uganda, as in other cases across Africa, war economies emerge as manifestations of local and regional coping strategies.

Conclusion

In his *East African* editorial, Charles Onyango-Obbo stated, "The fighting in the north [is] Uganda's political equivalent of the genie in children's fairy tales. Once the genie escapes, it takes a miracle to put it back in the bottle" (Onyango-Obbo 2003). There is considerable wisdom in this statement. Perhaps the primary reason it is so hard to get the genie back in the bottle—in this case, bring about a resolution to the LRA conflict—resides in the multiple reasons that the war started and its dramatic evolution into an institutionalized lifestyle of violence in a rather marginalized corner of the world. As Richards notes, "War only makes sense as an aspect of social process," and monocausal explanations are unsatisfactory and dangerously misleading (Richards 2005a: 12).

The LRA's struggle emerged in relation to patterns of violence already embedded in Ugandan society. Alice's Holy Spirit Mobile Forces emerged for a variety of complex, and sometime conflictual, reasons. Developing a coherent belief system that legitimized a certain degree of violence and a particular performative discourse of violence (from kidnapping to maiming), Alice Lakwena created a movement that drew upon established symbolic languages and memories of the northern people and offered an alternative to the abuses of the central government and the vagaries of modernity. As the indirect descendant of that movement, Joseph Kony's LRA performed a similar function for a narrow constituency of the politically and socially dispossessed. In the decades that have followed, the LRA has helped create a culture of violence throughout northern Uganda. It was not alone in this creation but was accompanied by the Museveni government, members of military and paramilitary organizations, government operatives from Sudan, and various elements within the civilian population.

To continue Onyango-Obbo's metaphor, it will seemingly take a miracle to put the genie back in the bottle because the genie has so dramatically transformed. On one level, the LRA has created something of a historical trap. Since their founding, LRA forces have committed many atrocities and have lost the support of the general local population, so that now they seem to fight just for survival. Government-sponsored amnesty programs have met with only limited success. In part, this is because of suspicions that government is not serious about allowing the integration of LRA fighters and that they will be arrested upon their return. This situation was further complicated by the International Criminal Court's (ICC) warrants against Kony and four of his commanders as well as the ICC's subsequent refusal to honor the amnesty offered by Museveni. But LRA fighters also deal with guilt for their past murders, and many also maintain a strong belief in the power of Kony. Finally, many seem to prefer remaining in the bush to life in IDP camps.[5] On another level, it must be recognized that numerous elements in the army and government benefit materially from the conflict. Museveni and his government also benefit politically from the conflict. The conflict provides the government political opportunities for the entrenchment of its power in much the same way that the George W. Bush administration exploits its self-declared "war on terror" for political purposes. In fact, after 11 September 2001 the LRA was quickly named to the US list of terrorist organizations. Since then, Museveni has increasingly emulated the Bush strategy, to the point of directly appropriating the same rhetoric and making direct appeals to the United States as a fellow combatant in the war on terror.[6]

As this book went to press, Joseph Kony had just stepped into a jungle clearing full of LRA soldiers and journalists near the DRC-Sudan border to announce that he would not attend the formal peace talks taking place in Juba, Sudan. Despite his denials, Kony's actions suggest that he is closer to ending his fight than he has ever been before. What is unclear is whether the Museveni government will be willing to peacefully resolve the conflict on anything but its own terms. To date, Museveni has seemed pointedly uninterested in a peaceful resolution to the conflict. Museveni's success in winning a third presidential term is likely to further embolden him, as well as to give rise to further northern distrust and animosity toward the government.

Perhaps the LRA would collapse if Kony were to be arrested or die, as did União Nacional para Independência Total de Angola (UNITA) after Jonas Savimbi's death. But there is no reason to anticipate such a turn of events. Despite heightened expectations, the massive self-repatriation of thousands of displaced persons in the north, and evidence that the LRA leadership seems to have reached a level of exhaustion with their struggle, nothing indicates that the conflict will reach a conclusive resolution soon. Given the history of the struggle, it is likely that the underlying roots of the conflict will continue to keep both sides emboldened and embittered.

Notes

1. It is estimated that the LRA war has created close to 20,000 child-soldiers (Cederna 2003: v)
2. To my knowledge, the most extensive research on this history has been conducted by the anthropologist Heike Behrend (1998a, 1998b, 1999), and I am heavily indebted to her work on this subject. I adopt her practice of distinguishing between "Alice Auma" and "Lakwena," employing the latter when referring to actions credited to the spirit itself.
3. In her article "The Stories We Must Tell: Ugandan Children and the Atrocities of the Lord's Resistance Army" (1998), Rosa Ehrenreich sets out a similar framework for examining the narratives of the war. While my approach is notably different and I reach different conclusions, I am indebted to Ehrenreich's piece for helping me organize my own thoughts on some issues.
4. During this time the Acholi also suffered a devastating wave of lethal cattle raids by Karamojong in which most of their cattle were lost, furthering the disarray in Acholiland and adding to their sense of desperation and resentment. My thanks to an anonymous reviewer for pointing this out.
5. My thanks to David Newton of Quaker Peace and Social Witness for providing me with this information, based on interviews with returnees.

6. During the US buildup to its war on Iraq in 2003, many Ugandans suggested that northern Uganda would be a more suitable target in the US war against terrorism. Tellingly, the Museveni government quickly rejected the possibility of receiving US assistance in the struggle against the LRA (BBC News 2003c).

9

Sudan:
The Janjawiid and
Government Militias

Øystein H. Rolandsen

A common feature of media reports from Darfur has been detailed accounts of atrocities committed by the Janjawiid militia.[1] More than anything else it is the activities of the Janjawiid that have made the Darfur conflict "the largest ongoing humanitarian disaster" and provided Sudan international attention similar to that devoted to the famines of the 1980s. While the numbers of deaths and of refugees caused by the conflict, and even how many people have been affected by the civil war, are not known, the terms *ethnic cleansing* and *genocide* have been used to describe situation (cf. Kasfir 2005; Prunier 2005: 148–152).[2] Who are these Janjawiid? How have they become the instrument of chaos and suffering in Darfur?

The Janjawiid hail mainly from the Abbala (camel herding) tribes of northern Darfur but also include ex-soldiers and criminals of other origins (Flint and de Waal 2005; Prunier 2005).[3] While the Sudanese army and air force have been active, the Janjawiid have been Khartoum's main weapon against Darfurian rebels. But far from ending the civil war in Darfur, Janjawiid activities have escalated the conflict and brought it the international attention that led to sanctions from the United Nations, investigation by the International Criminal Court, and the arrival of an 8,000-strong monitoring force from the African Union. Why did the Sudanese government resort to such a blunt and ineffective tool as the Janjawiid?

Most academic research on (and media attention to) civil wars focuses on the insurgents and their reasons for rebelling. Loyalists' motives receive less attention. Why do some choose to take up arms against neighbors who are fighting nondemocratic and predatory governments? Answers to such questions may be sought at different levels: within the particular history of Darfur; with reference to national politics and to other conflicts on Sudan's peripheries; and in regional dynamics, including the local impact of conflicts within and between neighboring countries.

Historical Roots of Today's Civil War in Darfur

The population of Darfur consists of many tribes, almost all of which are both cultivators and herders. But the tribes are often categorized as either farmers or pastoralists; a distinction between camel- and cattle-herders is also made. The major farming tribes are the Fur, who live in central Darfur, and the Masalit, who live to the west near the border with Chad. The major pastoralist tribes are the Zaghawa, straddling the Sudan-Chad border, and the Baqqara (cattle herders) in the south; there are several smaller Abbala tribes in the north.

It is important to point out that this is a crude simplification. How individuals in rural areas decide to prioritize modes of production is determined not by tribal affinity but by what appears most profitable at the moment. Furthermore, ethnic and tribal boundaries have historically been blurred. A family could decide to change its tribal affiliation and after a few generations become full-fledged members of another tribe, while members of different tribes could live within the same territory (O'Fahey 1980: 7–8). Intermarriage also took place. But despite fluctuations and unclear tribal boundaries, the Darfurian tribes have still been seen as distinct entities with recognizable traits.

In recent times, as a result of the increased influence of ideology in Darfurian politics, differences among the peoples of Darfur have taken on a racial dimension, whereby the semipastoralists have been portrayed as "Arabs" and the agriculturalists as "blacks" or "Africans."[4] If we disregard livelihood strategies, however, it is difficult to distinguish between two groups that share the same religion and have few differences in physical traits.[5] The main divider is that the Arab tribes speak Arabic while the Africans—who also mostly speak Arabic—have local languages as their mother tongues.

Darfur as a political entity has deep historical roots. The Fur sultanate—*Dar Fur* means "the Fur homeland"—dominated the region from the seventeenth century until 1874. The center of the sultanate was the middle and western parts of Darfur, where elevated areas surrounding the mountain range of Jebel Marra provide a favorable climate for farming. The pastoralist tribes living on the northern and southern peripheries of the sultanate were sometimes tributary, at other times hostile.[6] The non-Muslim regions south of the Baqqara belt were regarded as a legitimate sphere for slave raiding (O'Fahey 1980: 135–139). The sultan granted letters of marque, which endowed raid leaders with "sultanic" powers while raids lasted, a practice that indicates a historical precedent for delegating state power and violence to free agents. Moreover, the sultan often enlisted one peripheral tribe as auxiliary troops in his wars to subdue another, a policy that may be seen as a precursor to today's militias mobilized by Khartoum (Harir 1994: 152).

The integration of herding tribes into the Darfur sultanate varied in accordance with the fluctuations of the sultanate's power and with local factors.[7] Throughout the history of the sultanate, agriculturalist groups in central areas were more sophisticated in terms of culture, economy, and, at least until the nineteenth century, warfare and saw themselves as the natural rulers of Darfur.[8] This historical relationship continued into the colonial period and forms part of the ideological justification for the Janjawiid and their political counterpart, the secret society of the Arab Gathering, Tajammu al-Arabi.

Colonialism in Darfur

Neither the Egyptians nor the Mahdist state (1882–1898) managed to establish effective rule in Darfur. In 1898, as the Mahdist revolution came to an end at the battle of Omdurman and the Anglo-Egyptian Condominium was established (1899–1955), a Fur prince, Ali Dinar, reestablished the sultanate. Since Ali Dinar initially represented no threat to the condominium, the British refrained from occupying Darfur; the territory was a convenient buffer against French expansion from the west (Daly 1986: 171–172). This policy was altered at the onset of World War I, when the British feared Turco-German intrigues at the sultan's court (Daly 1986: 175–178). A relevant aspect of the ensuing British conquest, in 1916, was the effort to mobilize tribes hostile to the Darfur sultanate by handing out money and cheap rifles (Theobald 1965: 155–156, 159). This suggests a line of continuity from the sultanate's use of semiautonomous armed groups for warfare and slave raiding.

Darfur's late inclusion in Anglo-Egyptian Sudan, its remoteness from the center, and the condominium government's unwillingness to provide services beyond "care and maintenance" (Flint and de Waal 2005: 13) doomed the region to remain a loosely integrated periphery with few stakes in the political center. The condominium government's system of indirect rule offered little room for the development of a modern economy or of an educated elite in Darfur, and the people of Darfur hardly participated in the creation of the multiparty system of government centered in Khartoum. Nevertheless, the agriculturalist tribes remained the most significant within Darfur's political life, while the pastoralist tribes became a periphery of a periphery.

The condominium administrative policy contributed to the marginalization of the position of the pastoralists. Most tribes were granted their own homeland to be administered under local chiefs or shaikhs, but full-fledged nomads were not granted territory because they were considered to be always on the move and in no need of land allocation (de Waal 2004c: 5–6). Furthermore, the system of passage rights and livestock migration corridors was not formalized. Both nomads and seminomads were in most cases dependent on grazing their cattle during the dry season in areas that had been demarcated as the homelands of various farming tribes. When a pastoralist became destitute for one or another reason and had to resort to farming until a new herd could be accumulated, he had to ask the local *shartay*'s permission to cultivate land, and he had to pay rent. As long as there were enough natural resources for both groups, this system worked. The policy of granting homelands and establishing "native" structures for the governance of each tribe also contributed to fixing borders between the previously loosely defined tribes.

The Fur became subordinate to the central government and had to endure being ruled by British administrators, and traders from the Nile Valley who followed in their wake combined skills and personal networks to become wealthy and influential (Doornbos 1984; Ibrahim 1984). Minimal training or education was provided to enable Darfurians to manage their own affairs after independence. Thus began a system of outside economic and political dominance from Khartoum that is still in place.

Independence

Following Sudan's independence on 1 January 1956, tension increased in Darfur. Already during the colonial period antagonism had developed between the conquered local elite in Darfur and the national elite in Khartoum. An "internal colonisation" begun during the last years of the condominium period was expanded after independence (Harir 1994: 154–155). Educated administrators from the Nile Valley took over the positions previously held by the British. "The rulers, decision-makers, judges and, not least, the jailers were riverain Sudanese whom the Dar Furians generally regarded as alien to the region. With total and absolute power over the people they ruled, disdain, arrogance, and exploitation were part and parcel of the behaviour of the riverain overlords" (Harir 1994: 159). Ordinary Darfurians also experienced harsh conditions and discrimination as seasonal workers on large farming schemes in central parts of Sudan and as foot soldiers in Khartoum's war against southern insurgencies (Harir 1994).

After World War II, a few people from Darfur obtained higher education, and by the 1960s an intellectual elite was emerging. During this period, some began to forge secret resistance networks against the dominance of the riverain Sudanese. In 1964 the Dar Fur Development Front was established, but this soon merged with the national Umma Party.[9] The 1969 coup led by Jaffar Nimeiri ended the second period of multiparty politics in Sudan and introduced a single-party system under the Sudanese Socialist Union.

Competition for resources had been increasing since independence. Until 1970 local institutions for conflict settlement, whereby traditional leaders negotiated solutions to local disputes over land, women, and cattle, were still in place. When Nimeiri abolished these, he failed to provide adequate staffing and funds for the new formal government structure. The result was a governance vacuum at the local level. This contributed to the intensification of conflicts over natural resources in Darfur, as the traditional system of arbitration had partly broken down (Harir 1994: 168–170).

During the late 1970s and early 1980s conflicts intensified further as a global drought set in: this significantly decreased previous dry-land grazing areas just as the agricultural population was trying to expand land under cultivation (with motorized water pumps) in order to meet increased demand for food (Morton 1994). Herds of camels and cattle destroyed crops and ruined watering points. In retaliation and to discourage herders from entering farming areas, the farmers burned dry-land pastures. This in turn contributed to the extreme severity of the 1983–1984 famine and caused further animosity.

* * *

Although viewed from the Nile Valley Darfur appears to be a regional backwater, it has for several decades been central to an intricate game of domination and destabilization involving Chad, Libya, and Sudan (Burr and Collins 1999). "Africa's Thirty Years' War"—from the 1960s until 1989—between Libya and Chad affected Darfur in several ways.[10] Libya, Chadian opposition groups, and the Sudanese government all used Darfur as a training and recruitment ground and as a staging area for attacking Chad. The presence of ex-fighters, a proliferation of small arms, and the need to settle refugees intensified conflicts over increasingly scarce natural resources, in particular land and water. The Chad-Libya conflict was particularly damaging during the 1980s, when Chadian tribes sought refuge among related groups in Darfur (Harir 1994: 163). At the same time Libya recruited soldiers from other parts of the Sahelian belt. These were armed and trained in Darfur to form autonomous attack squads—"Islamic Legions"—to wreak havoc in Chad (Burr and Collins 1999: 137–138; Flint and de Waal 2005: 23; Harir 1994: 164).

Muammar Qaddafi, the Libyan leader, also generated Arabist propaganda, encouraging nomadic tribespeople to identify themselves as Arabs while regarding the farmers as *zurga* (black). This contributed to changes in the nomadic tribes' view of themselves, their surroundings, and their history. The propaganda encouraged them to see themselves as belonging to the historical tradition of Islam and the Arab expansion into Africa, which justified the rule of Arabs over "black" Africans and not vice versa. These views were promoted in the *Green Book,* Qaddafi's thoughts on Islam (Burr and Collins 1999: 113) and by the Arab Gathering (Flint and de Waal 2005;

Prunier 2005; Harir 1994: 166). Libyan propaganda may have been a factor in making the pastoralists more assertive vis-à-vis the agriculturalists and in fomenting their rebellion against a perceived subordination to the Fur and farming tribes (Harir 1994: 174–175; Johnson 2003: 140).

The conflict between Libya and Chad also intensified the struggle over productive resources in Darfur, because insecurity in the border areas compelled herders to move closer to the central highlands, thus increasing the number of people fighting over the meager resources in that area. This led to constant local conflicts; each village formed its own defense militia.

The Janjawiid: Intensified Ethnic Conflict, 1980–2002

Against this background, the tensions building in Darfur escalated during the period 1987–1989 into strife in many respects resembling today's civil war. The regional government lacked policing capacity, and as a consequence, it had long been common practice among all ethnic groups to arm and organize self-defense groups. The novelty of the late 1980s was the increased attention to ideology and the scale of the conflict, which led to a total collapse of security in most of central and western Darfur (Harir 1994; Flint and de Waal 2005). The combination of ethnically charged politics, increased competition over natural resources, and the breakdown of local mechanisms for arbitration caused the province to explode. Sharif Harir presents the following description: "The war soon took ideological and racist leanings which were heavily laden with tribal bigotry. Arab bands called *janjawid* (hordes) and *fursan* (knights) roamed the Fur areas, burning villages, killing indiscriminately and appropriating Fur property at will. The Arab *janjawid* slaughtered anyone whose tribal identity was Fur or looked like a Fur in complexion or facial appearance, whether on a highway or in a village. The Fur started developing their own groups, the *malihiyat* (militias) and responded in a similar manner" (1994: 165).[11]

This may be the first mention of the Janjawiid in the academic literature, and different translations of the word *janjawid* have been offered (see note 1). Other names for Arab militias, such as *fursan* and *murahalin* (in Kordofan), have a more positive ring, and it appears that *janjawid* is a term used mainly by their adversaries and victims (International Commission of Inquiry on Darfur 2005: 31–33).

The Janjawiid and the Arab Gathering may be uniquely characterized as ideologically driven as a consequence of their link to Islamist currents in northern Africa and their religious and supremacist rationales for action, including Qaddafi's notion of the need to expand the "Arabic belt" in Africa. In Darfur this has meant the expansion of "Arab" territory in areas controlled by the Fur and Masalit particularly. According to Harir, a corresponding strategy was adopted by the Fur, to broaden the "Africanist belt" (Harir 1994: 170).

The political system of Darfur did not recover from the damage caused by the conflict in the late 1980s. In May 1989 a peace conference was held in El Fasher, and a settlement was reached (Harir 1994; Flint and de Waal 2005: 56). But although the level of violence declined after 1989, the settlement was not implemented, and the new National Islamic Front (NIF) government in Khartoum immediately started to recruit pastoralists into progovernment militias and arm them (Harir 1994: 170; Flint and de Waal 2005).

Agriculturalists in central Darfur, in particular the Fur and Masalit, were under pressure from two sides. Locally they continued to have conflicts over access to land and water with neighboring nomads, conflicts increasingly mixed with the ideological overtones of "Arabs" versus "Africans." Moreover, the agriculturalists, in particular the Fur, became increasingly marginalized under the repressive Sudanese state. The advent of the NIF regime meant that tribal tensions in Darfur and the growing antagonism between the local elite and Khartoum become increasingly interlaced: the new government's radical Islamism suited (at least in theory) the nomadic people, and the NIF regime saw them as useful allies and proxy soldiers. When a Fur intellectual, Daud Bolad, brought the Sudan People's Liberation Movement/Army (SPLM/A) to Darfur in 1991, Khartoum allied itself with the Beni Halba tribe and its *fursan* militia; the SPLM/A task force was routed, and Bolad was killed (Flint and de Waal 2005: 25–26; Johnson 2003: 140). The Sudanese government increasingly sided with Arab groups against "African" agriculturalists in local disputes.

In 1994, a local government reform split the Fur homeland into three parts, making the Fur a minority in each region, while the relative strength of the pastoralist groups was increased (Flint and de Waal 2005). Eight new *amirs* were appointed among the pastoralists living in Dar Masalit, most of them recent Chadian immigrants, so that they had a majority on the council electing the sultan of Dar Masalit even though pastoralists constituted only 25 percent of the population. These appointments also implied entitlement to land (Flint and de Waal 2005: 58–59).

In the mid-1990s, growing unrest in western Darfur erupted into open conflict. The violence provided the central government with an opportunity to introduce strict military rule in the area and to repress Masalit politicians and intellectuals (Human Rights Watch 2004a: 6–7). The regional government, under instructions from Khartoum, used local militias recruited among pastoralists, combined with regular army troops and the air force.[12] Initially these armed groups were officially recognized as Popular Defence Forces (PDF), but they later evolved into one part of the Janjawiid (Flint and de Waal 2005: 59).[13] By 2000 there were four Janjawiid bases, the largest at Misteriha in northern Darfur (Flint and de Waal 2005: 63–64).

The late 1990s saw in turn the beginning of armed resistance among the African tribes, Fur, Masalit, and Zaghawa (International Crisis Group 2005b: 2; Flint and de Waal 2005: 65–76). Small groups of fighters were organized among the Fur and the Masalit; a secret network was established in Khartoum. The Zaghawa started to organize resistance in 2001. These armed groups were thus formed in response to official discrimination and Janjawiid raids, which were conducted with material support of the government and the appearance of impunity. It was not until 2001 that the various groups managed to join forces.

Civil War in Darfur

In the current conflict the main adversaries are the central government and the rebel forces fighting for political and economic concessions. The Janjawiid and their local conflicts with rebellious tribes are used by the central government as a means of fighting the insurgents.

The rebels were consolidated in October 2002, when representatives of the "African" tribes met in the village of Boodkay in Jebel Marra (Flint and de Waal 2005). They decided to divide the leadership of a joint resistance among representatives of the Masalit, Fur, and Zaghawa.[14] Rebels had already in 2001 started to attack police stations and army outposts, but in the spring of 2003 the scale of attacks and their number radically increased. The initial phase was typical of a young guerrilla movement using hit-and-run attacks to acquire arms and win spectacular but inconsequential skirmishes (Flint and de Waal 2005). The surprise attack on El-Fasher airport in April 2003, when the Sudan Liberation Movement/Army (SLM/A) destroyed several planes and helicopter gunships, represented an intensification of the conflict. This humiliating blow for Khartoum demonstrated that the resistance was organized and had considerable military capabilities. Several battles between the rebels and government forces took place later in 2003, and the government began to use fighter planes and helicopter gunships to attack villages as well as rebel positions (Human Rights Watch 2004a: 17–20).

The Sudanese government had only a limited capability for war in Darfur, because its forces were worn out and stretched thin in the southern Sudan, Nuba Mountains, and southern Blue Nile regions. Strategists in Khartoum therefore increasingly relied on the Janjawiid as their main weapon in fighting the insurgents. Beginning in late 2002, the number and intensity of Janjawiid attacks increased dramatically. Apparently, there were considerable numbers of Janjawiid already trained and armed at that time, and more were recruited in the spring and summer of 2003 (Flint and de Waal 2005). The main difference between the Janjawiid attacks of the 1980s and those taking place since the late 1990s is that now the militias operated under direction from the regional and national government and with the assumption of impunity.[15]

The Janjawiid have mainly targeted civilians in villages believed to be backing the "African" resistance. They seldom attacked rebels directly. Their standard tactical approach has been to encircle a village at dawn and then attack from several directions. The village would then be looted and destroyed, and women and girls raped (e.g., Flint and de Waal 2005: 101–106). The role of the regular army in most cases has been to provide transport and ammunition; it has only rarely participated directly. The air force has on many occasions participated in the attacks with gunships and bombers (Flint and de Waal 2005: 106–108). Though the Janjawiid kill in their attacks, it appears that the main purpose is to displace, loot, and humiliate. Human Rights Watch reports that the attacks were less violent in the beginning, when the Janjawiid were content with looting cattle, shooting in the air, and threatening people (Human Rights Watch 2004a: 20). More recently the Janjawiid have to an increasing degree also killed, usually men, but also women and children.

The "African" resistance was politically inexperienced but got assistance from the SPLM/A leadership in the south (Flint and de Waal 2005: 81–84), and in late spring 2003 the SLM/A emerged in Darfur. At this time it became clear that another group, the Justice and Equality Movement (JEM), was fighting alongside the SLM/A. The JEM's launch had been announced in the Netherlands in August 2001. At first it fought only through political means, but the activities of the Janjawiid and the NIF government spurred it into military action. The core demands of the JEM and the SLM/A are local autonomy, improved economic development for Darfur, better representation at the national level, and an end to ethnic discrimination (SLM/A 2003; JEM n.d.).

The motives for beginning outright insurgency in early 2003 are debated, but it appears that several factors were involved. The most important was increased discrimination against—and in many cases downright oppression of—the Fur and other "African" groups. It is also possible that the north-south peace negotiations at the time prompted an escalation of the Darfur insurgents' attacks: the rebels may have feared that Darfur would be shortchanged if they remained quiescent, while Khartoum, for its part, may have feared that concessions to the southern Sudan would show the other peripheries that rebellion pays off and lead them to follow suit. Still, the most important consequence of the north-south peace negotiations appears to have been international reluctance to expand existing sanctions or use other methods of coercion against Khartoum. Though US secretary of state Colin Powell went so far as to describe the systematic targeting of "Africans" in Darfur as "genocide," he still concluded that this did not necessarily prompt any action from the United States (Prunier 2005: 140). This policy seems to have given the Sudanese government confidence to continue supporting ethnic cleansing in Darfur.

The role of the SPLM/A in the conflict of Darfur may also help to explain the uncompromising attitude of the Sudanese government: it feared a grand alliance between the SLM/A and the SPLM/A and that Darfur would be dragged into the north-south conflict in the same way as the Nuba Mountains and the southern Blue Nile had been. Although it failed, the above-mentioned SPLA Darfur task force in 1991 had confirmed suspicions of the movement's intention of expanding the civil war and its influence to Darfur. Darfur rebels had been trained in SPLA bases in Eritrea in the late 1990s, and the SLM/A received political advice and weapons from the SPLM/A (Flint and de Waal 2005: 85).[16] SPLM/A involvement in the Darfur resistance may also have fueled the "Arab" groups' fear of a grand conspiracy to expand the "African belt" in Darfur with the aid of the stronger and more organized rebel forces of the south.

There have been several attempts to end the conflict through negotiation. The president of Chad, Idriss Deby, mediated an agreement signed on 8 April 2004, but the parties did not adhere to it. The Sudanese government agreed, however, to the establishment of an African Union monitoring mission in Darfur, and it arrived in June 2004. Owing to a lack of funding and a narrow mandate, this mission achieved only limited results in its first two years on the ground (International Crisis Group 2005a, 2006a, 2006b). After President Deby's intervention, seven rounds of peace talks took place in Abuja under the auspices of the African Union (AU). Until recently these negotiations made little progress because of a lack of coordination among the rebels, their political inexperience, Khartoum's unwillingness to end the conflict, and insufficient attention and pressure from the international community.

In early 2006, the SLM/A started to disintegrate. At the time of writing (January 2007), two main factions had emerged. One is dominated by the Zaghawa under the leadership of Minni Minawi and, in terms of firepower, is the strongest of the factions (International Crisis Group 2006a: 3). The other faction is dominated by the Fur leader Abdul Wahid but also seems to include the Masalit rebel groups. This group is militarily weak but so far enjoys stronger popular support than Minawi does.

Mainly due to this weakened position and increased pressure from the international community, the United States in particular, the negotiations gained momentum in March 2006. Khartoum signed a comprehensive draft peace agreement prepared by the negotiation team, later referred to as the Darfur Peace Agreement (DPA).[17] Minawi's faction decided to sign, but none of the other factions did. It is too early to predict any long-term impact of the DPA, but so far it has not contributed significantly to improve the situation in Darfur.

Chadian president Deby declared "a state of belligerence" between Chad and Sudan in the wake of an attempted assassination and an attack on the capital (International Crisis Group 2006a, 2006b). While Khartoum is accused of backing armed opposition in Chad, Deby has established a close relationship with the Darfurian rebels, in particular JEM. In this way the Darfur conflict has contributed to destabilization in Chad and increased tension between neighbors. The extent to which any of Khartoum's Darfur-based militias have been involved remains uncertain at this point.

Why Janjawiid?

The Janjawiid's main area of operation is central and western Darfur, in areas inhabited by "African" tribes. It has been established that the main bulk of Janjawiid fighters have been recruited from camel-herding tribes in northern Darfur, although they are not regarded as representing those tribes (Flint and de Waal 2005; Human Rights Watch 2004b: 22–23; International Crisis Group 2004b: 16); the recruits are mainly young men mobilized by clan and tribal leaders. The Baqqara of southern Darfur have until now been less involved (Flint and de Waal 2005). It has been alleged that criminals and mercenaries from Chad and Libya are also involved (Prunier 2005: 97).[18] Janjawiid leaders seem to be persons of high standing in the local community, with the ability to exploit loyalty to tribal structures in persuading young men to join (Flint and de Waal 2005). The best known of the Janjawiid leaders is Musa Hillal, shaikh of a small northern Abbala tribe, who wears a colonel's uniform in the field (Flint and de Waal 2005; Human Rights Watch 2004a: 4).[19]

The utility of the Janjawiid as a tool of counterinsurgency is debatable. There is almost no historical precedent to indicate that attacking a civilian population will quell an uprising, and there is little evidence that Darfur will represent an anomaly in this regard. On the contrary, Janjawiid attacks have not stopped the JEM and SLM/A from asserting themselves on the battlefield and at the negotiating table. Further, the Janjawiid attacks and the central government's involvement initially helped the rebels to gain the moral high ground: their own attacks on noncombatants were, until quite recently, negligible in comparison to the havoc caused by the Janjawiid and the Sudanese armed forces (Human Rights Watch 2004a: 36). The escalating conflict in Darfur threatened to bring down further international sanctions on the regime and to create new political tensions with the former rebels in southern Sudan, the SPLM/A, which entered the national government in 2005.

By encouraging local groups to attack their neighbors, Khartoum's strategy creates animosities and grievances and deepens existing conflicts among the Darfurian peoples. There is reason to believe, moreover, that the conflict between the government and the rebels would have passed nearly unnoticed by the international community had it not been for the humanitarian disaster caused by Janjawiid attacks on civilians. If the government of Sudan wanted to deal with the Darfur insurgents swiftly, with minimal damage to the population and the local political and social fabric, unleashing the Janjawiid militia appears to have been counterproductive. Even worse, putting the leash back on may prove to be extremely difficult (deWaal 2006; cf. Lacey 2005).

Government Militias in Sudan

In recent decades the Sudanese government has in fact systematically exploited local animosities by arming and enticing local warlords and their followers to fight rebels and harass civilians in hot spots around the country. What has made Darfur different from previous cases is the scale of the militia attacks, although even this is not totally unprecedented, and the level of international attention the conflict has received.[20] To explain fully the role of the Janjawiid in Darfur, it is necessary to examine this phenomenon in the context not only of Darfur's history but also of conflicts elsewhere in Sudan. There was ample historical precedent for a Sudanese government to outfit and employ autonomous armed groups as part of a military effort (cf. Johnson 2003: 83). When the second civil war in the south started in 1983, mobilization of tribal militias had already begun. In the mid-1980s, Khartoum used militias on a large scale in the northern Bahr el-Ghazal and western Upper Nile. Since then, militias have been used all over the south and in southern parts of the north. These militias fall into two different categories.

One type consists of local armed groups or factions of the southern rebels that were induced to go over to the government side. All three southern regions have been affected, but in particular Upper Nile and Equatoria.[21] The most notorious example is the Anyanya 2, commanded by Paulino Matiep in the western Upper Nile.[22] In the early 1980s Matiep fought against Khartoum together with other local groups, but he later changed sides partly for economic reasons but also to gain protection against the SPLM/A. Matiep's forces were instrumental in protecting oil installations in the Bentiu area and displacing the local population in the 1990s (Human Rights Watch 2003: 152–154). While Matiep remained loyal to Khartoum, other groups drifted between the two sides in the civil war. Khartoum's alliances with local militias in southern Sudan, as well as Joseph Kony's Lord's Resistance Army (see Chapter 8; Prunier 2004: 366–367), were not in most cases part of any systematic plan to win back territories; their main purpose was to divert the attention and resources of the SPLM/A and to hinder the formation of a unified military front in the south.

The second type of militia consists of those developed from scratch by the government of Sudan. Bearing a close resemblance to the Janjawiid, these have been drawn from semipastoralist Arab tribes in northern Sudan, in particular southern Darfur and southern Kordofan, and have been employed in northern Bahr el-Gazal, western Upper Nile, and the Nuba Mountains. The most widely known and best documented are the *murahalin* of the Baqqara tribes in southern Kordofan and Darfur, who beginning in the mid-1980s attacked various Dinka subtribes in the northern Bahr el-Ghazal (de Waal 1993; Salih 1989). Combined with severe drought and crop failure, these strikes caused a humanitarian disaster of unprecedented dimensions as the militias raided civilian settlements in order to loot, steal cattle, and enslave people. Many who fled from these attacks still live in shantytowns outside the cities of the north or in refugee camps in neighboring countries. These raids were finally stopped by SPLA counterattacks, in some places as late as 2001.

It has been argued that Khartoum, the militia leaders, and their followers were motivated by a desire to expand the territory controlled by "Arabs" (de Waal 1993), thus paralleling the Arabist-Africanist discourse in Darfur. And indeed, after the coup in 1989, the new NIF regime attempted to formalize relations with the militias by including them in the paramilitary Popular Defence Forces. But this move had only a limited impact on the militias' organization and modus operandi.

It is therefore possible to distinguish between Arab militias and local progovernment armed groups in the south. The former could be seen as a dormant weapon that the government chose to activate, while the latter militias were not created but co-opted. Still, the Janjawiid transcend this categorization. In its ethnic composition and its shared goal with the Islamist regime in Khartoum, it resembles Arab militias elsewhere. But to a much higher degree than other Arab militias, the Janjawiid were co-opted by the Sudanese government, which not only sanctioned their activities but also provided training and weapons.

Government Rationale

Why does the government of Sudan choose to use a weapon that appears to be ineffectual, and even counterproductive, in fighting insurgencies? Some disincentives connected specifically to the Janjawiid militia were mentioned above. Creation of militias increases hostility and distrust among tribes that are dependent on each other in peacetime. The Sudanese state is weak, and the central government's legitimacy is limited. Giving carte blanche to irregular forces erodes the state's monopoly over the legitimate use of violence (Salih 1989). Moreover, the government lacks control over the militias, and it may prove difficult to demobilize and disarm the Janjawiid and others who want to stay armed and can easily run away or hide their weapons. To be sure, "Khartoum knew well that it could not disarm the Janjawiid even if it wanted to, despite repeated promises to do just that in 2004. 'We will not retreat,' Musa Hilal warned in a statement sent to 'the leaders of the state' early in 2004 and copied to 'the loyal, honourable fighters of the masses of our nation.' The 'cowardly, invalid decision' to disarm the Janjawiid would be 'impossible' to enforce" (Flint and de Waal 2005: 122).

The government in Khartoum has at different points in time committed itself to demobilize and disarm the Janjawiid, the last time being under the DPA (see below), but Khartoum has so far not demonstrated any will to take these promises seriously. In the event that the government attempts in earnest to control the militias, it is likely that these groups will refuse to hand in their weapons and may even decide to use them against their previous benefactor. An indication of this was seen on 18 September 2005, when Janjawiid forces surrounded a police station in Geneina, near the Chadian border, roughed up government officials, and freed several of their members from jail (Lacey 2005: 1).

Following *murahalin* attacks in Bahr el-Gazal in the late 1980s, various explanations were adduced for them. According to Alex de Waal, the militias were recruited by Sadiq al-Mahdi's government (1986–1989) from among tribes that had been loyal to the Umma Party and the Mahdi family since the Mahdist revolution of the 1880s, and they were intended as a counterbalance against growing disloyalty within the regular army (de Waal 1993: 143–144). This strategy proved futile, since the military seized power in 1989. While the special influence of the Umma Party and al-Mahdi may have been instrumental in the process of mobilizing and directing the *murahalin* attacks, that influence cannot of course explain the NIF government's reliance on militias.

As de Waal points out, militias are cheap and easy to recruit and hence represent an inexpensive way to keep insurgents occupied and to disrupt their sources of supplies from sympathetic civilians. However, it may be just as important that the Sudanese state lacks the ability to mobilize and train an adequate fighting force to deal with insurgencies in various places in the country, and as a consequence Khartoum sees the militias as a necessary supplement to the regular forces. Nevertheless, considering the militias' inefficiency as a counterinsurgency measure and the negative effects of their deployment, it appears that, even though they are cheap, for the government these represent a poor investment.

Later de Waal presents militarism itself and a propensity to solve political issues by force as a factor in explaining actions and policies in Sudan's recent history (2004c: 19–20).[23] It can be argued that leaders in Khartoum prefer to meet political and military threats with any type of armed force available, rather than seeking a less costly nonviolent solution. This notion challenges the rational actor model for explaining political actions and borders on dismissing decisionmakers in Khartoum as irrational. More empirical research is required to establish the presence of this factor in the Khartoum government's decisionmaking circles.

It is also important to bear in mind the short-term benefits of the divide-and-rule strategy related to the co-option of militias in the south and the strengthening of "Arab" groups at the expense of "Africans" in Darfur and the north-south border areas. By recruiting and arming tribes in the south, Khartoum distracted the SPLM/A in its fight against government forces, but, perhaps more important, it also managed to keep southerners divided by creating resentments and distrust. This may also be a motivation for using Arab militias, whose tribes otherwise might have found nonviolent solutions to local disputes with their neighbors in Darfur, the Nuba Mountains, Bahr el-Ghazal, and the Upper Nile. These then might have remained neutral or even have joined the rebels. Although militias provide immediate advantages to the government, the long-term negative consequences for building state legitimacy and a constructive political atmosphere after a conflict has been resolved are only too obvious.

A certain degree of political convenience is also connected to the employment of militias, since the government has on several occasions denied involvement and referred to conflicts as local ones involving tribes fighting each other. But in most cases government involvement has eventually been revealed and has resulted in bad publicity and international indignation, which clearly outweighed the short-term benefits of the initial smokescreen.

A final aspect to consider is the current government's Islamist agenda. With regard to the southern militias, Khartoum appears to be indifferent to which armed group or tribe it supports as long as its objective—division and hostility—is achieved. But in the border areas between the north and the south as well as in Darfur, the tribes identifying themselves as "Arabs" are preferred as militia groups. To some extent this is a result of their availability and their political preferences, but it must also stem from a desire to strengthen these groups within local political settings. This is achieved by allowing "Arabs" to raid "African" groups and to expand their territories at the expense of displaced "Africans."

It is also worthwhile to consider historical precedent. Throughout the history of Sudan as a state, autonomous armed groups have been employed as slave raiders, auxiliary troops, border police, and, since the 1980s, tools in government counterinsurgency campaigns. It appears that employing militias has become a standard procedure for successive regimes in Khartoum, and it may be that their ultimate utility or long-term consequences are not considered in a systematic manner. Put differently, militias have become a familiar and readily available short-term solution to immediate problems.

Militia Members' Motivation

The central question of why the Sudanese government uses militias leads us to another: Why is the militia weapon available? What makes the leaders and the foot soldiers decide to fight Khartoum's wars against neighboring tribes? The case of the Janjawiid illustrates that these questions should be answered by reference to factors unique to each case, as well as to factors related to the political, cultural, and social dynamics between the central state and marginalized areas in general.

Douglas Johnson suggests that there were economic reasons for people to join the *muharalin* in the mid-1980s: they had become destitute as a consequence of drought and lost their land to mechanized farming schemes (Johnson 2003: 82). In this setting, joining the *muharalin* was a way out of poverty. While de Waal and Mohamed Salih refer in different degrees to cultural factors, they provide diverging and partly complementary analyses of why tribesmen decided to join militia groups in the 1980s. De Waal suggests—through an instrumentalist, rational behavior point of view—that the motivation of militiamen is rooted in the desire to gain the upper hand in local disputes and to achieve personal enrichment (1993). Salih provides a more culturalistic explanation that focuses on a warrior tradition among the Baqqara (1989). Alluding to Thomas Hobbes, he suggests that raids are undertaken not only for gain but also for safety and reputation. By attacking neighboring tribes, young men bring wealth to themselves and the tribe through what have traditionally been seen as legal and even ennobling deeds. The weakening of neighbors means security for the tribe, and according to Salih, stealing their property has been considered a permissible way to increase one's own fortune. However, it has also been pointed out that the introduction of modern weaponry and ideology and the central government's exploitation of these cultural traits have led to a hollowing out, if not a straight-out distortion, of warrior traditions in southern Sudan (cf. Hutchinson 1998).

What is known about the composition of the militia groups is insufficient for a full analysis of the motives of their members. Based on existing knowledge, a tentative conclusion is that in Darfur, southern Kordofan, and those areas in the south where Khartoum has managed to co-opt local militias, the exploitation of local disputes seems to be central, at least at the beginning. Later, the cycle of attacks and retaliations may provide sufficient incentive for continuing the local conflicts. However, in the final analysis—as illustrated by the discussion of the background of the Janjawiid and the Darfur conflict—in each case there is a unique mix of general factors and local idiosyncrasies that makes it necessary to investigate each case on its own terms.

Conclusion

Do state-sponsored militias belong within the study of insurgency in Africa? Judging from experiences of Sudan's modern history, we must answer yes. Although these militias fight particular insurgency groups, they have much in common.

The leaders of insurgencies in Sudan have come from among educated elites or the armed forces, and some, like John Garang, from both. Among the militias, leaders have often been ex-soldiers or prominent tribesmen but also intellectuals. Lam Akol, foreign minister of Sudan, and Riek Machar, vice president of the government of southern Sudan, both have Ph.D.s, and during most of the 1990s their SPLM/A factions were allied with the government and fought against Garang's SPLM/A. The men behind the Arab Gathering, such as Janjawiid commander Musa Hilal, appear to combine modern education with tribal authority.

There are also similarities between rebels and government militias when it comes to methods of recruitment and relations with the host society. The southern insurgencies—both the Anyanya (see note 22) and the SPLM/A—relied on a hard core of government-trained foot soldiers, combined with a much larger number of recruits drawn from sympathetic tribes through a system of informal conscription with chiefs as interlocutors. This system was a remnant of the indirect rule established by the condominium government. Little is known about the SLM/A's and JEM's social composition and methods of recruitment, but there are reasons to believe that these would resemble those of the southern insurgents. Turning to the militias, we see that the co-opted ones in the south have much in common with the rebels. The "Arab" militias mobilized by Khartoum use systems of tribal mobilization but also, as we have seen with the Janjawiid, attract outlaws and mercenaries. In many cases, members of the militias do not participate throughout the year but are mobilized for a series of raids, in contrast to the rebel armies, whose foot soldiers often stay with their units permanently. The Janjawiid are an anomaly in this regard, since they have been trained over a long period and are located in specific bases.

The most important differences between the rebels and the government militias are their roles and the way they operate. Rebels in Sudan have all been fighting the central government in order to achieve either secession or government reform, and they have directed their military activities against government forces and, when necessary, allied militias. Although the issue of foreign support and war by proxy is relevant for the discussion of rebel autonomy, it is still fair to say that it is the rebel leaders who set the priorities for the movements and their activities. The militias, on the contrary, exist mainly as instruments of the government. In most cases the government decides when and where they fight. However, in contrast to regular armed forces, the militias, depending on their political backing, strength, and mobility, have some veto power, and the government makes sure to give orders that are as far as possible consistent with the short-term interests of militia leaders. Moreover, only to a very limited degree do the militias participate in attacks on the rebels. Their role is to punish civilians believed to support the rebels, and in this way they have contributed heavily to making Sudan's civil wars more intractable humanitarian crises.

Notes

Although they are not to blame for any errors and shortcomings, I would like to thank Dr. Endre Stiansen and Professor R. S. O'Fahey for their extensive and insightful comments on earlier drafts.

1. The exact meaning of the word *janjawid* is debated, but it appears that there is a common agreement that it is a derogatory word referring to a group of armed riders. O'Fahey (2004: 2 n. 4) presents the following analysis: "from the Arabic, jann (jinn) 'spirit, devil' and jawad 'horse.'"

2. Exactly when a local conflict reaches the level of civil war may be difficult to pinpoint, but it can be argued that the scale of the conflict in Darfur means that *civil war* is the best description. This categorization is also supported by the fact that the rebels' (SLM/A and JEM) political programs and military actions are primarily directed against the national government and its official army and police. This does not, however, deny that local animosities play an important part in the overall conflict. Close to 2 million displaced and at least 200,000 killed or died from secondary effects of the civil war are figures that have been floating in the media sphere in 2005 (cf. Kasfir 2005: 196–197).

3. *Tribe* is a commonly used term within Sudanese studies for "an ethnic group that is hierarchically organized. That is, the [Kababish] are a tribe while the Nuba are an ethnic group, or even a collection of small ethnic groups" (Stiansen and Kevane 1998: 9). Stiansen and Kevane 1998 is by far the most detailed and well-researched publication on the current civil war in Darfur. However, the book is intended for a broader audience and is confined in terms of references and discussion of sources. For the writing of this chapter, I have been able to check the facts presented in the book only to a limited degree, but the two authors' extensive fieldwork and intimate knowledge of the region render the book trustworthy, though a bit one-sided. Also, there is a high degree of coherence between it, Flint and de Waal 2005, and International Crisis Group 2005b, all published at approximately the same time and based on different investigations.

4. Unfortunately, this division has also been imposed on the Western public by reporters and advocacy groups that either do not have the opportunity to conduct in-depth research or find the division useful when attempting to raise sympathy for the victimized civilians.

5. Even livelihood strategy is not an absolute divider, as the Zaghawa, while being camel herders, are regarded as "African" and fight the "Arabs" in the ongoing civil war.

6. To the north: Meidob, Zaghawa, Northern Rezaiqat, and Zayadiya. To the south: Baqqara Arabs (Rizaigat, Habbanyia Taisha, and Beni Halba; Harir 1994: 153).

7. E.g., the southern tribes were more difficult to control than their northern counterparts, as the former could escape the sultan's forces by moving further south while the latter were barred from movement further north by the Sahara Desert (O'Fahey 1980).

8. In addition to the Fur, other smaller tribes were gradually absorbed. These included the Berti, Marareet, Mima, Daju, Birgid, Tunjur, and Dadinga (Harir 1994: 152).

9. Sharif Harir claims that the Dar Fur Development Front (DDF) was a regional movement that "made the whole region its base of recruitment" (1994: 156). Even though the funding members belonged to "diverse ethnic groups," the DDF's appeal to the rural population and pastoralist tribes in particular may need to be investigated further. Given the low level of education and the lack of a democratic tradition in the area, it appears plausible that in the 1960s the DDF was confined to the urban educated elite of Darfur.

10. This name was introduced by Burr and Collins 1999.

11. It must be noted, however, that the scale of destruction between the two "sides" was rather unequal. At the reconciliation meeting in 1989, the Fur claimed that 400 Fur villages had been burned and they had lost 2,500 people and 40,000 head of livestock, while the Arabs claim to have lost 500 people, 700 tents, and 3,000 livestock (Flint and de Waal 2005: 56).

12. More than 60 Masalit villages were burned in 1998, and 125 was destroyed in 1999 (Human Rights Watch 2004a: 6–7), and more than 100,000 people became refugees or internally displaced (Johnson 2003: 141).

13. Amirs from the Beni Halba tribe are mentioned as leaders of the local militias. Flint and de Waal also suggest that militias from Quwait al Salaam in southern Kordofan were brought to Dar Masalit to train local militias and that from then on tribal leaders began to be paid as commanders of unofficial militias (2005: 60).

14. Abdel Wahid (Fur) chairman, Abdalla Abakir (Zaghawa) chief of staff, and Khamis Abakir (Masalit) deputy chairman (not appointed until 2005; Flint and de Waal 2005: 85).

15. Human Rights Watch claims it has proofs that the Janjawiid have been given impunity by the government of Sudan (Human Rights Watch 2005).

16. International Crisis Group 2005b is a bit more vague on the issue of military assistance from the SPLM/A to the SLM/A, but it also confirms strong ties between the two movements. However, ICG believes these have been weakened by the death of SPLM/A leader John Garang in July 2005.

17. Both Alex de Waal (in fifteen parts, available at http://allafrica.com/search .html?string=%22Alex+de+Waal%22+%2B+%22Darfur+Peace+Agreement%22) and International Crisis Group 2006a provide in-depth analyses of the contents and possible consequences of the DPA.

18. In fact, Gérard Prunier suggests six different types of background for the Janjawiid members: "former bandits and highwaymen . . . ; demobilized soldiers from the regular army; young members of the Arab tribes having a running land conflict with neighbouring 'African Groups' . . . ; common criminals who were pardoned and released from gaol . . . ; fanatical members of the Tajammu al Arbai [the Arab Gathering]; and young unemployed 'Arab' men" (2005: 97–98).

19. In a widely distributed video interview by Human Rights Watch, Musa Hilal, despite overwhelming evidence, denied being a Janjawiid leader; see Human Rights Watch 2005.

20. The attacks on the Dinka people in northwest Bahr el-Ghazal in the mid-1980s and on the Nuba people in the Nuba Mountains also caused enormous human

suffering and numerous refugees and internally displaced (African Rights 1995).

21. For instance, armed groups among the Nuer, Shilluk, Topas, Mundari, and Murle have at different times during the civil war been allied with the central government.

22. Anyanya was originally the name of the armed groups fighting against the Sudan government during the first civil war in the south (1955–1972). When armed groups, often composed of Anyanya veterans, appeared during the late 1970s and early 1980s, they called themselves Anyanya 2 (later merged with other progovernment militias into South Sudan Defense Force).

23. Without mentioning Sudan in particular, de Waal's edited collection outlines these ideas more comprehensively (2002).

10

Senegal:
The Resilient Weakness of
Casamançais Separatists

VINCENT FOUCHER

The Mouvement des Forces Démocratiques de Casamance (MFDC), which has been fighting since 1982 for the independence of the region of Casamance, southern Senegal, draws an interesting contrast to the other guerrilla groups of recent African history. First, it is separatist, an oddity in a continent where, despite predictions to the contrary, separatism has remained rare.[1] Second, while it soon emerged that it could not seriously endanger Dakar's control over most of Casamance, and while its internal divisions weakened its capacities, the MFDC has struggled over a long period against the state of Senegal, a state that, despite its difficulties in the 1980s and 1990s, was nowhere near the deliquescent or shadowy states of Liberia or Sierra Leone. Third, the MFDC has endured despite a war economy in rags, dependent on a little cannabis and a variety of labor-intensive forest products such as charcoal and cashew nuts. Fourth, it has largely refrained from employing the violent methods that have been noted in recent African wars, from child soldiers to mass rapes or amputations. Fifth, since the signing of the first cease-fire in 1991, it has been engaged with the Senegalese authorities in a process of negotiation and accommodation that has become bizarre: to take but an example, in September 2005, President Abdoulaye Wade of Senegal dispatched the head of the gendarmerie in Casamance to "reassert his trust" in Father Augustin Diamacoune, the leader of the MFDC.[2] None of these features is in itself unique, but their combination seems to be: a movement both fragile and resilient, waging a war with weak resources against a powerful adversary, a movement that has largely escaped degeneration into ultraviolence, the little-known MFDC provides a fascinating and somewhat counterintuitive case study that may help us refine our interpretation of how armed conflicts develop in Africa and elsewhere.

After a brief historical overview, I will focus on the emergence of the MFDC mobilization, highlighting its rootedness in a broad social movement. The next two sections will discuss the MFDC's relative lack of international support and the weak war economy on which the movement has survived. The ambiguous and varied relationships that developed between civilians and guerrillas in the context of a rather immobile war are discussed in the following section. After that we shall examine the fragmentation of the MFDC, a fragmentation further reinforced by Dakar's somewhat contradictory handling of the conflict, discussed in the next section. Next we shall consider how civilian pressure on the MFDC has been mounting over the past years. The last section presents the broader conclusions that can be drawn from the case.

A Historical Overview

The separatist mobilization in Casamance, southern Senegal, went public in December 1982, when a peaceful protest took place in Ziguinchor, the regional capital, calling for independence in the name of the MFDC. Faced with repression by Senegalese forces, some MFDC supporters went underground and organized a *maquis,* a guerrilla group, under the name Atika ("fighter" in the Diola language). The *maquis* really took off toward the end of the 1980s, and in March 1991, a first cease-fire was agreed upon. Key figures of the MFDC, including its inspiration, Father Augustin Diamacoune Senghor, a Catholic priest, and Sidy Badji, the founder of Atika, then settled in Ziguinchor under Senegalese ward for discussions. Soon after, tensions split Atika open: the Front Nord, a detachment based north of the Casamance River, kept to the cease-fire, while the Front Sud proved less accommodating; these two factions fought one another on a number of occasions. Another rift appeared in 1994, when Atika's new leader, Léopold Sagna, was de facto replaced by a triumvirate of younger fighters, among whom Salif Sadio took a lead role.

While the peace process has been going on since then, with many more agreements signed between the Senegalese state and the MFDC political wing, the Front Sud has fought on and off. In June 1998, the Senegalese army intervened in neighboring Guinea-Bissau, supporting President João Bernardo Vieira against mutinous Brigadier Ansumane Mané, who in turn enlisted the support of Front Sud fighters. Through 1999, meetings were held in Banjul, Gambia, to try to reunify the MFDC. Mané's eventual victory in Bissau failed to reduce tensions within Front Sud, and violent internal fighting broke out between the partisans of Sadio and those of Sagna.

The election to the Senegalese presidency in March 2000 of Abdoulaye Wade, a historical opponent of Presidents Léopold Sédar Senghor and Abdou Diouf, raised high hopes, but Wade's calling into question of his predecessor's policies actually resulted in a worsening of the situation throughout

2001. Mané's death in November 2000 had nevertheless given Senegal the upper hand, and since 2003, Atika has almost given up military strikes. Dakar has been fostering a tightly controlled peace process, as well as a silent demobilization policy, but the guerrillas are still out there, as was demonstrated by the several attacks they staged between May and August 2005. A reunification of the *maquis* was being attempted, whose success and direction remain unpredictable. Over the twenty years of conflict, while a precise count is difficult to reach, several thousand people, combatants and noncombatants altogether, have been killed in Casamance.[3]

A Movement of (Some of) the People

Unlike many guerrilla movements elsewhere in Africa (e.g., Mozambique, Liberia, and Sierra Leone), the MFDC did not start as the enterprise of a small group of disgruntled politicians, soldiers, and mercenaries but resulted from a significant prewar effort at political mobilization and indoctrination, related to a broader social protest. This does not mean that we can accept uncritically the MFDC's self-description as the evident and immediate trustees of a unanimous population. From its inception, the MFDC was enmeshed in a complex set of conflicts and competitions that provided its substance. These conflicts were very local, and it took some time for the MFDC to broaden its constituency. Through what mechanism could the idea of Casamance progressively become entrenched in the minds of many people as a solution to their life problems? The answer is found in the social and political history of the region.[4]

The standard version of the social history of the region, in both its academic and lay versions, is essentially a narrative of loss and exclusion. In fact, it would seem that there is not much of a history to be found, for both the separatists and the government—and many external observers as well—tend to picture the Casamançais as primeval peasants. There are basically two main lines of argument. The first insists on the deep cultural misunderstanding between north Senegal and Casamance, highlighting civilizational differences (e.g., Sufi Islam versus Catholicism and animism; millet versus rice; savannah versus forest and swamps; hierarchy versus egalitarianism). There is of course some truth in these distinctions (though some are simply mistaken), and the weird geography of Casamance, separated as it is from north Senegal by Gambia, surely does nothing to facilitate its inclusion (objective and imagined) in Senegal.[5] The other approach describes the political and economic domination that north Senegalese migrants, traders, and civil servants exert over Casamance: based on their control of state, capital, and Sufi orders, north Senegalese newcomers exploit the region. Here again, these explanations are caricatural but carry an element of truth.

Many of the same characteristics are found in other regions of Senegal—for instance, in the Senegal River Valley or eastern Senegal. Even in Casamance, the mobilization has essentially been focused in the westernmost part of the region, populated by the Diola ethnic group, around the regional capital city of Ziguinchor. Indeed, almost all known members of the MFDC are of Diola origin, as are its symbols and deployment areas; only a few guerrillas hail from other Casamançais ethnic groups, such as the Peulhs.[6]

If one stands back from this description of the MFDC as a peasant rebellion—a description that, interestingly enough, is offered both by the separatists and by the Senegalese state—and looks into the history of the mobilization, one is struck by a combination of two elements: the role of the literati and the context of unstable legal politics. First, the westernmost portion of Casamance, which coincides with both the area of the MFDC mobilization and that of the Diola ethnic group, far from being the locus of primeval peasants, has long stood out as having the highest level of primary education in Senegal, as well as a very strong migration, both male and female, toward urban centers, and particularly Dakar. To be even more specific, MFDC mobilization was initially strongest among the Diola of Buluf (district of Bignona), precisely the portion of Lower Casamance where both education and migration were most developed—a peculiarity that is not without importance in the subsequent divisions of the MFDC.[7] In Casamance, the crisis of the state since the late 1970s produced a large set of youth with education but without future, a situation that has been identified as a major element in many other conflicts.[8] But this link between disenfranchised educated youth and political violence is not specific enough: as far as Casamance is concerned, the state is at the heart of educational issues, because it has long been the provider of both education and the formal sector jobs that make it profitable. Young Diola were faced with increasing difficulties with getting into the civil service and the army, where their elders had earlier secured attractive positions. The frustrated expectations of education and uneasy migration to urban centers with which it is associated thus provided a common experience that gave plausibility to the claims that Casamance was ill-treated. But the Diola expectations also pointed to the source to this ill-treatment: the state, which was inexplicably reneging on its implicit promises. The words of an MFDC supporter who attended the meetings of the early 1980s are clear on this:

> Q: What were people talking about in the meetings?
> A: We were talking about unity; they explained about the creation of Casamance, and how Casamance had become a part of Senegal. . . . They told us to compare Ziguinchor to Dakar and the other regions. If you go to Dakar, they call you "the Casamançais," never "the Sénégalais." Even in court. About Ziguinchor, we would talk about roads, administrative problems, taxes. About the way our students were dealt with. About people who had graduated and the kind of jobs they would get.

Q: Did you experience these kinds of problems?

A: Yes. My younger brother, who is now a teacher. He got the bac B [*baccalauréat* in economics], with honors; he was the third in Ziguinchor. He was supposed to get a foreign scholarship. He was accepted. But they replaced his name with someone else's. Almost all my younger brothers, it was the same. My other younger brother, he repeated his second year [at university], and he was told that there was no room for clever people, especially if they were Casamançais, that he had better find another job or set up a plantation. He was unemployed for four or five years before getting a job as a teacher. I too went to Dakar, I had the same problem, I left school. I was there around 1977 and 1978. In 1978, I came back. I could not finish the year. My elder sister managed to pay for school, at the Sacré-Coeur [a Catholic school]. It cost 9,000 CFA francs per month. My elder sister, she was working as a maid. I preferred to go back home, to manage on my own.[9]

Education did much to provide the shared frame of mind that could give shape to protest. Indeed, in the very same years, the Diola literati themselves played a key part in all sorts of traditionalist enterprises—in the state, the Catholic Church, and the developing tourist industry. A strong interest in the history and culture of Casamance developed among the literati, and until this day, when one meets with Casamançais separatists, one can rarely fail to notice their evident passion for these topics. It seems, for example, that Father Diamacoune's inability to provide the archives that he had insisted supported Casamance's claim to independence played a part in the subsequent "moderation" of a number of important MFDC figures, including Atika's chief of staff, Sidy Badji.[10] The two founders of the movement, a Casamançais migrant in France, Mamadou Sané Nkrumah, and Father Diamacoune, were heavily involved in cultural activism. In 1981, Sané himself, with fellow literati, including a young Diola who was completing a doctoral thesis at the Sorbonne on Diola culture and colonial intrusion, founded a magazine on Diola culture, *Kelumak,* which was central to the formation of the first separatist circles.[11] The specific experience of Lower Casamance with education and the state was thus crucial in endowing the MFDC with its key resources: a large group of men deprived of a future, who identified the Senegalese state as the source of their difficulties, and an ideology based on autochthony and cultural self-valorization. Thus Casamance could be made into a credible political symbol.

This was all the easier as the transfer of traditionalism and autochthony into the sphere of politics was effected not by the guerrillas-in-the-making but by the legal political sphere itself. Regionalism was a classic feature of Senegalese politics, and in Ziguinchor, a former Portuguese possession ceded to the French in 1886, the Portuguese mestizos and the French settlers structurally resented the Quatre Communes, the four historical French settlements found along the coast of north Senegal.[12] This took a peculiar turn when, in the late colonial period, Léopold Sédar Senghor built up a coalition of regionalisms against the dominant Quatre Communes elites. In fact, the current MFDC draws its name from a regionalist Casamançais movement that, in the late 1940s, allied itself (and later fused) with Senghor's party. But in the context of the early and partial liberalization initiated by President Senghor from the mid-1970s, this classic bring-the-pork-barrel-home-type regionalism made growing reference to autochthony—an early instance of the connection between democratization and debates on autochthony and nationality noted in the 1990s.[13] In Senegal, the legalization of the first opposition party, the Parti Démocratique Sénégalais (PDS) in 1974 and Senghor's 1980 handover of power to Prime Minister Abdou Diouf were key steps in the mounting of legal political competition both within and without the then-ruling Parti Socialiste (PS). In the regional capital city of Ziguinchor, whose steady growth was stimulated by the massive arrival of north Senegalese migrants and educated and politicized rural Diola, bitter disputes and scandals developed around land; these land issues pointed the way of autochthony, and various politicians vied for legitimacy by playing the card of Casamançais natives against north Senegalese "invaders."[14] Thus with the opening of the political scene over issues of representation and regional development, autochthony became a matter for argument in legal politics—and turned into a rallying point for separatist mobilization.

Interviews with separatists give a clear sense of this combination of elements: the associations and networks among Diola literati together in Ziguinchor, Dakar, and France resounded with arguments on the history and culture of Casamance; the opening of political competition both inside and outside the ruling Socialist Party allowed these reflections on identity to penetrate into politics; linkages were established among the educated youth, politicians, amateur historians, and cultural activists; other groups, such as football fan clubs and female religious associations, were also brought in. A Casamançais mythicohistory became entrenched, which stirred enthusiasm and resonated with local politics in Ziguinchor. Thus, Casamançais separatism was initially rooted in a lively political civility, in contact with legal politics.

This accounts for the way the movement chose to express itself initially: a peaceful demonstration in Ziguinchor, held on 26 December 1982. Though many militants were arrested following the demonstration, the movement did not turn immediately into guerrilla warfare; throughout 1983, and despite the pressure exerted by the Senegalese security forces, discreet discussions and meetings were held. As is often the case, repression actually fed mobilization. Targeting its repression on the Diola, the state seemed to confirm the MFDC's claim that they were second-class citizens in Senegal.[15] This was of no small importance, because the separatist version of history was new to Casamance and by no means undisputed. In a country with an unusually peaceful political history in West Africa, this self-fulfilling logic of state repression was particularly spectacular. In their narratives, most MFDC guerrillas mention that they joined the *maquis* to avenge the brutalities suffered by a relative; one *maquisard* confided: "I entered the *maquis* in 1992. . . . What I learned was that Casamance exists, that it has a right to independence. But what got me in was that my dad was taken right here [by the security forces], in front of me. He was beaten up in front of me."[16]

State repression had another effect: once most MFDC ideologues, including Diamacoune and Sané, had been arrested, a new group of men was in charge—Sidy Badji, Léopold Sagna, and Aliou Badji, veterans of the French or Senegalese armies, inclined toward the military rather than the political. Under these new leaders, on 18 December 1983, three groups of MFDC supporters, including men armed with bows, machetes, and hunting rifles, marched down on central Ziguinchor. Coming in the wake of the brutal killing of three Senegalese gendarmes in an MFDC meeting, they met with the heavy fire of the Senegalese forces. The death toll, officially twenty-four (including Badji and five members of the security forces), was in all likelihood far higher. By then, the proverbial spiral of violence had begun to roll: many participants in the march hid in the bush, where they later developed Atika, the MFDC's military wing. Militarization was thus, to a large extent, forced on the separatists. Their preparation had been minimal, and the movement, under pressure from Senegalese security, delayed years before engaging in aggressive actions. The MFDC thus has had to structure itself on the spot, with very limited resources.

The Limits of Extraversion

Guerrillas, in Africa and elsewhere, are keen on finding international backers. Whether to attract the support of the international community or to discard its responsibility in the matter, the Senegalese state has often pointed at the malevolence of other countries—its neighbors (Gambia, Mauritania, Guinea-Bissau) or the international rogue states of the day (Iraq, Taylor's Liberia, or Libya)—as supporters of the MFDC. Though there may be elements of truth in some of these accusations, what is really striking is in fact that, while international borders have played a central role in the MFDC's development, the separatists have so far attracted very little international support.

Senegal's close collaboration with the West might have earned it the status of a proper Cold War guerrilla movement.[17] But the MFDC came somewhat late to get its share of Cold War money. The suspected Libyan and Cuban connections do not seem to have been significant.[18] There are some indications of contacts between Liberian warlord-president Charles

Taylor and the MFDC, but these amounted to little more than decentralized, small-scale circulation of weapons and men, with no larger purpose. After the 1989 incidents between Senegal and Mauritania, the Mauritanian government did provide, on one occasion at least, automatic weapons to the MFDC, thus playing a key part in the increasingly aggressive behavior of Atika, but Mauritanian support for the MFDC quickly waned as Senegalo-Mauritanian tensions eased.[19]

There is a lot more to be said about the countries that border Casamance itself.[20] One only has to look at the geography of the MFDC bases and zones of control, between the tarmac roads of Casamance and the borders with Gambia and Guinea-Bissau. This is no surprise: border areas are an asset for guerrilla fighters, as they allow a measure of safety from pursuit and access to refugee camps and supply lines. The relationships between Senegal and its two small neighbors are complicated and marked by a measure of mistrust that occasionally verges on nationalist paranoia, but with the possible exception of the time of General Mané's brief hold in Bissau, neither Banjul nor Bissau has ever strongly supported the MFDC.[21] In any case, the Casamance policies of these two countries cannot be reduced to such formulas as "ethnic solidarity" and "anti-Senegalese strategy." These two countries have always been fragile and dependent on Senegal in many ways and have usually been keen on maintaining working relationships with Dakar. At the same time, in their diplomacy, economics, and politics, the conflict in Casamance has been a factor—a resource and a constraint. It is for instance clear that when the MFDC took to automatic weapons and land mines, many were coming from the huge stores of post-Soviet Guinea-Bissau. Gambia, an established entrepôt-state, was the alternative source for hardware. Also, both countries have been markets for the Casamançais war economy—booty (e.g., cattle and vehicles, TV sets and tin sheets) but also legal and illegal agricultural or forest productions, from charcoal to cannabis. Finally, refugee communities settled in both countries as a result of Senegalese repression have played a key part in providing a social basis for the MFDC.[22]

Despite the fact that MFDC guerrillas have been renting or buying weapons from Bissau-Guinean militaries of all ranks, one should not assume that there has been a consistent Bissau-Guinean policy of supporting the MFDC.[23] Weapon sales to the MFDC did become a major factor in Bissau-Guinean politics, but only rather late into the conflict: in June 1998, President Vieira of Guinea-Bissau launched accusations against his chief of staff, Brigadier Ansumane Mané, as a pretext to get rid of him, and thus stirred up a mutiny among the Bissau-Guinean forces. Eager to cut off the MFDC's supply lines, Senegal dispatched troops in support of Vieira. Ironically, it later emerged that Vieira's entourage was far more involved in business with the MFDC than Brigadier Mané had been. Dakar's major intelligence failure resulted in the MFDC rushing to Mané's aid.

Following Mané's victory, Dakar worked hard to establish good relations with the newly elected Bissau-Guinean president, Kumba Yala, going as far as providing funds to the Bissau-Guinean army; this was all the easier as banditry related to the Casamance conflict increasingly endangered Bissau's interests.[24] In November 2000, Brigadier Mané, resenting Yala's takeover of the armed forces, rebelled again. Sagna's Front Sud MFDC faction sided with Yala against Mané and took control of a major MFDC base in Kassolol, earning for itself the nickname Kassolol. Mané's subsequent death opened a new era, as Yala backed Kassolol against Salif Sadio's MFDC faction and took to the forceful repatriation of pro-Sadio refugees. Kassolol has since maintained better access in Guinea-Bissau, on the condition that it remain discreet and peaceful. The persistent fragility of Guinea-Bissau may provide the Front Sud factions new opportunities, but it seems Dakar has built enough influence among the Bissau-Guinean elites (particularly the military) to withstand the threat.[25]

The case of Gambia is equally complicated.[26] The breakup of the Senegambian confederation in 1989 left bitter memories on both sides, and things seemed to worsen in 1994 with the coming to power of Yahya Jammeh, a young Gambian officer of ethnic Diola origins. For Jammeh, Casamance matters on several counts. First, the fragile Gambian economy has increasingly benefited from the many trade links generated by the conflict. Also, as pressures toward democratization increased, Jammeh has tried to turn the vast Casamançais Diola community, old-time migrants and refugees together, into a support base (electoral and otherwise).[27] Occasionally MFDC fighters have been put to direct use, for instance when they were requested to search for and turn in anti-Jammeh activists or ordinary criminals who had taken refuge in Casamance. But one should bear in mind that the Diola are a minority group in Gambia, and this makes the Diola card an uneasy one for Jammeh to play.[28] Furthermore, over the past years, the Casamance conflict has increasingly been a liability for Jammeh, as MFDC-related banditry affected Gambia. Finally, in the context of the "war on terror" and the renewed trend to global peacekeeping, Jammeh has increasingly had to use his contacts with the MFDC to act as a broker between Dakar and the MFDC, thus building up a diplomatic credibility that had been damaged by his dictatorial style and (now defunct) alliance with Libya. Jammeh thus seems to be trying to strike a balance between Dakar and the MFDC, using the question of Casamance as both a nagging point and a bargaining chip. For all these reasons, Jammeh's policy is ambivalent and conservative: MFDC militants usually move about freely in Gambia provided they bear no weapons, but Banjul has been exercising a growing pressure, engaging in occasional arrest sweeps and "encouraging" the return of refugees to Senegal—or their removal away from the border—with some results.

Overall, while there is no doubt that access to international borders has been vital to the MFDC, Guinea-Bissau and Gambia have always been entangled in a set of contradictory links. The persistent difficulties of both countries and the increasing negative consequences of the conflict for them have given a greater leverage to Senegal in recent years. This became all the more true after the 2000 elections in Senegal, with the coming to power of Abdoulaye Wade, a veteran of the political opposition, which considerably strengthened Dakar's international standing. Western countries (notably the United States and Germany) and the international financial institutions have been putting increasing weight behind the peace process.[29]

Fasting for Guns: War Economy with Low Profits

As said above, the *maquis* had not been prepared for armed struggle; logistics were inexistent, and the movement had to begin with local resources, such as retired soldiers, bows and arrows, and hunting rifles.[30] Funding has always been a huge problem, as international support was never forthcoming. One MFDC guerrilla described his sense of disappointment when he joined the *maquis* in 1988: "They [the MFDC propagandists] said that there were many weapons. But it was false. So once you were there, you had to live like a man"; in his camp, young fighters went on a fast to save money for weapons.[31]

The MFDC has thus been fighting a "resourceless" war. Its economic base has developed through a three-step process. During most of the 1980s, the *maquis* relied on banditry and cattle rustling in the south of the Ziguinchor district, where they were based, and the support they could gather on visits to their families. At a later phase, as it became clear that war was there to stay and as guerrilla camps stabilized, a network of collectors was organized among the population. After state repression dissolved this network, the *maquis* developed a decentralized, low-profit economy, exploiting local resources.

In the late 1980s, with the release of many of the political activists arrested in 1982–1983, an underground MFDC political wing was organized under Father Diamacoune, for propaganda and forms of fundraising that occasionally verged on soliciting protection money; civilian sections of the MFDC were set up in many villages, MFDC membership cards were sold, and the money financed the *maquis*.[32] Centralization of fundraising was never quite complete: in the late 1980s, through his fighters, Sidy Badji, the chief of staff, had his own civilian funders, and when Bertrand Diamacoune, Father Diamacoune's brother and deputy in the political wing, claimed to centralize all resources, hinting that Badji was diverting money, the *maquis* briefly split. Progressively, fundraising capacities waned, as the conflict damaged the regional economy and as the political wing weakened. The Senegalese forces seized MFDC membership lists and targeted the political wing. Some members of that wing fled to the *maquis,* while others, such as Mamadou Nkrumah Sané, went abroad; their attempts to raise funds among the small Casamançais diaspora in Europe checked the downward financial trend only for some time.[33] Some among the most significant members of the political wing, including Father Diamacoune, his brother, and his four main lieutenants, settled in Ziguinchor under the ward of the Senegalese forces for negotiations. Unending negotiations and rumors (not always unfounded) of corruption and embezzlement challenged the credibility of the political wing, further reducing its fundraising capacity. The resource base of the *maquis* thus weakened, and from the mid-1990s on the *maquisards* were increasingly forced to manage on their own.

In their attempts to live off the land, the *maquisards* were faced with contrasting economic situations depending on whether they were settled along the Gambian or the Bissau-Guinean border. Along the latter, where the war was most intense, entire villages have been durably displaced, and the *maquis* have come to control significant areas, forests, and fields. Not infrequently, they have laid land mines to assert their monopoly over these areas; civilians (including legitimate owners) who trespass the limits have often been blown up by mines or killed by MFDC patrols. These areas are exploited by the *maquisards* themselves or by their refugee partners. While cannabis may yield higher profits, the produce exploited is often labor intensive and of mainly low value: cashew nuts, charcoal, timber, firewood, game, or palm products.[34]

In the other main MFDC area, along the Gambian border, the products are the same, but war took off later, and displacement has been far less massive and durable. Communities have been maintained and play a key part in business, though the guerrillas have often imposed "taxes" on local producers or incoming merchants.[35] It seems that in the area around Djibidione, cannabis-growing villagers asked for the deployment of MFDC fighters as a protection from the Senegalese gendarmerie. On this side of the Casamance River, business has benefited from the proximity of the Gambian market—a stronger economy and a provider of cheap manufactured goods—as well as from the historically better connections that the Casamançais Diola have had in Banjul.[36] Generally speaking, in the *maquis*-controlled areas along the Gambian border, Gambian products, currency, and transports have grown hegemonic. In fact, the long tradition of contraband with Gambia benefited immensely from the lifting of Senegalese border control that resulted from the guerrillas' presence. "Here, the market has been liberalized," proudly commented one Front Nord commander—and indeed, in some of these communities, money has been made, as the relative material wealth of households indicates.[37]

In both of these localized war economies, production and marketing are usually decentralized. One *maquisard* explained, "When I need to, I take leaves [from active duty]. If you have a wife and children, you must take care [of them]." This young guerrilla would regularly go work in various villages of Casamance for a few months as a fisherman or a woodcutter.[38] In most *maquis,* everyone fends for himself; taking leave from the camps for periods ranging from a few days to a few months, single fighters or groups of kin or friends go hunting, fishing, cultivating, cropping, or trading. Not infrequently, they go back to their village, but they may also find safety in anonymous temporary labor migration in Dakar, Ziguincho, or a neighboring country. Some may also use their weapons and know-how to engage in independent banditry, to the dismay of the impotent MFDC leaders—one fighter admitted to taking part in such operations, to such an extent that he chose to undergo purification rituals to protect himself from mystical sanctions.[39]

Because means of subsistence are not earned collectively, meals are not cooked or eaten collectively. The exception is in those groups that have, at some point of the peace process or another, secured the support of a major resource provider. Where food and money are made available to the commanders, collective meals can be organized. Where productive equipment, such as fishing boats, nets, or chainsaws, have been obtained, both production and consumption can be also more centralized. As support from the political and the external wings has been on the wane, the Senegalese state itself has become a major funding source for some of the *maquis;* from the early 1990s, it began providing "reinsertion funds" or "humanitarian assistance" to some MFDC groups, civilian or military, deemed to be "moderates." This is no small paradox that minimal forms of centralization in the MFDC have often resulted from the support of the Senegalese state!

When compared to the flamboyant war economies of the Mano River, Angola, and Congo conflicts, Casamance stands out for its ad hoc, decentralized, low-key system: it does not depend on a single, high-priced resource or marketing network; it is a labor-intensive, low-scale, low-productivity, low-profit business. As Martin Evans argues in his extensive survey, in this sense the war economy in Casamance represents "continuity with much 'normal' activity in the region" (2003a: 283). Such a weak, decentralized economic base is obviously not without political implications, as it has encouraged the economic autonomization of guerrilla groups, which has in turn reduced the leverage that the external or political wing can exert with the guerrillas. Interviews with guerrillas typically raise severe moral criticisms of the MFDC leaders, whose "good life" (e.g., refugee status in Europe, hotel life in Casamance or Gambia, children sent abroad on scholarships, possession of vehicles, private investments) is contrasted with the harsh conditions prevalent in the *maquis.* MFDC leaders thus stand regularly accused of treason, and whenever members of the political wings want to enter the *maquis,* they are actually expected to pay their way in.[40] Some have run into trouble.[41]

The fragmentation of the MFDC into competing factions, which renders the ending of the conflict difficult, thus finds an echo in its economic structures and in the culture of generalized suspicion prevalent among the fighters.

Localized War, Stable Frontline, Embedded Guerrillas?

Partly related to the nature of the Casamançais war economy is another important aspect: its strongly localized character. As mentioned above, the MFDC is essentially a Diola movement, and the administrative region of Ziguinchor, which corresponds more or less to the Diola-populated portion of Casamance, is small (7,400 square kilometers) and locked in by marshes and forests. In this context, the Casamance River is more of a link than an obstacle, as it allows for a lively riverborne traffic. The topography lends itself to the preservation of enclave territories—and this was made even easier by the importation of land mines. The Senegalese government learned at a price that its army's combing operations were costly in political, diplomatic, and human terms, and it has since tended to use alternative political strategies.[42] These elements and the nature of the war economy have combined to give this conflict a very localized character. The frontline has indeed remained extremely stable over the years and is marked on both sides by a series of earth bunkers and minefields. On this count again, Casamance differs from the wars in Angola, Mozambique, and the Mano River, where the frontline fluctuated widely.

One of the consequences of this is that MFDC *maquis* have usually settled. This has meant that while they do not necessarily hail from the villages around which they are stationed, and may move from camp to camp, guerrillas have embedded in the local communities. This is particularly true of refugee communities, since civilians who fled to Guinea-Bissau or Gambia often did so because they were sympathetic to the MFDC and felt threatened by Senegalese forces.[43] But even in those areas where guerrillas settled among stable civilian populations, connections were established. Links born from the necessary cooperation between civilians and guerrillas in the production and marketing of low-value agricultural or forest products played a part. As the years passed, fighters have married—frequently to women from a nearby village or refugee camp. Through all these links, the guerrillas have remained dependent on the population—or at least sections of it.

Borrowing from Mancur Olson's comments on warlords in revolutionary China, Thandika Mkandawire suggests a distinction between two styles of rebellion, stationary and roving (Mkandawire 2002). While the latter rampage their way through the countryside, the former have to build working relationships with the people among whom they operate, and thus they tend to be less violent. Surely the geographical stability of Atika classifies it among the stationary kind, and indeed, in Casamance, levels of violence cannot quite compare with those observed in other conflicts, such as those of Liberia, Sierra Leone, and northern Uganda. In Casamance, instances of sexual violence have been noted but seem not to have been very frequent; the MFDC does not recruit child soldiers; and while captured or killed Senegalese soldiers have been subjected to mutilations, civilians have usually been spared—with the exception of civilians from north Senegal, who have repeatedly been targeted.[44]

Working on other African conflicts, Paul Richards (1998) and Christian Geffray (1990) have suggested a different (though not contradictory) take on the issue of extreme violence: to them, extreme violence is the result of a transformation of rebel organizations into "war-oriented social bodies" or "sectarian" groups, that is to say enclaved communities, small groups removed from the larger society which fight merely to perpetuate themselves. The controlled nature of the violence in Casamance may seem to indicate that the MFDC has not quite reached this state, though perhaps in this regard again, one might draw a contrast between the *maquis* settled by the Gambian border and those by the Bissau-Guinean border. North of the Casamance River, because of the chronology and geography of the conflict, communities suffered only temporary displacements and have usually remained in place or at a short distance, a few miles beyond the border; ties have thus been maintained, and the guerrillas have demonstrated moderation. South of the river, the situation is different: the Front Sud operates in a deeply traumatized area, largely emptied of its population; its ties are primarily with the refugee communities that survive in difficult conditions in Guinea-Bissau, There perhaps sectarian tendencies can be noted, and MFDC operations have often been very violent.[45] Most massacres of civilians by the MFDC have taken place south of the river (Pointe Saint-Georges, November 1992, and Cap Skirring, October 1992), and those perpetrated in the Bignona district (Niahoump, February 2001, and Bélaye, March 2001) involved Front Sud fighters who had just moved north of the river.

Long after beginning its military actions, the MFDC enjoyed the support of large sectors of the population. As discussed above, this owed something to the attractive character of the Casamançais nationalist ideology in a society where young unemployed literati were abundant. The excesses of the Senegalese forces also initially did much to strengthen the movement, but it was when the *maquis* forced the government to a cease-fire and discussions in 1991–1992 that support for the MFDC reached its peak.[46] In villages, ardent discussions were held on the justifications for independence and what would happen after it was obtained; the imagined redistribution of state jobs and the riches of the north Senegalese became a major topic of discussion. During the first half of the 1990s, young men flocked to the *maquis,* uncoerced. Because of the noted fluidity of Atika, its constant shifting to and from civilian life, estimates are difficult to attain, but most accounts agree that at its high point in the first half of the 1990s, the *maquis* comprised a few thousand men—many more than could be provided for, as guerrillas often point out.

The aforementioned embeddedness and popular support should not be taken to mean that all has been well between villagers and guerrillas. Fighters have repeatedly been involved, collectively or individually, on or off duty, in antisocial behavior such as rapes, the murder of civilians, robbery, the breaking of ritual taboos, and petty racketeering. As one woman living under Front Nord control lamented, "Living with someone who has a weapon is never a good thing."[47] She explained how her family would always keep bowls of food ready, to placate passing guerrillas. There have been many instances of resistance by villagers. In zones beyond direct MFDC control, such as Coubanao, resistance was open, using both "mystical" and physical weapons, and MFDC guerrillas were killed.[48] In MFDC-controlled areas, villagers would resort to "weapons of the weak"; in one case, villagers moved a new school development project away from the MFDC camp, so as to limit the interactions between their daughters and the fighters.

If anything, what is striking is the variety of configurations of relations between guerrillas and civilians in Lower Casamance—a variety that echoes the amazing cultural and dialectal diversity of the region. But toward the end of the 1990s, MFDC internal divisions worsened, and the odds turned increasingly against the MFDC. Because they owed much to (some of the) people, the guerrillas were forced into an uneasy standoff. It is to this weakening that I now turn.

"Divided We Stand": The Fragmentation of Atika

As we have seen above, the MFDC did not start out as a military movement but as a loose, multilocal network of networks, with no evident leader. This lack of leadership was worsened as the most significant activists were quickly rounded up by the Senegalese security forces. The MFDC has somehow never recovered from this initial fragmentation, and it increased over the years, as a result of a series of factors. As pointed out in the historical overview, leadership struggles within the MFDC resulted in repeated internal violence in which many fighters were killed. The situation was such that since the late 1990s the Senegalese government has been encouraging the reunification (on its own terms) of the MFDC as a prerequisite for the peace process. The present section will explore this fragmentation.

First, one should insist on the extent of this fragmentation: the initial Front Sud–Front Nord division in 1992 was followed by a Front Sud internal

division. Then around 2003–2004, the Front Nord split into two over negotiations with conflicting Front Sud factions. Most of these divisions have
been accompanied by violence; indeed such violence within the movement
has probably become the main cause of death for MFDC guerrillas in recent
years. Salif Sadio's adversaries accuse him of having literally starved to
death more than a dozen of his captured opponents, including Léopold
Sagna himself, in the course of this internal conflict.

It is difficult to find a guiding principle to the fragmentation of the
MFDC. MFDC leaders have frequently been reproached for prioritizing
their subgroup, religion, or area of origin. The first division of the *maquis*
apparently resulted from the struggle, discussed above, between Sidy Badji
and Bertrand Diamacoune over the control of funds and paved the way for
the Front Nord–Front Sud divide. This division seems to have arisen from
multiple cleavages, as the splinter groups that rebelled against Badji, a Muslim Diola from Buluf (district of Bignona), were led by Sagna and Maurice
Adiokane Diatta, two Catholic Diola from, respectively, Bandial (district of
Ziguinchor) and Kasa (district of Oussouye). Among the Diola from Buluf,
a group that, for reasons discussed above, provided many of the first militants and guerrillas as well as much of the initial funding for the *maquis,*
there was a sense of ownership of the movement. As a result of their contribution, they would often resent the growing influence of the Diamacoune
brothers, who were Diola from Kasa. This division provided the foundation
for the subsequent split of the Front Nord, and it has been looming in the
Front Sud too: apparently to counter the influence of Sagna and the Diamacoune brothers, all Catholics, Sadio, himself a Muslim Diola from Buluf,
seems to have played up the religious theme. How real this cleavage actually
is remains uncertain: subethnic and religious borders overlap in various ways,
and bonds of friendship (prewar or war-created) seem to matter a lot in determining factional affiliation. All these factional episodes can equally well be
interpreted as power struggles between aspiring leaders, with every one of
them mobilizing a variety of constituencies. This seems to be confirmed by
the fact that factions were never built purely on ethnoreligious affiliations and
that enough ties have persisted between the competing factions to allow for
repeated (and repeatedly failed) drives toward reunification.

Most people who, in one capacity or another, have been involved in discussions with the *maquis* note that these discussions are rarely individual but
are usually among several *maquisards,* not infrequently a dozen of them.
Accounts of the internal functioning of the *maquis* emphasize the importance of periodic fora in which current policy is reviewed. Indeed, this was
how the movement was born, during the countless meetings in Dakar, Paris,
and Ziguinchor, as Senegal's policies in Casamance were commented on in
open assemblies. This populist tendency has been maintained, and military
and political leaders can be targets of populist criticisms for their biases,

inefficiency, corruption, or authoritarianism. These criticisms have repeatedly led to changes in leadership that losers in the MFDC game describe as "coups." It was such a "coup" that decided on Sagna's replacement as the chief of staff of Front Sud in 1994. Attempts at reunification of the *maquis* proceed through the many contacts that MFDC fighters of all ranks, liaisons, and civilian supporters have with one another; indeed, in his own turn, Sadio was called into account in September 2005.[49] To many guerrillas, this egalitarian character is a source of pride; one of them insisted: "The Casamançais rebellion is the poorest rebellion in the world. And I like that. . . . The people would go of their own will. . . . This too I liked. And the democracy too, I liked. You are not paid, you fend for yourself, so you can quit anytime you want. So I really liked this thing, and I always will."[50]

This egalitarianism may have to do with the entrenched cultural logic of Diola society, which has long been characterized as acephalous; there is indeed no "natural," self-evident hierarchy among the Diola, and even that of "modern" education, one that is very respected among the Diola, quickly lost relevance in the *maquis*.[51] A good name among other fighters is the key to being a *maquis* leader. Beyond the culturalist explanation, it is clear that the movement owes something of its democratic tendency to its weak and decentralized structure. As noted above, neither the political nor the military leaders control much resources, and as the guerrilla quoted above explained, since fighters fend for themselves, they feel entitled to leave anytime and to have a say in all decisions. The *maquis* leaders are thus very reliant on the goodwill and motivation of the fighters, and disciplinary measures (e.g., detention in a prison bunker, beatings, or punishing training exercises, the "maneuvers") have remained largely unable to strengthen command and control. Indeed, some accounts have it that Sadio's decision to tighten the discipline and the budget, upon the advice of Brigadier Mané, a "classical" soldier, weakened his popularity among many of the guerrillas and was a key step to the breakup of the Front Sud.[52] But fragmentation owes also to external factors, and particularly to policies implemented by the Senegalese authorities, to which we shall now turn.

Dakarois Paradoxes

First of all, it is to be noted that Dakar took little time to realize the potential for trouble. The Senegalese government often gave the security forces much room, allowing for human rights abuses that in turn strengthened the MFDC. But although it was going through a hard time during the 1980s and 1990s, faced as it was with structural adjustment, Dakar nonetheless devised policies to try to deal with the grievances expressed by the MFDC: a new generation of autochthonous Casamançais politicians was quickly promoted, a commission for the settlement of land disputes was installed, some cultural claims were addressed. During the 1990s, attempts were made to limit the extent of human rights violations.[53] This surely did something to relativize the credibility of the separatist critique of Senegal, and hardcore separatists saw this clearly, as they violently denounced the loyalist Casamançais politicians whose careers received boosts from Dakar's new Casamance policy.

More generally, as negotiations began, money and promises of money started to flow. Most civilians who have been involved in one capacity or another with the *maquis* insist that "gifts" were made to the fighters.[54] As one such middleman commented, "How can one talk with someone who lives in the bush and who is hungry? If you want to talk to him, you must first make him feel good."[55] At various times, several *maquis* have agreed to direct or indirect assistance from the Senegalese authorities, officially as part of cease-fire money or demobilization and reinsertion policies or as incentive to refrain from banditry.[56] MFDC members provide all sorts of justifications for their acceptance of state monies, describing them alternatively as a "weapon of the weak," as a way to get Casamançais taxpayers' money back, or as a legitimate compensation for all the sacrifices they have agreed to.[57]

In any case, Dakar's willingness to hand money out to the MFDC is consistent with the great Senegalese political tradition, the art of the "reciprocal assimilation of elites" at which Senghor was adept.[58] Indeed, one can only be amazed at the density of ties that quickly developed in the shadow of Dakar's mixed policy of repression and cooptation.[59] On many occasions, local agreements could thus be negotiated for the release of captives or the retrieval of seized goods, the organization of elections or the advancement of public works.

But tensions within the MFDC also resulted from another aspect of Dakar's policy. This is not to say that Dakar consistently implemented a "divide and rule" policy: while there have been instances of such a policy, the process seems to have been largely unconscious, with internal tensions in Dakar's policymaking circles resonating with and aggravating tensions within the MFDC.[60] To sort the conflict out, Senegalese elites tried to develop links and contacts with the MFDC, but in the broader context of the Senegalese democratization, the Casamance peace process became a political issue, with legal politicians competing for a part. Thus, when a group of Diola MPs of the opposition PDS established contacts with the guerrillas and brokered the first cease-fire in 1991, their initiative was quickly countered by rival politicians both from within the PDS itself and from the ruling PS, who relied on the MFDC detainees released as a consequence of the cease-fire to play a part. Accusing the signatories of corruption and betrayal, the released detainees took over the MFDC and sidelined Badji, the leader of the armed wing.

This pattern was repeated over the years, as competing factions within the Senegalese establishment built up connections with opposing factions within the MFDC: the other middlemen's separatists would always be "false" and "corrupt," and one was always in touch with the only "true rebels" around.[61] Thus, during the first years of President Wade, a de facto competition was established between the Diola minister of the armed forces, Youba Sambou, and the minister of the interior, Lamine Cissé, an army general with Casamance experience. Each operated with his own sets of connections to the Casamançais "civil society" and the MFDC and thus, unwittingly or not, they mutually neutralized their interventions: for every step made, there were instant critics denouncing "corruption" or "lack of inclusiveness." As one middleman bitterly commented, "One should first reunify the reunifiers."[62] At some point, from about 2003 to 2005, President Wade seemed to try to regulate the Senegalese side of the peace process, setting one man, General Abdoulaye Fall, in charge and calling everybody else into line, but this policy later frayed.[63]

Out of a mixture of subtlety and maladroitness, Dakar's attempts at developing links with the MFDC thus did much to weaken a movement that was already structurally fragile. The paradox is that while many localized agreements could be reached and violence could be kept under control, every potential middleman and every MFDC leader has been cast into doubt in the eyes of everybody else. A credible pan-MFDC negotiation has become very difficult, and Dakar acknowledged as much when it began fostering drives toward reunification.

But fundamentally, Dakar has long been trying to dodge real negotiations, out of a mixture of conceit and realpolitik in unknown proportions. One may indeed ask what there is to negotiate between a powerful state and separatists who, no matter how divided and weakened, have repeatedly stated they would never settle for anything less than independence. Playing its advantage, Dakar has essentially been using MFDC factions and figures with whom it has links in order to declare the end of the conflict, hoping that the various *maquis,* eventually induced with "reinsertion money," will progressively evaporate. Evidently, the closer an MFDC faction gets to negotiating with Dakar or accepting Senegalese money, the less legitimacy it has and the less "useful" it becomes. Dakar's handling of the peace process and its partially successful attempt to "assimilate" the MFDC may thus have created a catch-22 situation, fragmenting the MFDC to such an extent that no MFDC figure can afford to publicly renounce the idea of independence without losing his clout, so each tends to encourage (and help) fighters to keep to the bush to increase his returns from an unending peace process.

The Water Against the Fish?

Stuck as it has become in these conundrums, the MFDC has seen the proverbial water silently withdrawn from around the fish of its rebellious enterprise. It no longer benefits from the legitimacy it enjoyed in the early 1990s, a good indication being its current lack of recruits.[64] On the military side, it progressively emerged that there would be no decisive victory on either side: while Senegal came to realize that it could not face the internal and international costs of a military solution, the MFDC saw that it could not extend its control much beyond the mined forested border areas Atika controlled.

Skepticism had actually dawned early on some MFDC militants: associates of Badji, Atika's chief of staff until 1992, insist that Badji's willingness to stick to the cease-fire was related to his growing pessimism regarding Atika's military prospects. This weakness of the MFDC was not lost on the population, particularly when, beginning in the mid-1990s, the movement took to planting land mines and engaging in banditry. The defeat and death in 2000 of Brigadier Mané of Guinea-Bissau, who was possibly the MFDC's first serious international partner, and its repercussions—renewed internal MFDC fighting, a new spate of attacks on civilians, renewed Senegalese army combing operations, significant displacements of civilians beyond the Gambian border—were additional wounds to the credibility of Casamançais separatism. The MFDC came under increasing criticism, even among those populations where its embeddedness was strongest.

Thus, along the Gambian border the communities that surrounded, for better or worse, the *maquis* have been using their leverage. In 2003, local religious leaders, pro-MFDC civilians, and development workers negotiated a de facto cease-fire and the return of refugees. The government followed suit, agreeing to a reduction of its military presence and supporting returning refugees; this led to the signing, in January 2004, of an agreement between General Fall, then the representative of the Senegalese authorities, and the "officials of the MFDC in Fogny"—in fact villagers who were partners of the local *maquis*.[65] The whole Bignona district was progressively stabilized, and refugees began coming back. Later, the same civilians pushed for the withdrawal of some hardline fighters who were considered troublemakers.[66]

Along the Bissau-Guinean border, the refugee communities that had been generally supportive of the MFDC were coming under pressure from the new Bissau-Guinean authorities. Supporters of Sadio were repeatedly harassed by Bissau-Guinean troops; on one occasion at least, a refugee village was burnt to the ground by Bissau soldiers. Those farther west, who backed the other Front Sud faction, have enjoyed greater stability as a result of their patrons' proximity to the post-Mané Bissau-Guinean army, but they have exerted a de facto pressure on "their" guerrillas to keep it quiet—and indeed they have: MFDC Kassolol fighters have since refrained from action against the Senegalese army. They have also continued cooperating with the Bissau-Guinean forces, and with significant Bissau-Guinean assistance, they have assaulted Sadio. In February 2005, they took over one pro-Sadio camp east of Ziguinchor; in March 2006, they launched a massive attack against Sadio's main camp near Baraka-Mandioca, next to the Bissau-Guinean town of Saõ Domingos. Chased from the Bissau-Guinean borders, Sadio's men have switched to the Gambian border, where, in May and June 2006, they seized several pro-Kassolol camps. In an international context unfavorable to rebellions, fragmented in both its political and military wings, faced with a Senegal that has gained considerable strength over the past years, increasingly called into question by the Casamançais population, the MFDC seems to be losing credibility. And because it had long remained like a fish in water, it could only feel the water's growing pressure.

But Casamance is never lacking in paradoxes: Senegal's current visible advantage has encouraged activists of various factions to make use of the cease-fire to try to reunify and refurbish the structures of the *maquis* and even rebuild a fundraising system. In typical MFDC fashion, this process has partly benefited from President Wade's cease-fire money. The trend toward MFDC reunification is partly related to the activism of young, Europe-based Casamançais émigrés who are not entangled in the bitter disputes of the past, and perhaps the current development of the international Diola diaspora will be an influential factor.[67] It is as yet unclear whether this rebuilding of the movement will succeed.

Conclusion

What broader lessons can one derive from the present study of the Casamançais insurgency? First, the case of the MFDC calls into question the idea of armed rebellion as a profit-led enterprise: though Casamançais separatism surely had to do with a sense of economic deprivation and "stolen" riches, mobilization started long before any serious "economic" consideration of its chances for success or returns.[68] It was grievances, and above all the way in which they were framed in the ideology of Casamançais nationalism, that were key to the separatist mobilization, and political and historical arguments have been playing a part all along. What also emerges clearly from the case study is the importance of the political economy in the later development of armed conflict. The absence of international backing and the incapacity of the political wing to preserve its fundraising capacity have been central in weakening the structure of command of the MFDC. In this situation, the *maquisards* have developed coping mechanisms arising from local contexts: a bit of banditry, with some exploitation of the low-profit local resources, thereby creating ties with civilians, whose war-weariness they had to confront sooner or later.

The paradox is that the survival of the MFDC as a guerrilla movement was made possible by its transformation into an embedded, decentralized, and ultimately weak structure. More than anything, the case of Casamance indicates that within a single movement there can be significant variations from one subgroup to another in terms of structure and embeddedness, and that these variations matter.[69] Thus, along the Bissau-Guinean border, the MFDC and its refugee communities live in difficult isolation and exhibit some signs of sectarianism. Along the Gambian border, the movement seems to persist more as a kind of mafia, embedded in and dependent on the rather prosperous local economy. Barely bureaucratized, relying on a series of constituencies with conflicting interests (e.g., the refugees, the civilian wing, the urban and diasporic supporters, the guerrillas, the villagers), the MFDC has been highly sensitive to personal links and struggles and amenable to Senegal's assimilation policies.

The nature of the state's reaction to the separatist challenge has been a crucial variable, producing mixed effects. The repression was unexpectedly violent, and while it confirmed in the eyes of many the plight of Casamance at the hands of Senegal, it eventually did much to break up the political wing. But Dakar has also, very early on, allowed for mechanisms of self-control, incorporation, and negotiation, however clumsy—a testimony to Senegal's rather peculiar political history of accommodation and mixed democracy.

The condition of the *maquis'* survival has thus been the very mechanism of its fragmentation: the MFDC survived through its connections "above" (with the state elites) and "below" (with sections of the population), but it survived only in a degraded, weak form. A movement of voluntary, part-time guerrillas, the MFDC was never able to escape its "amateur" (though militarily efficient) status, but it has nevertheless retained some of its constituency. These weaknesses, rebel fragmentation, and Dakar's search for a (favorable) soft landing all combine in explaining the duration of the conflict.

Notes

This chapter was written within the framework of the Centre d'Etudes d'Afrique Noire programme on African conflicts, a program jointly funded by the Aquitaine Regional Council and the French Ministry for Research. My research in Casamance has been facilitated over the years by many more people than I can thank here. I would like to mention O. Badiane, my research assistant, and M. Bøås, D. Cruise O'Brien, X. Crettiez, M. Davidheiser, K. Dunn, J.-H. Jézéquel, O. Journet, A. Klein,

F. Lecocq, F. Müller, J.-C. Marut, and K. Nwajiaku, whose comments were very helpful in the writing of the chapter. Participants in the African Politics and History Seminar at the University of Oxford provided useful feedback. Material was gathered through interviews with former or current MFDC fighters, activists, and supporters, Casamançais civilians, Senegalese officials, and members of the security forces, NGO workers, politicians, and diplomats in Casamance, Dakar, Gambia, Guinea-Bissau, and France between 1997 and 2005. Precise references are indicated here only in text quotes.

1. See Clapham 1998a.

2. See *Le Matin* 2595, 9 September 2005.

3. See Evans 2004: n. 7 for a discussion.

4. This first section summarizes elements presented elsewhere. See Foucher 2002a and 2002b.

5. While Islam is overbearing in most of Senegal, Casamance hosts minority Catholic and animist communities; this religious specificity is frequently described as a major factor, to the point of distorting the evidence. Some authors go as far as describing Casamance as a region populated by a *majority* of Catholics and animists. Though this is inaccurate, there is no doubt that the resentment of some involved Diola Catholics (including Father Diamacoune) at the invasion of north Senegalese Islam played a part in the formation of the Casamançais sentiment. On these issues, see Foucher 2003a and 2005.

6. One participant to the 1982–1983 meetings noted, "The movement was created only with Diola, and two Mancagne and one Peulh" (interview with MFDC militant, Ziguinchor, February 2005).

7. This specificity did not go unobserved by the MFDC leaders. One leading MFDC figure of the time recounted: "[In the late 1980s] I told him [Father Diamacoune] that the Kasa was not involved enough. The very area of origin of the leader, there was no one from there! It was Bignona mostly. And overall, in fact, the Buluf, because the Fogny [another part of the Bignona district] was not very present" (interview with member of the MFDC political wing, Serekunda, Gambia, 1 September 2005). As a result of this, a special effort was made to develop influence in other districts, and particularly in Kasa, Father Diamacoune's area of origin. Father Diamacoune's own brother Bertrand, a retired agricultural extension worker, was recruited for this.

8. See for instance Richards 1995; Abdullah and Muana 1998.

9. Interview with MFDC militant, Ziguinchor, February 2005.

10. Father Diamacoune, a self-made historian of Casamance, has long insisted that there existed documentary evidence that Casamance was juridically not part of colonial Senegal. MFDC supporters also claim that a secret pact was signed at Senegal's independence, in 1960, for a twenty-year association between Casamance and Senegal. Séverine Awenengo Dalberto has documented a plausible source for these claims: in the late 1950s, the French did toy with the idea of a separate Casamance, which they thought might be more favorable to them than the north Senegalese elites (Awenengo Dalberto 2005). A politician involved in the 1992–1993 peace process recounted that the loyalists had noticed the separatists' fascination with this issue and had pressed for France's word, so as to weaken Diamacoune's position. The MFDC's call for a French arbitrage was evidently suicidal: for obvious reasons, France could not take an official stand, and in December 1993, a French expert, Jacques Charpy, produced, in his own name, a report on the claims of the MFDC. See Charpy 1993 and the passionate hand-written, hundred-page-long answer by Father Diamacoune (1995).

11. See Sambou 1984.

12. On this colonial regionalism, see Foucher 2002a: 128–130 and Awenengo Dalberto 2005: chap. 3.

13. See Bayart, Geschiere, and Nyamnjoh 2001.

14. On land disputes in Casamance, see for instance Hesseling 1992.

15. There is, for instance, ample evidence that the Diola, who can be more or less identified by their patronymic names, were subjected to tighter controls by the security forces. Human rights NGOs have documented the extrajudicial killings and tortures (including beatings, electric shocks, burnings, and forced ingestion of harmful liquids) carried out by Senegalese forces. See for instance Amnesty International 1998.

16. Interview with Front Sud fighter, Ziguinchor, February 2005.

17. The armed uprising planned in southern Senegal by the Marxist Parti Africain de l'Indépendance (PAI) during the 1960s never materialized.

18. It seems some separatist fighters had trained in Libya's Mathaba camp as associates of Gambian leftist leader Kukoï Samba Sanyang, prior to their joining the MFDC.

19. Around 1990–1991, the MFDC tried and failed to install a bureau in Nouakchott, the Mauritanian capital.

20. For one of the rare, and already old, surveys of Senegal's relations with its neighbors, see Diop et al. 1994.

21. Partisans of Sadio maintain that General Mané reneged on the promises he had made to the MFDC after the Senegalese withdrawal from Bissau and refused to provide them with weapons.

22. It is difficult to ascertain precise figures regarding Casamançais refugees, given the ethnic overlaps and the long-standing presence of Casamançais migrants in Gambia. In the mid-1990s, it was claimed that there were up to 15,000 refugees in each country, but the figure may have been exaggerated by Gambian and Bissau-Guinean authorities so as to attract more (divertible?) aid. There have been many returnees over the past years.

23. The Bissau-Guinean National Assembly produced a report that indicates the activity of competing networks, ranging from the renting of individual weapons to large-scale purchases. One source indicated that around 2002–2003, an AK-47 cost 100,000 CFA francs and could be rented for a day for 10,000.

24. In July 2000, to protest against banditry, Senegalese villagers closed down the border, thus cutting off a major business road to Bissau.

25. While it openly supported the outgoing president, Kumba Yala, Dakar could rely on its good relationships with both the chief of staff, General Tagme Na Way, and the returnee president, Nino Vieira; Dakar did much to rally Yala to Vieira for the second round of the elections. The uneasy coalition of Yala, Vieira, and Na Way has thus far maintained.

26. For an interesting discussion of Gambia's policy regarding Casamançais refugees, and Casamance at large, see Baker 2002.

27. During the 2001 Gambian elections, Diola from all around the Bignona district (Senegal) were brought to Gambia to vote.

28. According to *Jane's Sentinel: West Africa,* February–July 2002, quoting the 1993 census figures, the Diola constituted about 10 percent of the Gambian population.

29. The United States' interest in Casamance began in 1999, in relation with Bill Clinton's African tour, and has not waned since.

30. This discussion of the war economy in Casamance owes much to texts by and discussions with Martin Evans. See Evans 2003a and 2003b.

31. Interview with Front Nord liaison, Bignona, July 2004.

32. Business interests and Casamançais elites and migrants were approached for contributions, and threats were at times explicit. One relatively well-off Casamançais migrant established in north Senegal told of receiving death threats for his refusal to contribute to the MFDC.

33. As noted above, Casamançais migrations long remained national or sub-regional, and until the 1990s, one found very few Diola in France, though it was home to significant and often long-standing communities of Senegalese migrants of other ethnicities.

34. Even this profitability should not be overestimated: Casamançais cannabis is of low quality, and international exports, which proceed essentially through Gambia or Dakar, are actually quite limited. Consumption is primarily local and subregional.

35. During a seminar around a presentation of this paper in Oxford in November 2005, David Anderson mentioned that drug dealers in Gambia had shown him receipts issued by MFDC guerrillas for cannabis taxes.

36. Gambia, rural and urban, has been a major destination for Diola migrants ever since the early twentieth century. The "national" Diola community is much more significant in Gambia than in Guinea-Bissau.

37. Interview with Front Nord commander, district of Bignona, August 2004.

38. Interview with Front Sud fighter, Ziguinchor, January 2005.

39. MFDC leaders of both the political and military wings claim that a number of attacks are the acts of off-duty guerrillas. Quote comes from interview with Front Sud fighter, Ziguinchor, February 2005.

40. A "moderate" member of the MFDC's external wing spoke of how he had overcome the hostility of the "radical" refugees by bringing along a container of secondhand clothes for them (interview with MFDC external wing member, Paris, July 2005). An MFDC liaison reported being robbed in an MFDC attack on public transportation vehicles; as he was protesting that he was himself an MFDC activist, guerrillas told him to report to Father Diamacoune, the MFDC head in Ziguinchor, who they said was failing to do anything for them (interview with Front Nord liaison, Bignona, July 2004).

41. In November 2001, Laurent Diamacoune, a Gambia-based "moderate" political wing member and nephew of Father Augustin Diamacoune, was killed during a visit to a pro-Sadio *maquis*.

42. On two occasions, the army acknowledged the loss of more than twenty soldiers (Babonda, July 1995, and Mandina-Mancagne, August 1997). Given the army's tendency to manipulate body counts, losses in these two incidents may have been higher, as some independent sources assert. Heavy losses resulted in a change in tactics: air and artillery bombings were increasingly employed before assaults. The political costs of repression became quickly evident, as human rights NGOs started to pinpoint abuses, endangering Senegal's major resource, its good international repute. Reacting to Amnesty International's damning reports in the 1990s, Dakar released two reports. See Republic of Senegal 1991 and 1998.

43. Symmetrically, internally displaced people who made it to Senegalese urban centers or to villages closer to the tarmac roads controlled by the Senegalese troops were often adversaries of the MFDC, village chiefs with connections to the ruling Parti Socialiste, or north Senegalese migrants. When the *maquis* emptied the villages along the Bissau-Guinean border in the early 1990s, villages would split in two, some villagers heading to Ziguinchor while others went to Guinea-Bissau, usually according to their proclivities.

44. In the rural areas, these north Senegalese civilians were usually civil servants, nurses, or schoolteachers. The state encouraged their replacement with autochthonous Diola, maintaining a partial access to public goods. More generally, the war has provoked a silent, unstudied exodus of north Senegalese from Casamance.

45. Contrary to communities along the Gambian border, those in Guinea-Bissau enjoy little security; while the former can rely on the large Diola migrant community in Gambia, the latter seem largely isolated from their host society, except perhaps near the small Bissau-Guinean Diola community near Eramé; they are frequently victimized by their landlords or other Bissau-Guineans and tend to form endogamic groups.

46. In typical MFDC fashion, the money that the government had given to the political wing to explain the cease-fire in the villages was actually spent building up support for the movement.

47. Interview with female civilian resident of a Front Nord–controlled area, district of Bignona, August 2004.

48. The partial disarmament of communities by the Senegalese security forces may have reduced the potential for such resistance. Coubanao is nevertheless a case in point. See the accounts in *Fagaru* 52 (June 1992) and *Le Nouvel Afrique Asie* 38 (November 1992). A further MFDC attack in 2002 against the local credit institution in Coubanao stirred villagers into armed mobilization; see *Sud Quotidien,* 29 May 2002.

49. See Mané 2005. Following the release of this information in the press, Sadio's men organized for an official refutation, in the form of an interview given by Sadio. But it is clear Sadio was being contested from within his own group.

50. Interview with Front Sud fighter, Ziguinchor, January 2005.

51. One educated ex-*maquisard* thus explained: "I had decided I would leave. It is very difficult for an intellectual, there, when you live with those guys who have another kind of [education] level" (interview with ex–Front Sud fighter, Ziguinchor, November 1998).

52. Sadio apparently tried to impose a "tax" in cashew nuts on fighters to finance the *maquis.*

53. To this effect, a joint staff, mixing the civil and military authorities, was created in Ziguinchor in December 1995. Many local notables, including Catholic priests, army officers, and politicians involved in the peace process mentioned interventions on behalf of detainees. This did not prevent, however, the frequent killing of guerrillas captured in combat, confirmed by ex–Senegalese army soldiers.

54. Researchers do not always escape such requests (however minimal) for assistance or gifts.

55. Interview with foreign development worker involved in the peace process, Ziguinchor, July 1999.

56. Such was the case of the Front Nord from 1992 to 2000 and of the Camp de la Paix, a splinter group from the Front Nord, from 2003 to 2005. When Wade withdrew assistance to the Front Nord in 2000, the Front Nord successfully lobbied the Comité des Cadres Casamançais, an association of Casamançais elites, to intervene on their behalf (source: author's archives). Front Sud factions also received Senegalese-sponsored assistance on several occasions; it is rumored that in 2005 Kassolol was receiving state support.

57. One *maquisard* thus commented, "The civilians from the shipwreck [of the Dakar-Ziguinchor ferry, which killed 2,000 people in September 2002], who did nothing, each family received ten millions [as compensation from the Senegalese

state, which ran the ferry]. So how much should there be for those young men who have spent their entire life in the *maquis*?" (interview with Front Sud fighter, Ziguinchor, August 2005).

58. On these political arts in the postcolonial situation, see Bayart 1989. On Senegal more specifically, see Cruise O'Brien 1975; Diop 2002; Diop and Diouf 1990 and 2002.

59. To take but one example, in the mid-1990s, Edmond Bora, a member of the MFDC political wing, was famous because his own daughter lived in Dakar in the house of General Wane, the Senegalese official then in charge of the peace process.

60. Though some people insist, for instance, that it was Dakar that informed the *maquis* on its secret meetings with their then chief of staff Sagna, so as to discredit him.

61. There were famous one-night stands, for instance when Abdoulatif Guèye, then an adviser to President Wade, bought his way into the peace process, in what may have been a desperate attempt to rebuild credibility shortly before his arrest in an AIDS medicine scandal.

62. Interview with Casamançais Catholic priest involved in the peace process, Ziguinchor, July 2004.

63. The December 2004 and February 2005 peace signings were marred by these tensions, with all sorts of agents (from the factions of the MFDC political wing, civil society, or legal politics) fighting Wade's handling of the matter, and Wade finally having it his way. For an account of the first three years of Wade's policy in Casamance, see Foucher 2003b.

64. The children of MFDC activists seem less and less inclined to enter the *maquis*.

65. Source: author's archives.

66. Phone interview with local development worker, October 2005.

67. While other Senegalese groups have long been migrating to Europe, the Diola have historically migrated essentially to Dakar and Gambia. Since the 1980s, however, they have increasingly been going to Europe and North America. The possibility of applying for refugee status has been a factor in this evolution. This has led to the development of a trade in MFDC certificates which may serve as a basis for refugee status applications.

68. The growing talk in the late 1970s and early 1980s of oil discoveries in Casamance deserves a special mention here. It seems as if in an oil-hungry age, oil would grant credibility to separatist enterprises. Modern Scottish nationalism and Cabinda are other cases in point.

69. On the same issue in Mozambique, see Geffray 1990: chap. 2, and Weissman 1993.

11

Angola: How to Lose a Guerrilla War

Assis Malaquias

União Nacional para Independência Total de Angola (UNITA) was one of Africa's most resilient insurgency movements. From a small guerrilla force created by Jonas Savimbi in 1966, this movement grew from its base in eastern Angola to become one of the two main players in postcolonial Angola, competing with the governing Movimento Popular de Libertação de Angola (MPLA) for supremacy in a protracted civil war and seriously threatening to achieve power—with bullets, if not ballots—until its implosion as a military force in the aftermath of Savimbi's death in combat in 2002.

Demilitarized and without Savimbi's charismatic leadership, UNITA now faces its greatest set of challenges. Internally, important fissures have surfaced within the leadership. In addition, UNITA seeks to retain its claim to be the only viable political alternative to the governing MPLA. This constitutes a major challenge due to the enduring popular perception of UNITA as the main perpetrator of the human suffering and physical destruction that befell Angola during the first twenty-seven years of independence. But throughout its history, UNITA has demonstrated a remarkable ability to successfully manage adversity and overcome many challenges. This, perhaps more than anything else, makes UNITA an important guerrilla group to study.

UNITA's trajectory sheds some light into unusual insurgency dynamics. Specifically, it provides insights into how an insurgency movement can skillfully survive major structural, contextual, and conjunctural pressures while making strategic miscalculations. UNITA's capacity to adapt to changing internal and international circumstances—particularly its peculiar knack for selecting strange bedfellows—enabled it not only to survive but to develop into a major threat to the government. Under Savimbi's leadership, UNITA dealt with major crises that periodically shook its foundations by reinventing itself and adapting to the new circumstances. First, UNITA responded to its early isolation from external sources of support by developing a relationship with the very colonial forces against which it was purportedly fighting.

Second, when faced with defeat in the early stages of the civil war in 1975, it entered into an alliance with apartheid South Africa, then one of the most despised and isolated regimes in the world. Third, after agreeing to participate in the first multiparty elections, held in 1992—one of its key demands throughout the long insurgency—UNITA refused to accept defeat at the polls and plunged the country back into war, now as a semiconventional army.

Ironically, the very flexibility that enabled UNITA to survive life-threatening challenges throughout most of its history also imbued the movement with an exaggerated sense of confidence that led it to make important strategic miscalculations that eventually brought its demise. UNITA successfully adapted to the collapse of its external alliance structure—especially the end of the apartheid regime in South Africa and the end of direct military assistance from the United States—by developing new relationships within international diamonds and arms networks. The diamonds produced within areas under rebel control more than compensated for any loss of external funds. Disastrously for UNITA, however, this newfound wealth precipitated its transformation from a peasant-based insurgency into a semiconventional army. This transformation, and the new type of insurgency it pursued to achieve power, ultimately led to its defeat.

This discussion of UNITA's insurgency is divided into five parts. The chapter first focuses on UNITA's main survival strategy: forging anomalous alliances. The second section explores how these relationships, combined with UNITA's intraparty conflicts, left the insurgents poorly positioned to participate in the electoral process designed to end the civil war. Thus, as discussed in the third section, UNITA was defeated at the polls and then, unwilling to accept this result, plunged the country back to war. The nature of this postelectoral insurgency is discussed in the fourth section. The chapter concludes by examining postwar, post-Savimbi options for UNITA.

UNITA's Unconventional Insurgency

In creating UNITA, Savimbi sought, first and foremost, to give a revolutionary political voice to the Ovimbundu—by far the largest ethnolinguistic community in Angola—of which he was a member. The Ovimbundu represent 35–40 percent of Angola's population and dominate the areas with the highest population density in the country, the central plateau provinces of Huambo, Bié, and Benguela. Many Ovimbundu believed that, as the largest community in Angola, they needed their own liberation movement to counterbalance the role and power of the movements representing the other two major ethnic communities—the Frente Nacional de Libertação de Angola (FNLA), which drew much of its support from the Bacongo, and MPLA, with its main power base among the Mbundu. In other words, there was a strong ethnic rationale behind the creation of UNITA.

This ethnic rationale notwithstanding, the birth and development of UNITA is inextricably associated with the determination and vision of one man: Jonas Savimbi. Early in his political career, Savimbi had been inclined to join Agostinho Neto's MPLA because of its progressive program (Bridgland 1987: 45). However, the dominance of mulattos in MPLA's leadership dissuaded the young nationalist leader from joining this already well established political organization. Explaining his reasons for not joining a mulatto-dominated MPLA, Savimbi argued that "it was very difficult for blacks to understand why mestiços should be leading a liberation movement to fight the Portuguese. It was not clear to us that mestiços were suffering in Angola; they were privileged people" (Bridgland 1987: 46). Although Savimbi did not say as much at the time, he was also deeply suspicious of the *assimilados,* Angolans who were voluntarily or coercively assimilated into a Portuguese way of life. He would later imply that both *mestiços* and *assimilados,* "having bitten off a piece of the good life," lacked both the legitimacy and the moral authority to lead the anticolonial liberation struggle (Bridgland 1987: 98). This simplistic view of Angolan society—ironically tinged heavily with its own brand of racism and classism—imbued Savimbi's organization with a peculiar character that eventually, like a deadly virus, corroded it from within and significantly contributed to its ultimate downfall.

After rejecting the MPLA, Savimbi joined the União das Populações de Angola (UPA) on 1 February 1961, even though he found Holden Roberto to be an uninspiring leader who could not adequately articulate the policy of his own organization (Bridgland 1987: 45). Savimbi climbed rapidly through UPA ranks; by the time this organization initiated its military campaign against Portuguese colonialism on 15 March 1961, he had risen to the rank of secretary general. In this capacity, he played an important role in the merger between UPA and the smaller Parti Démocratique de l'Angola to create FNLA in 1962. A week later, after FNLA formed a "government in exile," Govêrno Revolucionário de Angola no Exíto (GRAE), Savimbi was given the foreign secretary position. But he eventually became disappointed with Roberto's autocratic leadership style, and he resigned from FNLA/GRAE in July 1964.

UNITA was created on 15 March 1966. A year earlier, after resigning from FNLA/GRAE, Savimbi and several followers traveled to China and received four months of training in guerrilla warfare at Nanking Military Academy. This short stint in China profoundly shaped the new organization's political and military character. Although UNITA's struggles to survive later forced it to compromise on Maoist principles of self-reliance and the guerrillas' organic relationship with the people, Savimbi at least insisted on keeping the group's leadership within Angola. There Savimbi developed his own brand of autocratic leadership to build UNITA into a recognizable third force among the liberation movements.

Beyond leadership style, Savimbi committed some of the very same errors that were at the base of his rupture with Roberto's FNLA/GRAE. For example, UNITA never developed into an inclusive organization. Likewise, mirroring Roberto's practices, Savimbi ensured that UNITA's leadership was dominated by individuals from his Ovimbundu ethnic group. As mentioned earlier, UNITA was overtly racist and classist in the sense that it sought to represent the majority rural African populations against white colonial domination and positioned itself as a direct opposite to the mulatto-dominated, urban-based MPLA. Ominously, Savimbi defined domination very narrowly by conflating class and race. Thus, he regarded both mulattos and *assimilados* as agents of oppression, not much different from Portuguese settlers. Ultimately self-destructive, this peculiar understanding of who was the enemy led UNITA to regard MPLA—a liberation movement dominated by mulattos, *assimilados,* and even some leftist whites who constituted the radical anticolonial elite—as its natural enemy, with horrendous consequences for postcolonial governance. In the mid-1960s, however, Savimbi appeared to present a fresh alternative to MPLA and FNLA.

Initially, UNITA opted for spectacular military actions for maximum publicity. In December 1966, after its first commanders returned from military training in China, UNITA mounted its first two military attacks against Portuguese targets. The first attack, personally planned and led by Savimbi, was against the small town of Cassamba in Moxico province and proved to be disastrous (Bridgland 1987: 71). The second attack was on Teixeira de Sousa (Luau), an important town at the end of the Benguela Railway. This was an important propaganda coup because it disrupted for a week the shipment of Zambian and Zairian copper to the Lobito port via the Benguela Railway. However, from a military perspective, the attack could not be considered a success inasmuch as UNITA, using poorly armed recruits with little guerrilla training, lost half of its 600 fighters against six Portuguese killed, including the town's chief of the secret police (Marcum 1978: 191–192). Strategically, the negative consequences of this attack extended far beyond the casualty count. It led to UNITA's being "outlawed in Zambia" in early 1967 (Bridgland 1987: 75). Given its dependence on copper exports through the Benguela Railway as a source of foreign exchange, Zambia could not tolerate UNITA's disruption of this critical transportation link.

Zambia's actions against UNITA effectively forced it to operate completely inside Angola. This was its first adaptation test: how to survive without a reliable foreign base. Initially, UNITA made a virtue out of this necessity by claiming that unlike MPLA and FNLA, which operated from bases outside the country, it was the only liberation movement operating entirely with the people it sought to liberate. But this bravado hid an untenable situation. For the next two years, UNITA's main struggle was not against the Portuguese army but for its own survival. Strangely, UNITA ensured its survival until the end of the liberation war by forging an alliance with the Portuguese colonial army.

In Cahoots with the Enemy

By 1971, the Portuguese colonial army was in a position to eliminate the several hundred UNITA guerrillas who remained active in isolated pockets
around Moxico. However, the Portuguese army spared UNITA because "from
a military point of view it was better to use them against the MPLA" (Minter
1988: 18). William Minter quotes General Francisco da Costa Gomes—com-
mander-in-chief of the Portuguese forces in Angola from April 1970 through
August 1972 and president of Portugal after a 25 April 1974 coup—as saying, "It was understood that Portuguese and UNITA forces would not fight
against each other. UNITA captured food and armaments from the MPLA,
while the Portuguese gave them ammunition (not guns), as well as medical
and school equipment. The area reserved for UNITA was the Lungue-Bungo
river area, between Luso and Bié" (Minter 1988: 18). Minter also reproduces
documents indicating that Savimbi sought, and the Portuguese authorities
seriously considered, his group's "reintegration" into "the national community" (Minter 1988: 83–85).

The "gentlemen's agreement" between UNITA and the Portuguese
colonial army lasted from 1971 until early 1974, just before the military
coup in Portugal. Savimbi's calculations, it would seem, were accurate only
in the sense that UNITA did not pay a high political cost for cooperating
with the enemy. As he calculated, UNITA was given an equal place, alongside the other two liberation movements and the colonial power, at the table
where decolonization and the postcolonial frameworks were negotiated. But
the MPLA would never forgive UNITA for its treachery. This was an important contributing factor in igniting and sustaining the civil war.

The onset of the civil war—in reality, the continuation and aggravation
of interrivalries among the liberation movements—posed another existential challenge to UNITA. As the weakest of the three liberation movements,
UNITA had little hope of prevailing over the others. To avoid defeat, it survived as a proxy of external forces: apartheid South Africa and the United
States. Both countries, whose direct and indirect interventions ahead of
independence failed to prevent MPLA from gaining power, were still committed to overthrowing the newly installed government.

Survival as Proxy

South African troops were forced to withdraw from Angola in February
1976, after failing to prevent a postcolonial MPLA takeover. The withdrawal left UNITA virtually destroyed. But although MPLA had prevailed,
it had also failed to fully destroy its internal enemies and overcome its external threats. A severely battered UNITA withdrew into the countryside to
regroup and return to guerrilla warfare. At the regional level, South Africa

and Zaire still posed real threats. Internationally, the United States remained overtly hostile. The new MPLA regime viewed Angola's long-term security, including the elimination of the internal threat posed by UNITA, as being intrinsically tied to its ability to foster a friendlier regional environment. This strategic calculation—more than ideological solidarity—led MPLA to actively support domestic opponents of the regimes in South Africa and Zaire. Thus, the new Angolan government provided open and unconditional military and diplomatic support for South Africa's African National Congress (ANC), Namibia's South West Africa People's Organization (SWAPO), and Zaire's Front National pour la Libération du Congo (FNLC). Both South Africa and Zaire responded by supporting their own proxies in Angola. With FNLA out of commission as a military force, UNITA became the proxy of choice.

South Africa's response to the perceived threats emanating from the new Angolan state came in the form of the so-called total strategy, a set of policies aimed at ensuring the survival of the apartheid system through a combination of reform and repression at home and coercive regional intervention. Angola became one of South Africa's principal enemies in the region and suffered the brunt of apartheid's total strategy. South Africa used two main instruments against Angola: frequent and well-planned military invasions and the instrumentalization of UNITA as a proxy in its regional destabilization policies.

From 1976 until its final disengagement in 1988, the South African Defense Forces (SADF) carried out twelve major military operations in Angola. These incursions were crucial for UNITA's development as a major military force. Although virtually destroyed by MPLA and Cuban troops in 1975–1976, UNITA was reorganized into a significant military force by 1979. Beginning in 1980, UNITA was restructured "by the South Africans along the lines of a conventional army, with brigades (made up of several battalions), regular battalions (900–1,500 men), semi-regular battalions (300–500 men) and 'special forces' (small groups of a few dozen men normally used for sabotage operations)" (Conchiglia 1990: 45). Thus reorganized and revitalized, UNITA took advantage of South Africa's regular incursions to advance behind SADF lines, occupy "liberated" territory, and defend it with weapons captured by the South Africans. Furthermore, while SADF threats kept the government occupied, UNITA was able to expand its guerrilla activity throughout most of the country. In the process it seriously disrupted food production in rural areas, brought the vital Benguela Railway to a standstill, and moved into diamond-producing areas.

Seriously threatened, the MPLA regime sought to defeat UNITA militarily by mounting yearly offensives against the rebels' main bases in the southeastern corner of the country. These massive military operations commenced in 1985 and culminated with major conventional battles for the strategic towns of Mavinga and Cuito Cuanavale in 1987–1988 (Campbell 1989; Bridgland 1990). Mavinga was especially critical, as it represented UNITA's key defensive position north of its main headquarters at Jamba. MPLA was supported by large quantities of sophisticated heavy armaments from the Soviet Union, including jet fighters, tanks, combat vehicles, helicopter-gunships, and air defense systems. In addition, it could also count on about 45,000 to 50,000 Cuban troops to supplement its own increasingly capable army. To save UNITA, South Africa deployed equally heavy and sophisticated weaponry, including 127mm multiple rocket launchers, 120mm mortars, G-5 155mm heavy and high-precision artillery guns (with a range of 25 miles), tanks, armored cars, and combat troops like the notorious Thirty-Second "Buffalo" Battalion. The battle for Mavinga started on 10 September 1987 and entered its decisive stage on 3 October 1987. South African assistance as well as surface-to-air Stinger missiles provided by the United States thwarted MPLA plans to break UNITA's main line of defense. After stopping MPLA's advance, in December 1987, South African G-5 guns destroyed the airfield at Cuito Cuanavale, thus preventing MPLA from using it as a starting point for future offensives.

This was one of the bloodiest battles of the entire civil war. Clearly, the military option for dealing with UNITA had failed, at least temporarily. Yet SADF and UNITA could not claim victory. After failing to take Mavinga, MPLA and Cuban troops retreated to Cuito Cuanavale and took defensive positions. There SADF and UNITA were not able to replicate their successes at Mavinga and settled for a long siege starting in November 1987. Given the strategic importance of Cuito Cuanavale, the MPLA government mobilized much of its military strength and, with the help of its allies, was able to prevent the fall of the town. SADF could only use its large long-range G-5 guns to shell it from a distance. In January, February, and March, SADF and UNITA made unsuccessful attempts to take the town. But MPLA ultimately prevailed. The siege of Cuito Cuanavale ended with SADF disengagement, in the context of a wider regional arrangement that brought independence to Namibia.

By the end of the 1980s, then, both MPLA and UNITA faced important pressures to find a political end to the war. In combination, apartheid South Africa's twin strategies toward Angola—regular military invasions and support for UNITA—convinced the Angolan government that a regional settlement with South Africa was in its best interest. As a result, MPLA accepted the Reagan administration's "linkage" policy tying the withdrawal of Cuban troops from Angola to Namibia's independence on the basis of United Nations Security Council (UNSC) Resolution 435 of 29 September 1978. This resolution reaffirmed the legal responsibility of the United Nations over Namibia and approved a report from the UN Secretary-General containing a proposal for a settlement of the issue based on the withdrawal of South

Africa's illegal administration from Namibia and the transfer of power to the people of Namibia.

The New York Accord of 22 December 1988 was the culmination of this process. The peace accord signed by Angola, Cuba, and South Africa provided for the removal of Cuban troops from Angola in exchange for a South African commitment to implement UNSC Resolution 435. Angola saw this accord as a major foreign policy victory, inasmuch as it was expected to bring MPLA closer to finally achieving a measure of domestic security. The Angolan regime believed that full implementation of UNSC Resolution 435 (1978) would bring two important benefits: first, the removal of the South African threat from its southern border and, second, the collapse of UNITA as a military threat because its main supply routes via Namibia would be cut off by a SWAPO-led government. But this optimistic scenario, whereby UNITA would disappear due to discontinued South African support, did not materialize because of the insurgents' flexibility. UNITA was also a proxy within a wider global ideological war; it was an important instrument in the implementation of the "Reagan Doctrine."

By the late 1970s, a reorganized UNITA served important US security interests in Africa. Ironically, the reemergence of UNITA in this role is partly the result of strategic miscalculations on the part of the governing MPLA on how best to enhance its fragile security within a hostile regional environment. Seeing its security in terms of regional regime changes, as discussed above, MPLA encouraged and supported two invasions of Zaire by Katangese gendarmes who had been based in Angola since their defeat in Zaire's own turbulent transition to independence. These invasions seriously threatened the Mobutu regime and Western interests. Expectedly, therefore, Mobutu Sese Seko's allies—including the United States, France, Belgium, and Morocco—promptly came to his rescue and quickly pushed the invading forces back to Angola.

The invasions provided Mobutu and his Western allies with a convenient excuse for continuing intervention in Angola. Within a Cold War context, Angola's actions—regardless of whether they had been carried out with Cuban and Soviet consent or support—were seen as an attempt to expand the Soviet sphere of influence into Central Africa. Consequently, and predictably, the United States and its allies responded with massive military support for Mobutu. Even more significant for Angola, Western intelligence services accelerated efforts to provide training and weapons to UNITA through Zaire. This Western-Zairian-UNITA connection seriously weakened the new Angolan state and constituted a major threat to its territorial security—exactly the reverse of the outcome MPLA had expected. In seeking to bolster its own security by attempting to induce regime change in Zaire, MPLA had made UNITA even more relevant as a proxy. Thereafter, UNITA became an important player in the southern African theater of the Cold War, particularly as a tool in implementing the Reagan Doctrine. This US relationship with UNITA endured until the rebels' decision to return to war after losing both parliamentary and presidential elections in September 1992.

Prelude to Defeat

UNITA's electoral defeat can be attributed principally to the party's own internal idiosyncrasies. After its retreat to the rural areas in the aftermath of MPLA's takeover at independence, Savimbi's leadership became increasingly authoritarian, leading to UNITA's propensity for self-mutilation. Permanently bleeding at the subleadership level, it lost much of its characteristic flexibility to make fundamental self-corrections in the conduct of its insurgency. Ultimately, by emphasizing military over political means, UNITA alienated a significant segment of its traditional support base, with negative electoral consequences.

UNITA's internal weaknesses had been apparent since the start of the civil war in 1975 and became glaringly so during the electoral fiasco and the resumption of the conflict in 1992. However, the internal factors that ultimately led to Savimbi's death and UNITA's demise were apparent even earlier—in 1966, when the group joined the anticolonial struggle. Salient among them was Savimbi's failure to develop his organization into a true liberation army. This failure meant that UNITA's survival depended primarily on the degree to which it was useful as a tool in the hands of foreign powers—whether Portugal, South Africa, or the United States—with serious negative impacts on the internal dynamics of the organization. UNITA, unlike classical guerrilla insurgents, did not adequately resolve the relationship between political ends and military means. This partly explains why Savimbi apparently did not perceive the fundamental contradictions inherent in his organization's problematic relationships with the Portuguese army during the liberation struggle and, later—both during the decolonization process and after independence—with the South African apartheid regime and the US Central Intelligence Agency. Although it was winning the immediate battles for survival, it was undermining its ability to win the war.

Paradoxically, Savimbi's brand of leadership also robbed UNITA of the flexibility it needed to face changing political circumstances at both the domestic and international levels. By the time of its first major defeat in 1976 at the hands of MPLA and Cuban troops, UNITA was already undergoing an important transformation. It had evolved from a ragtag rebel group that barely survived the anticolonial armed struggle into a significant military force, masquerading as a political party, whose main functions were to promote and enforce a personality cult of its leader. A stronger and increasingly militarized UNITA also became an important tool for its leader to hold

the country hostage as he sought to grab national power. The first function—enforcing the personality cult—eventually led to a politics of fear
within UNITA. Although initially many people filled UNITA's ranks voluntarily, exit from those ranks was rarely an option. Given UNITA's military
character, deviance was dealt with harshly, particularly among those perceived by Savimbi as potential threats. Thus, Savimbi eliminated most of
his party's most promising political and military cadres, including Jorge
Sangumba (foreign secretary), Pedro "Tito" Chingunji (foreign secretary
and deputy secretary-general), Wilson dos Santos (international cooperation
secretary), Eunice Sapassa (UNITA's women's organization president),
António Vakulukuta (UNITA's top Ovambu leader), Valdemar Chindondo
(chief of staff), Jose Antonio Chendovava (chief of staff), and Mateus Katalaio (interior secretary), among others.

Bizarrely, Savimbi did not just kill his close assistants; he also had all
their families, including small children, killed. To instill fear in his followers,
he regularly meted out punishment in public, ranging from the mundane—
floggings and firing squads—to more horrific killing methods, including
burning at the stake. An infamous such episode took place at UNITA's former
headquarters in Jamba on 7 September 1983, when, after a group of women
and children were accused of witchcraft, they were burned alive under Savimbi's personal supervision. This level of intraparty violence was sympto-
matic of a seriously dysfunctional organization. But it represented only the
tip of a much larger structural problem that contributed to UNITA's defeat at
the polls in 1992.

Defeat at the Polls

Beyond the leadership problems and concomitant intraparty violence of the
early 1990s, UNITA faced serious structural challenges as it approached a
new era of multiparty politics. For much of its postindependence insurgency, UNITA had justified the war in terms of a struggle for freedom and
democracy. Thus, it attempted to present itself as the main catalyst for the
political transformations that took place in Angola, that is, the end of single-party politics. Ironically, UNITA itself was unprepared for the new realities of multiparty politics. Paralyzed by fear, it could not count on its legendary flexibility to make the adjustment from war to peace, from guerrilla
group to political party.

The complexities involved in UNITA's transformation from a guerrilla
group into a political party were colossal. As Savimbi made clear in a speech
to the Seventh UNITA Congress on 12 March 1991, "UNITA was not born
as a political party, but as a military force with a political outlook." The end
of the civil war required UNITA's transformation into an inclusive political

party with a coherent electoral strategy and a viable alternative program to the ruling party. Instead, the group's simmering internal struggles and contradictions boiled over publicly when two prominent UNITA figures—Tony da Costa Fernandes, who founded the movement with Jonas Savimbi in 1966, and Miguel N'Zau Puna, UNITA's long-time deputy leader—defected on 29 February 1992.

Fernandes and Puna accused Savimbi of serious human rights abuses, including the execution of prominent UNITA figures. Even more significant than the accusations of human rights abuses—which merely corroborated previous allegations by UNITA dissidents—the defection of Puna and Fernandes represented the first serious crack in UNITA's outward facade of unity. UNITA's unity, achieved through fear, could not survive in an open political system. No longer captive, many close Savimbi associates could now break away from UNITA's rigid and violent structures. In other words, openness would further erode flexibility.

In addition to corroborating information about the wickedness of Savimbi's leadership, Puna and Fernandes ominously publicized UNITA's lack of commitment to the peace process. The defections exposed for the first time the rebel group's intention to sabotage the peace process and block movement toward democracy in Angola. Fernandes and Puna claimed that UNITA was preparing to use military force to achieve power if it failed to win the elections. Fernandes attested, for example, that Savimbi maintained a secret army in UNITA-controlled areas on the border with Namibia.

Why would UNITA insist on pursuing a military path to power? Throughout the years of insurgency, UNITA did not demonstrate that it was any better equipped to establish democratic governance in Angola than was MPLA. Political participation in the vast areas UNITA controlled during the civil war was just as problematic as in government-held zones. UNITA's terror was indiscriminate and targeted populations living under government control and in rebel-dominated areas with equal ferocity. Several reasons account for this situation. First, although UNITA portrayed itself as a democratic organization, its practice suggested that this was a military organization masquerading as a political movement. Peculiarly, military structures dominated the organization in the sense that few civilians held leadership positions. For example, all members of UNITA's Politburo and Political Commission (the decisionmaking body) had a military rank. The primacy of the military over politics gave UNITA a particularly rigid and nonrevolutionary character that alienated a considerable segment of the population. Now, with the advent of multiparty politics, this same population had to be convinced that even after many years of committing atrocities, the rebel perpetrators still deserved a vote. Given the alienation of potential rural voters—a consequence of the nonrevolutionary nature of its postcolonial insurgency—UNITA faced the prospect of electoral defeat. War, therefore, remained its best option to achieve power.

There is a second key reason behind UNITA's insistence to use war as an avenue toward political power. Open multiparty political competition was not UNITA's favored option. It was a direct result of the major global and regional changes that took place since the late 1980s. The end of the Cold War and the collapse of the minority regime in South Africa, in particular, threatened to marginalize UNITA at the international and regional levels, even if not domestically. These momentous changes presented UNITA with important challenges. The rebels could no longer count on the generosity of external benefactors to ensure survival, let alone victory. Thus, UNITA reluctantly joined an externally driven peace process aimed at ending the civil war. Expectedly, UNITA did not completely abandon its long-term goal of capturing state power by force. But, unexpectedly, the peace process opened significant opportunities for the rebels to use the lull in fighting to reorganize and replenish their supplies for a planned new phase of the war. Savimbi believed that the MPLA regime was irremediably debilitated by long years of economic mismanagement, its own internal squabbles, and civil war. More important, the regime could no longer count on the 50,000 Cuban troops that had kept it in power since independence. Moreover, the peace process enabled Savimbi to move his best troops from southeastern and central Angola to effectively control the diamond-producing regions of Lunda Norte, Lunda Sul, and Malanje. The loss of US and South African support was more than offset by the newfound diamond wealth.

UNITA guerrillas initiated their northward movement immediately after the signing of the Bicesse Peace Accord in May 1991. The process of demobilizing excess government and UNITA soldiers as part of the peace deal provided the ideal pretext, inasmuch as both government and rebel troops were expected to assemble with their weapons in various predetermined sites around the country. But as Fernandes and Puna warned, UNITA did not send its best soldiers to the demobilization centers. They hid to fight another day. However, UNITA's postelectoral gambit was doomed to failure because, as mentioned above, it could not be assured of sufficient popular support, even from the Ovimbundu, who had also been alienated by UNITA's indiscriminate violence.

Unsurprisingly, Savimbi and his party lost the first multiparty elections of 1992. In the presidential election, incumbent president José Eduardo dos Santos received 49.6 percent of the vote while Savimbi received 40.1 percent. MPLA won the parliamentary election with 53.7 percent of the vote while UNITA received 34 percent. Before a second presidential run-off election could take place, Savimbi claimed that the elections had been rigged and reignited the war. This new war—even more so than the long insurgency—emptied UNITA of any legitimacy it could still claim as a political force engaged in a struggle to induce fundamental positive changes in the country. Without this legitimacy, the postelectoral phase of the rebellion acquired all the traits of a criminal insurgency.

Aftermath of Defeat: Criminal Insurgency

UNITA's return to the military option to seize power after the 1992 electoral fiasco was a colossal strategic blunder. At the political level, it was unsustainable because UNITA could no longer count on popular support—not simply due to war fatigue among the population but also because UNITA degenerated into a criminal insurgency. At the military level, UNITA miscalculated its ability to deploy troops in sufficient numbers and weapons of sufficient quality not only to withstand the national army's counterattacks but also to defeat it on the battlefield. Even at the height of UNITA's military power in the 1980s—when it could rely on steady logistical and air support from the SADF—the rebels could not topple the MPLA government. Now, in addition to lacking critical SADF support, UNITA had to confront new weaknesses especially in terms of its command structure—its best military leaders had been integrated into the national army under the terms of the failed peace accord.

UNITA's political and military miscalculations were magnified by important changes in the ways it was viewed both at home and abroad. At the domestic level, the election results denied UNITA the standard justification for its "resistance," for they showed that it did not have the popular support it had claimed. Now it was increasingly regarded as the main impediment to peace and development. At the international level, the end of the Cold War and the international community's readiness to reward MPLA for the major transformations it had engineered for Angola—especially the holding of free and fair elections—meant that UNITA's unwillingness to abide by the electoral results would not be tolerated. UNITA was now viewed internationally as a spoiler. In the end, without domestic legitimacy and international support, the postelectoral insurgency quickly acquired a criminal character.

Insufficient Conditions for Insurgency

After 1992, UNITA severely damaged its reputation by increasingly regarding civilians in contested areas—such as diamond-producing regions—as a burden, if not an obstacle, whose elimination by military means could be justified if this helped to secure a tactical victory. But unlike in the past, when the rebels aptly balanced their violence with propaganda, the criminal character of the postelectoral insurgency seemed to have robbed UNITA of the ability to articulate a coherent set of political objectives for the renewed fighting. Instead, UNITA pursued a strategy of rendering the country ungovernable to induce an implosion of the state. Thus, the rebels increased pressure on infrastructure targets, such as water and electricity, while continuing to attack small towns and villages throughout the country, resulting in countless civilian casualties and the displacement of 1.3 million people.

UNITA also stepped up terror actions against the population, including the use of torture, summary executions, indiscriminate killing of civilians in operational areas, forced displacement, and continuous mine laying. Peculiarly, for the first time since the civil war began in 1975, UNITA reversed its long-held practice of forcing people into its "liberated" areas. Instead, it pursued a policy of forcibly pushing civilian populations into government-held cities and towns to overwhelm already strained state structures and thus demonstrate governmental incapacity to provide the internally displaced with the basic means to survive—food, shelter, clothing, water, and medical assistance. Moreover, since government-held cities were easy targets for UNITA's long-range bombardments, the rebels could demonstrate the state's inability to provide security to its citizens. But this also demonstrated that the government's characterization of UNITA as a criminal insurgency was justified.

Precipitating Disaster: UNITA's Conventional Option

As mentioned earlier, throughout the 1980s UNITA had evolved as a powerful semiconventional army under the guidance of the apartheid regime in South Africa. This army also received large quantities of military materiel from the United States, delivered via the Kamina airbase in the former Zaire. By the late 1980s, UNITA was supplementing this external military assistance with its own military procurement program. Using its increasing stock of diamonds, UNITA was able to purchase additional weapons and logistical supplies, especially oil, food, and medicines, on the international black market and have them delivered to its bases via "friendly" African countries, especially Mobutu's Zaire. While UNITA participated in the Bicesse peace process, including the elections, it was also involved in a parallel program to finalize its conversion into a fully equipped conventional army. After UNITA's electoral defeat in September 1992, this army overran most government positions around the country and seriously threatened the capital city, Luanda. It took the Angolan government about two years to beat back UNITA's pressure. By November 1994, Angolan government forces were able to recapture Huambo, UNITA's main stronghold, only days before the two sides signed the Lusaka Peace Protocol to end the postelectoral round of fighting. Ominously, UNITA leader Savimbi did not personally endorse this accord. He retreated to Bailundo and Andulo to set up his group's new headquarters.

Gaining control of these two strongholds then became a top political and military priority for the government. First, its postelectoral strategy rested heavily on fully implementing the Lusaka Protocol, which provided the government with both a mandate and a timetable to reestablish state authority in all areas still under rebel control. Second, UNITA's headquarters were highly symbolic: Bailundo was regarded as the cradle of Ovimbundu nationalism, while Andulo was Savimbi's hometown. By retaking Bailundo and Andulo, the government intended to force UNITA forces to disperse to various unconnected regions, thus making communication, coordination, and control as well as logistical support extremely difficult for the rebels. Without its central headquarters, UNITA could not retain a conventional military posture. From the rebels' point of view, this meant that Bailundo and Andulo had to be defended at all costs.

Initially, guided by the provisions of the Lusaka Protocol, the government embarked on an attempt to regain control over these two areas through negotiations. However, after four years of failed efforts, it changed course. On the eve of its fourth congress, the governing MPLA decided to discontinue talks with the rebels and publicly indicted their leader as a "war criminal." The government also directed the armed forces to retake the two UNITA strongholds of Bailundo and Andulo. At the time, however, UNITA was strong enough to withstand this offensive. In fact, buoyed by newly acquired war materiel, the rebels responded by mounting military offensives of their own.

After successfully stopping the government's March 1999 offensive, UNITA escalated its military operations and brought them, as in 1992, close to the capital city. Thus, on 20 July 1999, UNITA rebels mounted a daring and surprise attack on the town of Catete, just sixty kilometers from Luanda. Catete represented a clear warning to the government that Luanda itself could be the next target. UNITA's military and political calculations, however, reflected its continuing inability to carefully assess the realities on the ground. For example, UNITA's pressure on Luanda could not be sustained for any prolonged period. First, the Armed Forces of Angola (FAA) had significant concentrations of military power in the capital. Second, the civilian population in Luanda was heavily armed as a result of the government's distribution of large quantities of light weapons to its sympathizers in the aftermath of the electoral fiasco of 1992. More important, while UNITA was putting pressure on Luanda, FAA was fortifying its positions in the central highlands, in preparation for its long-delayed *cacimbo* (cold season) offensive against Andulo and Bailundo.

Tactically, instead of putting pressure on Luanda—something the rebels could not sustain, given the difficulties of supplying conventional military units so far away from their main logistical bases—UNITA was in a better position to deny government troops the ability to mount the inevitable *cacimbo* offensive. This would have necessitated continuing the sieges of Huambo, Kuito, Malanje, and Menongue—all government-controlled cities where FAA concentrated its forces in the central highlands before attempting to strike out and evict Savimbi's troops from their bases in Andulo and Bailundo as well as the diamond mines around Nharea.

What led UNITA into such tactical blunders? Significantly, as mentioned above, UNITA had lost most of its top military leaders. Many of those who had survived the long guerrilla war had been integrated into the national army within the context of the demobilization and reintegration processes stipulated by the Bicesse Peace Accord and the Lusaka Protocol. In 1990 UNITA had had a sixteen-member top military command (UNITA 1990).[1] Of these, only generals Altino Sapalalo (Bock), Antonio Dembo, and Abilio Kamalata (Numa) remained with Savimbi when the civil war re-ignited in 1992. In other words, UNITA could only count on mostly second-tier military officers. Many of those who had commanded the bulk of UNITA troops were now commanding the very government troops that would later pursue Savimbi to his death.

Why had Savimbi allowed some of his best commanders to be integrated in the new army prior to the 1992 election, especially given his stature within the organization and his preference for war as a means to achieve power? In many respects, it was much easier for him to hide his organization's military hardware and financial assets than his top generals. Under the terms of the Bicesse Peace Accord, UNITA provided a comprehensive list of its top officers to be integrated into the national army—a process that was expected to take place before elections. This aspect of creating a national army was easier to achieve, given the relatively small number of individuals involved, than the more daunting process of integrating thousands of soldiers and their weapons. Also, many of UNITA's tops officers were members of the urban classes who enjoyed the comforts of urban living. Not even Savimbi could order them all to leave such comforts and return to guerrilla warfare.

The depletion of UNITA's command structure contributed to its diminished ability to interpret conflicting messages from senior FAA officers and members of the Angolan government regarding their perceptions and interpretations of the rebel military threat. Some FAA officers expressed overt pessimism about the government's prospects for defeating UNITA. For example, in June 1999, in a report to the Angolan Parliament, the army chief of staff, Lieutenant-General Jose Ribeiro Neco, admitted that "UNITA has the upper hand and the Angolan army is largely on the defensive" (Daley 1999; McGreal 1999). Even the Angolan president sought public support from his regional allies to deal with UNITA. Regardless of whether such signals were intended to confuse the rebels, they reinforced UNITA's misperceptions of its own military capacity.

UNITA exhibited this exaggerated sense of confidence when it claimed to control 70 percent of the country in the semicircular zone adjoining the Democratic Republic of Congo, Zambia, and Namibia while "the regime control[led] only 30 per cent of the territory, mainly the coastal band about 100–175 km wide" (BBC 1999a). From this delusional position of strength, Savimbi threatened to enter Luanda. In a letter to the ruling MPLA, he stated that "this time, UNITA may reach Futungo [the presidential palace] before the Angolan armed forces reach Andulo" (BBC 1999a). But government forces were not as unprepared as Savimbi believed. In fact, they were preparing for a decisive offensive against UNITA. Self-deceivingly, until the eve of their defeat in Bailundo and Andulo, UNITA rebels demonstrated a total disregard for the conditions on the ground and chose to believe only those reports portraying them as the stronger force. They did not appear to fully appreciate the previously mentioned political and military factors driving MPLA's strategy. Consequently, they seemed both surprised by and unprepared for the scale of FAA's much anticipated offensive, which began on 14 September 1999.

The government formally announced the capture of Bailundo and Andulo on 20 October 1999. The following day, Angolan television showed pictures of FAA chief of staff General João de Matos in Andulo. Despite UNITA's deployment of some of its most experienced troops back to Andulo for a final stand on the outskirts of the town, the government advance was so powerful that Andulo was evacuated without heavy fighting. In the disorderly evacuation, the rebels abandoned large quantities of war materiel, including heavy artillery guns and vehicles, and headed eastward into Moxico province toward a final dead end.

Savimbi was now moving on foot, heading back to where his journey as UNITA leader had began more than three decades earlier, taking his group into one last grand act of self-destruction. The insurgency was crushed and Savimbi killed within two years of the fall of Bailundo and Andulo. But the destruction of UNITA as a military force and Savimbi's death did not simply result from tactical mistakes, however costly these might have been. They were also a direct consequence of a fundamental shift in strategy: the abandonment of guerrilla war and the adoption of conventional warfare as the main approach for UNITA's attempt to achieve power. UNITA was convinced—in hindsight fatally incorrectly—that it was sufficiently strong to abandon its roots as a guerrilla movement and evolve into a conventional army, thanks in part to its access to great quantities of diamonds.

The Conventional Option: The Role of Diamonds

The loss of Bailundo and Andulo affected the insurgency in several important ways. It was a major political and psychological setback for UNITA. It proved its inability to hold on to two key symbolic bastions. From a military perspective, the loss of the two towns threw the insurgency into disarray because it robbed the rebels of important command, control, and communication systems. Beyond these two factors, however, the demise of UNITA's insurgency can be attributed to Savimbi's fateful decision to deemphasize guerrilla warfare in favor of more conventional military tactics to engage government forces. This decision was inspired by the rebels' control of important diamond revenues that could be used to purchase vast quantities of war resources. However, the rebels seriously misjudged the degree to which control of significant diamond revenues could be translated into military and political power. In the end, diamonds did not prove to be a guerrilla's best friend.

By the early 1990s, UNITA's resources were mainly drawn from its exploration for diamonds, a resource that is plentiful in much of Angola. Angola's diamonds are "ranked among the top three in the world" in terms of quality (Helmore 1984: 530). At independence, Angola was the world's fourth-largest producer of diamonds in terms of value. UNITA controlled this important source of foreign exchange almost uninterruptedly from 1992 until 1999 and obtained US$400–600 million per year in income from it (Global Witness 1998; Dietrich 2000: 275).

UNITA's wealth came at a time when the acquisition of military means to support guerrilla wars had become considerably less complicated. In the post–Cold War era, diamond smuggling from rebel-controlled areas took place within a context of an unprecedented worldwide proliferation of light weapons. While during the Cold War the United States and the Soviet Union had often supported their respective clients with massive quantities of weapons, such support—whether for governments or for liberation movements—took place mostly through "official" channels. In the post–Cold War era, however, many states and arms manufacturers were eager to empty their arsenals and warehouses of weapons that were no longer needed. For some states that had been involved in the Cold War, the momentous global political changes of the previous decade suggested that stockpiling weapons was a thing of the past. Arms manufacturers therefore had to seek clients elsewhere. Angola and other countries undergoing civil war were irresistible markets for arms traders.

The relatively easy availability of both diamonds and weapons created a particularly nightmarish situation in Angola. As mentioned, UNITA used its considerable diamond revenues to evolve from a guerrilla group into a conventional army, with near catastrophic consequences for the government. But the availability of such enormous amounts of money also generated premature overconfidence within UNITA, leading the rebels into committing major political and military errors.

At the political level, UNITA's control of important diamond mines induced the rebels into committing significant blunders, especially after signing the Bicesse Peace Accord. For example, as argued above, UNITA failed to build on its postindependence insurgency to position itself as the natural political alternative to the governing MPLA. Specifically, it did not offer a clear program to satisfy national aspirations for change, particularly in terms of good governance and respect for the fundamental rights of citizens. Instead, its misplaced confidence led UNITA to underestimate MPLA's strong desire to stay in power and willingness to employ all available means to achieve this objective. At the same time, UNITA's relationship with the population grew increasingly hostile, even vicious. For the rebels—no longer dependent on the population for food and other necessities because those commodities could now be purchased abroad with diamonds and flown into rebel-controlled areas—people became both dispensable and disposable. From a strategic point of view, control of resources, not people, became the rebels' primary concern. Tactically, this was consistent with a movement away from guerrilla warfare toward more conventional forms of combat to secure control of diamond-rich territory.

At the military level, control of diamond revenues led to an illusion of capacity. This illusion, in turn, caused serious strategic and tactical miscalculations: UNITA used its substantial diamond revenues to undertake a fundamental military reorganization away from its traditional posture as a guerrilla army into a more conventional disposition in preparation for delivering a final victorious blow against government forces and finally seizing state power. To this end, the rebels engaged in a major military procurement program.

The Fowler Report (UNSC 2000b), prepared in compliance with UNSC Resolution 1237 (1999), presented a detailed account of UNITA's activities in acquiring arms and military equipment. It established, for example, that UNITA used several international arms brokers as well as connections in several African states—including Burkina Faso and Togo—to facilitate delivery of large quantities of weapons imported from Eastern Europe, including "mechanized vehicles such as tanks and armored personnel carriers, mines and explosives, a variety of small arms and light weapons, and antiaircraft weapons, and a variety of artillery pieces" (UNSC 2000b: par. 48). This evidence corroborated previous reports that between 1994 and 1998 UNITA had purchased military hardware from Eastern Europe, particularly Ukraine and Bulgaria, including about fifty T-55 and T-62 tanks; a significant number of 155mm G-5, B-2, D-2, and D-30 guns; medium- and long-range D-130 guns; BMP-1 and BMP-2 combat vehicles; ZU-23s antiaircraft weapons; and BM-21 multiple rocket launchers (BBC 1999b; Gordon 1999).

Ultimately, UNITA's option to use conventional tactics of warfare—including the deployment of large infantry units, mechanized units, and heavy artillery—to face government forces proved fatal for the rebels. They were simply not ready to confront Angolan government forces in successive conventional battles. After all, since coming to power in 1975, the government had molded its own former guerrilla army into a powerful fighting force with the help of Cuba and the Soviet Union. Although UNITA also had important advantages—a plentiful supply of seasoned and disciplined troops and, by the early 1990s, access to important sources of revenue—the rebels grossly underestimated the government's military advantages, particularly in the air but also in artillery and logistics.

In sum, UNITA's own errors ultimately contributed to the Angolan government's victories both in the political arena and on the battlefield. The rebels, on the other hand, were left with only one viable option: another return to guerrilla warfare after the fall of Bailundo and Andulo. However, given the rebels' violent track record, the rural populations were particularly loath to aid them, making it impossible to return to the classical Maoist framework of guerrilla warfare. Defeat, in such circumstances, was just a matter of time.

Conclusion

Savimbi's death during a gunfight with government forces in February 2002 punctuated the rebels' defeat. Headless without its creator, UNITA quickly accepted the government's demand for surrender. A formal cease-fire agreement—the Luena Memorandum of Understanding—was signed on 4 April 2002. The key provisions of this document, negotiated as an addendum to the Lusaka Protocol, included the quartering in several camps around the country of an estimated 70,000 UNITA troops and more than 400,000 members of their families before 5,000 former guerrillas would be selected for integration into the National Army and the Police Force. The civil war thus ended with the quietest of whimpers. MPLA emerged as the clear victor, while a defeated UNITA faced yet another in a series of existential challenges.

At the political level, the government's magnanimous embrace of UNITA as "peace partner" has come to an end as MPLA now reverts to pointing to the war—and implicitly the rebels—as the main cause for the critical problems of postconflict governance and reconstruction confronting the country. UNITA, then, must continue to face its role as scapegoat—not entirely undeserved—while taking tentative steps in a long process of adapting to fundamentally new and difficult realities. These realities include, first, the sudden disappearance of UNITA's founding leader—its main source of energy and inspiration—and the collapse of the former rebels' once feared military structure. Second and critically important for its long-term relevance, if not survival, UNITA must generate a genuinely forward-looking political strategy to recast itself as a force for positive national renewal. This is necessary to change the popular perceptions of UNITA as an essentially destructive force incapable of providing an alternative to the governing MPLA.

Ironically, UNITA has a unique opportunity to reinvent itself partly because many individuals who occupied top positions within the organization under Savimbi have been killed or abandoned the party. In 1990, UNITA's leadership had the following structure and composition: the president, a ten-member secretariat of the central committee, a fifteen-member command of the armed forces (see note 1), a twenty-member administrative council, and a fourteen-member external mission (UNITA 1990).[2] By the end of the civil war, the rebels' leadership had been almost completely decimated or neutralized by internal purges or by government action. Savimbi was dead; of the ten-member secretariat of the central committee, only Alberto Mario Vasco Miguel (Kanhali Vatuva) and Armindo Moises Kassessa remain actively, although not centrally, involved in the party. Most of the former administrative council members are either dead or inactive. Most of the key military leaders who survived the war have integrated into the national army. Only the external mission survived the purges relatively unscathed and was thus in a position to produce Savimbi's replacement in the person of Isaias Henrique Ngola Samakuva.

Samakuva must now deal with how the aftermath of the civil war affects his organization. Specifically, he must focus on ways to help former UNITA guerrillas make the transition into civilian life. Another set of key issues revolves around the problematic postconflict relationship with the governing party. Samakuva must face a victorious and emboldened MPLA that has traditionally defined "partnership" with other national political forces in terms of co-optation, if not incorporation.

But UNITA's survival as a viable political force under Samakuva depends only partly on how it deals with current challenges. Equally important is how it deals with its recent past. How can it overcome the adverse side effects of its survival strategy? How can it bury the stigma of its past choices—the relationship with the colonial regime and, later, with apartheid South Africa? How can it come to terms with the killings of hundreds of thousands of innocent Angolans, most of them Ovimbundu, the very people UNITA claimed to represent? How can UNITA come to grips with the fundamental issues of reconciliation, both national and intraparty? To move UNITA forward, Samakuva must seriously look at its past. UNITA must, minimally, undergo a period of reflective soul-searching to ascertain the fundamental causes that led it to where it is today. This necessarily includes dealing openly and transparently with ethical and moral questions, including the degree to which collective responsibility can be assumed for the violence and devastation that UNITA directed against Angola after independence. This process may produce a cathartic outcome and place UNITA on the path toward rehabilitation.

Ironically, the governing MPLA is likely to work toward UNITA's rehabilitation. The "partnership" with UNITA serves MPLA's political purposes well, if only to remind potential voters that the former rebels remain the greater of two evils.

Notes

1. Jonas Savimbi, Arlindo Chenda Isaac Pena (Ben Ben), Andrade Chassungo Santos, Altino Bango Sapalalo (Bock), Renato Sianguenhe Sakato Campos Mateus, Augusto Domingos Lutoki Liahuka (Wiyo), Peregrino Isidro Wambu Chindondo,

Jeronimo George Ngonga Ukuma, Demostenes Amos Chilingutila, Geraldo Sachipengo Nunda, Antonio Sebastiao Dembo, Abilio Jose Augusto Kamalata (Numa), Carlos Tiago Kandanda, Jeremias Kussia Chihundu, Carlos Veiga Morgado, and Daniel Zola Luzolo (Mbongo-Mpassi).

2. *President:* Jonas Savimbi. *Secretariat of the central committee:* Miguel Nzau Puna, Pedro Ngueve Jonatao Chingunji (Tito), Alberto Mario Vasco Miguel (Kanhali Vatuva), Smart Gaston Mandembo Chata, Eugenio Antonino Ngolo (Manuvakola), Armindo Moises Kassessa, Odeth Ludovina Baca Joaquim Chilala, Noe Kapinala (Andulo), and Isalina Kawina. *Administrative council:* Jeremias Kalandula Chitunda, Elias Salupeto Pena, Jorge Alicerces Valentim, Tony Fwaminy da Costa Fernandes, Fernando Wilson Fernandes dos Santos, Aurélio João (Kalhas), Almerindo Jaka Jamba, Samuel Martinho Epalanga, Ana Isabel Paulino Savimbi, Nicolau Chiuka Biangu, Júnior Agostinho Benguela, Henrique Afonso Raimundo, Lourenço Pedro Makanga, Teodoro Eduardo Torres Kapiñala, Serafina Costa Pereira da Gama Paulo (Bebe), Judite Bândua Dembo, Georgina Clara Sapalalo, Germana Melita Malaquias (Tita), Alda Juliana Sachiambo, and Aniceto José Manuel Hamukwaya. *External mission:* Armindo Lucas Paulo (Gato), Adolosi Paulo Mango Alicerces, Domingos Jardo Muekália, Isaias Henrique Ngola Samakuva, Joao Miguel Vahekeny, Alcides Sakala Simões, Marcial Adriano Dachala, Ernesto J. Mulato, José Jaime Furtado Gonçalves, Honorio Van-Dunem de Andrade, Marcos Samondo, Abel Epalanga Chivukuvuku, Anibal Jose Mateus Candeia, and John Marques Gabriel Kakumba.

12

African Guerrillas
Revisited

CHRISTOPHER CLAPHAM

My book *African Guerrillas* (Clapham 1998a), to which the present book is in some degree a sequel, derived very largely from an awareness of my own ignorance. It was clear that armed insurgencies of one kind or another were transforming—often but not always for the worse—the lives of many millions of Africans. It was clear, too, that these movements, each embedded within the specific circumstances of different African societies, varied greatly from one to another, even though there were also significant linkages between them. At the same time, there was extraordinarily little literature available about them. Even the extant writing on the Eritrean People's Liberation Front, which had strong claims to be the most impressive of them all, was at that time—in the mid-1990s—largely restricted to the work of sympathizers with the Eritrean struggle for independence from Ethiopia. Written during or immediately after the struggle itself, this was understandably affected by what has been described as the "guerrilla groupie" phenomenon, in which the insurgents were regarded in the most uncritical terms and aspects of the conflict that might have reflected badly on them were deliberately or unconsciously suppressed (for example, Pateman 1990). When it came to less familiar and less well organized movements, like the National Patriotic Front of Liberia, the absence of material was almost total.

I therefore set about finding scholars who were carrying out original research on some of the most important and interesting movements and who could help to answer some of the basic questions that cried out for attention: Why did these insurgencies take place? Who formed them? How were they organized? What were their goals, overt and covert? How did they operate? What were their relations with the peoples among whom they fought? What determined their levels of success and failure? And, in the cases where their struggle had ultimately been victorious, how did their experiences in the field affect the ways in which they conducted themselves

221

in power? I was very fortunate indeed to be able to recruit a group of scholars, all of whom knew vastly more about the subject than I did, and to induce them to put their knowledge in print. Several of them—including Heike Behrend on northern Uganda, Stephen Ellis on Liberia, David Pool on Eritrea, and John Young on Tigray—were already engaged on much more substantial studies that have now been published, greatly extending the necessarily brief appraisals that appeared in the original book (Behrend 1993; Ellis 1999; Pool 2001; J. Young 1997). Thanks to these and other works, our understanding of African insurgencies has now been greatly improved.

A deliberate decision was made to exclude the insurgencies of southern Africa, about which much had already been written and which had indeed dominated the literature on the subject to a degree that might well obscure differences from other parts of the continent (for example, James 1992; Kriger 1992; Leys and Saul 1995; Minter 1994; Vines 1991). Southern African insurgencies almost invariably derived from the long struggle against colonial and white minority rule, or from attempts by the remaining settler regimes in the region (and eventually just apartheid South Africa) to secure their own survival by destabilizing their neighbors. Even though movements like UNITA in Angola and RENAMO in Mozambique evidently had their own agendas and domestic bases of support, rather than being merely the puppets of Pretoria, the peculiar configuration of southern Africa made them only very doubtfully representative of the whole continent. Elsewhere, with the exceptions of Guinea-Bissau and Algeria, guerrilla insurgencies had arisen within, and been directed against, established African-governed states and offered a better guide to the role of such movements in a continent from which alien rule had now entirely disappeared.

As a result, the focus of the earlier volume was on three regions, each with a set of interlinked conflicts: the Horn, which had long been the principal theater of guerrilla activity in Africa; the Great Lakes region, which was linked to the Horn through the arc of conflict that stretched through southern Sudan to northern Uganda and northeastern Congo/Zaire; and the geographically quite separate cases of Liberia and Sierra Leone. I had also hoped to include studies of the Casamance region of Senegal, admirably covered in this volume by Vincent Foucher, and also of the Touareg insurgency that has extended across several Saharan and Sahelian states and is quite exceptional in its transfrontier scope. These, however, did not materialize.

Typologies of Guerrilla Warfare

This still encompassed a very wide range of cases and in turn imposed the need for some set of criteria to distinguish one from another and create some basis for the evident comparisons that needed to be made. The typology that resulted, broadly grouping the cases into liberation, separatist, reform, and warlord insurgencies, was a rough-and-ready one, derived from convenience rather than from any strict set of defining elements. For a start, the "liberation" category was defined only in order for the movements within it to be discarded: it indicated a group of movements that we did not want to look at. Liberation movements directed against colonial and white minority rule, in Algeria, Angola, Guinea-Bissau, Mozambique, Namibia, and Zimbabwe, have themselves differed quite significantly from one another and could either be subdivided into further categories or incorporated into a broader classification.

Separatist insurgencies were likewise distinguished from the remainder by their objectives rather than by their structure, effectiveness, or relations with local societies: the Sudan People's Liberation Movement (SPLM) and the Eritrean People's Liberation Front (EPLF) did not necessarily have anything in common, by virtue of the fact that they sought independence or autonomy for particular regions within existing states. The EPLF indeed resembled the Tigray People's Liberation Front (TPLF), classed as a "reform insurgency," more than it did the SPLM.

The "reform insurgency" category nonetheless picked out a group of movements that were in the mid-1990s of quite exceptional interest. These were all highly disciplined formations, with a clear ideology and structure, which had as their goal the creation of a very different kind of state within an existing national territory from that which currently governed. Their leaders—Paul Kagame in Rwanda, Yoweri Museveni in Uganda, Meles Zenawi in Ethiopia—were indeed hailed as "new Africans" who, in collaboration with Nelson Mandela and the newly victorious African National Congress (ANC) in South Africa and the similarly disciplined and motivated EPLF led by Isaias Afewerki in Eritrea, might transform the continent as a whole (see Ottaway 1999). The collapse of the "new African" ideal, and with it of the idea that insurgent warfare might be the means through which a "second independence" could redeem the failures of the first, has been the single most important (and most dispiriting) development in the field of African insurgency between the publication of the earlier volume and the present one.

Finally, the "warlord insurgency" served as something of a residual category into which to lump those movements that failed to fit into any of the other three. The cases that it encompassed did have something in common, but this was defined as much in terms of what they lacked (notably discipline and ideology) as what they possessed (notably highly personalized leadership). The term *warlord* itself imposed an emphasis on leadership on movements in which the level of actual control varied a good deal from case to case, and it emphasized the benefits that a particular group of political entrepreneurs gained from their engagement in insurgent warfare, at the expense of the underlying social and economic conditions—such as political and economic decay and the crisis of alienated youth—that largely accounted for their appearance (see Charlton and May 1989; Reno 1998). These movements sometimes drew heavily on the spiritual or religious beliefs of the societies in which they operated, as Heike Behrend (1993) has found for the Holy Spirit Movement in northern Uganda and Stephen Ellis (1999) for the conflicts in Liberia.

The Decay of Ideology

Looking at the trajectory of African insurgencies since the earlier volume appeared, the most striking change—as Morten Bøås and Kevin Dunn note in their introductory chapter—has been the decline of ideologically motivated movements, or "reform insurgencies," as I termed them. I am aware of no significant guerrilla movement, anywhere in Africa, that has developed the kind of coherent ideology, linked to a project of state reconstruction, that distinguished the National Resistance Army (NRA) in Uganda, the EPLF in Eritrea, the TPLF/Ethiopian People's Revolutionary Front (EPRDF) in Ethiopia, or even—in the peculiar form made inevitable by the horrific circumstances of its accession to power—the Rwandan Patriotic Front (RPF) in Rwanda. This absence cannot merely be ascribed to the end of the Cold War. The NRA's struggle against the Obote and Okello regimes in Uganda was barely associated with global alignments, while the EPLF and the TPLF, though both Marxist in their own ideologies, fought against one of the Soviet Union's leading African client regimes. The RPF's initial invasion of Rwanda did not even take place until after the Cold War was over. More significant may be the fact that the leaders at least of the first three movements developed their own ideas in the ideologically charged atmosphere of the late 1960s and early 1970s, when "liberation war" on the Maoist model did indeed appear to offer the prospect of building, from the bottom up, an effective revolutionary state that would stand in dramatic contrast to the false independence of the early 1960s. Much too derived from the fact that these four movements operated within hierarchically ordered societies that, in contrast to much of Africa, had long-standing traditions of statehood. Laurent Kabila, after all, came from the same intellectual generation as and had even fought alongside Che Guevara during his futile attempt to lead a revolution on the Cuban model in Congo; but the prospects of establishing a disciplined reform insurgency in Congo were negligible, even had Kabila been the man to attempt it.

In one respect at least, the reform insurgencies have been very successful: all of them are still in power, after twenty years in the case of the Museveni regime, fifteen for Isaias Afewerki and Meles Zenawi. This might well make them an attractive model for other aspirant rulers to emulate. Further, their achievements have not entirely been limited to survival. They have indeed built fairly effective states, even though none of them have entirely overcome the threat of insurgency against their own regimes—and in Uganda, as Kevin Dunn points out, the continued survival of the Lord's Resistance Army (LRA) points either to the ineffectiveness or possibly even to the collusion of the Museveni regime. All of them have retained the core of their movement intact, even though all have likewise suffered damaging splits, due in part at least to a reaction against the centralized authoritarianism of the movement itself.

Where they have evidently failed, however, has been in creating any viable *political* structure that offers a long-term solution to the very evident political failures that brought them to power in the first place. None has been able to engineer a peaceful internal change of leadership, and all have reacted with increasing authoritarianism to the challenges that are bound to afflict any regime that has been in power for fifteen years or more. In Eritrea, the questioning of Afewerki's rule by a very senior group of leaders of the liberation struggle led to their imprisonment without trial in some undisclosed location, where (if they are still alive) they remain some three and a half years later. In Ethiopia, the unexpected success of the opposition in the May 2005 election that the ruling party had complacently expected to win led to a brutal reaction, with the killing of demonstrators and the imprisonment of opposition leaders on dubious treason charges. In Uganda, Museveni secured the reversal of term limits on his own presidency and the arrest of his most significant challenger. The deep underlying problems of Rwanda remain unresolved, while all four regimes, most obviously Uganda, are increasingly affected by corruption.

Underlying this political failure, which contrasts with the peaceful transfer of power in a number of countries with multiparty electoral systems, is a problem characteristic of successful insurgencies: those who have fought their way to power, often at great cost and after long and bitter struggle, acquire a sense of their entitlement to rule that overrides any acceptance of the people's right to choose their own leaders. In this respect, the leaders of the "second independence" all too clearly resemble those of the first, who likewise felt themselves to be the embodiment of the struggle and hence exempt from normal processes of accountability. Marina Ottaway was perfectly correct in identifying the leaders of reform insurgencies as being preoccupied with state reconstruction, under circumstances in which democracy was simply not—in the initial stages at least—on the agenda (Ottaway 1999). She could likewise plausibly argue that state reconstruction was an essential precondition for any process of democratization that might subsequently take place.

What has since become apparent, however, is that this reconstruction could not be engineered entirely from the top but must necessarily involve the creation of inclusive political institutions that (even if they did not meet the requirements of multiparty democracy) would engage the loyalty and support of the major elements in the population. In Eritrea, it was taken for granted that all other elements in the population should be subsumed within the iron frame provided by the EPLF, and the pretense that the EPLF itself could be turned into a democratic institution, renamed the People's Front for Democracy and Justice, was no more than cosmetic. In Uganda and Ethiopia, there was at least an initial recognition that the victorious guerrillas did not represent all of the population, and attempts were made—through the "movement" system in the first case and through the recognition of the rights of "nationalities" and the establishment of the EPRDF in the second— to create a broader political base. As a result of their failure to leave open any means to achieve a peaceful change of leadership, however, these systems proved to be fatally flawed. Regardless of how long any of these governments remain in power, therefore, their eventual demise is likely to leave the construction of effective political institutions as a task to be tackled all over again.

The Uncertain Future of Separatism

One thing that has *not* changed over the last decade, as Pierre Englebert points out, has been the extraordinary paucity of "separatist insurgencies." Despite the success of separatist movements especially in Europe and the former Soviet Union, where more than twenty newly independent states have emerged since the end of the Cold War, the loosening of the international conventions that have supported the "territorial integrity" of states worldwide, and the evident artificiality of many African states, it is difficult to find a single significant new separatist movement, even in countries like the Democratic Republic of Congo (DRC) that might well be expected to support them. In this light, the Mouvement des Forces Démocratiques de Casamance (MFDC) described by Foucher, with its close links to local populations, its lack of significant external support, and the absence of an extractive and exploitative "war economy," resembles a throwback to earlier patterns of rural insurgency.

Englebert is certainly right to identify the continued commitment to maintaining the existing structures of territorial statehood in Africa, and hence the calculations of those politicians who seek to benefit from insurgent opposition, as a major part of the explanation for the otherwise surprising absence of separatist insurgencies—and equally right to identify this support for territorial integrity as ultimately obstructing the emergence of more accountable African states. I am not sure, however, that this is the whole story. For one thing, although elite manipulation has been a significant element in African politics since the dawn of the independence era, many of the problems of alienation and state failure that underlie the growth of insurgencies are too inchoate and intense to be readily incorporated into rational strategies for political action. I doubt whether elites really control agendas in northern Uganda, for instance, or in Côte d'Ivoire, as much as this approach assumes.

Part of the explanation may lie in the ability even of some pretty improbable African states, with the DRC as the prime example, to foster a sense of national identity among their citizens; it is hard to believe that some at least of that country's regionally based faction leaders would not have tried the separatist option, had there been any support for it among the people of their own base areas. Instead, all of that suffering country's peoples appear to retain, against all rational calculation, an obstinate conviction that they are Congolese.

Another part may lie, as it were, in a failure of imagination. In Europe, where ethnic nationhood has been the normal basis for state formation, it is easy to conceive of a Slovak or Serb or Lithuanian or even Basque nation-state as a plausible political invention; it is far harder to imagine such an outcome in Africa, simply because the nation-state has not been the basis for African governance. The exceptions have been in Ethiopia, where that country's entirely exceptional political trajectory has fostered the idea of "nationality" as the basis for rule, in a way not found elsewhere in the continent, and in Somalia, in the form of postindependence pan-Somali nationalism rather than the post-1991 proclaimed independence of the Republic of Somaliland, which fits very clearly into Englebert's schema.

But most important of all, we can now see the development of a politics of identity in response to state failure, which—even though it is usually not explicitly directed against the territorial integrity of existing states—nonetheless threatens those states in a new and fundamental way. The clearest example, and the subject of Richard Banégas and Ruth Marshall-Frantani's excellent chapter in this volume, is Côte d'Ivoire, where paradoxically the forces of division derive from a doctrine of *Ivoirité* that explicitly seeks to build a sense of nationhood on the basis of the country's colonial boundaries. The problem, however, is that by building a substantive element into the concept of Ivorian nationality, and one that derives very heavily from the societies of the south of the country, this sense of nationhood presents a mortal threat to a state whose integrity depends on its artificiality. It seems plausible to suggest that Côte d'Ivoire can survive as a state only so long as it does *not* become a nation.

An analogous development is taking place in Nigeria, with the intensification of a politics of identity—always present in that massive state's inevitably fractured politics—in which movements that occupy a blurred position between legitimate political parties, ethnic or religious insurgencies, and criminal gangs are redefining the country's politics in ways that increasingly challenge the survival of territorial statehood. Not only in the oil states of the Niger Delta but also with the O'odua People's Congress in the southwest and the Sharia movement in the north, a populist (even if elite-manipulated) politics of identity strains against the peculiar territorial structures imposed by European colonialism (see Adebanwi 2005; Nolte 2004; Ukiwo 2003). Given the all but total dependence of Nigerian government on oil revenues, not only for the spectacular graft of incumbent politicians but also for public employment and services throughout the federation, the prospects of any peaceful breakup of Nigeria are negligible.

It is, however, inevitable that over time a people's sense of who they are should take precedence over administrative continuity or the limited interests of governing elites as the primary basis for governance, not only in Africa but throughout the world; and in cases like Nigeria where this sense of identity clashes with firmly established interests, the resulting conflicts may well become extremely violent. Those more fortunate or skillfully managed postcolonial states that have been able to capture this sense of belonging for themselves can use it to strengthen the foundations of democratic and accountable government. Where the state has been unable to establish its own cultural legitimacy, on the other hand, the same process can only promote movements that challenge the existing form of statehood, many of which will take an insurgent form. Even where it does not adopt an explicitly separatist agenda, insurgency is increasingly becoming a matter not just of elite manipulation but of struggle for inclusion in, or exclusion of others from, a state that is defined in terms of identity; and a state that is defined in these terms must also define populations that are excluded from it, in a way that a state defined merely in terms of colonial borders or colonized populations does not. In short, the very absence of accountability that, as Englebert argues, accompanies the survival of postcolonial statehood is itself an indication that the problem of separatist insurgency has merely been postponed and not resolved.

Beyond Warlords

Where does this leave the most varied and extensive category identified in the earlier volume, that of "warlord insurgencies"? It is certainly open to question, as already suggested, whether these constituted a category at all, in the sense that they can be regarded as broadly similar movements, open to some common pattern of explanation. While liberation, reform, and separatist insurgencies are broadly definable in terms of their goals, however great their variance in other respects, these other cases have no such commonality of purpose and may result from varying combinations of circumstances. Thandika Mkandawire's argument (Mkandawire 2002; see also Ellis 2003a) that these are essentially urban movements, compelled by circumstances to pursue their struggle in the countryside (and correspondingly indifferent to the fate of the peasantry, with whom they have nothing in common), may well strike a chord in Sierra Leone but prove far less convincing in neighboring Liberia—let alone in northern Uganda. Some elements, such as the crisis of marginalized youth to which Morten Bøås draws attention, are widespread across a large number of cases but do not in themselves explain why such youths should be drawn into widely differing movements. Child soldiers, to take a widely recognized aspect of this phenomenon, have been responsible for the most horrifying atrocities (as well as having such atrocities committed against them) in some movements, while in others (like the NRA in Uganda or the TPLF in northern Ethiopia) they have given rise to no special problems. The roles of leadership, and of economic entrepreneurship, have likewise differed considerably from case to case. The studies in this volume all place their emphasis on political factors as the key element in insurgencies, even (as Denis Tull argues) in the DRC, where the economic opportunities have been particularly tempting. At the same time, any insurgency needs to have some economic basis for its operations, and the extent to which this is merely a money-raising operation geared to its political goals (as was certainly the case with the EPLF and TPLF in pre-1991 Eritrea and northern Ethiopia), as against the extent to which it becomes an important element in the conflict in its own right, is open to considerable variation.

A further significant source of variance is the nature and level of external engagement. Guerrilla warfare is inherently subversive of state frontiers, simply because its operational requirements impose a need to use channels of communication (for finance, food, diplomacy, and information, as well as for purely military purposes) that are not controlled by the target government. The small size of the guerrilla-affected states in some cases, the difficulty of extending central government control over distant peripheries in others, the external origins of most African frontiers, and the close association of guerrilla warfare with the mass movement of refugees to places where they hope to find greater security all reinforce the regional aspects of the phenomenon. The activities of guerrilla movements therefore necessarily attract the attention of neighboring governments. In the two regions of the continent where guerrilla warfare was first established, the Horn and southern Africa, their engagement was greatly intensified by the fact that guerrilla warfare itself was simply one aspect of far more deep-seated issues in regional politics, with the result that the African conventions on "nonintervention" in the internal affairs of other states never fully applied.

All of the chapters in this volume emphasize the authentic domestic bases for insurgency: guerrilla warfare is such a high-cost option for the populations engaged in it that it must be extremely difficult, if not impossible, for any external state to promote it in any location that does not already suffer from chronically bad government. At the same time, they indicate—notably in Denis Tull's chapter on DRC and Will Reno's on Liberia—the strong elements of external engagement in at least some of Africa's current conflicts. The war in the Great Lakes has been deeply internationalized since the RPF first crossed the frontier from Uganda into Rwanda in 1990—just after the National Patriotic Front of Liberia (NPFL) similarly attacked Liberian territory from Côte d'Ivoire. The need to exercise control over such movements has since become increasingly great, not least because of the wash-back effects that they may have across the borders from which they operated. Even though, as Banégas and Marshall-Fratani make clear, the conflict in Côte d'Ivoire is overwhelmingly about issues of identity and power within the country itself, its manageability has been badly affected by Côte d'Ivoire's immediate proximity to Liberia. As the Lansana Conté regime in Guinea stumbles toward its close, so the conflicts in both Liberia and Sierra Leone become an element in Guinea's own domestic politics, prompting the need for closer control. Similar factors, as well as cruder economic motives, guide Rwandan and Ugandan involvement in the DRC. At the same time, Dunn does not discern any significant intensification of Sudanese engagement with the LRA in northern Uganda, while the MFDC in Casamance, as Foucher shows, continues to maintain a low-level but resilient insurgency that remains remarkably detached from regional politics and developments elsewhere on the continent.

I am skeptical about whether increased control by governments in one country over insurgent movements operating across their frontiers represents any enhancement of the capacity of the state system as a whole to manage these conflicts. Even if, as Reno suggests, individual warlords are less free to chart their own course than they once were, the involvement of neighboring states derives, as suggested above, from their weakness quite as much as from their strength and may carry intensified dangers of general regional disorder. For a start, this engagement marks the breakdown of the "nonintervention" rule that once helped to insulate conflicts within a country from its neighbors. It necessarily blurs the effective territorial jurisdiction of states and is likely to foment retaliatory intervention in the state that fostered and controlled the insurgency, once the chance arises. States that are themselves secure feel little need to try to extend their activities across the frontier: it is striking, for example, that while Côte d'Ivoire's civil war engages participation from Liberia, Guinea, and Burkina Faso, there appears at least to be no sign of involvement by arguably the country's most important neighbor, Ghana. Reasonably secure both in their own sense of statehood and in their domestic political structure, Ghanaian governments could only lose from meddling in the affairs of their western neighbor.

The militia movement, here illuminated by Øystein Rolandsen's chapter on the Janjawiid in eastern Sudan, exemplifies the usefulness of guerrilla-style military organizations, under some circumstances at least, for the governments of the state in which they operate. The "progovernment guerrilla" is not merely a paradox: it is also a phenomenon that carries intense dangers for the states that promote it. The classic example of this is Somalia, where the enfeebled dictatorship of Mohamed Siyad Barre hastened the total collapse of the Somali state by arming clan-based militia movements in an attempt to control opposition insurgencies and keep itself in power as the national army crumbled. What happened instead was that these movements pursued their own agendas, were divided by internal splits, shifted back and forth between government and opposition camps, and eventually ensured that when the Siyad Barre regime fell, it was replaced not by a single movement capable of reestablishing an effective state but by a plethora of clan-based factions that have been unable to create any viable government in the subsequent fifteen years. In the north of the country, by contrast, opposition to the regime was monopolized by the Somali National Movement, which in consequence was able to establish its own independent and reasonably stable (though internationally unrecognized) Republic of Somaliland, in the aftermath of the collapse of government in Mogadishu.

The Janjawiid militia in Sudan derives from precisely the same imperatives as the Somali militias—the need for a weak government to counter armed opposition in territories beyond the reach of its own state institutions—and its consequences have been equally catastrophic for local populations, even though the very different political geography of Sudan and notably the insulation of Darfur from the rest of the country mean that it does not carry the same threat to the survival of the state as a whole. As Rolandsen makes clear, militia operations represent a rational response to the intense problems of projecting power over long distances in territories with sparse populations and decaying (or simply nonexistent) institutions— a problem that Jeffrey Herbst has identified as the central weakness of African governance (2000). It may not make a great deal of difference, except in terms of formal diplomatic norms, whether militias are deployed within the territories of the governments that use them or—as with Liberians United for Reconciliation and Democracy (LURD) in Reno's contribution—beyond its frontiers. In either case, this reversion to precolonial forms of warfare carries terrifying implications for the maintenance of political order on the continent.

Conclusion

Since the mid-1980s, the forms of guerrilla warfare in Africa have continued to evolve, and the countries and regions of its greatest incidence have shifted. Southern Africa and the Horn, at one time by far the most important locations for it on the continent, have seen quite a marked reduction in insurgent activity. In southern Africa, the enormous impact of the peaceful transfer of power in South Africa provides every hope that this demilitarization of regional politics can be sustained. The Mozambique settlement continues to hold, and despite the impact of misgovernment on Zimbabwe, there is as yet at least no sign that opposition to the Mugabe and Zimbabwe African National Union–Patriotic Front (ZANU-PF) regime is taking an insurgent form. Angola was always the most isolated from South Africa of the regional insurgencies, despite the heavy involvement of the apartheid regime in the later 1970s and 1980s, and this helps to explain how UNITA was able to survive and reinvent itself after 1994. Assis Malaquias's chapter ascribes its eventual failure much more to its own strategic blunders than to its loss of external support; and the continued weaknesses of the Movimento Popular de Libertação de Angola (MPLA) regime, not least its corruption, make it by no means impossible that an Ovimbundi-based insurgency might eventually recur. The situation in the Horn remains altogether more fragile, with the EPLF government in Eritrea and the EPRDF one in Ethiopia each testing the limits of authoritarian control while at the same time promoting further insurgencies in its rival's territory.

In the Great Lakes, by contrast, the Second Congo War from 1998 onward proved far more destabilizing than the first war of 1996 that culminated in the removal of Mobutu. Whereas the first war remained broadly under the control of a regional alliance that was united in support of the insurgents (and, in the case of Rwanda, furnished much of what was ostensibly an indigenous opposition army), the second fractured the regional diplomatic consensus (and even eventually the alliance between Uganda and Rwanda) and led to a vastly more damaging mobilization of indigenous factions. Despite intensive efforts to engineer political solutions to the various internal conflicts that provide much of the impetus to regional instability, notably in DRC and Burundi, any general settlement to the problems of the region appears to be far away.

The most worrying development of the last decade, however, has been the increasing level of insurgency in West Africa, despite the apparent pacification of the two states, Liberia and Sierra Leone, that were previously the major focus of armed conflict in the region. In Sierra Leone, peace appears to rest on the deterrent presence of a foreign military force, and although formal stability reigns, there is little sign that the Kabbah government has been able to reestablish an effective political and institutional base from which to tackle the underlying problems of development. The inauguration of President Ellen Johnson-Sirleaf in Liberia, after an election in which representatives of the insurgent factions demonstrated a remarkable (and welcome) lack of popular support, may provide a stronger political basis for reconstruction, even though a vast amount remains to be done. The focus of regional insurgency has shifted to Côte d'Ivoire, where its resolution remains deeply problematical, while the long-drawn-out demise of the Lansana Conté regime in Guinea raises further dangers of extension. All these, however, pale into insignificance by comparison with the threat of insurgency in Nigeria.

Guerrilla warfare, in short, not only remains a continuing phenomenon in Africa but has been becoming a more clearly threatening one. Whereas in the 1990s it was possible to discern in at least some insurgent movements the genesis of more effective (and possibly, in time, more democratic and accountable) states, that prospect has now disappeared. The continent is left instead with a plethora of movements, for the most part locked into regional patterns of conflict, which generally suffer from weak internal organization and poorly articulated goals and can be far less readily incorporated into stable political settlements than earlier liberation insurgencies (whose goals were in any event always clear and limited) and reform insurgencies. Out of the conflicts described in this volume, and especially perhaps out of those where as in Côte d'Ivoire new identities are being forged, new structures of African politics are emerging. But this emergence is likely to be protracted and may well become extremely violent.

ACRONYMS

ADF	Allied Democratic Forces
ADIACI	Association of Defense of Autochthons' Interests of Côte d'Ivoire
AENF	Alliance of Eritrean National Forces
AFDL	Alliances des Forces Démocratiques pour la Libération du Congo
AFRC	Armed Forces Revolutionary Council
ANC	African National Congress
APC	All People's Congress
ARLPI	Acholi Religious Leaders' Peace Initiative
ATU	Anti-Terror Unit
AU	African Union
BBC	British Broadcasting Corporation
BCP	Battalion of the Commando of Parachutists
CCCE	Commission Consultative Constitutionnelle et Électorale
CDF	Civil Defense Force
CIA	Central Intelligence Agency
DDR	disarmament, demobilization, and reintegration
DPA	Darfur Peace Agreement
DRC	Democratic Republic of Congo
ECOMOG	Economic Community of West African States Monitoring Group
ELF	Eritrean Liberation Front
EPLF	Eritrean People's Liberation Front
EPRDF	Ethiopian People's Revolutionary Democratic Front
EU	European Union
FAA	Armed Forces of Angola
FAN	Forces Armées du Nord
FANCI	Forces Armées Nationales de Côte d'Ivoire

FAR	Forces Armées Rwandaises
FDLR	Forces Démocratiques de Libération du Rwanda
FESCI	Fédération Estudiantin et Scolarie de Côte d'Ivoire
FLEC	Front for the Liberation of the Enclave of Cabinda
FLGO	Front de Libération du Grand Ouest
FNLA	Frente Nacional de Libertação de Angola
FNLC	Front National pour la Libération du Congo
FPI	Front Populaire Ivoirien
FSCO	Forces de Securité du Centre Ouest
GDO	Government Diamond Office
GPP	Groupement Patriotique pour la Paix
GRAE	Govêrno Revolucionário de Angola no Exílo
HSM	Holy Spirit Movement
HSMF	Holy Spirit Mobile Forces
ICC	International Criminal Court
ICG	International Crisis Group
ICJ	International Court of Justice
IDP	internally displaced person
IMF	International Monetary Fund
JCL	Justice Coalition for Liberia
JEM	Justice and Equality Movement
LDF	Lofa Defence Force
LPC	Liberian Peace Council
LRA	Lord's Resistance Army
LURD	Liberians United for Reconciliation and Democracy
MASSOB	Movement for the Actualization of the Sovereign State of Biafra
MFA	Mouvement des Forces de l'Avenir
MFDC	Mouvement des Forces Démocratiques de Casamance
MINURCA	United Nations Mission in the Central African Republic
MJP	Mouvement pour la Justice et la Paix
MLC	Mouvement pour la Libération du Congo
MODEL	Movement for Democracy in Liberia
MONUC	United Nations Organization Mission in the Democratic Republic of the Congo
MP	member of Parliament
MPCI	Mouvement Patriotique de la Côte d'Ivoire
MPIGO	Mouvement Populaire du Grand Ouest
MPLA	Movimento Popular de Libertação de Angola
NCO	noncommissioned officer
NIF	National Islamic Front
NPFL	National Patriotic Front of Liberia
NPRC	National Provisional Ruling Council

NRA	National Resistance Army
NRM	National Resistance Movement
OAU	Organization of African Unity
ONI	Office National d'Identification
PAI	Parti Africain de l'Indépendance
PDCI	Parti Démocratique de Côte d'Ivoire
PDF	Popular Defence Forces
PDS	Parti Démocratique Sénégalais
PS	Parti Socialiste
RCD	Rassemblement Congolais pour la Démocratie
RCD-ML	RCD–Mouvement de Liberation
RDR	Rassemblement des Républicains
RENAMO	Resistëncia Nacional Mocambicana
RFDG	Rassemblement des Forces Democratiques de Guinée
RPF	Rwandan Patriotic Front
RUF	Revolutionary United Front
SADF	South African Defense Forces
SAP	structural adjustment program
SCNC	South Cameroon's National Council
SCSL	Special Court for Sierra Leone
SLM/A	Sudan Liberation Movement/Army
SLPP	Sierra Leone People's Party
SPAF	Sudan People's Armed Forces
SPLM/A	Sudan People's Liberation Movement/Army
SSU	Sudanese Socialist Union
SWAPO	South West Africa People's Organization
TPLF	Tigray People's Liberation Front
TWP	True Whig Party
UDPCI	L'Union Pour la Démocratie et la Paix en Côte d'Ivoire
ULIMO	United Liberation Movement of Liberia for Democracy
ULIMO-J	United Liberation Movement of Liberia for Democracy–Johnson faction
ULIMO-K	United Liberation Movement of Liberia for Democracy–Kromah faction
UN	United Nations
UNAMSIL	United Nations Mission in Sierra Leone
UNDP	United Nations Development Programme
UNITA	União Nacional para Independência Total de Angola
UNLA	Uganda National Liberation Army
UNMIL	United Nations Mission in Liberia
UNOCI	United Nations Operation in Côte d'Ivoire
UNSC	United Nations Security Council
UPA	Uganda's People Army

UPA	União das Populações de Angola
UPDA	Ugandan People's Democratic Army
UPDCA	Ugandan People's Democratic Christian Army
UPDF	Ugandan People's Defence Forces
US	United States of America
USAID	United States Agency for International Development
WNBF	West Nile Bank Front
ZANU-PF	Zimbabwe African National Union–Patriotic Front

BIBLIOGRAPHY

Abbink, Jon, and Ineke van Kessel, eds. 2005. *Vanguard or Vandals: Youth, Politics, and Conflict in Africa.* Leiden: Brill.

Abdullah, Ibrahim. 1998. "Bush Path to Destruction: The Origin and Character of the Revolutionary United Front/Sierra Leone." *Journal of Modern African Studies* 36, no. 2: 203–235.

———, ed. 2004. *Between Democracy and Terror: The Sierra Leone Civil War.* Dakar: Council for the Development of Social Science Research in Africa (CODESRIA).

Abdullah, Ibrahim, and Patrick Muana. 1998. "The Revolutionary United Front of Sierra Leone: A Revolt of the Lumpenproletariat." In Christopher Clapham, ed., *African Guerrillas.* Oxford: James Currey, pp. 172–193.

Adebajo, Adekeye. 2003. "Africa and America in an Age of Terror." *Journal of Asian and African Studies* 38, no. 2–3: 175–191.

Adebajo, Adekeye, and Ismail Rashid, eds. 2004. *West Africa's Security Challenges: Building Peace in a Troubled Region.* Boulder: Lynne Rienner.

Adebanwi, Wale. 2005. "The Carpenter's Revolt: Youth, Violence and the Reinvention of Culture in Nigeria." *Journal of Modern African Studies* 43, no. 3: 339–365.

Africa Confidential. 1998. "Entrenched and Overstretched." 9 October.

———. 1999a. "Complex War, Ambitious Peace." 10 September.

———. 1999b. "Precious Little Peace." 5 November.

———. 2003. "Peace or Bust." 5 December.

———. 2004. "Militant Diplomacy." 5 November.

———. 2005. "Peace Is Pricey." 4 February.

African Rights. 1995. *Facing Genocide: The Nuba of Sudan.* London: African Rights.

———. 1997. *Food and Power: A Critique of Humanitarianism.* London: African Rights.

———. 2000. *The Cycle of Conflict: Which Way Out in the Kivus?* London: African Rights.

Aliro, Ogen Kevin. 1998. "Death on the River Congo." *Monitor,* 6 October.

All Parliamentary Group on the Great Lakes Region and Genocide Prevention. 2002. *Cursed by Riches: Who Benefits from Resource Exploitation in the DR Congo?* London: APGGLR.

Allen, Tim 2006. *Trial Justice: The International Criminal Court and the Lord's Resistance Army.* London: Zed.

Amnesty International. 1998. "Sénégal: La terreur en Casamance." Paris: Amnesty International.
———. 2001. "Uganda." *Annual Report 2001.* Available at http://web.amnesty.org.
———. 2003. *Côte d'Ivoire: A Succession of Unpunished Crimes, from the Massacre of Gendarmes at Bouaké to the Mass Graves of Daloa, Monoko-Zohi, and Man.* AFR 31/007/2003, 27 February 2003.
Atkinson, Ronald 1994. *The Roots of Ethnicity: The Origins of the Acholi of Uganda Before 1800.* Philadelphia: University of Pennsylvania Press.
Awenengo Dalberto, S. 2005. "Les Joola, la Casamance et l'etat, 1890–2004: L'identisation joola au Sénégal." Ph.D. diss., Université Paris 7, Denis Diderot.
Bach, Daniel C., ed. 1999. *Regionalisation in Africa: Integration and Disintegration.* Oxford: James Currey.
———. 2003. "New Regionalism as an Alias: Regionalization Through Trans-state Networks." In J. Andrew Grant and Fredrik Söderbaum, eds., *The New Regionalism in Africa.* Aldershot, UK: Ashgate, pp. 21–30.
Baker, Bruce. 2002. "Political Sensitivies in Gambian Refugee Policy." *Journal of Humanitarian Assistance,* 23 June. Available at www.jha.ac/articles/a091.htm.
Banégas, Richard. 2003. "La guerre en Côte d'Ivoire: Les enjeux d'une crise régionale." *Questions Internationales* 1, no. 3: 91–100.
Banégas, Richard, and Ruth Marshall-Fratani, eds. 2003. *La Côte d'Ivoire en guerre: Dynamiques du dedans, dynamiques du dehors.* Special issue of *Politique Africaine,* no. 89, March.
Banégas, Richard, and René Otayek. 2003. "Le Burkina Faso dans la crise ivoirienne: Effets d'aubaine et incertitudes politiques." *Politique Africaine,* no. 89: 71–87.
Bartkus, Viva Ona. 1999. *The Dynamic of Secession.* Cambridge: Cambridge University Press.
Bayart, Jean-François. 1989. *The State in Africa: The Politics of the Belly.* London: Longman.
———. 1993. *The State in Africa: The Politics of the Belly.* London: Longman.
Bayart, Jean François, Peter Geschiere, and Francis Nyamnjoh. 2001. "Autochtonie, démocratie et citoyenneté en Afrique." *Critique Internationale* 10: 177–194.
Bazenguissa-Ganga, Remi, and Patrice Yengo. 1999. "La popularisation de la violence au Congo." *Politique Africaine,* no. 73: 186–192.
BBC. 1999a. "Angola: UNITA Leader's Letter to Ruling Party Calls for Dialogue." 7 October.
———. 1999b. "Radio Notes British Study of UNITA's Military Resources." BBC Summary of World Broadcasts, 17 August, quoting Radio Nacional de Angola, 14 August 1999.
———. 2005. "DRC War May Cost Uganda Billions." 19 December.
BBC Monitoring. 1998a. "African Foreign Ministers Meet Rebel Leaders in Goma." 20 August.
———. 1998b. "DR Congo Minister Urges International Condemnation of Rebels." 24 August.
———. 1998c. "Human Rights Leader on Situation in Rebel-Held Bukavu." 9 October.
———. 1998d. "Minister, Rebel Counterpart Speak to Belgian Paper About Health Situation." 6 October.
———. 1998e. "Rebel Leader Denies Backing from Rwanda or Angolan Ex-Rebels." 12 September.
———. 1998f. "Rebel Leader Leads Delegation to Washington." 19 October.

———. 1998g. "Rebel Leader Ngoma Praises French, Western Stance on Rebellion." 20 August.

———. 1998h. "Rebel Leader on Foreign Armies, Rebel's Reception in Conquered Towns." 16 September.

———. 1998i. "Rebel Leader Says Kabila Selling Off the National Heritage." 2 October.

———. 1998j. "Rebel-Held Territory to Be 'Showpiece' of Good Management, Kahara Says." 7 September.

———. 1998k. "US Envoy Susan Rice Holds Talks in Rwanda with DR Congo Rebels." 6 November.

BBC News. 2003a. "DR Congo Plunder Denied." Available at http://news.bbc .co.uk/go/pr/fr/-/1/hi/world/africa/3161034.stm.

———. 2003b. "Republished Former Interview with Maskita." 14 April.

———. 2003c. "Uganda Seeks US Military Aid." 3 September.

———. 2005. "Ugandan Civilians Killed by Army." 27 December.

BBC News Online. 1999. "Old Alliance Under Strain in Kisangani." 17 August.

BBC Two. 2006. "Uganda Rebel Leader Breaks Silence." *Newsnight,* 28 June.

BBC Worldwide Monitoring. 1999. August 31, quoting SAPA news agency website, Johannesburg, 30 August.

Behrend, Heike. 1993. *Alice und die Geister: Krieg in Norden Ungandas.* Munich: Trickster.

———. 1998a. "The Holy Spirit's Movement's New World: Discourse and Development in the North of Uganda." In Holger Bernt Hansen and Michael Twaddle, eds., *Developing Uganda.* Oxford: James Currey, pp. 245–255.

———. 1998b. "War in Northern Uganda: The Holy Spirit's Movements of Alice Lakwena, Severino Lukoya, and Joseph Kony, 1986–1997." In Christopher Clapham, ed., *African Guerrillas.* Oxford: James Currey, pp. 107–118.

———. 1999. *Alice Lakwena and the Holy Spirits: War in Northern Uganda, 1986–97.* Oxford: James Currey.

BERCI (Bureau d'Etudes de Recherches et de Consulting International). 2002. *Le Rassemblement Congolais pour la Démocratie: La biographie d'un mouvement et de ses leaders.* Kinshasa: BERCI.

Berdal, Mats. 2003. "How 'New' Are 'New Wars'? Global Economic Change and the Study of Civil War." *Global Governance* 9, no. 4: 477–502.

———. 2005. "Beyond Greed and Grievance—and Not Too Soon." *Review of International Studies* 31, no. 4 (October): 687–698.

Berdal, Mats, and David M. Malone, eds. 2000. *Greed and Grievance: Economic Agendas in Civil Wars.* Boulder: Lynne Rienner.

Berner, Boel, and Per Trulsson. 2002. "Structural Change and Social Action in Sub-Saharan Africa: An Introduction." In Boel Berner and Per Trulsson, eds., *Manoeuvring in an Environment of Uncertainty: Structural Change and Social Action in Sub-Saharan Africa.* Aldershot, UK: Ashgate, pp. 3–28.

Bøås, Morten. 1997. "Liberia—the Hellbound Heart? Regime Breakdown and the Deconstruction of Society." *Alternatives* 22: 350–380.

———. 2000. "Borgerkrigen i Sierra Leone." *Internasjonal Politikk* 58, no. 4: 559–582.

———. 2001. "Liberia and Sierra Leone—Dead Ringers? The Logic of Neopatrimonial Rule." *Third World Quarterly* 22, no. 5: 697–723.

———. 2002. "Civil Society in Sierra Leone: Corruption, Destruction, and Reinvention?" *Democracy and Development: Journal of West African Affairs* 3, no. 1: 55–68.

————. 2003a. "Conclusion: The Task Is Always to Revise." In James J. Hentz and Morten Bøås, eds., *New and Critical Security and Regionalism: Beyond the Nation State.* Aldershot, UK: Ashgate, pp. 203–212.

————. 2003b. "Weak States, Strong Regimes: Towards a "Real" Political Economy of African Regionalization." In J. Andrew Grant and Fredrik Söderbaum, eds., *The New Regionalism in Africa.* Aldershot, UK: Ashgate, pp. 31–46.

————. 2004a. "Rebels with a Cause? Africa's Young Guerrillas." *Current History* 103, no. 673: 211–214.

————. 2004b. "Uganda in the Regional War Zone: Meta-narratives, Pasts and Presents." *Journal of Contemporary African Studies* 22, no. 3: 283–303.

————. 2005. "The Liberian Civil War: New War/Old War?" *Global Society* 19, no. 1: 73–88.

Bøås, Morten, and Karin Dokken. 2002. *Internasjonal Politikk og Utenrikspolitikk i Afrika sør for Sahara.* Oslo: Universitetsforlaget.

Bøås, Morten, and Anne Hatløy. 2005. *Alcohol and Drug Consumption in Post War Sierra Leone: An Exploration.* Oslo: Fafo.

————. 2006a. *After the Storm: Economic Activities of Children in Return Areas in Liberia: The Case of Voinjama.* Oslo: Fafo.

————. 2006b. *Living in a Material World: Children and Youth in Alluvial Diamond Mining in Kono District, Sierra Leone.* Oslo: Fafo.

Bøås, Morten, and Kathleen M. Jennings. 2005. "Insecurity and Development: The Rhetoric of the Failed State." *European Journal of Development Research* 17, no. 3: 385–395.

Boone, Catherine. 2003. *Political Topographies of the African State: Territorial Authority and Institutional Choice.* Cambridge: Cambridge University Press.

Braathen, Einar, Morten Bøås, and Gjermund Sæther. 2000. "Ethnicity Kills? Social Struggles for Power, Resources, and Identities in the Neopatrimonial State." In Einar Braathen, Morten Bøås, and Gjermund Sæther, eds., *Ethnicity Kills? The Politics of War, Peace, and Ethnicity in Sub-Saharan Africa.* Basingstoke, UK: Macmillan, pp. 3–22.

Brabazon, James. 2003. *Liberia: Liberians United for Reconciliation and Democracy, LURD.* London: Royal Institute of International Affairs.

Bridgland, Fred. 1987. *Jonas Savimbi: A Key to Africa.* New York: Paragon.

————. 1990. *The War for Africa: Twelve Months That Transformed a Continent.* Gibraltar: Ashanti.

Burr, J. Millard, and Robert O. Collins. 1999. *Africa's Thirty Years War: Libya, Chad, and the Sudan, 1963–1993.* Boulder: Westview.

Callaghy, Thomas M. 2001. "From Reshaping to Resizing a Failing State? The Case of the Congo/Zaïre." In Ian Lustick, Brendan O'Leary, and Thomas Callaghy, eds., *Right-Sizing the State: The Politics of Moving Borders.* Oxford: Oxford University Press, pp. 102–137.

Campbell, Horace. 1989. "The Military Defeat of South Africans in Angola." *Monthly Review* 40, no. 11: 1–15.

Cederna, Giulio. 2003. "Gulu's Night Commuters' Walk to Escape Kony's Murderous Campaign." *East African,* 2–8 June, p. 5.

Chabal, Patrick, and Jean-Pascal Daloz. 1998. *Africa Works: The Instrumentalization of Disorder.* Bloomington: Indiana University Press.

Charlton, Roger, and Roy May. 1989. "Warlords and Militarism in Chad." *Review of African Political Economy,* no. 45/46: 12–25.

Charpy, Jean. 1993. "Casamance et Sénégal au temps de la colonisation française." Mimeo.

Chauveau, Jean-Pierre. 1997. "Jeu foncier, institutions d'accès à la terre et usage de la resource: Une ètude de cas dans le Centre-Ouest ivoirien." In Bernard Contamin and Haris Mèmel-Fotê, eds., *Le modèle ivorien en questions: Crises, ajustements, recomposition.* Paris: Karthala-Orstom, pp. 325–360.

———. 2000. "Question foncière et construction nationale en Côte d'Ivoire: Les enjuex silencieux d'un coup d'ètat." *Politique Africaine,* no. 78: 94–125.

———. 2002. *Une lecture sociologique de la nouvelle loi sur le domaine foncier rural. Formalisation des "droites coutumiers" et contexte socio-politique en milieu rural ivoirien.* Montpellier: IRD Documents de travial UR RÈFO No. 6.

Chauveau, Jean-Pierre, and Koffi Samuel Bobo. 2003. "La situation de guerre dans l'arène villageoise: Un exemple dans le Centre-Ouest ivoirien." *Politique Africaine,* no. 89: 12–32.

Clapham, Christopher. 1996. *Africa and the International System: The Politics of State Survival.* Cambridge: Cambridge University Press.

———, ed. 1998a. *African Guerrillas.* Oxford: James Currey.

———. 1998b. "Introduction: Analysing African Insurgencies." In Christopher Clapham, ed., *African Guerrillas.* Oxford: James Currey, pp. 1–18.

Clark, John F., ed. 2002. *The African Stakes of the Congo War.* New York: Palgrave Macmillan.

Collier, Paul. 2000. *Economic Causes of Civil Conflict and Their Implications for Policy.* Washington, DC: World Bank.

Collier, Paul, and Anke Hoeffler. 1998. "On Economic Causes of Civil War." *Oxford Economic Papers* 50, no. 4: 563–573.

———. 2002. "The Political Economy of Secession." Mimeo. Washington, DC: World Bank Development Research Group and the Center for the Study of African Economies.

Comaroff, Jean, and John Comaroff. 2000. "Reflexions sur la jeunese: Du passe á la postcolonie." *Politique Africaine,* no. 80: 90–110.

Conchiglia, Augusta. 1990. *UNITA: Myth and Reality.* London: European Campaign Against South African Aggression on Mozambique and Angloa (ECASAAMA/ UK).

Cowell, Alan. 2003. "US Bases in Djibouti." *New York Times,* 21 May, p. A19.

Crawford, James. 1997. "State Practice and International Law in Relation to Unilateral Secession." Available at http://canada.justice.gc.ca/en/news/nr/1997/factum/craw_pt4.html.

Cruise O'Brien, Donal. 1975. *Saints and Politicians. Essays in the Organisation of Senegalese Peasant Society.* London: Cambridge University Press.

Crummey, Donald. 1986. "Introduction: The Great Beast." In Donald Crummey, ed., *Banditry, Rebellion, and Social Protest in Africa.* Oxford: James Currey, pp. 1–32.

Dahlitz, Julie, ed. 2003. *Secession and International Law: Conflict Avoidance— Regional Appraisals.* The Hague: T.M.C. Asser Press.

Daley, Suzanne. 1999. "Hunger Ravages Angolans in Renewed Civil War." *New York Times,* 26 July, p. A1.

Daly, Martin W. 1986. *Empire on the Nile: The Anglo-Egyptian Sudan, 1898–1934.* Cambridge: Cambridge University Press.

Daly, Martin W., and Ahmad Alawad Sikainga, eds. 1993. *Civil War in the Sudan.* London: British Academic.

De Villers, Gauthier, et al. 2001. *République Démocratique du Congo: Guerre et politique.* Tervuren, Belgium: Institut Africain.

De Waal, Alex. 1993. "Some Comments on Militias in the Contemporary Sudan." In Martin W. Daly and Ahmad Alawad Sikainga, eds., *Civil War in the Sudan*. London: British Academic, pp. 142–156.

———, ed. 2002. *Demilitarizing the Mind: African Agendas for Peace and Security*. Trenton, NJ: Africa World Press.

———. 2004a. "Counter-insurgency on the Cheap." *London Review of Books* 26, no. 15: 34–35.

———. 2004b. "Prospects for Peace and Security in the Horn of Africa." In Gunnar M. Sørbø and Siegfried Pausewang, eds., *Prospects for Peace, Security, and Human Rights in Africa's Horn*. Bergen, Norway: Fagbokforlaget, pp. 12–36.

———. 2004c. "Tragedy in Darfur." *Boston Review*, October/November, pp. 5–9.

———. 2006. "Darfur's Fragile Peace." *Open Democracy*. Available at www.open democracy.net/content/articles/PDF/3709.pdf

Dembélé, Ousmane. 2002. "La construction économique et politique de la catégorie 'éntranger' en Côte d'Ivoire." In Marc le Pape and Claudine Vidal, eds., *La Côte d'Ivoire: L'année terrible, 1999–2000*. Paris: Karthala, pp. 123–190.

Deng, Francis 2002. "Beyond Cultural Domination: Institutionalizing Equity in the African State." In Mark R. Beissinger and Crawford Young, eds., *Beyond State Crisis? Postcolonial Africa and Post-Soviet Eurasia in Comparative Perspective*. Washington, DC: Woodrow Wilson Center Press, pp. 359–384.

Diamacoune, Senghor A. 1995. "Casamance, pays du refus: Réponse à Monsieur Jacques Charpy." Mimeo, Ziguinchor.

Dietrich, Christian. 2000. "UNITA's Diamond Mining and Exporting Capacity." In Jakkie Cilliers and Christian Dietrich, eds., *Angola's War Economy: The Role of Oil and Diamonds*. Pretoria: Institute for Security Studies, pp. 275–294.

Diop, Momar-Coumba, ed. 2002. *Le Sénégal contemporain*. Paris: Karthala.

Diop, Momar-Coumba, et al., eds. 1994. *Le Sénégal et ses voisins*. Dakar: Sociétés-Espaces-Temps.

Diop, Momar-Coumba, and Mohammed Diouf. 1990. *Le Sénégal sous Abdou Diouf: Etat et société*. Paris: Karthala.

———. 2002. "Léopold Sédar Senghor, Abdou Diouf, Abdoulaye Wade, et après?" In Donal Cruise O'Brien, Momar-Coumba Diop, and Mohammed Diouf, eds., *La construction de l'etat au Sénégal*. Paris: Karthala, pp. 101–141.

Doom, Ruddy, and Koen Vlassenroot. 1999. "Kony's Message: A New *Koine*? The Lord's Resistance Army in Northern Uganda." *African Affairs* 98: 5–36.

Doornbos, Paul. 1984. "Trade in Two Border Towns: Baida and Foro Boranga, Darfur Province." In Leif O. Manger, ed., *Trade and Traders in the Sudan*. Bergen, Norway: University of Bergen, pp. 139–187.

Dozon, Jean-Pierre. 2000. "La Côte d'Ivoire entre démocratie, nationalisme et ethnonationalisme." *Politique Africaine*, no. 78: 45–62.

Drogin, Bob. 1996. "Ugandan Rebels Terrorize in the Name of the Lord." *Los Angeles Times*, 1 April, pp. A1–A9.

Duffield, Mark. 2001. *Global Governance and the New Wars: The Merging of Development and Security*. London: Zed.

Dunn, Kevin C. 2001. "MadLib #32: The Blank African State; Rethinking the Sovereign State in International Relations Theory." In Kevin C. Dunn and Timothy M. Shaw, eds., *Africa's Challenge to International Relations Theory*. Basingstoke, UK: Palgrave, pp. 46–63.

———. 2003. *Imagining the Congo: The International Relations of Identity*. New York: Palgrave Macmillan.

———. 2007. "Sub-Saharan Africa and American Power in the Era of the Bush Doctrine." In Roger Kanet and Edward Kolodziej, eds., *Consensual or Coercive*

Hegemon—Either or Neither? American Power and Global Order. Athens: University of Georgia Press.

East African. 2003. "Who's Behind the Civil War?" 23–29 June, p. 12.

Economist. 1999. "Call Off the Dogs of War." 11 December.

———. 2005. "Africa's Unmended Heart." 9 June.

Ehrenreich, Rosa. 1998. "The Stories We Must Tell: Ugandan Children and the Atrocities of the Lord's Resistance Army." *Africa Today* 45, no. 1: 79–102.

Ellis, Stephen. 1999. *The Mask of Anarchy. The Destruction of Liberia and the Religious Dimension of an African Civil War.* London: Hurst.

———. 2003a. "Violence and History: A Response to Thandika Mkandawire." *Journal of Modern African Studies* 41, no. 3: 457–475.

———. 2003b. "The Old Roots of Africa's New Wars." *International Politics and Society* 62: 29–43.

Englebert, Pierre. 2003. *Why Congo Persists: Sovereignty, Globalization, and the Violent Reproduction of a Weak State.* Working Paper 95. Oxford: Queen Elizabeth House.

European Union. 2003. *The European Security Strategy—A Secure Europe in a Better World.* 12 December. Available at www.consilium.europa.eu/uedocs/cms Upload/78367.pdf.

Evans, Martin. 2003a. *The Casamance, Senegal: War Economy or Business as Usual?* Ph.D. diss. London: King's College, University of London.

———. 2003b. *Ni paix ni guerre: The Political Economy of Low-Level Conflict in the Casamance, Senegal.* Background Paper. London: ODI Humanitarian Policy Group.

———. 2004. *Senegal: Mouvement des Forces Démocratiques de la Casamance (MFDC).* Armed Non-state Actors Project Paper. London: Chatham House.

Finnström, Sverker. 2003. *Living with Bad Surroundings: War and Existential Uncertainty in Acholiland, Northern Uganda.* Ph.D. diss. Uppsala: Acta Universitatis Upsaliensis.

Fithen, Caspar. 1999. "Diamonds and War in Sierra Leone: Cultural Strategies for Commerical Adaptation to Endemic Low-Intensity Conflict." Ph.D. diss. University College, London.

Fithen, Caspar, and Paul Richards. 2005. "Making War, Crafting Peace: Militia Solidarities and Demobilisation in Sierra Leone." In Paul Richards, ed., *No Peace, No War: An Anthropology of Contemporary Armed Conflicts.* Oxford: James Currey, pp. 117–136.

Flint, Julie, and Alex de Waal. 2005. *Darfur: A Short History of a Long War.* London: Zed.

Foucher, Vincent. 2002a. "Cheated Pilgrims: Migration, Education, and the Birth of Casamançais Nationalism (Senegal)." Ph.D. diss. School of African and Oriental Studies, University of London.

———. 2002b. "Les 'évolués,' la migration, l'école: Pour une nouvelle interprétation de la naissance du nationalisme casamançais." In Momar-Coumba Diop, ed., *Le Sénégal contemporain.* Paris: Karthala, pp. 375–424.

———. 2003a. "Church and Nation: The Catholic Contribution to War and Peace in Casamance." *Le Fait Missionnaire: Missions et Sciences Sociales,* no. 13: 7–40.

———. 2003b. "Pas d'alternance en Casamance: Le nouveau pouvoir sénégalais face à la revendication séparatiste casamançaise." *Politique Africaine,* no. 91: 101–119.

———. 2005. "La guerre des dieux? Religions et séparatisme en Casamance." *Canadian Journal of African Studies* 39, no. 2: 361–388.

Galy, Michel. 2003. "Les espaces de la guerre en Afrique de l'Ouest." *Hérodote,* no. 111: 41–56.

Gasser, Geneviève. 2002. "Manger ou s'en aller: Que veulent les opposants armés casamançais?" In Momar-Coumba Diop, ed., *Le Sénégal contemporain*. Paris: Karthala, pp. 459–498.

Geffray, Christian. 1990. *La cause des armes au Mozambique. Anthropologie d'une guerre civile*. Paris: Karthala.

Gérard-Libois, Jean. 1963. *La sécession katangaise*. Brussels: Centre de Recherche et d'Information Sociopolitique (CRISP).

Geschiere, Peter 2004. "Ecology, Belonging, and Xenophobia: The 1994 Forest Law in Cameroon and the Issue of Community." In Harri Englund and Francis B. Nyamnjoh, eds., *Rights and the Politics of Recognition in Africa*. London: Zed, pp. 237–259.

———. 2005. "Autochthony and Citizenship: New Modes in the Struggle over Belonging and Exclusion in Africa." *Forum for Development Studies* 32, no. 2: 371–384.

Geschiere, Peter, and Francis Nyamnjoh. 2000. "Capitalism and Autochthony: The Seesaw of Mobility and Belonging." *Public Culture* 12, no. 2: 423–452.

Gleditsch, Nils Petter, et al. 2002. "Armed Conflict, 1946–2001: A New Dataset." *Journal of Peace Research* 39, no. 5: 615–637.

Global Witness. 1998. *A Rough Trade: The Role of Companies and Governments in the Angolan Conflict*. London: Global Witness.

———. 2005a. *An Architecture of Instability: How the Critical Link Between Natural Resources and Conflict Remains Unbroken*. London: Global Witness.

———. 2005b. *Making It Work: Why the Kimberley Process Must Do More to Stop Conflict Diamonds*. London: Global Witness.

Gordon, Chris. 1999. "Eastern Europe Aid Bolsters UNITA." *Africa News Online*, 15 January.

Gorenburg, Dmitry. 2001. "Nationalism for the Masses: Popular Support for Nationalism in Russia's Ethnic Republics." *Europe-Asia Studies* 53, no. 1: 73–104.

Gluckman, Max. 1963. *Order and Rebellion in Tribal Africa: Collected Essays with an Anthropological Introduction*. London: Cohen and West.

Hagberg, Sten. 2004. "Ethnic Identification in Voluntary Associations: The Politics of Development and Culture in Burkina Faso." In Harri Englund and Francis B. Nyamnjoh, eds., *Rights and the Politics of Recognition in Africa*. London: Zed, pp. 195–218.

Hale, Henry E. 2000. "The Parade of Sovereignties: Testing Theories of Secession in the Soviet Setting." *British Journal of Political Science* 30: 31–56.

Hansen, Ketil Fred. 2003. "The Politics of Personal Relations: Beyond Neopatrimonial Practices in Northern Cameroon." *Africa* 73, no. 2: 202–224.

Harir, Sharif. 1994. "Arab Belt Versus African Belt: Ethno-political conflict in Darfur and the Regional Cultural Factors." In Sharif Harir and Terje Tvedt, eds., *Short-Cut to Decay: The Case of the Sudan*. Uppsala: Nordic Africa Institute, pp. 144–185.

Harir, Sharif, and Muhammed A. M. Salih. 1994. "Tribal Militias: The Genesis of National Disintegration." In Sharif Harir and Terje Tvedt, eds., *Short-Cut to Decay: The Case of the Sudan*. Uppsala: Nordic Africa Institute, pp. 186–203.

Harris, David. 1999. "From 'Warlord' to 'Democratic' President: How Charles Taylor Won the 1997 Liberian Elections." *Journal of Modern African Studies* 37, no. 3: 431–455.

Helmore, Richard. 1984. "Diamond Mining in Angola." *Mining Magazine*, June, pp. 530–537.

Herbst, Jeffrey. 2000. *States and Power in Africa: Comparative Lessons in Authority and Control*. Princeton, NJ: Princeton University Press.

Hesseling, G. 1992. *Pratiques foncières à l'ombre du droit: L'application du droit foncier urbain à Ziguinchor, Sénégal.* Leiden: African Studies Centre (ASC).

Høibjerg, Christian Kordt. 2005. "Masked Violence: Ritual Action and the Perception of Violence in an Upper Guinea Ethnic Conflict." In Niels Kastfelt, ed., *Religion and African Civil Wars.* London: Hurst, pp. 147–171.

Honwana, Alcinda, and Filip de Boeck, eds. 2005. *Makers and Breakers: Children and Youth in Postcolonial Africa.* Oxford: James Currey.

Howe, Herbert. 1998. "Private Security Forces and African Stability: The Case of Executive Outcomes." *Journal of Modern African Studies* 36, no. 2: 307–333.

Huband, Mark. 1998. *The Liberian Civil War.* London: Frank Cass.

Human Rights Watch. 1997. *The Scars of Death: Children Abducted by the Lord's Resistance Army in Uganda.* New York: Human Rights Watch.

———. 2001. *Uganda in Eastern DRC: Fueling Political and Ethnic Strife.* New York: Human Rights Watch.

———. 2003. *Stolen Children: Abduction and Recruitment in Northern Uganda.* New York: Human Rights Watch.

———. 2004a. *Darfur Destroyed: Ethnic Cleansing by Government and Militia Forces in Western Sudan.* Washington, DC: Human Rights Watch.

———. 2004b. "Video Transcript: Exclusive Video Interview with Alleged Janjaweed Leader." New York: Human Rights Watch, pp. 1–7. Available at http://hrw.org/english/docs/2005/03/02/darfur10225.htm.

———. 2005. *Youth, Poverty, and Blood: The Lethal Legacy of West Africa's Regional Warriors.* New York: Human Rights Watch.

Humanité. 1999. "Wamba coincé entre Kigali et Kampala." 18 August.

Hutchinson, Sharon E. 1998. "Death, Memory, and the Politics of Legitimation: Nuer Experiences of the Continuing Second Sudanese Civil War." In Richard Werbner, ed., *Memory and the Postcolony: African Anthropology and the Critique of Power.* London: Zed, pp. 58–70.

Ibrahim, Abdel Rahman A. 1984. "Trade and Regional Underdevelopment in Sudan." In Leif O. Manger, ed., *Trade and Traders in the Sudan.* Bergen, Norway: University of Bergen, pp. 109–137.

ICG (International Crisis Group). 1999. *Africa's Seven-Nation War.* Brussels: ICG.

———. 2000. *Scramble for the Congo: Anatomy of an Ugly War.* Brussels: ICG.

———. 2001. *Rwanda/Uganda: A Dangerous War of Nerves.* Brussels: ICG.

———. 2002. *Liberia: The Key to Regional Instability.* Brussels: ICG.

———. 2003a. *Côte d'Ivoire: The War Is Not Yet Over.* Brussels: ICG.

———. 2003b. *The Kivus: The Forgotten Crucible of the Congo Conflict.* Brussels: ICG.

———. 2003c. *Liberia: Security Challenge.* Brussels: ICG.

———. 2003d. *Tackling Liberia: The Eye of the Regional Storm.* Brusels: ICG.

———. 2004a. *Côte d'Ivoire: No Peace in Sight.* Brussels: ICG.

———. 2004b. *Darfur Rising: Sudan's New Crisis.* Brussels: ICG.

———. 2005a. *Darfur: The Failure to Protect,* Brussels: ICG.

———. 2005b. *Unifying Darfur's Rebels: A Prerequisite for Peace,* Brussels: ICG.

———. 2006a. *Darfur's Fragile Peace Agreement.* Brussels: ICG.

———. 2006b. *To Save Darfur.* Brussels: ICG.

IMF (International Monetary Fund). 2000. *Liberia: Staff Report for the 1999 Article IV Consultation and Staff Monitored Program.* Washington, DC: IMF.

———. 2002. *Liberia: Staff Reports for the 2001 Article IV Consultation and Overdue Financial Obligations to the Fund.* Washington, DC: IMF.

International Commission of Inquiry on Darfur. 2005. *Report to the United Nations Secretary-General.* Geneva: United Nations.

IRIN News (Integrated Regional Information Networks News). 1998. "Who Is Who: Key Members of the Rebellion." 20 August.

———. 1999. "Rebel Leader Says Political Rivals Threaten RCD." 5 January.

Jackson, Stephen. 2003. *War Making: Uncertainty, Improvisation, and Involution in the Kivu Provinces, DR Congo, 1997–2002.* Ph.D. diss. Princeton, NJ: Princeton University.

Jackson, Robert H., and Carl G. Rosberg. 1982. "Why Africa's Weak States Persist: The Empirical and the Juridical in Statehood." *World Politics* 35, no. 1: 1–24.

James, Walter M. 1992. *A Political History of the Civil War in Angola, 1974–1990.* New Brunswick, NJ: Transaction.

Johnson, Douglas. 2003. *The Root Causes of Sudan's Civil Wars.* Oxford: James Currey.

Joseph, Richard. 1984. "Class, State, and Prebendal Politics in Nigeria." In Nelson Kasfir, ed., *State and Class in Africa.* London: Frank Cass, pp. 21–38.

JEM (Justice and Equality Movement). N.d. "Proposal for Peace in Sudan in General and Darfur in Particular." Available at www.sudanjem.com/english/english .html.

Kaiza, David. 2003. "Why Won't M-7, Kony Give Peace a Chance?" *East African,* 23–29 June, p. 36.

Kaldor, Mary. 2001. *New and Old Wars: Organized Violence in a Global Era.* Oxford: Polity.

Kaplan, Robert D. 1994. "The Coming Anarchy." *Atlantic Monthly,* February, pp. 44–76.

———. 1996. *The Ends of the Earth: A Journey at the Dawn of the Twenty-First Century.* New York: Random House.

Kasfir, Nelson. 2005. "Sudan's Darfur: Is It Genocide?" *Current History,* May 2005, pp. 195–202.

Kastfelt, Niels. 2005. "Religion and African Civil Wars: Themes and Interpretations." In Niels Kastfelt, ed., *Religion and African Civil Wars.* London: Hurst, pp. 1-27.

Keen, David. 2000. "Incentives and Disincentives for Violence. In Mats Berdal and David M. Malone, eds., *Greed and Grievance: Economic Agendas in Civil Wars.* Boulder: Lynne Rienner.

———. 2005. *Conflict and Collusion in Sierra Leone.* Oxford: James Currey.

Kielland, Anne, and Maruizia Tovo. 2006. *Children at Work: Child Labor Practices in Africa.* Boulder: Lynne Rienner.

Kirk-Greene, A. H. M. 1991. "His Eternity, His Eccentricity, or His Exemplarity." *African Affairs* 90, no. 358: 163–187.

Klare, Michael T. 2001. *Resource Wars: The New Landscape of Global Conflict.* New York: Henry Holt.

Konan, André Sylver. 2003. "Dissolution du GPP, enrichissement des leaders 'patriotes': Le rêve brisé des suiveurs," *Le Nouveau Réveil,* 21 October.

Konaté, Franck. 2004a. "Daloa, Duekoué, Guiglo et Bloléquin: L'ouest militarisé se prepare à la guerre." *24 Heures,* 4 November.

———. 2004b. "Gagnoa, Ouragahio, Bayota, Sinfra . . . : Dans le couloir de la terreur." *24 Heures,* 12 March.

———. 2005. "Bouaflé, Oumé, Diégonéfla, Hiré . . . : Les milices préparent un coup." *24 Heures,* 16 February.

Konaté, Yacouba. 2003. "Les enfants de la balle: De la Fesci aux mouvements de patriots." *Politique Africaine,* no. 89 (March): 49–70.

Kpundeh, Sahr John. 1995. *Politics and Corruption in Africa: A Case Study of Sierra Leone.* Lanham, MD: University Press of America.

Kriger, Norma. 1992. *Zimbabwe's Guerrilla War: Peasant Voices.* Cambridge: Cambridge University Press.

Lacey, Mark. 2005. "Chaos Grows in Darfur Conflict as Militias Turn on Government." *New York Times,* 18 October.

Lair, Eric, and Gonzalo Sánchez, eds. 2004. *Violencias y estrategias colectivas en la región andina.* Bogotá: IFEA, Editorial Norma.

Lapoti, Lucy. 2003. "Pader Boss Says Kony War Now a Big Business." *Monitor,* 3 June.

Le Pape, Marc, and Claudine Vidal, eds. 2002. *La Côte d'Ivoire: L'année terrible, 1999–2000.* Paris: Karthala.

Lemarchand, René. 1962. "The Limits of Self-Determination: The Case of the Katanga Secession." *American Political Science Review* 56, no. 2: 404–416.

———. 1999. *Ethnicity as Myth: The View from Central Africa.* Occasional Paper. Copenhagen: Centre of African Studies.

———. 2001. *The Democratic Republic of Congo: From Collapse to Potential Reconstruction.* Occasional Paper. Copenhagen: Centre of African Studies.

Lettre du Continent. 1999. "Etats-Unis/Congo-K: Emile Ilunga." 28 October.

Leys, Colin, and John S. Saul. 1995. *Namibia's Liberation Struggle: The Two-Edged Sword.* Oxford: James Currey.

Losch, Bruno, ed. 2000. *Côte d'Ivoire: La tentation ethnonationaliste.* Special issue of *Politique Africaine,* no. 78.

Lusaka Ceasefire Agreement. 1999. Available at www.usip.org/library/pa/drc/drc_07101999_toc.html.

MacLean, Sandra S. 2005. "Discordant Discourses: Southern African Narratives on Zimbabwe's Crisis." In Morten Bøås, Marianne H. Marchand, and Timothy M. Shaw, eds., *The Political Economy of Regions and Regionalisms.* Basingstoke, UK: Palgrave Macmillan, pp. 129–146.

Mamdani, Mahmood. 1996. *Citizen and Subject: Contemporary Africa and the Legacy of Late Colonialism.* Princeton, NJ: Princeton University Press.

———. 2001. *When Victims Become Killers: Colonialism. Nativism and the Genocide in Rwanda.* Princeton, NJ: Princeton University Press.

———. 2002. "Citizenship and African States." *International Affairs* 78, no. 2: 493–506.

Mané, Mamadou Papo. 2005. "Chef de l'aile combattante du MFDC: Salif Sadio mis aux arrêts par de jeunes maquisards," *Wa Fadjri,* 29 September.

Marchal, Roland. 2002. "Libéria, Sierra Léone et Guinée: Une guerre sans frontières?" *Politique Africaine,* no. 88 (December): 5–12.

Marchal, Roland, and Christine Messiant. 1997. *Les chemins de la guerre et de la paix: Fins de conflits en Afrique Orientale et Australe.* Paris: Karthala.

Marcum, John. 1978. *The Angolan Revolution,* vol. 2, *Exile Politics and Guerrilla Warfare, 1962–1976.* Cambridge, MA: MIT Press.

Marshall, Anne, and Comfort Ero. 2003. "L'ouest de la Côte d'Ivoire: Une conflit libérien?" *Politique Africaine,* no. 89 (March): 88–101.

Marshall-Fratani, Ruth. 2004. "Liaisons dangereuses: Les implications régionales de la guerre ivorienne." In *Côte d'Ivoire: Consolidation d'une paix fragile.* Ottawa: Partnership Africa Canada, pp. 25–35.

———. 2006. "The War of 'Who Is Who': Autochthony, Nationalism and Citizenship in the Ivorian Crisis." *African Studies Review* 49, no. 2 (September): 9–43.

Mayanja, Vincent. 2003. "Sudanese Army Now Assisting Kony: Uganda." *East African,* 23–29 June, p. 8.

Mbembe, Achille. 1992. "Provisional Notes on the Post-colony." *Africa* 62, no. 1: 3–37.

———. 2001. *On the Postcolony.* Berkeley: University of California Press.

McGreal, Chris. 1999. "Profits Fuel Angola's War." *Guardian Weekly,* 14 July, p. 3.

Médard, Jean-Francois. 1991. *États d'Afrique Noire: Formations, mecanismes et crisis.* Paris: Karthala.

———. 1996. "Patrimonialism, Neopatrimonialism, and the Study of the Postcolonial State in Sub-Saharan Africa." In Henrik Secher Marcussen, ed., *Improved Natural Resources Management: The Role of Formal Organisations and Informal Networks and Institutions.* Roskilde, Denmark: Roskilde University Press, pp. 76–97.

Migdal, Joel. 1988. *Strong Societies and Weak States: State-Society Relations and State Capabilities in the Third World.* Princeton, NJ: Princeton University Press.

Minter, William. 1988. *Operation Timber: Pages from the Savimbi Dossier.* Trenton, NJ: Africa World.

———. 1994. *Apartheid's Contras: An Enquiry into the Roots of War in Angola and Mozambique.* London: Zed.

Misser, François. 1998. "Die im dunkeln sehen am besten." *Tageszeitung,* 22 October.

Mkandawire, Thandika. 1999. "Crisis Management and the Making of 'Choiceless' Democracies." In Richard Joseph, ed., *State, Conflict, and Democracy in Africa.* Boulder: Lynne Rienner, pp. 119–136.

———. 2002. "The Terrible Toll of Post-colonial Rebel Movements in Africa: Towards an Explanation of the Violence Against the Peasantry." *Journal of Modern African Studies* 40, no. 2: 181–215.

Monitor. 2003. "Kony Rebels Enclose Boy's Ear in Letter." 2 June, pp. 1–2.

———. 2004. "Sudan Magazine Interviews Kony." 15 April, p. 12.

Morton, James. 1994. *The Poverty of Nations: The Aid Dilemma at the Heart of Africa.* London: I. B. Tauris.

Muggah, Robert. 2002. *Development Held Hostage: Assessing the Effects of Small Arms on Human Development.* Geneva: United Nations Development Programme.

Mulumba, Kin-Kiey T. 2003. "Le RCD sacque son ème président Adolphe Onusumba et nomme Me Ruberwa à sa place." *Soft,* 17 June.

Münkler, Herfried. 2005. *The New Wars.* Cambridge: Polity.

Museveni, Yoweri Kaguta. 1997. *Sowing the Mustard Seed.* Oxford: Macmillan.

Neuberger, Benyamin. 1991. "Irredentism and Politics in Africa." In Naomi Chazan, ed., *Irredentism and International Politics.* Boulder: Lynne Rienner, pp. 97–109.

Newbury, David. 1998. "Understanding Genocide." *African Studies Review* 41, no. 1: 73–97.

New Democrat (Freetown). 2000. "Liberia V.P.'s Mysterious Death." 11 July, pp. 2–4.

New Vision. 2003a. "Museveni Rejects Calls for Mercenaries to Fight Kony." 28 June, pp. 1–2.

———. 2003b. "UPDF Captures Kony Hideouts." 28 June, pp. 1–2.

Nguya-Ndila Malengana, Célestin. 2001. *Nationalité et citoyenneté au Congo-Kinshasa: Le cas du Kivu.* Paris: L'Harmattan.

Nolte, Insa. 2004. "Identity and Violence: The Politics of Youth in Ijebu-Remo, Nigeria." *Journal of Modern African Studies* 42, no. 1: 61–89.

Norwegian Refugee Council and Global IDP Project. 2003. *Profile of International Displacement: DR Congo.* Geneva: Global IDP Data Base, 20 May.

Nouveau Réveil. 2005. "Dons d'ambulance à Guiglo, à Bloléquin et à Toulepleu: Le ministre Mabri Toikeusse bloqué par les 'jeunes patriotes.'" 28 February.

Nzongola-Ntalaja, George. 2002. *The Congo from Leopold to Kabila: A People's History*. London: Zed.

O'Brien, Kevin A. 2000. "Private Military Companies and African Security, 1990–98." In Abdel-Fatau Musah and J. Kayode Fayemi, eds., *Mercenaries: An African Security Dilemma*. London: Pluto, pp. 43–75.

Observatoire de l'Afrique Central. 2003. "Kigali, Rwanda: Plus jamais le Congo." Vol. 6, no. 10 (9 March).

O'Fahey, Rex Sean. 1980. *State and Society in Darfur*. London: C. Hurst.

———. 2004. "A Distant Genocide in Darfur: Historical and Contemporary Perspectives." Typescript.

Olson, Mancur. 2000. *Power and Prosperity: Outgrowing Communist and Capitalist Dictatorships*. New York: Basic Books.

Omara-Otunnu, Amii. 1987. *Politics and the Military in Uganda, 1890–1985*. New York: St. Martin's.

Onyango-Obbo, Charles. 2003. "New Genie of Uganda: The Man with the Gun." *East African,* 23-29 June, p. 13.

Ottaway, Marina. 1999. *Africa's New Leaders: Democracy or State Reconstruction?* Washington, DC: Carnegie Endowment.

Pateman, Roy. 1990. *Eritrea: Even the Stones Are Burning*. Trenton, NJ: Red Sea.

Patriote. 2003. "Nous avons tué pour le pouvoir et il nous rejette aujourd hui." 23 September.

———. 2004. "Menace sur le processus de paix: Gbagbo prépare la guerre depuis le Libéria." 27 January.

Peters, Krijn. 2005. "Reintegrating Young Ex-Combatants in Sierra Leone: Accommodating Indigenous and Wartime Value Systems." In A. Abbink and I. van Kessel, eds., *Vanguards or Vandals: Youth, Politics and Conflict in Africa*. Brill: Lieden, pp. 267–296.

Peters, Krijn, and Paul Richards. 1998. "Jeunes combattants parlant de la guerre et la paix en Sierra Leone." *Cahiers d'Études Africaines,* no. 150–152: 581–617.

Pole Institute. 2002. *The Coltan Phenomenon in War-Torn North Kivu Province*. Goma, DRC: Pole Institute.

Pool, David. 2001. *From Guerrillas to Government: The Eritrean People's Liberation Front*. Oxford: James Currey.

Prunier, Gérard. 1999. "L'Ouganda et les guerres Congolaises." *Politique Africaine,* no. 75: 43–59.

———. 2004. "Rebel Movements and Proxy Warfare: Uganda, Sudan, and the Congo, 1986–99." *African Affairs* 103, no. 412: 359–383.

———. 2005. *Darfur: The Ambiguous Genocide*. London: C. Hurst.

Reed, William Cyrus. 1998. "Guerrillas in the Midst: The Former Government of Rwanda and the Alliance of Democratic Forces for the Liberation of Congo-Zaire in Eastern Zaire." In Christopher Clapham, ed., *African Guerrillas*. Oxford: James Currey, pp. 134–154.

Reno, William. 1995. *Corruption and State Politics in Sierra Leone*. Cambridge: Cambridge University Press.

———. 1998. *Warlord Politics and African States*. Boulder: Lynne Rienner.

———. 2000. "Shadow States and the Political Economy of Civil Wars." In Mats Berdal and David M. Malone, eds., *Greed and Grievance: Economic Agendas in Civil Wars*. Boulder: Lynne Rienner, pp. 43–68.

———. 2001. "How Sovereignty Matters: International Markets and the Political Economy of Local Politics in Weak States." In Thomas Callaghy, Ronald Kassimir, and Robert Latham, eds., *Intervention and Transnationalism in Africa: Global-Local Networks of Power*. Cambridge: Cambridge University Press, pp. 197–215.

———. 2002. "The Politics of Insurgency in Collapsing States." *Development and Change* 33, no. 5: 837–858.

———. 2003. "The Changing Nature of Warfare and the Absence of State-Building in Africa." In Diane Davis and Anthony Pereira, eds., *Irregular Armed Forces and Their Role in Politics and State Formation.* Cambridge: Cambridge University Press, pp. 322–345.

Republic of Senegal. 1991. *Les faits en Casamance: Le droit contre la violence.* Dakar: République du Sénégal.

———. 1994. *Historical Testimony of Casamance.* Dakar: Ministry of Education.

———. 1998. *La vérité sur la Casamance.* Dakar: République du Sénégal.

Reyntjens, Filip. 1999. *La Guerre des Grands Lacs.* Paris: L'Harmattan.

Richards, Paul. 1995. "Rebellion in Liberia and Sierra Leone: A Crisis of Youth?" In Oliver Furley, ed., *Conflict in Africa.* New York, I. B. Tauris, pp. 134–170.

———. 1996. *Fighting for the Rain Forest: War, Youth, and Resources in Sierra Leone.* Oxford: James Currey.

———. 1998. "Sur la nouvelle violence politique en Afrique: Le sectarisme séculier en Sierra Leone?" *Politique Africaine,* no. 70: 85–104.

———. 2005a. "Green Book Millenarians? The Sierra Leone War Within the Perspective of an Anthropology of Religion." In Niels Kastfelt, ed., *Religion and African Civil Wars.* London: Hurst, pp. 119–146.

———. 2005b. "New War: An Ethnographic Approach." In Paul Richards, ed., *No Peace, No War: An Anthropology of Contemporary Armed Conflicts.* Oxford: James Currey, pp. 1–21.

Richards, Paul, Steven Archibald, Beverlee Bruce, Watta Modad, Edward Mulbah, Tornorlah Varpilah, and James Vincent. 2005. *Community Cohesion in Liberia: A Post-war Rapid Social Assessment.* Social Development Paper 78. Washington, DC: World Bank.

Rodriguez, F. Carlos. 2003. "Sudan Still Helping LRA Kill Acholi." *Monitor,* 2 June, p. 13.

Rolandsen, Øystein. 2005. *Guerrilla Government: Political Changes in the Southern Sudan During the 1990s.* Uppsala: Nordic Africa Institute.

Rone, Jemera. 2003. *Sudan, Oil, and Human Rights.* Washington, DC: Human Rights Watch.

Ross, Will. 2003. "Lord's Terror." *BBC Focus on Africa* 14, no. 2: 20–21.

RUF (Revolutionary United Front). 1994–1995. *Footpaths to Democracy: Towards a New Sierra Leone.* Gola Forest, Sierra Leone: RUF.

Salih, Mohamed M. A. 1989. "Tribal Militias, SPLA/SPLM, and the Sudanese State: New Wine in Old Bottles." Paper presented at conference on Sudan, Bergen, Norway.

Sambou, E. D. 1984. "La Casamance Sénégal et les forces du mal." Ph.D. diss. Université Paris 1, Sorbonne.

Scott, James C. 1985. *Weapons of the Weak: Everyday Forms of Peasant Resistance.* New Haven, CT: Yale University Press.

Sesay, Max. 1993. "Interdependence and Dependency in the Political Economy of Sierra Leone." Ph.D. diss. University of Southampton.

Shaw, Martin. 2005. *The New Western Way of War.* Cambridge: Polity.

Sklar, Richard L. 1963. *Nigerian Political Parties: Power in an Emerging African Nation.* Princeton, NJ: Princeton University Press.

SLM/A (Sudan Liberation Movement and Sudan Liberation Army). 2003. Political declaration, 14 March. Available at www.sudan.net/news/press/postedr/214.sht.

Smith, Stephen. 2002. "Côte d'Ivoire: Le vrai visage de la rébellion." *Monde,* 11 October.

Special Court for Sierra Leone. 2003. Case SCSL-03-I, The Prosecutor Against Charles Ghankay Taylor. Freetown, 3 March.

Standard Times (Freetown). 2000. "Profile: Gbagbo Zumaningie." 20 October, pp. 1–2.

Stiansen, Endre, and Martin Kevane. 1998. "Introduction: Kordofan Invaded." In Endre Stiansen and Martin Kevane, *Kordofan Invaded: Peripheral Incorporation and Social Transformation in Islamic Africa.* Leiden: Brill, pp. 1–45.

Strakes, Jason. 2005. "The Social Context of War and Peace." *International Studies Review* 7, no. 3: 475–477.

Taylor, Ian. 2004. "The 'All-Weather Friend'? Sino-African Interaction in the Twenty-First Century." In Ian Taylor and Paul Williams, eds., *Africa in International Politics.* London: Routledge, pp. 83–101.

———. 2005. "The Logic of Disorder: Malignant Regionalization in Central Africa." In Morten Bøås, Marianne H. Marchand, and Timothy M. Shaw, eds., *The Political Economy of Regions and Regionalisms.* Basingstoke, UK: Palgrave Macmillan, pp. 147–166.

Tegera, Aloys. 2003. *Une rébellion dans une rébellion?* Goma, DRC: Pole Institute.

Theobald, Alan B. 1965. *Ali Dinar: Last Sultan of Darfur, 1898–1916.* London: Longmans.

Touré, Seydou, ed. 1996. *L'ivoirité, ou l'espirt du nouveau contrat social du Président Henri Konan Bédié.* Acts of the Cellule Universitaire de Recherche et de Diffusion des Idées du Président Henri Konan Bédié (CURDIPHE) forum, 20–26 March. Abidjan: Presses Universitataires d'Abidjan.

Tull, Denis M. 2003. "A Reconfiguration of Political Order? The State of the State in North Kivu DR Congo." *African Affairs* 102, no. 408: 429–444.

———. 2005. *The Reconfiguration of Political Order in Africa: A Case Study of North Kivu DR Congo.* Hamburg: Institute for African Studies.

Ukiwo, Ukoha. 2003. "Politics, Ethno-religious Conflicts, and Democratic Consolidation in Nigeria." *Journal of Modern African Studies* 41, no. 1: 115–138.

UNDP (United Nations Development Programme). 2003. *Human Development Report 2003.* New York: Oxford University Press.

———. 2005. *Human Development Report 2005.* New York: Oxford University Press.

UNITA (União Nacional para Independência Total de Angola). 1990. *The UNITA Leadership.* Jamba: UNITA.

United Nations. 2000. *Report of the Panel of Experts Appointed Pursuant to Security Council Resolution 1306 (2000), Paragraph 19, in Relation to Sierra Leone.* S/2000/1195. 20 December.

———. 2003a. *Final Report of the Panel of Experts on the Illegal Exploitation of Natural Resources and Other Forms of Wealth of the Democratic Republic of Congo.* S/2002/1146. New York: UN Security Council.

———. 2003b. *Second Special Report of the Secretary-General on the United Nations Organization Mission in the Democratic Republic of Congo.* New York: United Nations, 27 May.

———. 2004. *Report of the Group of Experts Pursuant to Resolution 1533 2004, Concerning the DR Congo.* New York: UN, 15 July.

———. 2005. *Seventeenth Report of the Secretary-General on the United Nations Organization Mission in the Democratic Republic of the Congo.* S/2005/167. 15 March.

UNSC (United Nations Security Council). 2000a. *Report of the Experts Appointed Pursuant to Security Council Resolution 1306 2000, Paragraph 19, in Relation to Sierra Leone.* New York: UN.

————. 2000b. *Report of the Panel of Experts on Violations of Security Council Sanctions Against UNITA.* S/2000/203. New York: UN, 10 March.

————. 2002a. *Report of the Panel of Experts Appointed Pursuant to Security Council Resolution 1395 2002, Paragraph 4, in Relation to Liberia.* New York: UN.

————. 2002b. *Report of the Panel of Experts Appointed Pursuant to Security Council Resolution 1408 2002, Paragraph 16, Concerning Liberia.* New York: UN.

————. 2003. *Second Report of the Secretary-General Pursuant to Security Council Resolution 1408 2002, Regarding Liberia.* New York: UN.

————. 2004. *Fourth Progress Report of the Secretary-General on the United Nations Mission in Liberia.* New York: UN.

US Congress, House of Representatives, Committee on International Relations, Subcommittee on Africa. 1999. *Sierra Leone: Prospects for Peace and Stability.* Washington, DC: US Congress, 23 March.

Utas, Mats 2003. *Sweet Battlefields: Youth and the Liberian Civil War.* Uppsala: Uppsala University Dissertations in Cultural Anthropology.

————. 2005. "Building a Future? The Reintegration and Remarginalisation of Youth in Liberia." In Paul Richards, ed., *No Peace, No War: An Anthropology of Contemporary Armed Conflicts.* Oxford: James Currey, pp. 137–154.

Van de Walle, Nicolas. 2001. *African Economies and the Politics of Permanent Crisis, 1979–1999.* Cambridge: Cambridge University Press.

Vines, Alex. 1991. *RENAMO: Terrorism in Mozambique,* London: James Currey.

Vlassenroot, Koen. 2000. "Identity and Insecurity: The Building of Ethnic Agendas in South Kivu." In Ruddy Doom and Jan Gorus, eds., *The Politics of Identity and Economics of Conflict in the Great Lakes Region.* Brussels: Brussels University Press, pp. 263–288.

Weisman, Stephen R. 2006. "US Policy Entangled by Rising Price of Oil." *International Herald Tribune,* 24 July, p. 2.

Weissman, F. 1993. "Mozambique: La guerre du ventre." In F. Jean and J.-C. Rufin, eds., *Économie des guerres civiles.* Paris: Hachette. pp. 299–341.

White House. 2002. *The National Security Strategy of the United States of America.* Washington, DC: US Government.

Willame, Jean-Claude. 1999. *L'odyssée Kabila: Trajectoire pour un Congo nouveau?* Paris: Karthala.

Wolters, Stephanie. 2004. *Continuing Instability in the Kivus: Testing the DRC Transition to the Limit.* Pretoria: Institute for Security Studies.

Young, Crawford. 1994. "Zaire: The Shattered Illusion of the Integral State." *Journal of Modern African Studies* 322: 247–263.

————. 2002. "Nationalism and Ethnicity in Africa." *Review of Asian and Pacific Studies* 23: 7–17.

Young, Crawford, and Thomas Turner. 1985. *The Rise and Decline of the Zairian State.* Madison: University of Wisconsin Press.

Young, John. 1997. *Peasant Revolution in Ethiopia: The Tigray People's Liberation Front, 1975–1991.* Cambridge: Cambridge University Press.

Zartman, William. 1995. *Collapsed States. The Disintegration and Restoration of Legitimate Authority.* Boulder: Lynne Rienner.

THE CONTRIBUTORS

Richard Banégas is professor of political science at the Université Paris 1, Sorbonne. He is also director of *Politique Africaine* and a member of Centre d'Étude des Mondes Africains (CEMAf).

Morten Bøås is a senior researcher at the Fafo Institute for Applied International Studies in Oslo, Norway. Recently published books include *Multilateral Institutions: A Critical Introduction* (with Desmond McNeill, 2003) and the edited volumes *Global Institutions and Development* (with Desmond McNeill, 2004) and *The Political Economy of Regions and Regionalisms* (with Marianne H. Marchand and Timothy M. Shaw, 2005).

Christopher Clapham is an associate of the Centre of African Studies at Cambridge University and editor of *The Journal of Modern African Studies*. His books include *Africa and the International System: The Politics of State Survival* (1996) *and African Guerrillas* (1998).

Kevin C. Dunn is assistant professor of political science at Hobart and William Smith Colleges, Geneva, New York. He is author of *Imagining the Congo: The International Relations of Identity* (2003) and editor of *Africa's Challenge to International Relations Theory* (with Timothy Shaw, 2001) and *Identity and Global Politics: Theoretical and Empirical Elaborations* (with Patricia Goff, 2004).

Pierre Englebert is associate professor of politics at Pomona College in Claremont, California. He is author of *State Legitimacy and Development in Africa* (2000).

Vincent Foucher is a researcher in political science at the Centre National de la Recherche Scientifique at the Centre d'Etudes d'Afrique Noire, Bordeaux, where he coordinates a research program on African conflicts. He has published chapters and articles in leading journals and teaches a course on African conflicts at the Institut d'Etudes Politiques de Paris. He is editor-in-chief of the French academic journal *Politique Africaine.*

Assis Malaquias is associate dean of international and intercultural studies and associate professor of government at St. Lawrence University in Canton, New York. Professor Malaquias has written extensively on issues pertaining to security and governance in Africa.

Ruth Marshall-Fratani is associate researcher at the Centre d'Etudes des Mondes Africains at the Université Paris 1, Sorbonne. Resident in Côte d'Ivoire in 2000–2003, she has published several academic papers on that nation's crisis and has acted as consultant for the International Crisis Group and the United Nations. She is currently undertaking a research project as a Guggenheim Fellow on youth militias, autochthony, and violence in southern Côte d'Ivoire.

William Reno is associate professor of political science at Northwestern University. He is author of *Corruption and State Politics in Sierra Leone* (1995) and *Warlord Politics and African States* (1998) and is currently working on a new book, *The Evolution of Warfare in Independent Africa.*

Øystein H. Rolandsen is a researcher at the International Peace Research Institute, Oslo (PRIO). He is author of *Guerrilla Government: Political Changes in the Southern Sudan During the 1990s* (2005) and was Horn of Africa adviser for the NGO Norwegian People's Aid in 2003–2005.

Denis M. Tull is research associate at the German Institute for International Affairs and Security in Berlin. He is author of *The Reconfiguration of Political Order in Africa: A Case Study of North Kivu (DR Congo)* (2005), which explores insurgency politics and the politics of survival in war-torn eastern Congo.

INDEX

Abbala, 151, 152, 161
Abdullah, Ibrahim, 13, 14, 28–29, 39, 140
Abidjan, 98; anti-French violence, 101; attacks in, 87, 89–90, 93; militarization and paramilitarization of youth patriots of, 106–108; paramilitary strategy of, 101; patriotic radicalism, 95. *See also* Yopougon massacre
Abuja Agreement, 71, 73
Abuja peace talks, 160
Accra, 79, 81, 87
Acholi, 14, 28, 33, 131, 133, 137, 138, 139; acquisition of state power, 131–132; atrocities against, 139; discontent with Ugandan government, 132, 138–140; displacement of peoples, 34, 131; economic role, 28
Acholi Religious Leaders Peace Initiative (ARLPI), 135, 139, 142
Addis Ababa, 125
Adek, Yusuf, 144
ADF. *See* Allied Democratic Forces
ADIACI. *See* Association of Defense of Autochthons' Interests of Côte d'Ivoire
Adjumani, 24
AENF. *See* Alliance of Eritrean National Forces
AFDL. *See* Alliances des Forces Démocratiques pour la Libération du Congo
Afewerki, Isaias, 223, 224, 225
AFRC. *See* Armed Forces Revolutionary Council

African Guerrillas (Clapham), 3, 8, 221
African National Congress, 204, 223
African state: composition of, 11; characteristics of, 55–56; illegitimate states, 25; obstruction of accountable state, 226; perceived bankruptcy of state model, 23; resolving border disputes, 57; state failure to provide for its population, 45; weakness of, 61; weak status upheld through sovereignty, 59, 66
African Union: monitoring mission in Darfur, 151, 160
African youth, 5, 10; diamond laborers in Sierra Leone, 42; involvement in insurgency movements, 39, 45; militarization of, 6, 45, 100, 103, 105–107; patriots, 104–106; unemployed males, 13. *See also* Lumpens
Agriculturalists, 14, 152, 157; autochthonous claims in Darfur, 153
Agricultural products: cannabis, 171, 178, 181; cashew nuts, 171, 181; charcoal, 171, 178, 181; cocoa, 84, 95; coffee, 84, 95; timber, 181
Ahmed Tejan Kabbah, 76
Akol, Lam, 167
al-Bashir, Omar, 20, 142
Algeria, 16, 222
Alice Lakwena, 133, 134, 141, 147
Al-Qaida, 19, 20
Alliances des Forces Démocratiques pour la Libération du Congo (AFDL), 115, 116, 117, 128

Alliance des Jeunes Patriotes pour le Sursaut National, 106, 107
Alliance of Eritrean National Forces (AENF), 20
Allied Democratic Forces (ADF), 36
All People's Congress (APC), 13, 43
Al-Mahdi, Sadiq, 164
Amin, Idi, 88, 134, 139
Amnesty, 27, 144, 147
Amnesty International, 131
Anaconda Company, 94
Andulo, 212–215, 218, 220
ANC. *See* African National Congress
Anglo-Egyptian condominium government, 153–154
Angola, 2, 7, 14, 63, 182, 183, 203, 204, 206, 232; Angolans as foreign mercenaries, 97, 100; intervention in Congo, 115, 117; peace process, 210; struggle for Cabinda, 55
Anyanya, 2, 162, 167
APC. *See* All People's Congress
Arab Gathering, 153, 155, 167
Armed Forces of Angola (FAA), 213, 214–215, 217
Armed Forces of Liberia, 72
Armed Forces Revolutionary Council (AFRC), 40, 50
Assimilados, 201, 202
Association of Defense of Autochthons' Interests of Côte d'Ivoire (ADIACI), 86
Atika, 172, 177, 178, 184, 185. *See also Maquis*
Auma, Alice, 133, 134, 141, 147. *See also* Alice Lakwena
Autochthony, 5, 6, 10, 24, 31, 32, 33, 85, 103; autochthons in Côte d'Ivoire, 86; ideology of, 83, 87, 123; as a politicized discourse, 33; in Senegalese politics, 175–176
Azawad People's Movement, 55, 65

Bach, Daniel, 23
Badji, Aliou, 177
Badji, Sidy, 172, 175, 177, 186, 189, 190
Bah, Ibrahim, 97
Bahr el-Ghazal, 162, 165; attacks, 163, 164
Bailundo, 212–215, 218

Bakayoko, Soumaila, 94
Baluf, 186
Bandial, 186
Banjul, 172, 178, 179, 181
Banque Centrale des Etats de l'Afrique de l'Ouest, 95
Banyamulenge, 14, 32, 117, 123, 124
Banyarwanda, 123. *See also* Hutu; Tutsi
Baoulé, Ivorian, 84, 86, 89, 101, 103, 104, 110
Baqqara, 152, 161, 163, 166
Baraka-Mandioca, 191
Barotse, 56, 60, 68
Barre, Mohamed Siyad, 231
Basque, 227
Battalion of the Commando of Parachutists (BCP), 101
BBC, 74, 136, 137
BBC Africa, 18, 40
BCP. *See* Battalion of the Commando of Parachutists
Bédié, Henri Konan, 85, 87, 88, 89, 90, 91, 93, 94
Behrend, Heike, 133, 138, 139, 141, 146, 222, 224
Belgium, 206; settlers in Congo, 63
Bemba, Jean-Pierre, 118, 119
Benguela, 200, 202
Beni Halba, 157, 168, 169
Bentiu, 162
Berdal, Mats, 145
Bélaye, 184
Besigye, Kizza, 20
Bété region, 100, 101
Biafra, 65
Biaka, Hippolyte Légré, 101
Bicesse Peace Accord, 210, 212, 214
Bié, 200, 203
Bignona, 174, 184
Bigombe, Betty, 143
Bloléquin, 98, 104, 105, 248, 250
Bobo, Koffee Samuel, 102–104, 111, 243
Bockarie, Sam "Maskita": death of, 40, 51, 52, 99; employed by Charles Taylor, 51; participation in Ivorian civil war, 51, 91, 97; regional warlord, 51–52; youth experiences, 41–42, 44
Bolad, Daud, 157

Boley, George, 71
Bomaru, Sierra Leone, 47
Bombet, Denis, 98
Boodkay, 158
Bouaké, 93, 94, 95, 98, 110, 240
British: colonial relationship to Darfur,
  153; colonial system in Uganda, 139;
  intervention force in Sierra Leone,
  50, 75; invasion of Iraq, 79;
  involvement in Liberia, 74
Bro-Grébé, Geneviève, 106
Buchanan, 98
Buganda, of Uganda, 28, 33
Bulgaria, 217
Buluf, 174, 186, 193
Bululu, Lunda, 117, 119
Bush devils, 47, 49. *See also*
  Revolutinary United Front
Bush, George W., 147–148
Burkinabé, 81, 86, 98, 101; autochthon
  recruits, 103; government, 93
Burkina Faso, 57, 92, 105, 217; direct
  support of MPCI, 91
Burundi, 2, 35, 124, 232

Cabinda, 55
Caistab (Caisse de Stabilisation des
  Produits Agricoles), 84
Cameroon, 16
Camorra, 89, 92, 93
Camp Johnson Road incident, 73, 76
Camp Lemonier, 20
Casamançais: autochthonous
  leadership, 187–188; educational
  discrimination of, 174–175; Euro-
  pean diaspora, 181, 191; identity,
  173; nationalist ideology, 184, 191;
  political roots of separatism, 176;
  war economy, 183. *See also* Diola;
  Peulhs
Casamance, 14, 28, 55, 58, 65, 171,
  222; degree of violence, 184; geog-
  raphy, 173; low-scale war economy,
  182; separatist claims, 63; social
  history, 173; social marginalization,
  27; unique localized conflict, 183
Casamance River, 172, 181, 183
Cassamba, 202
Catete, 213
CCCE. *See* Commission Consultative
  Constitutionelle et Électorale

CDF. *See* Civil Defense Force
Cederna, Giulio, 136
Cen, 133
Central Africa, 6, 11, 35, 206
Central African Republic, 35
Central Intelligence Agency, 207;
  operations from Djibouti, 20; alleged
  relationship with Charles Taylor, 74
Chad, 2, 9, 155, 161; immigrants in
  Darfur, 157
Chad-Libya conflict, 155–156
Chauveau, Jean-Pierre, 102–104
Chayee, Amos, 98
Chendovava, Jose Antonio, 208
Child soldiers, 137, 171, 184, 229. *See
  also* Lord's Resistance Army
Chingunji, Pedro "Tito," 208
China, 16, 183, 201, 202; role in
  Africa, 20
Chindondo, Valdemar, 208
Cissé, Lamine, 189
Citizenship: claims to, 32; colonial
  concept of, 31; conceptions of, 83;
  contested in African politics, 31, 90;
  nativist conception of, 87; questions
  of citizenship in Côte d'Ivoire, 83, 91
Civil Defense Force (CDF), 45; support
  from Sierra Leonean government, 49
Clapham, Christopher, 3, 4, 8, 15, 55;
  insurgency thesis, 119; on warlord
  insurgencies, 23, 69; scholarly
  contributions, 55
Clientelism, 67, 84, 88
Cockney Rejects, 52
Cold War, 2, 6, 17, 20, 29, 177, 206,
  216. *See also* Post–Cold War
Colonialism: in Africa, 12; common
  colonial subjugation, 56; concept of
  African citizenship, 31; documents
  granting liberation, 57; legacy of
  racially inherited privilege, 22
Coltan, 10, 126, 127
Commission Consultative
  Constitutionelle et Électorale
  (Consultative Constitutional and
  Electoral Commission; CCCE), 106
Compaoré, Blaise, 92
Congo, 10, 16, 18, 182, 224; Congolese
  war, 17; Congolese secessions,
  64–65; Congolese statehood, 129;
  Kwilu district, 16; northeastern

Congo, 118; sovereignty of, 65; UN intervention, 64–65
Congress of Pan-African Youth, 107
Conneh, Ayesha, 77, 80
Conneh, Sekou, 77
Conté, Lasana, 76, 97, 99; demise of regime, 230, 233; distribution of arms along Liberian border, 77–78
Convention des Patriotes pour la Paix, 107
Corruption, 14, 88, 181; consequences of state corruption, 44, 46; corrupted institutions, 5, 43; corrupt elites, 11; corrupt states, 46; Liberian state under Doe, 26; in northern Uganda, 145–146, 225; Sierra Leone under Stevens, 43–44
Cosa Nostra, 89, 92, 93
Côte d'Ivoire, 2, 3, 6, 14, 227, 233; agricultural development, 84; attempted coup d'état (2002), 81, 93; autochthons, 86; autochthonous conflict, 32, 33, 36; cease-fire line, 81, 92; conceptions of citizenship, 83; coup d'état (1999), 88; downfall, 82; economic crisis, 84; freelance militias, 25; Houphouetist state, 29; identity cards, 81, 87, 102; immigration history, 91; intergenerational relations, 108; internationalization of conflict, 230; junta, 89; legislative elections, 90; Liberian involvement in conflict, 91, 95–99; migration history, 91; militarization of, 83, 88–89, 100–102, 105; nature of conflict, 82–83; northern control by New Forces, 29; post-Boigny, 57; reconciliation government, 81, 94, 95, 107–108; resident cards, 87, 102
Coubanao, 185
Coulibaly, Ibrahim, 89; military career; 93
Cry Freetown, 50
Cuba, 177, 206, 217; troops in Angola, 204, 205, 207, 210
Cuito Cuanavale, 205

Dacoury-Tabley, Louis, 92
Dagbeson, Eric, 98
Dakar, 171, 176, 178, 186, 187; attempts at developing links with

MFDC, 189; policies in response to separatist action, 187–189; strategy to fight militias, 173
Dakoury, Richard, 106
Danané, 97, 110
Daola, 104
Dar Fur Development Front, 154
Dar Masalit, 157
Darfur, 3, 7, 25, 166; "African" resistance, 159; colonial period, 153–154; Darfurian rebels, 151; ethnic conflict, 152, 156–157; ideology, 156–157, 166; international attention, 162; media reports, 151
Darfur Peace Agreement (DPA), 160, 164
de Waal, Alex, 164, 166
Deby, Idriss, 160–161
Dembelé, Ousmane, 85
Dembo, Antonio (Bock), 214
Democratic Republic of Congo (DRC), 2, 11, 136, 214, 226, 229, 232; ceasefire, 125; fostering of national identity, 227; government asset stripping, 60; Hutu refugees in, 123; internal displacement, 116; local conflicts, 123; nationality laws, 123; peace negotiations, 125; second war, 113, 129; state mining sector, 128; withdrawal of foreign armies, 116; zones of influence, 115
Democratic Republic of Congo, eastern, 6, 136; autochthonous conflict, 33; Kivu provinces, 7, 113, 127; occupied by RDC, 121–122; Rwandan military presence in, 123–124; UN arms embargo, 127; violence in, 116. *See also* North Kivu; South Kivu
Dennis, Kuku, 97
Depelchin, Jaques, 117
Détente, 143
Diamacoune, Bertrand, 180, 186
Diamacoune, Father Augustin (Senghor), 171, 172, 175; liberalization policies, 176; organization of MFDC political wing, 180–181, 177
Diamonds, 7, 10–11; extraction economy, 34; fields in Koidu, 50; funding for RUF arms, 18, 50;

Kailahun, 35; Kono district, 35, 41; mines and producing areas in Angola, 204, 212; mining in Sierra Leone, 41; smuggling in Sierra Leone, 44; UNITA's control of, 200, 210, 216–217
Diara, Seydou, 107
Diatta, Maurice Adiokane, 186
Dinar, Ali, 153
Dinka, 163
Diouf, Abdou, 172, 176
Diola, 64, 81, 179, 181; egalitarianism, 187; literati, 174–175; mobilization by MFDC, 174–276; as stranger in Côte d'Ivoire, 86; diaspora, 191
Dioulasso, Bobo, 93
Djibidione, 181
Djibouti, 20
Djué, Eugene, 106, 107
Doe, Samuel, 26, 71–72
Dogolea, Ennoch, 74
Doh, Felix, 91, 99
Dolo, Adolphus, 97
dos Santos, José Eduardo, 210
Dououd, Emile Boga, 81, 87
Doué, Mathias, 98
DRC. *See* Democratic Republic of Congo
Duo, Roland, 97

East African, 143, 146
Eastern Europe: recruitment of foreign mercenaries, 97, 100; weapons exported to UNITA, 217
Economic Community of West African States Monitoring Group (ECOMOG), 40; liberation of Freetown, 50
Economist, The, 135
Egypt, 153
Ehrenreich, Rosa, 135, 137, 138, 141, 143
Elections: international monitoring, 76; irregularities in Côte d'Ivoire, 104; postelection violence in Ethiopia, 225; in Sierra Leone, 49, 78; in Senegal, 180; UNITA's participation in Angolan elections and electoral process, 208–211
Elites, 5; African political, 19, 23, 67; corrupt, 11; distribution of state resources, 57; economic, 10; exploitation of citizens through sovereignty, 58–59, 66; intra-elite conflict, 13, 154; manipulation, 226; political networking of elites in Liberia, 72; practice of hegemony over local populations, 60; reciprocal assimilation, 23, 57, 188; recycled elites in African society, 29–31; ruling elites strategy to maintain power, 24–25, 61–62, 66; Ugandan, 28
Ellis, Stephen, 26, 27, 222, 224
ELF. *See* Eritrean Liberation Front
Endundo, José, 117, 119
EPLF. *See* Eritrean People's Liberation Front
EPRDF. *See* Ethiopian People's Revolutionary Democratic Front
Equatoria, 162
Eritrea, 16, 25, 222, 225, 226; insurgency in, 25; secession of, 62–63; SPLM/A bases, 160; war on terror rhetoric, 20
Eritrean Liberation Front (ELF), 62
Eritrean People's Liberation Front (EPLF), 9, 15, 59, 221, 223, 224, 229, 232; renaming of, 226
Ethiopia, 9, 16, 55, 226; emphasis on nationality, 227; government war on terror rhetoric, 20; postelection violence, 225; struggle for independence, 221
Ethiopian People's Revolutionary Democratic Front (EPRDF), 9, 224, 226, 232
European Union (EU), 75
Evans, Martin, 182
Executive Outcomes: in Angola, 24; support of Sierra Leonean army, 49

FAA. *See* Armed Forces of Angola
Fall, Abdoulaye, 189, 190
FAN. *See* Forces Armées du Nord
FANCI. *See* Forces Armées Nationales de Côte d'Ivoire
FAR. *See* Forces Armées Rwandaises
Fédération Estudiantin et Scolarie de Côte d'Ivoire (FESCI), 90, 92, 94
Finnstrom, Sverker, 140
FLEC. *See* Front for the Liberation of the Enclave of Cabinda

FLGO. *See* Front de Libération du
    Grand Ouest
Flomo, Nowai, 74
FNLA. *See* Frente Nacional de
    Libertaçâo de Angola
Force d'Intervention Rapide Para-
    Commando, 94
Forces de Securité du Centre Ouest
    (FSCO), 101, 108
Forces Armées du Nord (FAN), 9
Forces Armées Nationales de Côte
    d'Ivoire (FANCI), 88, 97, 98, 100,
    103, 108
Forces Armées Rwandaises (FAR),
    117
Forces Nouvelles, 94
Foreign aid, 58; block of aid package
    to Liberia, 75; direct investments, 58
Forum for National Reconciliation, 90
Fowler Report, 217
Fozié, Tuo, 92, 94
FPI. *See* Front Populaire Ivoirien
Francafrique, 84
France, 92, 93, 105, 106, 175, 176,
    206; anti-French demonstrations,
    107; intervention in Côte d'Ivoire,
    34; military assistance in Côte
    d'Ivoire, 88; settlers in Senegal,
    175–176; used as foreign
    mercenaries, 100
Freetown, Sierra Leone, 40; creation
    of LURD, 73; deployment of UN
    peacekeepers, 50–51; "liberation" of,
    50; recruitment for NPRC, 48; RUF
    offensive; 50
Frente Nacional de Libertaçâo de
    Angola (FNLA), 200, 201
Front de Libération du Grand Ouest
    (FLGO), 97, 98, 108
Front for the Liberation of the Enclave
    of Cabinda (FLEC), 63
Front National de Libération Totale de
    Côte d'Ivoire, 107
Front Nord, 172, 181, 185; internal
    division, 186
Front Sud, 172, 179, 184, 185, 187,
    190; internal division, 186
Front Populaire Ivoirien (FPI), 81, 85,
    87, 90, 92, 100–104
FSCO. *See* Forces de Securité du
    Centre Ouest   .

Fund for the Stabilization of Agricul-
    tural Production. *See* Caistab
Fur, 152, 154, 156–158; discrimination
    against, 159

G7 coalition, 81, 82, 103
Gbagbo, Laurent, 25, 81, 82, 85, 87,
    92, 108; antinorthern discrimination,
    94; arms distribution, 98; creation of
    ONI, 87; election as president, 89;
    extension of colonial policy, 84;
    influence on youth patriotic move-
    ments, 105; recruiting anti-Taylor
    forces, 97; support of MODEL, 99,
    100; ultranationalist propaganda,
    100; ultranationalist regime, 83;
    usage of Houphouët's rhetoric, 85
Gagnoa region, 101
Gambia, 173, 177; economic trade on
    Gambian border, 181–182;
    relationship with MFDC, 178–180
Gammi, Diomandé, 102
Garamba, 136
Garang, John, 167
GDO. *See* Government Diamond Office
Geffray, Christian, 184
Geneina, 164
Genocide, 60, 151, 159
Germany, 180
Geschiere, Paul, 31
Ghana, 17, 98, 230
Gio, 36, 74, 98
Gnatoa, Bertrand, 101, 108
Goma, 120
Gomé, Hilaire, 106
Gorenburg, Dmitry, 64
Goudé, Charles Blé, 105–108, 111
Government Diamond Office (GDO),
    44
Govêrno Revolucionário de Angola no
    Exílo (GRAE), 201
Gowan, Yakubu, 65
GPP. *See* Groupement Patriotique pour
    la Paix
GRAE. *See* Govêrno Revolucionário de
    Angola no Exílo
Great Lakes: conflict zone, 6, 35;
    crisis, 82; internationalization of
    conflict, 230; pattern of conflict, 36,
    232; region, 124, 222
Green Book (Qaddafi), 16, 72, 155

Groghué, Charles, 107
Groupement Patriotique pour la Paix (GPP), 107
Gueï, Robert, 88; death of, 92; junta, 92; loss of control to young militia groups, 89; regime of, 87
Guepard Company, 94
Gueu, Michael, 94
Guevara, Ché, 224
Guiglo, 98, 102
Guinea, 2, 70, 230; cross-border raids by LURD, 74; indigenous social structures, 78; politics under Conte, 77–78
Guinea-Bissau, 86, 172, 177, 190–191, 222; refugee communities, 191, 192; relationship with MFDC, 178–180; weapons sales to MFDC, 178
Gulu, 131, 133, 134, 145
Gyude, Bryant, 79

Habré, Hissen, 9
Hale, Henry, 64
Harir, Sharif, 156–157
Hassan el-Tourabi, 142
"Heart of darkness," 25, 138
Herbst, Jeffrey, 65, 231
Hillal, Musa, 161
Hobbes, Thomas, 166
Holy Spirit Mobile Forces (HSMF), 133–134, 147
Holy Spirit Movement, 141, 224
Horn of Africa, 222, 231, 232
Houphouët-Boigny, Félix, 32, 33, 109; death of, 57, 83; exploitation of "rents," 84; extension of colonial policy, 84; Houphouëtist state, 29; liberal land policy, 85; regional interventionalism, 91
HSMF. See Holy Spirit Mobile Forces
Huambo, 200, 212, 213
Human rights abuses, 122, 187, 188, 209
Human Rights Watch, 30, 159
Hunde, 123
Hutu, 33,123; rebels, 125, 126; refugees, 123; regime, 117
"Hutu Revolution," 31

ICC. See International Criminal Court
Identity: determined through autochthony, 33; ethnic, 12; explaining African conflicts, 31; identification cards, 81, 87, 102; Ivorian identity, 81; politics of, 32, 227; questions of, 37; reflections of identity in politics, 176; as social construction, 12, 29
Ideology: in Darfurian conflict, 156–157; decline of ideology in African insurgencies, 224–226; ideologically informed movements, 15; Maoism, 16, 17, 224; Marxism-Leninism, 16; Marxist, 224; Nativist, 6, 83, 85; nationalism, 56; of autochthony, 87, 123, 175; recession of ideological alternatives for African states, 72; revolutionary ideological discourse, 16
IDPs. See Internally displaced persons
Igbo, of Nigeria, 65
Ilunga, Emile, 117, 118
IMF. See International Monetary Fund
Intercongolese Dialogue, 116, 125
Interahamwe militias, 117, 129
Internally displaced persons (IDPs), 132; camps, 147; recruitment into patriotic self-defense groups, 103
International Criminal Court (ICC), 27, 136, 144, 147, 151
International Crisis Group, 102
International Monetary Fund (IMF), 44
Iraq, 20, 138, 177
Islamic Arab Front of Azawad, 65
Israel, 100
Italy, 62, 63
Ituri, 14, 17, 130
Ivorite, 84, 86; doctrine of, 227

"Jack the Rebel," 97
Jackson, Robert, 56, 61
Jamba, 204, 208
Jammeh, Yahja, 179
Janjawid, 156. *See also* Janjawiid
Janjawiid, 7, 153, 156, 157, 162, 167, 230–231; atrocities committed by, 151; characteristics of, 161; civilian attacks, 159, 161; co-opted by Sudanese government, 158–159, 163; modus operandi, 159
JCL. See Justice Coalition for Liberia
Jebel Marra, 152, 158
Jeunes Patriotes, 25
Jinja, 134

Johnson, Douglas, 166
Johnson-Sirleaf, Ellen, 232
Jopadhola, 133
Juba, 132, 144, 148
Justice and Equality Movement (JEM), 159, 161, 167
Justice Coalition for Liberia (JCL), 76

Kabare, James, 117, 129
Kabbah, Achmed Tejan, 49, 232
Kabila, Joseph, 116, 125, 126, 224
Kabila, Laurent, 18, 113, 115–117, 121, 232; assassination of, 116; exploitation by RCD, 120; insurrection against, 115
Kadet, Bertin, 101, 102
Kagame, Paul, 118, 223
Kahara, Bizima, 117, 119
Kailahun, 47, 48
Kaiza, David, 145
Kalangala Action Plan, 139
Kaldor, Mary, 12
Kalonji, Albert, 65
Kamalata, Abilo (Numa), 214
Kamina, 212
Kampala, 30, 133, 134, 140, 141, 145
Kanu, Abu, 47–48
Kaplan, Robert, 26
Karefa-Smart, John, 43
Kasa, 186
Kasai, 55, 114
Kasavubu, Joseph, 64
Kassessa, Armindo Moises, 219
Kassolol, 179, 191
Kassy, Serge, 106
Katalaio, Mateus, 208
Katanga, 55, 63, 64, 128, 206
Kazini, James, 136
Kelumak, 175
Kenya, 16, 134
Khartoum, 3, 142, 146; alliance with LRA, 163; animosity toward Museveni, 141–143; attempts at demobilizing Janjawiid, 164; dominance over Darfur, 154, 231; employment of Janjawiid, 151, 158; Islamist agenda, 163, 165; multiparty government, 153; usage of militias, 7, 25, 151, 158, 161
Khobe, Maxwell, 76
Kigali, 116, 117, 120, 125

Kinshasa, 113,115, 116, 121, 127, 128
Kitgum District, 134
Koidu, Sierra Leone, 41, 48; diamond extraction by RUF, 50
Kolo, Samuel, 136
Komakech, Yakobo, 146
Koné, Massamba, 94
Kony, Joseph, 7, 29, 131–148; formation of LRA, 134–135
Kordofan, 156, 163, 166
Korhogho, 94
Krahn, 36, 97, 98
Kromah, Alhaji, G. V., 24, 72
Kuito, 213

Lagoni, Olanya, 144
Lalogi, IDP camp, 139
Landmines, 183, 190
Langi, 133
Latek, Odong, 135
Latin America, 5, 55, 100
LDF. *See* Lofa Defense Force
Legré, Thierry, 106
Le National, 106
Leopoldville, Congo, 6
Liberia, 2, 51, 74, 82, 138, 171, 173, 177, 184, 222, 229, 230, 232; Americo-Liberians, 36; autochthonous conflict, 33; Bong county, 77; civil war, 10, 12, 15, 36, 69, 91; corruption under Samuel Doe, 26; extreme violence in Ivorian conflict, 96, 98; FSCO training host, 101; humanitarian crisis, 74; Liberian fighters in Côte d'Ivoire, 91, 95–99; Liberian refugees in Côte d'Ivoire, 91; Lofa County, 14, 24, 73; Mandingo issue, 32; Nimba County, 36; post-Taylor government, 79
Liberian Peace Council (LPC), 71, 72
Liberians United for Democracy and Reconciliation (LURD), 3, 6, 17, 97, 231; anti-Taylor movement, 97; characteristics of, 69, 72; creation, 73; cross-border raids of Guinea, 74; as disciplined entity, 77; exploitation of state resources, 80; Fake LURD, 70, 73–76; increased military offensives, 77; internal fighting, 80; Krahn branch, 97; naming practices, 72; political aftermath of Charles

Taylor, 79; as a proxy, 77; Real LURD, 70, 76–79; recruitment, 69–70

Libya, 16, 30, 120, 155, 156, 161, 177, 179

Linas-Marcoussis, 81, 87, 92, 93, 95, 106

Lira, 24

Lofa County, Liberia, 14, 24, 36

Lofa Defense Force (LDF), 24

Lomas, 14, 24, 36

Lomé peace talks, 92, 97; agreement, 76

LPC. *See* Liberian Peace Council

Lord's Army, 134

Lord's Resistance Army (LRA), 7, 10, 24, 25, 131, 135, 148, 163; agenda of, 137; attacks on northern Uganda, 131, 135, 136, 184, 227, 229; cease-fire, 144; characteristics of, 14, 34; child soldiers, 137; communication strategy, 18; expansion to eastern Uganda, 141, 142; evolution of, 147–148; formation of, 134–135; longevity and survival of insurgency, 2, 28, 143, 225; military practices, 137–138; targeting of children, 131, 136; theories of existence, 132, 137

Los Angeles Times, 138

LRA. *See* Lord's Resistance Army

Luanda, 212, 213, 214

Lubanga, Thomas, 121

Luena Memorandum of Understanding, 218

Lukoya, Severino, 134

Lumpens, 13, 14, 28–29, 39

Lumumba, Patrice, 64

Lunda, 63, 64

Lunda Norte, 210

Lunda Sul, 210

Lunga-Bungo River area, 203

LURD. *See* Liberians United for Democracy and Reconciliation

Lusaka accords, 120–121, 212; cease-fire agreement, 115; implications for Rwanda, 125; post-Lusaka insurgencies, 120. *See also* RCD-Movement de Liberation

Lusaka Protocol, 212, 213, 214; addendum, 218

Luso, 203

Luwero triangle, 133, 139

Machar, Riek, 132, 136, 167

Mbundu, 200

Mahdist state, 153, 164

Mai Mai, 10, 15, 17, 24, 123–124

Makandu, 49

Makondu Hills, 49

Malanje, 210, 213

Mali, 55, 81, 86, 98, 103; indirect support of MPCI, 91; Tuareg separatism, 65

Malinke, 86

Malihyat, 156

Malone, David M., 145

Mamadou Sane Nkrumah, 175, 177, 181

Mamdani, Mahmood, 31

Mandela, Nelson, 223

Mandingo, 14, 24, 32, 36

Mané, Ansumane, 172, 173, 178, 179, 187

Mano River, 30, 35, 82, 91, 93, 96, 182, 183

Mansaray, Rashid, 48

Mao Glofei, Denis, 102

Mao, Nobert, 144

Mao Zedong, 16, 36, 201, 218

Maquis, 172, 173, 177, 181, 192; assistance from Senegalese authorities, 188; corruption, 181; democratic tendency, 187; embedded in local communities, 183–185; lack of preparation for armed struggle, 180; sustainability through low-profit economy, 180–183

Marchal, Roland, 96

Margai, Albert, 43

Margai, Sir Milton, 43

Masalit, 152, 157–158, 160

Masiaka Junction, 49

Masisi, 125

Massaquoi, Francois, 24

Matiep, Paulino, 162

Mauritania, 177, 178

Mavinga, 205

Mbabazi, Amama, 142

Mbembe, Achille, 61

Médard, Jean-Francois, 22

Media: attempts to explain African state, 26, 138; hate, 85; international

news, 10; international journalists
denied access to Liberian civil
conflict, 74; reports from Darfur,
151; Western reporting of LRA,
14, 131
Mende, 43
Menongue, 213
Mercenaries, 24, 30, 40, 82, 93, 97, 99,
100, 108, 141, 161, 167, 173
MFDC. *See* Mouvement des Forces
Démocratiques de Casamance
Middle East, 55
Migdal, Joel, 59
Miguel, Alberto Mario Vasco (Kanhali
Vatuva), 218
Militarization: of Côte d'Ivoire, 83,
88–89; of DRC politics, 128; of rural
space, 100, 102; of urban space, 107;
of youth, 105
Militias, 3, 5, 230–231; freelance, 25;
motivation for joining, 166; role of
authorities in mobilization of, 102;
rural, 100, 101; self-defense, 103;
sociological make up of local
militias, 102–103, state-sponsored,
167; urban, 89
Minawi, Minni, 160
Minter, William, 204
MINURCA. *See* United Nations
Mission in Central African Republic
Misteriha, 157
MJP. *See* Mouvement Pour la Justice et
la Paix
Mkandawire, Thandika: distinction of
stationary and roving rebels, 33–34,
183–184; urban conflict thesis,
13–14, 28–29, 30, 39, 228–229
MLC. *See* Mouvement Pour la
Libération du Congo
Mobutu Sese Seko, 17, 18, 22, 25,
29–30, 33, 35, 114, 123, 128;
intervention in Angola, 206;
Mobutuists, 29, 118, 119
Mogadishu, Somalia, 231
Momoh, Joseph, 22, 44
Monaco, 71
Monrovia, 43, 74, 78, 79
MONUC. *See* United Nations Organi-
zation Mission in the Demaratic
Republic of the Congo
Moore, Emmanuel, 74

Morocco, 16, 25, 63, 206
Mouvement des Forces Démocratiques
de Casamance (MFDC), 7, 171, 226,
230; acceptance of state money, 188;
accusations of internal corruption,
189; border relations with Gambia
and Guinea-Bissau, 178–180;
civilian massacres, 184; contradiction of, 191; coup, 187; economic
hierarchy of leadership, 182;
formation as "Diola" movement,
183; fragmentation of, 172, 183,
185–187; geographic positioning,
178; inception, 173; internal violence, 185–186; lack of international
support, 172, 177–180; legitimacy,
189, 190; lessons of, 191; membership cards, 180–181; militarization,
177–178; mobilization, 172, 173–
177; relationship between civilians
and guerrillas, 172, 183–185;
relationship with Dakar, 182,
187–189; "resourceless" war, 180;
as roving rebellion, 34; survival in
weak war economy, 172, 180–183,
192; weapons sales from Bissau-
Guinean militaries, 178
Mouvement Patriotique de la Côte
d'Ivoire (MPCI), 15, 90, 91; direct
support by Burkina Faso, 91, 230;
indirect support by Mali, 91; military
objective, 92; organizational discipline, 95; political image, 95;
recruitment, 93; youth leadership, 94
Mouvement Populaire du Grand Ouest
(MPIGO), 91, 97
Mouvement Pour la Justice et la Paix
(MJP), 91, 97
Mouvement Pour la Libération du
Congo (MLC), 115, 118
Movement for Democracy in Liberia
(MODEL), 3, 97, 98; fighters in Côte
d'Ivoire, 99; naming practice, 72;
support from Gbagbo, 99
Movimento Popular de Libertação de
Angola (MPLA), 199, 201, 210, 211,
213, 232; desire to stay in power,
216; invasions of Zaire, 206; post-
colonial takeover of Angola and
security strategy, 203–204; victory
over UNITA, 218

Moxico province, 202, 203, 215
Mozambique, 2, 173, 183, 232
MPCI. *See* Mouvement Patriotique de la Côte d'Ivoire
MPIGO. *See* Mouvement Populaire du Grand Ouest
MPLA. *See* Movimento Popular de Liberataçáo de Angola
Mudumbi, Joseph, 117
Mugabe, Robert, 20, 232
Mulattos, 201, 202
Mulele, Pierre, 16
Murahalin, 156, 163, 164, 166
Museveni, Yoweri, 9, 117, 131, 136, 223, 224; animosity toward Khartoum government, 141–143; implementation of economic reform, 140; indifference to Ugandan conflict, 132, 143–144; involvement in corrupt political behavior, 225; political benefits from LRA conflict, 147; response to peace talks, 144; war on terror rhetoric, 20, 148

Nairobi, 146
Nairobi Agreement, 135
Namibia, 2, 115, 120, 204–206, 214
Nande, 123
Nankabirwa, Ruth, 136
Nanking Military Academy, 201
National Islamic Front (NIF), 157, 163, 164
National Patriotic Front of Liberia (NPFL), 221
Nationalism: nationalist discourse, 61–62; postcolonial, 16, 67; territorial nationalism, 56; xenophobic, 96
National Patriotic Front of Liberia (NPFL), 3, 6, 15, 69, 76, 230
National Provisional Ruling Council (NPRC): election defeat, 49; offensive against RUF, 48; recapture of mining towns in Sierra Leone, 48
National Resistance Army (NRA), 9, 27, 139, 224, 229; local control based on local legitimacy; 59; ousting of Obote, 132
National Resistance Movement (NRM), 28, 139
Navigué, Konaté, 106

Neco, Jose Robeiro, 214
Neopatrimonial state, 2, 10; crisis of, 22–23, 25; distribution of, 57; neopatrimonial practice, 22–23, 30
Netherlands, 159
Neto, Agnostinho, 200
Newbury, David, 35
New Forces, 29, 34, 57
New Horizons, 72
New York Accord, 206
Ngoma, Zahidi, 117, 118, 119, 120–122
Nharea, 213
Nicla, 98
Niger, 55, 65
Niger Delta, 228
Nigeria, 3, 16, 233; Biafran civil war, 16, 65; coup, 65; forces in Sierra Leone, 40; politics of identity, 227–228
Nile Valley, 154, 155; southern Blue Nile, 158, 160
Nilotic, of Uganda, 27–28
Nimeiri, Jaffar, 154, 155
Nisitu, 142
Nongovernmental organizations, 17, 146
North Kivu, 115, 116; conflict with RCD, 122–124; election of Eugene Serufuli, 125
North Korea, 120; Juche idea, 72
NPFL. *See* National Patriotic Front of Liberia
NPRC. *See* National Provisional Ruling Council
NRA. *See* National Resistance Army
NRM. *See* National Resistance Movement
Nuba Mountains, 158, 160, 163, 165
Nyamwisi, Mbusa, 121
Nyanga, 123
Nyarugabo, Moise, 117, 119

O'odua People's Congress, 228
OAU. *See* Organization of African Unity
Obote, Milton, 28, 132, 139, 224
Office National d'Identification (ONI), 87
Ogaden rebellion, 55
Ogoni, Okot, 144
Ojukwu, Odumegwu, 65

Okello, Bazello, 132
Okello, Tito, 27, 132, 224
Okumu, Reagan, 144
Olson, Mancur, 33, 183
Omdurman, battle, 153
Onusumba, Adolphe, 118
Onyango-Obbo, 146–147
Operation Clean Slate, 45
Operation Iron Fist, 136, 142, 145
Organization of African Unity (OAU): Liberation Committee, 72; resolution on African border disputes, 57; rules, 58; usage of territorial integrity, 65; view of decolonization, 62
Organization of Displaced Liberians, 76
Orientale Province, 118
Oris, Juma, 134
Oromo, 20, 55
Ottaway, Marina, 225
Ouagadougou, Burkina Faso, 92, 93
Ouattara, Alassane, 85, 87, 90, 92, 93
Ouattara, Issiaka (Wattao), 94
Oulaï, Hubert, 102
Oumé region, 102, 104
Ousmane, Chérif, 94
Ovimbundu, 200, 202, 210, 212–213, 219
Oyike, 144

Pajule, 144
Pamelap, Guinea, 75
Paramilitarization: of Côte d'Ivoire, 83, 100, 102; of urban space, 107
Paris, 120, 186
Parti Démocratique de Côte d'Ivoire (PDCI), 85, 89, 104, 105, 109
Parti Démocratique Sénégalais (PDS), 176, 188
Parti Socialiste (PS), 176, 188
Paye-Layleh, Jonathan, 74
PC-Crise, 89
PDCI. *See* Parti Démocratique de Côte d'Ivoire
PDS. *See* Parti Démocratique Sénégalias
Pendembu, Sierra Leone, 48
People's Front for Democracy and Justice, 226
Peulhs, 174
Polisario Front, 15

Pool, David, 222
Popular Defense Force (PDF), 157, 163
Populist leadership, 186–187
Portugal, 63, 175, 201, 203, 206, 207
Post–Cold War: African politics, 2, 233; consequences for Africa, 18–19; decline of Western interest in Africa, 129; emergence of independent states, 226; end of Cold War effect in DRC, 113; end of Cold War effect on UNITA, 210; light arms proliferation, 216; regional conflict zones, 2; secessionist aftermath, 65–66
Powell, Colin, 159
Pretoria, South Africa, 116, 222
Prince Johnson, 72, 74
PS. *See* Parti Socialiste

Qaddafi, Muammar, 16, 72, 155, 156
Quatre Communes, 175–176

Rape, 95, 139, 140, 159, 171
Rawlings, Jerry, 17
RCD. *See* Ressemblement Congolais pour la Démocratie
RCD-Goma, 127
RCD-Mouvement de Liberation (RDC-ML), 121
RDR. *See* Ressemblement des Républicains
Realpolitik, 119, 189
Reagan, Ronald, 205–207
Red Brigades, 89, 92
Reed, William Cyrus, 36
Reform insurgencies, 3, 15, 55, 223, 233; success and failure of, 224–225
Refugees, 31, 91, 115, 123; communities, 191, 192
Regional conflict zones, 6, 10, 82. *See also* Great Lakes; Mano River; West Africa
Religion, 138, 224; animism, 173; Catholicism, 173; Christian spirit Lakwena, 133; evil spirits, 141; Holy Spirit, 141; Sufi Islam, 73; and Ten Commandments, 137
RENAMO. *See* Resistencia Nacional Mocambicana
Réseau Ivorien des Organisations Féminines, 106

Resistencia Nacional Mocambicana (RENAMO), 18, 222
Resources: appropriation of by elites, 59; coltan, 10, 126; control over natural resources, 11; diamonds, 10, 126, 200; exploitation by foreign companies, 61; gold, 10, 126; ivory, 10; oil, 10, 162, 212. *See also* West Africa, oil
Ressemblement Congolais pour la Démocratie (RCD), 6, 7, 29, 113, 115; assemblage of insurgency, 117–118; collaboration with Rwandan army, 122–123; Congolese rebels of, 57, 113; elite leadership, 118–119; insurrection of Kabila, 115; international diplomacy of, 120; motivation of, 127; occupation of eastern DRC, 121–122; political strategy, 113, 119; quest for international legitimacy, 119–121; statist approach, 122
Ressemblement des Forces Democratiques de Guinée (RFDG), 74
Ressemblement des Républicains (RDR), 89, 92
Revolutionary United Front (RUF), 10, 12, 15, 24, 140; attacks on Kambia, 75; brutal characterization, 28; burning of villages, 47, 49; common example of armed insurgency, 51; diamond trading, 48; demise of, 35; election participation, 49; exile in bush camps, 48, 49; exploitation of diamond resources, 18, 50; expulsion from Freetown, 50; funding from Charles Taylor, 71, 74; means to control diamond fields, 46, 50; portrayal of, 138; recruitment of youth, 45, 48; territorial control of Sierra Leone, 48
RFDG. *See* Ressemblement des Forces Démocratiques de Guinée
Rhodesia, 25
Rice, Susan, 74, 120
Richards, Paul, 26, 30, 184; characterization of RUF, 27; enclave formations, 34–35; theories on war, 4, 12, 14, 147; on youth and war in Sierra Leone, 39, 138
Rick's Institute, 79

Roberto, Holden, 201, 202
Rodriguez, Carlos, 135, 142
Rosberg, Carl, 56, 61
RPF. *See* Rwandan Patriotic Front
Ruberwa, Azaria, 117, 118, 119, 126
RUF. *See* Revolutionary United Front
Rural patriotic organizations, 103; internal hierarchy, 102; youth patriots, 101, 104–106
Rutshuru, 125
Rwanda, 2, 6, 113, 124, 232; exploitation of minerals in Congo, 126–127; invasion of DRC, 117, 230; military commercialism, 127; military presence in eastern DRC, 123–124; military support for RCD, 115, 116, 122–123; sponsorship of Eugene Serufuli, 126; violation of UN arms embargo, 127
Rwandan genocide, 31, 114; refugee crisis from, 115, 123
Rwandan Patriotic Front (RPF), 31, 224
Rwarkabije, Paul, 126

SADF. *See* South African Defense Forces
Sadio, Salif, 172, 179, 186, 187, 190
Sagna, Léopold, 172, 177, 179, 186, 187
Sahli, Mohamed, 166
Sambou, Youba, 189
San Pedro port, 97
Sangumba, Jorge, 208
Sankoh, Foday, 15, 47, 51; leadership qualities, 29; usage of communications technology, 18
Sapalalo, Altino, 214
Sapassa, Eunice, 208
Savimbi, Jonas, 2, 17, 148, 199; death of, 207, 215, 218; decision to de-emphasize guerrilla warfare for conventional military, 215–217; election results, 210; leadership style, 29, 201–202, 207–208; political shortcomings, 207; question of military decision, 214; racist view of Angolan society, 201, 202; replacement, 219; violent actions, 208
Sawyer, Amos, 74
Senegal, 7, 27, 55; army, 172, 176, 177; autochthony in politics,

175–176; cease-fire agreement, 171, 172, 184; democratization, 188; elections, 180; elites, 188; engagement with Mauritania, 178; funding of *maquis* and MFDC, 182, 188; peace process, 189; policies in Casamance, 186, 188; regionalism as a political feature, 175–176; relationship with West, 177; repression of Diola, 176–177; state responses to separatist action, 187–189, 192

Senghor, Léopold Sédar, 172, 175–176

Senoufo, 86

Separatism, 5; absence in African regions 56, 65; secessionist moments in Africa, 64–66; separatist claims by former African colonies, 62–63; separatist warfare, 55

Separatist insurgencies, 3, 15, 55, 223; scarcity of, 226–228

Serufuli, Eugene, 125–126

Sharia movement, 228

Sierra Leone, 2, 10, 11, 82, 171, 173, 184, 222, 229, 230; abandonment by international community; 49; army, 49; autochthonous conflict, 33; brutality of conflict, 12; corruption under Siaka Stevens, 43–44; death zone, 49; diamond mining, 41–42; diamond smuggling, 44; dysfunctional state, 51; economic crisis, 47; elections, 49; exploitation of minerals by RUF, 18; fighters in Côte d'Ivoire, 95; former agricultural economy, 41; Kailahun district, 47; Kamajors, 15; Kono district, 41, 44, 50; marginalization of young men 13, 40, 45, 52; mineral economy, 41; one-party state, 43; Operation Clean Slate, 45; origin of civil war, 47; peace process, 49, 235; poverty, 41; rebellion against corrupt state, 36; State of Economic Emergency Declaration, 44–45; 2002 elections, 78

Sierra Leone People's Party (SLPP), 43, 49

Shaba invasions, 115

Slanger, Edward, 98

SLPP. *See* Sierra Leone People's Party

Smith, Ian, 25

Social marginalization, 5, 9, 10; of African urbanized youth, 6, 13, 15, 17, 40, 45, 229; motivation of insurgency movements, 27, 29, 45

Somali National Movement, 231

Somalia, 138, 231; pan-Somali nationalism, 227; unilateral withdrawal of Somaliland, 55, 63, 65

Somaliland, Republic of, 55, 63, 65, 227, 231

Sorbonne, 106, 175

Soro, Guillaumme, 29, 92

Soroti, 24

South Africa, 25, 204, 206, 222, 232; arming of UNITA, 205; employment of UNITA as a proxy, 204, 205–207; Executive Outcomes, 24, 49; military presence and strategies in Angola, 204–206; South African mercenaries, 97, 100

South African Defense Forces (SADF), 204, 205

South Kivu, 115, 116, 127; RCD conflict, 122–124; Rwandaphone minority, 117

South West Africa People's Organization (SWAPO), 204, 206

Soviet Union, 2, 16, 224; absence of Soviet threat, 18; breakup of, 64; military support of MPLA, 205; military support to proxy clients, 216, 217; sphere of influence, 206; Soviet autonomy, 64; success of separatist movements, 226

SPAF. *See* Sudan People's Armed Forces

Spain, 63

SPLM/A. *See* Sudan People's Liberation Movement/Army

Stevens, Siaka, 22, 43–45

Strakes, Jason, 4

Strasser, Valentine, 48, 49

Structural adjustment programs, 21, 84, 140, 187

Sudan, 2, 3, 7, 134; aiding Joseph Kony, 141–143, 230; difference between rebels and government militias, 167–168; exploitation of local conflicts, 162, 166; historical precedence for employing militias, 162, 165; independence, 154–155;

internal colonization, 154; international attention, 151; Islamist agenda, 163, 165; militarism as means for solving conflicts, 164–165; military, 151, 157, 159; north-south peace negotiations, 159; protocol with Uganda, 134; rationale for employment of militias, 163–166; reliance on Janjawiid, 158; southern Sudan, 58, 158, 160
Sudan Liberation Movement/Army (SLM/A), 158–161, 167
Sudan People's Armed Forces (SPAF), 142
Sudan People's Liberation Movement/Army (SPLM/A), 157, 159, 160, 161, 162, 163, 165, 223; factions, 167; relations with LRA, 135, 142
Sudanese Socialist Union, 154
SWAPO. *See* South West Africa People's Organization

Taha, Ali Othman, 142
Tajammu al-Arabi, 153
Taylor, Charles, 3, 40, 177–178; alleged relationship with United States and British officials, 74, 78; amnesty agreement, 79; Anti-Terror Unit (ATU), 20; creation of MPIGO, 97; electoral strategy 73, 76; employment of Sam Bockarie, 51; exile to Nigeria, 79; exploitation of Nimba conflict, 36; exploitation of LURD, 70, 73; failure to help the RUF, 78; involvement in Côte d'Ivoire, 91; political rule over economic markets, 71; political strategy, 75; support of the RUF, 74–75, 77; war on terror rhetoric, 20
Teixeira de Sousa (Luau), 202
Tembo, 123
Teso, 133, 134
Thambwe, Alexis, 117, 119
Thirty-Second Buffalo Battalion, 205
Tibasima, Jean-Baptiste, 120
Tigray People's Liberation Front (TPLF), 222, 223, 229
Togo, 217
Toikeusse, Mabri, 104
Torture, 95, 212
Toshombe, Moise, 64, 65

Touareg insurgency, 222
Toulepleu, 98, 101, 104
Touré, Moussa, 107
Touré, Sékou, 88
TPLF. *See* Tigray People's Liberation Front
Tubman, William V. S., 30
Tutsi, 31, 33, 123, 124

Uganda, 2, 7, 9, 10, 226, 232; aiding SPLA, 141–143; amnesty bill, 135; bureaucratic elite, 28; corruption of Ugandan officers, 145–146; ethnic division under colonial administration, 27–28, 139; geopolitical rivalry with Sudanese government, 132, 141–143; invasion of DRC, 117, 230; media depictions of Kony, 137; military support for RCD, 115, 116; Ministry of Finance, 145; "night commuters," 131; peace talks, 132, 144; Rwandan refugees in, 31; Ugandan's theory on LRA conflict, 143–145
Uganda, northern, 2, 14, 131, 222; belief systems of, 140; civilians in displacement camps, 131; distrust of central government, 139–140; marginalization of, 138, 139; political economy of conflict, 132, 145–146; regional marginalization, 27
Uganda National Rescue Front, 143
Ugandan People's Defense Forces (UPDF), 135–136, 145
Uganda-Sudan agreement, 142
Uganda National Liberation Army (UNLA), 133
Ugandan People's Democratic Army (UPDA), 133, 134
Uganda People's Democratic Christian Army (UPDCA), 135
Uganda's People Army (UPA), 133, 134
Ukraine, 217
ULIMO-K. *See* United Liberation Movement of Liberia for Democracy–Kromah faction
ULIMO. *See* United Liberation Movement of Liberia for Democracy
Umma Party, 154, 164
União das Populações de Angola (UPA), 134, 201

UNLA. *See* Uganda National Liberation Army
Union of Democratic Forces of Liberia, 76
UNMIL. *See* United Nations Mission in Liberia
UNAMSIL. *See* United Nations Mission in Sierra Leone
União Nacional para Independência Total de Angola (UNITA), 2, 6, 7, 148, 222, 232; absence of US funding, 18; alliance with colonial forces, 199, 203; as a criminal insurgency, 211–212; attempt at forming conventional army, 213–217; control of diamond revenue, 216–218; demise of insurgency, 215; formation of insurgency 200–202; future of movement, 218–219; increased militarization, 207–208; intraparty violence, 208; military attacks against Portuguese, 202; miscalculations and tactical blunders, 213, 215–217; participation in elections and electoral defeat, 200, 207, 208–210; proxy for apartheid South Africa, 200, 203–206, 207; proxy for United States, 205–207; restructuring and reorganization of, 204, 206; semiconventional army, 212; as a stationary rebellion, 34; territorial control, 214; trajectory of movement, 199–200; transformation from guerrilla movement to political party, 208–209; usage of war to obtain power, 209, 210–211
Union pour la Libération Totale de la Côte d'Ivoire, 106
UNITA. *See* União Nacional para Independência Total de Angola
United Liberation Movement of Liberia for Democracy–Kromah faction (ULIMO-K), 24
United Liberation Movement of Liberia for Democracy (ULIMO), 72
United Nations, 105, 127; General Assembly Resolution 1514, 15, 57; intervention in Côte d'Ivoire, 34, 81; investigation of Charles Taylor, 71, 75, 77, 78; lifting of sanctions, 20; Panel of Experts, 127; sanctions against Taylor, 71; sanctions in Darfur, 151; Security Council Resolution 435, 205; Security Council Resolution 1237, 217; Security Council Resolution 1306, 75; war crimes tribunal, 79
United Nations Mission in Central African Republic (MINURCA), 94
United Nations Mission in Liberia (UNMIL), 96
United Nations Mission in Sierra Leone (UNAMSIL), 50
United Nations Organization Mission in the Democratic Republic of the Congo (MONUC), 115, 124, 126
United Nations peacekeepers: in Freetown, 50–51; in Liberia, 80; operations in Côte d'Ivoire (UNOCI), 96
United Nations Secretary-General, 205
United States, 148, 159, 160, 180; concern for African failed states, 19; economic interests in Africa, 20; external technological support to African insurgents, 18, 212, 215; foreign policy, 19; invasion of Iraq, 79; military support to proxy clients, 20, 205, 216; naming of terrorist organizations, 148; national security strategy, 19; pressure on Sierra Leonean government, 76; proxy relationship with UNITA, 205–207; sanctions, 20; stoppage of economic support to African insurgents, 20, 200
United States Agency for International Development (USAID), 20
UPA. *See* União das Populações de Angola
UPDA. *See* Ugandan People's Democratic Army
UPDCA. *See* Uganda People's Democratic Christian Army
UPDF. *See* Ugandan People's Defense Forces
Upper Nile, 162, 163, 165
USAID. *See* United States Agency for International Development
US Congress, 74
US Department of State, 74
US Secretary of State, 159

US Undersecretary of State for Africa, 74, 120

Vakulukuta, Antonio, 208
Vieira, João Bernardo, 172, 178
Voinjama, 52, 74

Wade, Abdoulaye, 171, 172, 180, 189, 191
Wahid, Abdul, 160
Wamba dia Wamba, Ernest, 117, 118, 120
War on terror, 19, 20, 147, 179; effect on African guerrilla insurgencies, 21; effect on global politics, 19, 179; rhetoric, 20
Warlord insurgencies, 3, 15, 25, 55, 72, 95, 223, 228–231. *See also* Lord's Resistance Army; Liberians United for Democracy and Reconciliation; Mai Mai; National Patriotic Front of Liberia; Revolutionary United Front
Waterloo, Sierra Leone, 48
Wayoro, Sery, 87
Wesseh, Conmany, 74
West Africa, 11, 176; combatants, 30; increased insurgency, 232; oil, 20; pattern of conflict, 36; recruitment zone for LURD, 69–70; regionalized conflict zone, 2, 6, 35
West Nile, 133
West Nile Bank Front (WNBF), 134
Western Bas Congo Province, 115
Western Sahara, 16, 25, 63
WNBF. *See* West Nile Bank Front
Wodié, Victorine, 107

World Bank, 43, 84
World War I, 153
World War II, 56, 154

Xenophobia, 82, 86, 124; and nationalism, 96; politics of, 98

Yahi, Octave, 102
Yala, Kumba, 179
Yamoussouko, Côte d'Ivoire, 81
Yemen, 20
Yopougon: massacre, 90; shootout, 107
Young, Crawford, 17, 56
Young, John, 222
Yugoslavia, 64

Zaghawa, 152, 158, 160
Zaire, 2, 22, 25, 113, 128, 204, 211; army, 114; informalization and privatization of state, 114; invasion of, 206; patronage networks, 128; Zairian copper, 202; Zairianization, 114
Zambia, 202, 214; western province, 60; Zambian copper, 202
Zenawi, Meles, 223, 224
Ziguinchor, 172, 174, 175, 181, 182, 186; administrative location of MFDC, 183; peaceful demonstrations, 176; violent conflict, 177
Zimbabwe, 2, 25, 115, 120, 232
Zimbabwe African National Union–Patriotic Front (ZANU-PF), 232
Zoumaniqui, Gbago, 76, 78
Zwedru, 98

ABOUT THE BOOK

At the center of many of Africa's violent conflicts are movements that do not seem to fit any established theories of armed resistance. *African Guerrillas* offers new models for understanding these movements, eschewing one-dimensional explanations.

The authors build on—and in some cases debate—the insights provided in Christopher Clapham's groundbreaking work. They find a new generation of fighters—one that reflects rage against the machinery of a dysfunctional state. Their analysis of this phenomenon, combining thematic chapters and a range of representative case studies, is a crucial contribution to any effort to understand Africa's war-torn societies.

Morten Bøås is researcher at Fafo Institute for Applied International Studies in Oslo. His recent publications include *Global Institutions and Development: Framing the World?* and *New and Critical Security and Regionalism: Beyond the Nation State.* **Kevin C. Dunn** is assistant professor of political science at Hobart and William Smith Colleges. He is author of *Imagining the Congo: The International Relations of Identity* and coeditor of *Identity and Global Politics: Theoretical and Empirical Elaborations.*